CCH BUSINESS OWNER'S TOOLKIT

WIN GOVERNMENT CONTRACTS

FOR YOUR SMALL BUSINESS

Third Edition

A *CCH Business Owner's Toolkit* Publication

John DiGiacomo

James Kleckner

CCH TAX AND ACCOUNTING
Chicago

A WoltersKluwer Company

This publication is designed to provide accurate and authoritative information in regard to the subject matter covered. It is sold with the understanding that the publisher is not engaged in rendering legal, accounting, or other professional service, and that the authors are not offering such advice in this publication. If legal advice or other expert assistance is required, the services of a competent professional should be sought.

Cover designed by Tim Kaage, Laurel Graphx, Inc.

Books may be purchased at quantity discounts for educational, business or sales promotion use. For more information please contact:

Consumer Media Group
CCH Tax and Accounting
2700 Lake Cook Road
Riverwoods, Illinois 60015

ISBN 0-8080-1225-8

Printed in the United States of America

THE CCH BUSINESS OWNER'S TOOLKIT TEAM

Drew Snider, Publisher, Consumer Media Group (*dsnider@cch.com*) has over 25 years experience with business-information services (SRDS), consumer magazines (*Golfweek*), and home-based software applications (Parsons Technology).

Joel Handelsman (*jhandels@cch.com*) has over 25 years of experience writing about business, tax, and financial topics. He has been involved in multiple new product and business ventures in the publishing industry, and has held a variety of management positions. Joel holds degrees from Northwestern University's Medill School of Journalism and DePaul University College of Law.

Alice H. Magos (*amagos@cch.com*) has over 35 years of experience running the operations of numerous small businesses. She is the author of the *CCH Business Owner's Toolkit*™ online advice column "Ask Alice." Alice is a popular instructor at small business seminars on accounting, financial planning, and using the Internet; is an accountant and a Certified Financial Planner; and holds degrees from Washington University in St. Louis and Northwestern University.

John L. Duoba (*jduoba@cch.com*) has more than 15 years of small business experience in book and magazine publishing, fulfilling various roles in editorial and production management. He has been involved in the publication of scores of titles, with multiple editions and issues raising the total well into the hundreds. John is a professional journalist and holds a degree from Northwestern University's Medill School of Journalism.

Paul N. Gada (*pgada@cch.com*) has over 10 years of legal publishing experience, primarily in dealing with federal and state tax issues. He has helped create numerous editorial products, including newsletters, journals, books and electronic information systems. Paul is an attorney and holds degrees from the John Marshall Law School (LLM. - Tax and Employee Benefits), Southern Illinois University (JD), Northern Illinois University (MBA) and Loyola University of Chicago (BA).

Catherine Gordon (*cgordon@cch.com*) has over 15 years of experience in the tax, business, and financial publishing field and has worked as a tax consultant providing services to individuals as well as large and small companies. Catherine holds a juris doctorate degree from the State University of New York at Buffalo School of Law and a BA in sociology from the State University of New York at Stony Brook.

ABOUT THE AUTHORS

John DiGiacomo is director of the Procurement Technical Assistance Center (PTAC) at Rock Valley College in Rockford, Illinois, assisting companies in working with the federal government. Under his watch, more than 400 different companies have been awarded over $427 million in contracts. John is a former owner of a business that sold to the government, at both the state and federal levels. After selling his business, he consulted internationally with companies in the U.S., Germany, and England, helping to find, negotiate and win $70 million in contracts. After leaving the private sector, he joined the PTAC and, among other things, has initiated small business workshops and conferences on using e-commerce and EDI to do business with the government, and is in the process of creating an online, real-time video conferencing network within the state of Illinois.

James L. Kleckner is a private consultant specializing in federal government procurement and small business, and also works with the Illinois PTAC program. Prior to starting his own consulting business, James was for 37 years part of various federal procurement activities, including former buyer and staff officer in the Procurement Policy Office of the HQ U.S. Army Weapons Command in Rock Island, Illinois; Small Business Specialist at DCASR Dallas; associate director of Small Business, DCASR Chicago; and deputy for Small Business, DCMAO Chicago. He also was appointed to the Illinois Small Business Council of 100 in 1996, which helps set state policy to foster the growth of small business in Illinois. In all, Jim has worked with over 1200 businesses that were awarded $17.5 million in contracts.

Both authors are members of the Association of Procurement Technical Assistance Centers (APTAC), Illinois Small Business Development Association (ISBDA), and the National Contract Management Association (NCMA). They are also Certified Contract Assistance Specialists by APTAC and Certified Business Specialists with ISBDA.

DEDICATION

Jim would like to thank his loving wife Janet and his family for their continued support and patience during this rewrite of the book. John would like to thank his family for their support.

Thanks to the entire CMG team at CCH for their support. A special thanks to Drew Snider and John Duoba who continue to support our efforts to educate those people and businesses that need to know how the government acquisition process works.

We would like to thank the experts who contributed to the third edition of this book: John Lanpher, of Lanpher, Shappert and Associates; Andy Pinon, of Alado Development; and Barb Woodruff, EDI specialist, of Triton-Tek.com. Special thanks to Ann Johns, GSA FSS Specialist, for her work on the GSA portion of this book. These exceptional people provided added insight and information in the creation of this book.

FOREWORD

If you are a small company, there has never been a better time to do business with the federal government. Changes in the laws and regulations that define federal government contracting and the procurement process have made it easier than ever for your business to participate in this $365 billion industry.

Even if you have little or no experience in selling to the federal government and have little or no knowledge of the contracting process, there is no reason you can't share in the opportunities that this huge market offers.

And this guidebook can help you do just that. It is written by expert authors who do what they write about. Together they have 60+ years of experience and have helped over 6,000 businesses secure government contracts to the tune of over $2 billion. They take you, step by step, through the process of doing business with the government—from how and where to find government buying opportunities to how to read, price out, and write a successful proposal. They also tell you about the types of resources that are available to help you as you go through the process and provide listings of buying offices, useful web site addresses, and all the other information that you need to make the government your new best customer.

Experience has shown that just about any business with the desire and perseverance can do it. And, with the help of this book, you can too.

A caution and an invitation—the discussions of the laws, web sites, procedures, and other information contained in this book are current as of the date of publication. But remember, things continue to change. To keep abreast of the latest news affecting your business, visit the *CCH Business Owner's Toolkit*™ (www.toolkit.cch.com). Take a look at the interactive information and tools that we offer to assist you in running your business. You can also ask follow-up questions of the authors. We welcome and look forward to your questions and comments.

Drew Snider

Publisher, Consumer Media Group

Table of Contents

Part I

Leap of Faith

You and your business are about to embark on a brand new venture. You are getting ready to enter a new $300+ billion market and to pursue a new, rather daunting customer—the federal government of the United States. Seem a bit overwhelming? Not if you understand the rules, the process, what to do and when to do it, and where to go for help. And that's exactly what this book is about.

So, let's get started. In this Part, we will first give you a feel for the magnitude of the opportunity available to small businesses in doing business with the government. Then we will show you how to assess whether you have "what it takes" to take on the government as a customer. Lastly, we will help you understand the government's game plan, the basis of the contracting process, and the rules and the rulebook that you have to know about and abide by.

Chapter 1, What Are the Opportunities?: Find out how much the government spends on the products and services it needs, where it spends its dollars, and whether there is real opportunity for small businesses.

Chapter 2, But Is There Real Opportunity for You?: Here we help answer an important question: What are the chances that the government needs and will buy the product or service that your company offers? We also tell you what government contracting can—and cannot—do for you.

Chapter 3, Do You Have What It Takes?: Here's your chance to find out whether you have the "right stuff" to do business with the government. We look at the resources, equipment, technology, and all of the other things that you need to be successful.

Chapter 4, Government Rules You Need To Know. Doing business with the government is really just "selling to a customer"—the same rules of business generally apply. But to minimize any problems, you need to know what the differences are.

Chapter 1

What Are the Opportunities?

How much opportunity is there in doing business with the government? Some statistics from fiscal year 2003 will give you an idea of how much opportunity there is. (While Fiscal Year 2004 figures were not yet available, recent reports indicate that procurement spending continues to grow about 10 percent per year.)

In Fiscal year 2003, the federal government wrote 11.5 million "actions," commonly referred to as "contracts," for products and services needed during the year. In addition to this activity, the federal government's use of credit cards resulted in another 26.5 million transactions. This is a lot of activity, but what are the dollars? The contracts represented over $305 billion, while the credit cards amounted to sales of an additional $16.4 billion. Looking at it from a different perspective, 91.5 percent of the contacts were under $25,000 in value and were reserved for only small business participation. That is a lot of "bread and butter" for your table. An interesting trend emerging from the data was the service area reported more dollars than the supply/equipment area.

Since any contracts that fall between $2,500 and $100,000 are reserved for small, small disadvantaged, small women-owned, and small veteran-owned businesses, that means that *almost 11 million contracts were reserved for small businesses in just one year!* Only 5 percent of the contracts were for more than $100,000 in value, and many of those were for major weapon systems, information management services, or large construction projects.

Government Prime Contract Goals

The government has the following designated goals for awarding prime contracts to small businesses:

23% to small businesses

5% to small disadvantaged businesses for prime and subcontracts

5% to small women-owned businesses for prime and subcontracts

3% to HUBZone small businesses

3% to small service-disabled-owned businesses

*Keep in mind that these are government goals, not government quotas. Quotas are set objectives that one must achieve; goals are set objectives that one must attempt to achieve. In any event, you probably will not get a contract just to help the government reach its goal. As in any commercial setting, contracts are awarded on the basis of what makes good business sense, with price, quality, and performance being the ruling factors.

CONTRACTING OPPORTUNITIES

Now let's get a better picture of where the government spends its money.

Fiscal Year 2003 (10/1/02 - 9/30/03)
Total Federal Actions and Contract Dollars

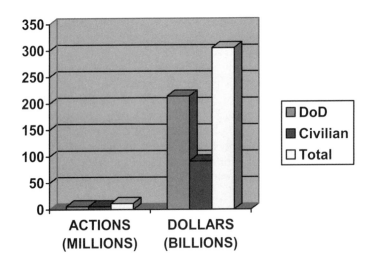

Agency	Actions	Dollars
DoD	5,801,573	$214,102,980,750
Civilian	5,721,087	$91,357,016,177
Total	11,522,660	$305,459,996,927

As you can see, there are two basic areas in which the government spends its contract dollars: the Department of Defense (DoD) and civilian agencies, such as the Department of Veteran Affairs and Department of Justice. And, as you can also see, the government contracted for almost $306 billion in products and services in fiscal 2003 alone. Based on the numbers, it looks like DoD is the biggest opportunity, but remember that many of the dollars went toward major systems and thus to larger companies.

Next let's look at what small businesses have done for the same period.

Fiscal Year 2003 (10/1/02 - 9/30/03)
Small Business Government Contracting

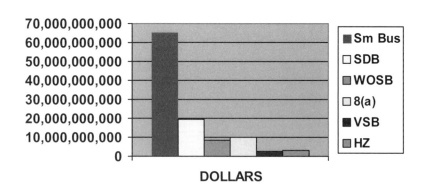

DOLLARS

Small Business Contracts by Method of Award

Noncompetitive	Restricted Competition	Open Competition
* $4,600,000,000	* $5,400,000,000	*$17,900,000,000

*These figures do not add up to the total figure of $65.5 billion because they do not reflect buys for under $25,000, which amounted to $37,600,000,000 and are automatically reserved for small businesses.

As this graph shows, small businesses, overall, did very well at almost $65.5 billion. It also shows that businesses that can be classified as small disadvantaged businesses (SDB) or as women-owned small businesses (WOSB) have a lot of room to grow.

It is also interesting to note that one-quarter of the total dollars awarded to small business (i.e., $17.9 billion of the total $65.5 billion) was received in open competition. In other words, the little guys and gals beat out the big ones for $17.9 billion in government contracts. Not a bad return for the effort!

And how many small businesses were new to the game? In fiscal 2003, a total of 19,658 small businesses received their first federal contract with the government. These businesses were either women-owned or disadvantaged-owned, and were split almost 65/35 between female and male ownership.

Who are the government's big spenders? Here's the top ten government agencies looking for contractors. For a more detailed breakdown of the figures, below, for each agency or department, go to the Federal Procurement Data Center site at http://www.fpdc.gov.

Top 10 Federal Agencies

Agency	Number of Contracts	Dollars
Department of Defense	5,801,573	$214,102,980
Department of Energy	13,880	$ 21,102,619
NASA	21,322	$ 11,806,861
Department of Veteran Affairs	3,694,837	$ 8,523,338
General Services Administration	616,852	$ 8,407,635
Department of Health & Human Services	239,449	$ 6,746,469
Department of Agriculture	178,030	$ 4,258,233
Department of Justice	277,584	$ 4,045,426
Department of Interior	87,892	$ 3,704,164
Department of Transportation	44,084	$ 3,382,456
Top Ten Totals	**10,975,503**	**$286,080,181**

Note: Although the number of contracts decreased by some 200,000, the dollars rose substantially by almost a $100 billion comparing FY 2001 with FY 2003 data. The Department of Homeland Security reported in at 11th position with $3.3 billion. This figure will likely increase in FY2004..

The complete data for FY 2003 and prior years is available in Acrobat Reader format at the Federal Procurement Data Center website http://www.fpdc.gov. Select the Fiscal Year of interest and download.

CREDIT CARD OPPORTUNITIES

In addition to government contracting, there is a whole new area of opportunity that isn't included in the figures above—credit card buying, often referred to as "micro-purchasing."

In Fiscal Year 2003, the federal government spent an additional $16.4 billion in credit card purchases. Yes, you read that right, $16.4 *billion* in business just using that little old piece of plastic money. Since 1984, when credit card purchases were first authorized, the number of credit card transactions has grown from 4.2 million to 26.5 million in Fiscal Year 2003. This means that, on average, over 72,587 transactions were placed each day. The amount of dollars spent with credit cards by government personnel—not just official government buyers—grew from $1.6 billion to almost $16.4 billion.

Example

In all, about 70 percent of all procurement transactions in government are for micro-purchases (i.e., sums under $2,500) and are done with a credit card. This is similar to the situation in the corporate world.

Although the largest credit card users were the Department of Defense, the Department of Veterans Prime Vendors and the Department of Veterans Affairs, accounting for almost $12.1 billion, every government office utilizes the credit card for almost everything it needs. That means that you can potentially have a government customer right next door.

Does your company accept credit cards? If not, you might want to think about the advantages of offering credit card purchasing as a part of your business strategy. Remember that the private sector is also increasing its use of the credit card.

Work Smart

Getting a merchant account is different today than it was years ago. The first time I asked my bank for an account, they literally almost threw a credit card swiper and everything else I needed at me. A couple of years ago, I wanted to use one again, but when I approached my bank, they wanted to know what I was going to use it for, who my customers were, how many charges there might be monthly, etc. Actually what they wanted was a business plan.

Your bank might ask for the same thing, and if they do you might find that creating a plan is a great exercise in thinking about what your business is going to be doing, where you might be going, and how you're going to get there.

The government most often uses MasterCard or Visa, but does use others like American Express and Discover. If you decide to set up your account for either MC or Visa, you should be OK. It is best to shop around because the charges vary significantly. Something else to consider is using the newer wireless systems that allow you to use it where needed without being hard-lined to a given location. Depending on the usage level, it may pay to buy the hardware rather than rent. Choose the most cost-effective method for you.

You can also check out the CCH Business Owner's Toolkit™ at http://www.toolkit.cch.com for more tips on merchant accounts

Chapter 2

But Is There Real Opportunity for *You?*

Although you may be starting to get an idea of the magnitude of government contracting opportunities for small businesses, you may be wondering—and possibly even doubting—whether the government has any need for *your* particular product or service. Of course, we can't tell you with certainty that it does, but what we can tell you is that the government needs—and stands ready to buy— more types of products and services than you can imagine.

If you think this is too difficult for you, maybe this data will encourage you. In fiscal year 2003, there were 19,658 small businesses that received their first government contract valued at $25,000 or more. If they can do it, so can you.

WHAT THE GOVERNMENT NEEDS

If you think that your company doesn't provide anything that the government needs, think again. Here are just a few examples about real-life companies much like yours. Notice that they didn't focus on what they made or the services they were currently providing. Instead they focused on entering the government market: They simply found out what the government needed that they were capable of supplying, and then supported those needs.

- What are the chances of a one-woman company making clothing for special-needs individuals getting a government contract? As it turned out, pretty good. She simply kept looking for something that the government needed that she was capable of supplying, and she found it. Today the one-person company has grown to 40 employees and reports a gross income of $2.5 million making coveralls for the military.

- A small, three-employee business started supplying fasteners to the military about 16 years ago. They started slow, but continued to make the effort to become more knowledgeable about the market and kept growing to where today they gross about $1 million a year. Not bad income for keeping the military fastened together.

- A few years ago, a nine-employee precision machine shop looked to the government market to replace some of their lost commercial work. They decided to concentrate on opportunities where drawings are available and require precision work. Today, the company is making tooling for the aerospace and pharmaceutical industries.

If you don't think the government needs *all* types of products and services, read on! These examples show that there is every chance that you provide, *or have the capability to provide*, a product or service that the government is looking for right now. (Believe it or not, all of these are fact—not fiction.)

- What use would the government have for old wrecked cars? A small business owner who owns a junkyard near an Air Force base had that same question and actually found out the answer. He was awarded a repeat contract for his junk cars, which were used to train Air Force rescue personnel in the use of the "jaws of life" and other emergency situations.

- Just a few years ago, the Department of Interior, U.S. Fish and Wildlife Service awarded an artist in Oregon an indefinite federal contract for wildlife artist services. This contract was awarded for various paintings portraying a variety of subjects.

- How about pork rinds? A small business received a contract for manufacturing and providing pork rinds, tasty treats that lots of people love, to several military base stores that needed someone to supply them. The owner won the contract based on price, delivery, and his status as a minority business contractor

- What's that about shooting pigs? An avid bow hunter who sold archery supplies and organized hunting trips won a bid from the Tennessee Valley Authority to get rid of the wild pigs that were living in and around the site and creating a safety problem. (Wild pigs tend to be a bit on the grouchy side!) Instead of bidding against firms that were going to charge and have employees do the work, he bid $1.00 and then scheduled hunters to go out and do the job. After clearing the hunters with the government to enter the area, he made his profit by charging the hunters just as he did for any other hunting trip to any other wilderness area.

- The Fish & Wildlife Services in Atlanta, Georgia, awarded a federal contract for walking the beach, specifically "PR for Beach Patrol of Leatherback Sea Turtles." If you're going to walk on the beach anyway, you may as well get paid for it.

WHAT CONTRACTING CAN DO FOR YOU

So, just maybe, the government might want to buy what you have to offer. But will a government contract really be worth the trouble? What can it really do for your business?

While winning a federal contract is not akin to winning the lotto, as some would have you believe, in some cases, it can help you accomplish other goals, from jump-starting your business to helping to finance your retirement.

- In just a few years, a small Midwest business that we know of went from being a one-man operation with a couple of thousand dollars in contracts per year to almost 70 employees with more than $75 million in contracts per year. The owner was able to take his expertise in MRO items (Maintenance, Repair and Operations materials) and win a major supply distribution contract from the Defense Department.

- A larger business that manufactured wood products had tried for some time, although unsuccessfully, to get a government contract for wooden handles for stretchers. The owners even bought a special machine that could put out hundreds of handles a day. But a one-man operation—a semi-retired wood maker who worked just a few hours each day making the handles—won the contract and accomplished his goal of keeping busy while earning extra retirement money. He put out a quality product that the government was happy with and, because he had virtually no overhead, was able to quote a much more competitive price.

- A small business owner who distributed diesel engines and engine parts, and was knowledgeable in government procedures, started a thriving business out of his dining room. He started with one client who wanted to supply the government, but didn't want to deal with the government. So he cut a deal with the client to do the government paperwork, organize the packing and shipping, take care of the problems with the government and become, in fact, the client's "contracting office." He now has several clients that supply different types of goods and works to various government agencies to the tune of several million dollars a year.

But even if your results are not as dramatic, getting a government contract can work to your advantage. What it can do is level out the hills and valleys during the business year. The usual margin of profit is never large, but if you utilize that portion of your business with the government for paying the overhead (i.e. lights, heat, a/c, etc.), you will find that the other contracts you have will be much more profitable. This is a very basic principle: If you can cover your costs with government contracts, you can be more selective with other, higher margin contracts.

WHAT CONTRACTING CAN'T DO FOR YOU

On the other hand, if your company has fallen on hard times and is in financial trouble, a government contract will not be able to save you. In fact, a contract might push you over the edge and put you completely out of business if you cannot fulfill its requirements.

You also need to keep in mind that the government does not finance contracts upfront. You must be able to handle the financing of the contract until you are paid, just like you do with your commercial customers. If you need financial assistance, perhaps you can meet with your banker to arrange a loan.

The government may sometimes allow for incremental payments based on incremental shipments or milestones of performance, but only if the value and duration of the contract are large enough. To receive any type of advance payment or progress payment, there must be a compelling reason, and not just the fact that a contractor needs money to stay in business.

Work Smart

Contrary to some late night talk show advice, the government does not have loads of free money to give to you that will set you up in any old business you want. It does have some programs that will help you find low interest loans, but that's a different book. (See CCH Business Owner's Toolkit Online: www.toolkit.cch.com.*)*

Chapter 3

Do You Have What It Takes?

So, are you ready to begin doing business with the government? Do you have the "right" resources, finances, equipment, computer skills and whatever else it may take? Here's a chance to find out. We'll tell you what you need and then give you the opportunity to rate yourself so that you can better see where you stand and in which direction you need to be moving.

IS YOUR BUSINESS BIG ENOUGH?

One question that often plagues small business owners at the start is, "Is my business big enough to handle a government contract?" Actually, there are many companies with fewer than five employees that have received a contract. In fact, some companies that have only one person in their entire operation have been awarded a contract. In one case, mentioned earlier, it kept the owner busy for an entire year and amounted to his total year's salary.

In other words, size is not necessarily important. Any business—regardless of size—has the potential to get a contract with the government. But which companies stand the best chance of actually getting a contract? The answer is simple—any business that sells a product or service and is:

- responsible

- competitive

- patient in dealing with the bureaucratic process

- committed to invest and apply the resources that are needed to market to the government.

How Small Is Small?

The United States Small Business Administration establishes the size standards used to identify a company considered small. As a general rule, a small business is one that:

- Is organized for profit

- Has a place of business in the United States

- Makes a significant contribution to the U.S. economy by paying taxes or using products, materials or labor

- Does not exceed the numerical size standard for its industry

Maybe that definition leaves you scratching your head. Here is another "rule of thumb" to use. If you deal with a product (i.e., manufacture, deal, or distribute), then the size standard is based on the average number of employees over a 12-month period, typically 500 or less. If you are in a service industry, then the standard is based upon the average annual sales over a three-year period, ranging in dollars from $750,000 to $28.5 million.

The following chart, which you also can find on the SBA website, will help you decide where you fall. Just remember this is a summary of industry groups. Go to the SBA website, http://www.sba.gov, for more detailed information. A business in one of the following industry groups is small if it is not greater than the size standard indicated.

SBA Small Business Size Standards

Company Classification	Criteria
Manufacturing	500 employees
Wholesale Trade	100 employees
Agriculture	$750,000
Retail Trade	$6 million
General and Heavy Construction (except Dredging)	$28.5 million
Dredging	$17 million
Special Trade Contractors	$12 million
Travel Agencies	$3 million (commissions and other income)
Business and Personal Services, except: -- Architectural, Engineering, Surveying and Mapping Services -- Dry cleaning and Carpet Cleaning Services	$6 million $4 million $4 million

For specific size standards, refer to the size regulations in 13 CFR § 121.201 or the table of small business size standards.

If the size of a business exceeds the size standard for its overall industry classification, it may still be a small business under the North American Industrial Classification System (NAICS) code (pronounced "nakes") for that group. Some industries have higher size standards than the general one for the entire industry group. SBA has a Table of Size Standards on its website at www.sba.gov. The SBA uses NAICS codes to identify industrial categories and make size determinations. Just remember that the SBA does revise the size standards from time to time based on changes in the data used to determine size. NAICS codes, as well as other government coding systems, are discussed in detail in Part II.

Work Smart

While you can use these general standards to make an educated assessment, only the Small Business Administration has the authority to make an official size determination. Anyone can challenge a company's size declaration, but it is the SBA that will settle the issue.

Again, the important thing to remember is that it doesn't matter whether a company is classified as large or small. The companies that successfully sell to the government are the ones that do their homework and "keep at it," while companies that just "give it a try" almost never succeed.

Be the innovator—the government is looking for an item—you have a better way or process. Don't just sit on the sideline. Get out and sell yourself.

We know of a contractor that helped a buyer by sending a form with all the information the buyer would need to prepare a good quote, along with his company information and point of contact printed on it. The buyer made copies of the form and gave it to the other buyers as well. Be helpful if you see a better way and work with the government. If you do have a better way you may be surprised at the "pay off."

DO YOU HAVE THE FINANCIAL RESOURCES?

What is the financial situation of your business? Is your business financially stable or are you just starting out and short on cash flow? Are you able to make payroll and other payments with no problem? In other words, is your business financially healthy?

As we mentioned earlier, if you are in financial trouble, a government contract would be more likely to put you out of business than to save your business.

Example

Small business owners primarily look to their own personal resources for capital. The predominant sources of financing are:

Small business owners themselves	*41%*
Cash advances from personal credit cards	*36%*
Personal lines of credit	*25%*

DO YOU HAVE A QUALITY ASSURANCE PROGRAM?

The terms of a government contract generally require you to assure the quality of the product or service that your business will be providing. To do that, you need to show that you have some kind of formal, documented quality control plan in place.

Your plan could consist of anything from a general quality assurance manual to a full quality assurance program that complies with a recognized commercial quality standard, a government standard, or the international ISO standard for your industry. (See Part III of this book for a detailed explanation of quality standards.)

IS YOUR OFFICE UP TO SPEED?

To be ready for the government, you need to be sure you have the proper office skills. You need to be organized, maintain accurate files and records, document important transactions and meetings, know where everything is, and generally be able to keep things humming.

DO YOU HAVE THE TECHNOLOGY?

We can't stress enough the importance of this area. Simply put, if you are not capable of doing business using some kind of electronic commerce (e-commerce) or electronic procurement (e-procurement), you will not be doing business with the government.

Why? Because the law, beginning with the Government Paperwork Elimination Act of 1995, requires that the government use electronic means to issue and award small business contracts, specifically those between $2,500 and $100,000. Furthermore, in a continuous effort to streamline the procurement process, government buyers are using new options in making purchases, such as multiple-award schedules, purchase cards, reverse auctions, etc., almost all of them technology-based.

The goal of electronic procurement is to allow the exchange of information, such as purchase orders, invoices, or shipping notifications in an electronic, paperless format. The benefits for the government are the elimination of manpower costs associated with processing paper, reduction in errors, and speeding up the process of ordering and paying for goods and services. You can now get government bids automatically sent to you via e-mail, decide which ones you want to bid on, download the technical information from the Internet, and then bid on the requirement without using one sheet of hard paper.

In order to do business with the federal government, you must have the following at your disposal. (If you are waiting for the next "best" or "latest" thing before you buy, grit your teeth and go ahead and get the one that's best for you *now*. There will always be something better or newer. And while you wait, opportunity passes you by.)

- *A personal computer, Pentium or higher, using a Windows, Linux or Macintosh operating system* — The faster and more RAM you have in your computer, the better off you will be. If you are in the process of shopping, we encourage you to buy as much "oomph" (otherwise known as RAM or memory) as you can afford, but don't get carried away with "goodies" you don't need for business. Remember that you want a computer to satisfy your business needs, not for multi-media or games, unless of course this is your business.

- *An Internet Connection* — If you use a modem, make sure that it uses the latest technology and is at least 56k baud rate. A better choice would be broadband giving you better Internet speed—a big plus when it comes to downloading large files. We feel the best setup is broadband. This gives the greatest speed and ready access to the Internet.

- *Internet Protection* — If you use either DSL or broadband, you also need to set up protection for your system with good anti-virus and firewall software. This software reduces the chances of getting hit with a virus or by a hacker. Remember, with a DSL or broadband connection, you are always connected to the Internet, so system security is an issue.

Work Smart

If you are not moving into new technology and new ways of doing business using e-commerce and the Internet, consider taking classes or attending workshops and conferences on these subjects. In this day and age, keeping up with and knowing how to use new technology in your business is crucial to your success.

ELECTRONIC PROCUREMENT

The concept of electronic procurement for a small business not yet comfortable with new technology can be overwhelming. E-procurement takes many forms and has become a requirement for doing business with the government.

But the electronic procurement requirements that we describe here are not unique to the government. They are the same as a large private-sector business requires of its suppliers. Therefore, it is essential that any business at least consider these issues, whether it does business with the government or not.

Electronic procurement with the government typically takes two forms: e-commerce web sites and/or Electronic Data Interchange (EDI).

- *Doing Business via Government Web Sites* — As a consumer, you've most likely purchased a product or service such as an airline ticket or an item of clothing on one of the many e-commerce web sites. When you complete your order by entering the required information and electronically submitting your order via a web site instead of calling or mailing in your order or visiting a store location, you are participating in electronic procurement. The information that you provided is electronically connected into the merchant's internal systems. The benefit to you as the consumer is saving time; the benefit to the merchant is saving the costs associated with processing a paper order, paying phone order takers, printing a catalogue, and maintaining a store location.

  When it comes to government-sponsored, e-commerce web sites, the set-up is similar to the one described above, except that in this situation, the government agency is the consumer, you are the merchant, and it is the government that provides the web site for performing various procurement transactions, such as displaying requests for proposals, submitting bids, delivering invoices, etc. This is a great benefit if you have a limited number of order transactions because the only technology it requires of you is a computer, Internet connectivity, and a web browser. A contractor will need to speak with the buyers of each agency to determine if an e-commerce web site is available, where it is located (the web address), and what procurement functions can be performed. Also, you may need to obtain a username and password from the agency to access the site.

- *Doing Business via EDI* — Government agencies that do not offer an e-commerce web site will most often require a contractor to communicate order transactions via EDI, the second form of electronic procurement with the government. EDI is a set of standards that defines how data/information is presented in an electronic form, thereby allowing the electronic equivalents of common business documents, such as invoices, forms, bids, requests for quotes, purchase orders, etc., to be transmitted electronically between the computers of what are called "trading partners." A trading partner can be the federal government, a prime contractor, or another commercial business.

Why Are EDI Standards Necessary?

For purposes of illustration, let's say that the government has contracted with you for certain supplies and wants to receive your invoice electronically. You go ahead and oblige by sending your invoice file in a format that is unique to your system. Since the way that data is presented in the government's system is also unique, in order to import your file into its system, it must first convert the data into the format that matches the format required by its system's database. Now imagine how difficult it would be for the government to manage this process if each of the thousands of government contractors were each to send electronic invoices in a format unique to their system.

So, instead, the government asks its contractors to convert their files into a standardized format (EDI) prior to sending into a standardized format. Using EDI as the standard, the government receives only one standardized format for all invoices and only has to manage converting files into one file format for each document type (invoice, purchase order, shipping notification, etc.).

Who sets EDI standards? There are nonprofit committees that define EDI standards for the country. The set of standards most often used is called ANSIIx12 4010. Within that set of standards, there are many documents, referred to by versions and numbers (e.g., 810 is the standard invoice document, 850 is the standard purchase order document, and 997 is the standard functional acknowledgement that confirms the receipt of the files by each party).

An explanation of these standards and the specifications for each version can be found at http://www-edi.itsi.disa.mil.

Converting Data into EDI

There are three basic options for getting your data into EDI format. It's best to check out all options, as prices and functionality vary greatly.

- *Translation Software* — There are many EDI companies that offer software that allow you to "map" the various data conversions that need to occur in order to convert your files. There will be upfront costs to purchase and install the software, and you will also have to pay an employee, often called an EDI coordinator, to manage the software or pay a consultant to do so.

- *Third-Party Solutions* — Many EDI companies offer services that take your paper or electronic files, convert those files to the required EDI format, and then deliver those files to the right location. Typically the fee for this type of service would be based on the number of transactions and the number of unique formats being translated (called "templates"). For instance, an 810 invoice is one template and an 850 purchase order is a second template.

- *Hosted Software* — Finally, some EDI companies offer solutions that allow you to take advantage of the translator software technology without the cost of purchasing and maintaining the software. You simply send your electronic files over the Internet in the format you normally use to the EDI host company. The EDI host converts your files into the EDI format required and then delivers the files to the specified location. Charges for this service typically include a one-time set-up fee for each trading partner and a smaller monthly fee that may or may not be based on the number of transactions.

Which is the best option for you? In order to define a return on investment for any of the options, you should take the following factors into account:

- *Transaction Volume* — Certain solutions will have a per transaction fee. Understanding the number of transactions your business will perform will allow you to estimate your monthly costs.

- *Employee Costs* — It is helpful to find out the cost to process a paper document in order to determine savings that may occur by implementing an EDI solution.

- *Opportunity Cost/Cost of Not Doing Business* — You should understand the dollar impact if you choose not to do business with the government (or with another trading partner). This helps greatly in determining what your business can "afford" to spend on a solution.

What EDI Can Do for You

Here are just some of the advantages of being EDI-capable:

- increased business opportunities; remember that once you've mastered EDI with the government, you can use the same technology to provide EDI to your larger, private-sector trading partners

- faster and more accurate processing of orders, resulting in improved inventory management and, best of all, greater customer satisfaction

- faster billing; since orders are filled and delivered sooner, billing and closeout can occur sooner

- lower mailing costs, a reduction in mailroom sorting/distribution time and elimination of lost documents

- improvements in overall quality through better recordkeeping and fewer errors in data

- better information for decision-making; EDI provides accurate information and audit trails of transactions, enabling you to identify the areas offering the greatest potential for efficiency improvement or cost reduction

Exchanging EDI Files

To manage various security and tracking issues associated with exchanging the high volume of files the government exchanges, it uses what is called a Value Added Network (VAN). In simplest terms, a VAN is a for-profit private-sector business that provides and manages a collection of secure mailboxes that are used to deliver and receive order files.

If you are doing business with the government, via EDI, you will need to acquire a VAN mailbox from which you will pick up and deliver files from and to the government via a dial-up connection. The VAN of your choice will offer you technical assistance in this area.

It is not a requirement that your mailbox be located on the same VAN as the government's. Most VANs have agreements with one another that enable them to exchange files. However, there is a cost for this, referred to as an Interconnect Fee. If you're doing business with only one government agency, you may decide to obtain a mailbox on that agency's VAN to avoid Interconnect Fees.

There are many other fees for optional ancillary services VANs offer. The main fee incurred is the "per kilo character" charge (per 1000 characters). VANs are becoming more competitive these days, so be sure to compare prices. As an ancillary service, most VANs also offer third-party translation services.

In closing, our advice is to use the information we have provided to perform a methodical appraisal of all the solutions available to you, and then choose the best one for your company.

Work Smart

It always amazes us how most people willingly and unhesitatingly give out their credit card number, Social Security number, address, and almost anything else that is asked for when placing an order by phone. Yet, when it comes to ordering over the web, people will hesitate to give out any information, thinking that anyone "out there" could access and misuse it. However, the truth is that most e-commerce sites are completely secure and safe. Just know the site you are dealing with.

E-Government and Security Issues

As previously discussed, all branches of federal government are required by law to migrate their business practices to a paperless operation. In implementing the new e-procurement way of contracting, it is clear that there is a need to ensure the confidentiality, security, and authentication of information exchanged between government and its contractors in the electronic environment.

The DoD, the buying giant of the federal government, has addressed the need for security in the e-government environment by adopting a mandatory system, referred to as "public key infrastructure" (PKI). PKI allows DoD to electronically communicate with industry by enabling paperless, secure, private electronic business contracting. In addition to adoption by DoD, PKI use is expanding at all levels, including federal, state, and local levels of government as well as in the private sector.

What is PKI? It works much like a realtor's lockbox. Under this arrangement, the seller has agreed to "trust" the realtor to gain access, via a key or combination to a lockbox, and show the home to prospective buyers when the seller is away.

PKI uses a process similar to the realtor's lockbox, although in this case the lockbox is digital and is stored on computers. For government contracting purposes, a unique PKI digital identity certificate file is issued to a contractor's authorized officer or agent. In essence, this PKI digital certificate file verifies that the contractor is in fact authorized to conduct business electronically with the government contracting office. In this way, PKI helps the contracting parties to establish a "trust relationship" while doing business via computers in a virtual world, and digitally protects the information assets of both parties in much the same way a lockbox protects the seller from allowing just anyone to enter the home while still providing access to the "trusted" parties and potential buyers.

In addition to ensuring the security of the electronic information at all times during transit through shared networks and storage on network servers and desktop hard drives, it ensures that the document being signed and sent online is from the company or person authorized to provide the information within the electronic document, that the document is legally signed in accordance with current federal and state laws, that the document has not been altered since being completed and electronically signed, and that the electronic document is time-stamped and requires an electronic return receipt.

What PKI Means to You

At this point, you may be wondering how all of this could affect you. Here are answers to the questions businesses most often ask about PKI.

Why not just use a PIN number? While a number of government agencies have successfully used PINs to provide security in innovative applications, particularly the Securities and Exchange Commission for regulatory filings and the Internal Revenue Service for tax filings, they are planning for an eventual transfer to digital signatures. PKI technology fosters interoperability across numerous applications— PIN numbers can't do that.

Are you required to get PKI-certified in order to do business with the government? No, not at this point. But the plan under federal e-government initiatives is to ultimately provide all U.S. citizens with a single entry point to all government online services and information through www.FirstGov.gov, a web portal from which anyone can access virtually all federal government information. The ability for a citizen to access information will be based on the nature and sensitivity of the information being accessed. Government contracting with federal agencies falls into the area that will require a PKI digital certificate authenticating the identity of the online user and insuring they have the authority to access and provide secure online data and documentation when required.

Does it cost anything to get PKI certification? There is no charge. It's just a matter of downloading and filling out a form from one of various sites. How do you get a digital ID or learn more? Microsoft Corp. in conjunction with Verisign.com has enabled their e-mail applications,

Outlook Express and Outlook 2000, to install PKI certificates. Microsoft and Verisign have also enabled Office XP and a number of versions of Internet Explorer browsers to include PKI digital certificates.

You can get a detailed explanation of how Verisign's PKI digital certificates work as well as instructions for how to obtain a PKI certificate for your Outlook email at http://www.verisign.com/support/tlc/per/clientHelp/help/toc.htm.

You can also download a Microsoft Word Document explaining the security features of Outlook 2000 entitled "Out2000SR-1.doc" at http://www.microsoft.com/office/ork/2000/download/Out2000SR-1.doc.

The following web sites can give you more detailed information on the various PKI programs for GSA, DoD, and the State of Illinois:

- The Rise of the e-Citizen: How People Use Government Agencies' Web Sites at http://www.pewinternet.org/reports/pdfs/PIP_Govt_Website_Rpt.pdf

- GSA's ACES, What is ACES at http://www.gsa.gov/Portal/content/offerings_content.jsp?contentOID=120787&contentType=1004

- DoD eMall at http://www.emall.dla.mil

- DoD e-Business Exchange System at http://eblibrary.jecpo.anvi.com/ec/debx/index.html

- DoD DFAS Wide Area Workflow at https://ecweb.dfas.mil/notes

- State of Illinois PKI Digital Signature Project at http://www100.state.il.us/tech/pki

Security is, and will continue to be, an issue in many aspects of our lives, including e-business. Although digital authorization is not currently a requirement, it certainly may be one day. It's a good idea to keep yourself informed about changes and developments. In the next several years, you will start to see more adoption of digital identities through the government implementation of Homeland Security policies.

DO YOU KNOW HOW TO USE THE INTERNET?

Folks, we are not talking here about knowing how to play games or surf the World Wide Web looking for sports scores. We are talking about knowing how to use search engines, download *and* upload files, use viewers like Adobe Acrobat, and communicate via e-mail.

You also need to know how to access a CD-ROM file so you can look at government bids. (We used to get a box the size of an orange crate with bids from the Corps of Engineers every other day. Now we get one CD with all the information, and it's so nice! It's easy to keep track of all the bids because all the information is in one place.)

Rate Your Readiness To Be a Contractor

This "quiz" is not meant to be a serious scientific assessment. Its main purpose is to get you thinking about the government market, what areas you may need to work on, and what will be expected of you and your company. So, with that in mind, here are the categories for scoring:

Criteria	Score
Size of Business	
If you have 1-500 employees and are committed to winning a government contract and willing to do your homework, **give yourself +10**. *If you get impatient quickly or plan on making only a half-hearted attempt to win a contract,* **give yourself -10**.	
Financial Capability	
If you are financially capable of performing a contract and are going after the government market in order to increase or stabilize sales, **give yourself +10**. *If you are going after a contract just to stay in business,* **give yourself -20**.	
Quality Assurance Program	
If you have a general QA manual, **give yourself +5**. *If your manual complies with a commercial quality or government standard,* **give yourself +10**. *If your quality assurance program complies with the international standard (referred to as an ISO standard) for your industry,* **give yourself +25**. *If you have no formal, documented quality assurance program,* **give yourself -10**.	
Office Efficiency	
If you keep good records and have an efficient way of finding information, **give yourself +10**. *If it takes you a while to put your hands on a piece of needed information and you run your office on the "I know it's here somewhere" principle,* **give yourself -10**.	
EDI and E-Commerce	
If you have the necessary equipment for doing business using e-commerce, **give yourself +25**. *If you don't have a computer and modem, count yourself temporarily out of the game. Start shopping now.* **Lose all points!**	

Internet	
*If you know how to do all the tasks we just talked about, **give yourself + 10**. If you can only play games, **give yourself −10**. If you lose to your kids, **subtract another -5 points**. If you know enough to go to your teenager and get some help, **give yourself 5 points**.*	
Bonus Points	
*Do you know how to get "specs & stds"? If you think that getting "specs & stds" means getting something out of your eye, **give yourself -10**. If you know that a spec is a specification or standard for a specific product or service, **give yourself + 10**.* *Do you believe that all you have to do is send in a bid and no matter what price you quote, it will be approved (like that $300 hammer you heard about 25 years ago)? If you do, **give yourself -25**. If you believe that your price needs to be competitive, **give yourself + 25**.*	

OK, now for the rating.

If you scored 0-50, you might want to either rethink your idea for getting a government contract or work on acquiring the necessary resources and skills.

If you scored 51-75, you are heading in the right direction and probably just need a little assistance.

If you scored 76-100, you are ripe and ready to go after a government contract.

If you scored 100+, you have everything you need to start winning contracts. (If your score fell into this range, please call us. We might have some money to invest!)

Chapter 4

Government Rules You Need To Know

You've heard it said many times, "Government contracting seems hard—so many rules and regulations. And, if you don't follow them, the government is just waiting to take you down!"

Actually, nothing could be further from the truth. The government not only actively seeks out small business participation when it buys products and services, but it also goes to great lengths and spends lots of money in outreach programs to find good, qualified small businesses to be its suppliers. For example, it will provide information that will help you bid with minimal risk. Just for the asking, you can find out how much the government bought the last 5 to 10 times, who they bought from, and how much they paid. Try asking for that kind of information from your commercial customers and see what they say!

In reality, there are many similarities in selling your products or services to commercial customers and selling them to the federal government—the same basic business principles and strategies generally apply. Both want a quality product or service at a reasonable price, delivered on time. And in both cases, you need to know your customers' needs, how they buy and who buys what. You need to do your market research. And whether it is a commercial customer or a buying agency of the federal government, you need to arrange face-to-face meetings so you can better clarify what they want and so they can better understand what your company can do to help them.

However, although the approach to the commercial and government market is similar, the procedures and rules of doing business in the government arena are different—and if these differences are not understood, it is here that problems can occur.

However, all of these problems can be minimized if you take the time to gain some basic knowledge of these procedures and rules and to learn how the process works. (Note that we said "minimized," not "avoided," because Murphy's law is always out there waiting to challenge your commitment to the task.)

GOVERNMENT PROCEDURES

Let's get started by looking at some of the differences in procedures. First of all, the federal government conducts its business through authorized agents, called contracting officers:

- The Procurement Contracting Officer (referred to as the "PCO") places contracts and handles contract terminations when the contractor defaults.

- The Administrative Contracting Officer (referred to as the "ACO") administers the contracts.

- The Termination Contracting Officer (referred to as the "TCO") handles contract terminations when the government terminates for its convenience.

Depending on the situation, the same person may be all three.

Because the government is a sovereign entity (in other words, it is the ruling power), it has rights that commercial businesses do not have. For example, the government has the right to unilaterally revise the contract, so long as changes are within the parameters of the contract.

This means the government can change the quantity it is contracting for, or how it is packaged or how it is being shipped. The contractor is entitled to equitable cost adjustment, but must comply with the changes. The government also has the right to cancel the contract if the need for the product or service no longer exists. Here again, the contractor would be entitled to reimbursement for costs incurred.

Because taxpayer dollars are being spent, the government can impose extensive audit and surveillance requirements under the terms of a contract. However, extensive and stringent requirements are usually imposed only on higher priced contracts (i.e., contracts of $100,000 or more in value) and thus are not usually applicable to contracts with small businesses.

One of the big fears that small business owners have is that the government will come in and audit their books, go through their files with a vacuum cleaner, and tell them how to run their business. That fear is totally unfounded and far from the truth.

GOVERNMENT LAWS AND REGULATIONS

Now let's take a closer look at the laws and regulations that will affect you when you do business with the government. Maybe the easiest way to begin is with a brief history lesson.

Before the earliest law was passed, private individuals furnished from their own resources whatever supplies and materials the government needed. (How well do you think that would work today?) But that all changed with the Purveyor of Public Affairs Act of 1795, which allowed the government to buy needed supplies and materials.

At the beginning of the Civil War, which created monumental needs for the federal government, the Civil Sundry Appropriations Act of 1861 became law, and this continued the principle of advertised procurements for the next 86 years.

When it became apparent that small companies and their labor force needed protection, the Sherman Antitrust Act of 1890 was enacted.

Finally, the Armed Services Procurement Act, signed into law in 1947, continued the sealed bid as the preferred method of procurement, with specific exceptions. It also attempted to place procurement rules in one location. The result was the Armed Services Procurement Regulation (ASPR).

In addition, there are many other laws and Executive Orders that affect how you must conduct your business if you want to contract with the federal government.

For example, the Eight-Hour Work Law of 1892 set the eight-hour workday. The Davis-Bacon Act of 1931 set the minimum wage on the construction site at the local prevailing wage. In 1933, the Buy American Act required the government to buy only American products. The Walsh-Healey Public Contracts Act of 1936, drastically changed in 1994, required a supplier to certify that it was the manufacturer or a regular dealer. This was an attempt to do away with the broker.

Later on, the Small Business Act of 1953 was passed, which established the Small Business Administration. The Truth in Negotiation Act of 1962 required both prime and subcontractors on contracts over $500,000 to certify the cost data submitted under the solicitation. Public Law 95-507, which amended the Small Business Act of 1978, formalized the Small Business Subcontracting Plan requirement in contracts over $500,000 to large businesses. At that time, this law was considered a significant change in government procurement practices.

Now we come to the recent laws. The Federal Acquisition Streamlining Act of 1994 (FASA) was revolutionary in its impact on the federal acquisition process. It repealed or substantially modified more than 225 statutes and pushed the contracting process into the 21st century.

Among other things, it simplified the federal procurement process, reduced paperwork burdens, and transformed the simplified acquisition process to electronic commerce. Before the law could be fully implemented, the Federal Acquisition Reform Act of 1996 (FARA, also known as the Clinger-Cohen Act) was passed to correct some deficiencies in the earlier legislation and to make more changes. These last two laws were significant events because of the vast changes they made in the way that the government conducts it business. The system is continuing to make adjustments to the new, more open environment.

Example

What prompted the changes in the procurement process as contained in FASA and FARA? The story goes that Motorola was contacted by the Defense Department to supply mobile communication devices to be used by our military in "Desert Storm." The company was more than willing to supply the product, and the price quoted was not an issue.

However, at that time, the law did not allow the government to contract for a basically commercial item. Motorola told the government to take the product and give them a check for the amount agreed upon. The government couldn't do that without a signed contract, an impasse. As hard as the government tried to remove the problem clauses, it couldn't do it.

An ally country, supposedly Japan, came to the rescue. They bought the product and then furnished it to the U.S. government as part of its support of Desert Storm.

After all of this, the powers in Washington finally realized that the procurement process needed some major changes to get in step with the marketplace.

For your easy reference, we have created a chart summarizing the most significant laws and their provisions at the end of this chapter.

How FASA Affects You

What was so significant about FASA to the interests of small businesses? Here are some of the specific changes that this law made:

- Changed the small purchase level from $25,000 and under to between $2,500 and $100,000, and provided that all these purchases can enjoy "simplified acquisition procedures," which in effect reserves all of these purchases for small business. Two of the main purposes of the simplified acquisition procedures are to reduce administrative costs and to improve contract opportunities for small, small disadvantaged, small service-disabled-veteran, and small women-owned businesses.

- The government was mandated to use electronic means to issue and award small purchases (termed by the law as "Simplified Acquisition Procedures" or "SAP"). That means that for contracts under $100,000, there is now a tremendous effort by the government to go "paperless." What does paperless mean? Well, it simply means that the government is entering the era of electronic commerce and technology for doing business. So much for the myth of being buried by government paperwork and red tape.

- Encouraged government buying offices to use credit cards on all requirements under $2,500. Basically, the intent was to get these "nuisance" buys out of the buying office and simply let the government user buy what was needed quickly and efficiently. This means two things for small businesses: minimal paperwork and a real opportunity for any business that accepts credit cards to increase its business. As we mentioned earlier, in 2003 alone, the federal government spent almost $16.4 billion in credit card purchases in the under-$2500 range. The government now just goes to a local store and buys what it needs.

Government Purchasing Thresholds

Micro-purchases (credit cards)	*for contracts up to $2,500*
Simplified Acquisition Procedures (SAP)	*for contracts for $2,501 to $100,000*
Simplified Commercial	*for contracts $100,000 to $5,000,000*
Commercial Off the Shelf (COTS)	*no dollar limits, any dollar size contract*
Commercial Items	*for contracts over $2,500*
Sealed Bids/Negotiations	*FAR Parts 14 & 15 apply for contracts $100,000 and up*

- Established commercial items as the preferred products for the government to buy if they meet the government need; to do otherwise requires a justification as to why it is necessary. This last little change is having a major impact on the process. First of all, it has meant a reduction in government personnel that small businesses have to deal with. The more the government buys commercial items, the less it will need buyers, production specialists, pricing specialists, quality assurance specialists and other personnel that were required when the government designed to its own specifications. Second, it has meant that only if the commercial market cannot satisfy the government's need can the government buyer require that items be built to government specifications. In other words, most government specifications and standards will be used only with contracts greater than $100,000, so you, the small business contractor, will have fewer government requirements to worry about.

Laws that Affect Government Contracting

Public Law	Result
Purveyor of Public Affairs Act of 1795	Allowed the government to buy needed supplies and materials to perform government functions.
Civil Sundry Appropriations Act of 1861	Continued the principle of advertised procurements for the next 86 years.
Sherman Antitrust Act of 1890	Protected small companies and their labor force from large business.
Armed Services Procurement Act of 1947	Continued the sealed bid as the preferred method of procurement, placed procurement rules in one location and gave us the Armed Services Procurement Regulation (ASPR), which was the beginnings of today's rulebook, the FAR.
Eight-Hour Work Law of 1892	Set the eight-hour workday.
The Davis-Bacon Act of 1931	Set the minimum wage on the construction site at the local prevailing wage.
Buy American Act	Required the government to buy only American products.
Walsh-Healey Public Contracts Act of 1936 (note that this law was drastically changed in 1994)	Required a supplier to certify that it was the manufacturer or a regular dealer. This was an attempt to do away with the "broker."
Small Business Act of 1953	Established the Small Business Administration.
Truth in Negotiation Act of 1962	Required both prime and subcontractors on contracts over $500,000 to certify the cost data submitted under the solicitation.
Public Law 95-507, Amendment to the Small Business Act (1978)	Formalized the Small Business Subcontracting Plan requirement in contracts over $500,000 to large businesses. Set goals for large primes.
Federal Acquisition Streamlining Act of 1994 (FASA)	Revolutionary in its impact on the federal acquisition process. It repealed or substantially modified more than 225 statutes and pushed the contracting process into the 21st century. Among other things, it simplified the federal procurement process, reduced paperwork burdens, and transformed the simplified acquisition process to electronic commerce.

Federal Acquisition Reform Act of 1996 (FARA) or (Clinger-Cohen Act)	*Before FASA could be fully implemented, this Act became law and corrected some deficiencies in the earlier legislation and made more changes.*

THE RULEBOOK AND BIBLE—THE FAR

No discussion of government procedures and rules is complete without talking about the basic rulebook for government contracts: the Federal Acquisition Regulation, commonly known as "the FAR."

The FAR, which had its beginnings in the Armed Services Procurement Regulation established in 1947, is considered the Bible for federal government contracting. The FAR contains all the rules governing the contracting process as well as all the forms and clauses used in contracts.

The FAR has recently gone through a significant rewrite to reflect and implement all of the changes made by all the recent laws. In order to do business with the federal government, you definitely need to have a basic knowledge of what is in the FAR and how to use it. (See Appendix 4 for a general Table of Contents for the FAR.)

Work Smart

The FAR is designed to be a guide, not a limiting rulebook. Under recent changes in the law, contracting officers can use "good business practices" that make sense in making decisions and in negotiating terms instead of having to consult a rulebook on each decision.

The FAR is divided into 53 parts, each part dealing with a separate aspect of the acquisition process. The first six parts deal with general government acquisition matters and the next six parts deal with aspects of acquisition planning. The rest of the FAR deals with other topics, such as simplified acquisition threshold (formerly known as small purchases), large dollar value buys, labor laws, contract administration, applicable clauses and forms.

Relevant parts for small businesses include Part 19, Small Business Programs, and Part 52, which contains the standard terms and conditions contained in a government contract.

Although the FAR is the primary acquisition regulation for the federal government, each government agency may issue an agency acquisition supplement to the FAR. We therefore have the Defense Federal Acquisition Regulation Supplement (DFARS), the General Services

Acquisition Regulation Supplement (GSARS), and the National Aeronautics Space Administration FAR Supplement (NASFARS), just to name a few. Many of these are on the Internet at the agency's web site (see Appendix 3 for a list of web sites that you might find useful).

These supplements are not stand-alone documents, but must be read in conjunction with the FAR. Therefore, when preparing a proposal or quote, remember to look at the relevant supplement, in addition to the FAR, to make sure added requirements don't apply. The FAR has more than 1000 pages and a supplement may be another 1000 pages, but only a relatively small portion is used in any single contract. That is why it's important, when dealing with a government office, to ask which regulation governs their acquisition procedures. Make sure that you read any changes to the rule before you quote. Don't assume, ask!

Caution

Congress gave the Federal Aviation Administration (FAA) the authority to develop its own acquisition regulations; therefore it is not bound by the FAR. Although the FAA has chosen to adopt or adapt many parts of the FAR, don't assume that its provisions are all just like those in the FAR. Some quasi-government agencies, like the Tennessee Valley Authority or United States Postal Service, are not bound by the FAR, but many of their acquisition regulations are adaptations of FAR provisions.

You can buy a copy of the FAR in hard copy from the Government Printing Office (GPO), read it on the Internet at http://farsite.hill.af.mil, or buy it from a third party like CCH Tax and Accounting (business.cch.com).

Work Smart

If you order the FAR from the Government Printing Office, make sure that the price includes all updates, as they occur, so you will always have current information when you prepare a proposal. Updates are important because of the potential impact on the way you will bid. It could change the cost and therefore your quote!

When you view the FAR on the Internet, make sure that you check the update date for the same reason. The softbound type, such as the CCH version, is current until the next update.

Just remember that the government is ready to do business, on a competitive basis, with competent, qualified companies that can supply the products or services it requires at a reasonable price. You, the new contractor, must know what their game plan is. Once you have some understanding of the federal buying process, you can enter this market with greater confidence and be successful and profitable.

Work Smart

The Department of Defense is transforming a significant portion of the DFARS to the DFARS Procedures, Guidance and Information (PGI). The PGI is a companion resource to the DFARS. DFARS PGI is a new, web-based tool so the entire acquisition community can simply and rapidly access non-regulatory Department of Defense (DoD) procedures, and guidance and information relevant to FAR and DFARS topics.

The DFARS still remains the source for regulation and implementation of laws, as well as DoD-wide contracting policies, authorities and delegations. In other words, DFARS will answer the questions, "What is the policy?" and "What are the rules?" DFARS PGI will connect the acquisition community to the available background, procedures and guidance, answering the questions, "How can I execute the policy?" and "Why does this policy exist?"

It is believed DFARS PGI will not only provide a rapid method of disseminating non-regulatory material to contracting officers and the entire acquisition community, it will also serve as a real-time training tool by making relevant information available on your topic of interest. DFARS PGI is new and will be evolving in the months ahead. It'll be in simpler language, in an easy-to-follow format, and with new tools for searching and retrieving current and past information on FAR and DFARS requirements.

Part II

Go For It!

OK, so what do you have to do to actually sign that first deal with the government? We have broken down the actions you need to take into ten steps. In the following chapters, we will guide you through the process of completing each one.

Caution

Although we are presenting the actions you need to take in a step-by-step fashion, it does not mean that they need to be done one at a time. They can be done simultaneously or in a different order, depending on your circumstances.

Chapter 5, Think Like the Government: Start thinking about your business the same way the government does—as the provider of an end product. By thinking in terms of output, and not process, you'll be more likely to make a connection leading to a deal.

Chapter 6, Identify Your Customers: The buying offices of the federal government don't know you're out there, but you can find them if you know where to look.

Chapter 7, Get Registered: Before you can start bidding on contracts, the government needs to know who you are and what you do. A mistake or omission at this point could severely hurt your chances of landing a contract, so we'll tell you what to do step-by-step, including how to decipher all the government codes involved in such a process.

Chapter 8, Find Bid Leads: The government is required by law to inform all potential contractors of what they're looking for, but are you listening? There are a number of outlets for this information, and one is best for you and your company.

Chapter 9, Get the Bid Package: You've got the lead, now you need to get your hands on the specifics. Find out how to get the bid package and how to understand its particular pricing arrangement.

Chapter 10, Review the Bid: The solicitation you've just received has the potential to be a binding contract. Know what to read and how to read it to maximize your chances for success.

Chapter 11, Get Technical Data: To successfully complete your bid, you'll need to do some research. Learn what types of specs may apply and how to get the correct data to comply with the order.

Chapter 12, Price It Out: In a competitive bidding process, price is the determining factor. And if your bid is accepted, it will literally make or break your company—so know what factors to consider.

Chapter 13, Write Your Proposal: This is a formal procedure that must be completed exactly. We take you through it line-by-line, explaining it all.

Chapter 14, Submit Your Bid: Submission of your bid is the final step in a contracting process full of fine print. Know the best ways to keep your bid from being kicked out at the last second.

Chapter 5

Think Like
The Government

You are now ready to get started. You might imagine that the first thing you should do is get out there out and look for all those government buyers and bid opportunities, right?

Not so fast. Before you take any action at all, there is one thing you need to do that will greatly increase your rate of success in finding opportunities and winning contracts: Learn to think the same way the government does when it does business.

A commercial company and a government buyer may need the same item, but their approach is very different. For example, when a commercial company looks to buy an item, the buyer is very familiar with the item being bought and knows exactly what type of process— be it welding or stamping or extrusion or metal finishing—is used in making the particular item. Therefore, when it is looking for a supplier of that item, it thinks in terms of the process and looks for a welding company or a stamping house or metal finisher, as the case may be.

On the other hand, when the government buys, it knows the item it needs (e.g., a gear, a resistor, a coffee cup, a spring, a bolt, a pencil), but it does not know the process or type of company that makes the item. The buyer is merely given a requirement (one or more items of some kind) and the technical data package and puts them out for bidding. Therefore, when the government is looking for a supplier, it thinks in terms of the item and looks for companies that have indicated that they can produce that item.

Think about it this way: In the commercial world, a buyer usually has a good idea of what they are buying, what the processes are, what machines are used, etc. On the other hand, government buyers, while very good at getting the job done—on time, in budget and when needed—are acquisition specialists first and not engineers. In other words, they buy the product, not the process.

Example

At a recent Congressionally sponsored government procurement conference, the owners of a company that made various items for the railroad industry were telling us how disappointed they were in the event, because there were no government offices at the conference that bought railroad items.

After talking with them a while, we got them to realize that they could use their same equipment and skills to make items for the military, such as tanks and off-road vehicles. They went over to the Army booth and found there were indeed some opportunities for them to support the Army's needs for heavy equipment. It turned out to be a good conference after all!

As you look for contracting opportunities, it is crucial that you think the same way. Think of your business in terms of your output—the products or items that you make and, perhaps more importantly, the items that you are capable of making. Think of how you can use your same equipment and process to make things that the government needs and wants—perhaps things you never even considered before.

If you think in terms of your process—for example, if you think of your company as a screw machine shop—you will be facing a much bigger challenge in trying to find government opportunities. Why? Because the government does not purchase items described as "screw machine products"—it buys nuts, bolts and screws.

How you think of your business can affect your success more than you imagine! What are your company's capabilities?

Work Smart

Before you can address what the government is looking for, identify what you really want to offer. We have counseled more companies than we would care to admit that come in and want to know what the government wants because they can provide it. That is not a good business plan. Target what you can do best and go for it

Chapter 6

Identify Your Customers

Now that you are thinking of your business in terms of the end items that you are capable of providing, you are ready to identify prospective customers—the buying offices within the federal government that have a need for your product or service.

A simple rule of thumb is that if the item is a commercial-type or general-purpose item, there is a good chance that the General Services Administration (GSA) buys it for both the military and civilian offices. Think of the GSA as the "Sears and Roebuck" of the government. This doesn't mean that the military or a civilian office won't be using the product; it just means that the GSA may issue the contract, and other government offices—both military and civilian—can buy off of that contract.

If the item or service is predominately military in nature, then one of the Department of Defense buying offices would be the place to go. The same is true for civilian agencies; if energy related, you may want to check out the Department of Energy as a probable customer. There are a number of ways to find the appropriate buying offices:

- Search FedBizOpps

- Use the personal touch

- Subscribe to a bid-matching service

- Work with a Procurement Technical Assistance Center (PTAC)

- Do your best to get to know the GSA

Work Smart

If your company produces or provides an item or service that is commercial or general purpose in nature, there is a good chance that you will be marketing your company to the General Services Administration (GSA) instead of individual government buying offices.

The GSA negotiates contracts for these sorts of products and services with commercial businesses, and then both the military and civilian government offices buy off those contracts. (Examples of such products and services could be anything from furniture products and services; cleaning supplies; copier equipment; hardware and appliances to marketing, media, and public information services; paints; pest control; financial services; training and travel services, just to name a few.)

SEARCH FEDBIZOPPS

One way to locate potential government customers is through FedBizOpps (Federal Business Opportunities), the official web site listing of all federal government contracting opportunities and awards over $25,000. Government buyers are able to post information about their business opportunities directly to FedBizOpps via the Internet at www.fedbizopps.gov.

This web site is updated every business day, with approximately 500-1000 new notices being posted on a daily basis. In addition to identifying specific government buying offices (your potential customers), you can also use this web site to find the person within each buying office who is there to answer questions and provide information to small businesses looking to sell to that office.

Here's how to proceed. For demonstration purposes, let's assume that you want to identify the government buying offices for the Department of Energy:

1. Go to http://www.FedBizOpps.gov.

2. Click on the FedBizOpps VENDORS button.

3. Choose whether you want to find an agency by acronym (e.g., DOE) or alphabet listing. Note: To get to information about the Department of Energy (or any other "Department of …" listing), look under "D" for Department, not "E" for Energy. Also note that you can get a listing for the Department of Defense (DoD) only in the "Alphabetic Order" area.

4. If you choose to find the agency by Acronym, the government buying offices for the agency you chose will be listed on the left-hand side of your screen. If you choose to find the agency by Alphabetic Order, click on the appropriate alphabet group, scroll down to the agency that interests you (e.g., Department of Energy), and click on "Offices" next to the agency to get to the list of buying offices.

5. To find the Small Business Office liaison or coordinator for the buying office you are interested in, click on either the "Posted Dates" or "Class Codes" heading that appears next

to the particular office to get a list of current bid opportunities for that office. If you open any one of the synopses, it will list Point of Contact information for that particular opportunity. Just contact the person who is listed and ask for the Small Business Office associated with that government buying office. The Small Business Office can answer any questions and provide more information about that buying office's requirements.

Work Smart

Now that you have identified your customers within the agency that interests you, it is useful for you to note, for future reference, that there is a variety of other meaningful information available to you here. Although you aren't quite ready to pursue live bids quite yet, when the time comes, you can also get synopses of current bid opportunities for that particular office grouped by posted date or classification code, as well as the location of the buying office.

USE THE PERSONAL TOUCH

One way to locate government buying offices is to pick up your local phone book, search the blue or yellow pages under "Government, federal," and then look for a listing for the purchasing office or small business office. If neither of these offices is identified, then call the office(s) listed and make an appointment to meet with them.

Once there, introduce yourself and your company, and provide the buyer with your business card and a listing of the supplies and services you can offer. If you have one, also provide the URL of your business's web page. This gives buyers another opportunity to see who you are and what you can do.

Don't be afraid to ask questions. Find out what products and services they buy. If they don't buy the product or service that you are offering, ask them to refer you to an office and a person that does.

Then later, use the first contact as a referral to the next. For example: "I recently talked to Joe/Mary and they suggested I talk to you for help in bidding on government contracts. What products and/or services do you buy?" This helps establish credibility with the new contact. It is important to get names and numbers for future use.

If you have already registered your business with the government in CCR, let the buyer know that. Over time, be sure to follow-up with the buyer to see if there are any new solicitations you can bid on and, in addition, to ingrain your company's name in the buyer's mind.

SUBSCRIBE TO A BID-MATCHING SERVICE

Instead of doing the work yourself, you can subscribe to a "bid matching" service to provide you with leads on bids and prospective customers. The bid service, with your help, will develop a company profile using keywords and government product and service codes to help match your company's capabilities to the needs of the government.

Using that profile to screen for suitable leads, the bid service will then search on the Internet for opportunities and will also get bid opportunity information directly from the government. You will receive the leads by e-mail, and all you have to do is decide whether to bid. However, keep in mind that this service only provides the leads; it will not help you understand a particular bid. Also, remember that they are getting this information from the same sources you can search on the Internet yourself. If your going to pay someone, make sure you get some added value.

You can locate a bid-matching service by searching on the Internet under "bid matching" or "bid matching service," or by asking for a referral from the small business specialist in the government buying office or from your local PTAC. Since bid lead services are usually not close by, contact is by phone or e-mail.

WORK WITH A PTAC

This method works much the same way as a bid-matching service, but costs you nothing (you already pay for it with your tax dollars). Stop in the Procurement Technical Assistance Center nearest you, sign up to be a client, and get your prospective buyers and bid leads through the PTAC.

As you go through the process, the PTAC will be available to answer your questions or will refer you to someone who can. It can also get copies of specifications and standards at minimum cost and do some market research. In addition, it offers training in government procurement practices through seminars/conferences and assistance with e-commerce. To locate the PTAC nearest you, go to http://www.sellingtothegovernment.net or www.aptac-us.org, which have listings with up-to-date contact information. To learn more about the services that PTACs provide, see Part IV.

Work Smart

Using a bid-matching service or a PTAC actually identifies customers and gets bid leads in one step. Some leads will not prove to be biddable for a variety of reasons, but the leads themselves will give you a lot of useful information on an item, including the buying office. It "jump starts" you in the process.

As you identify government buyers, keep in mind that there are two parts of the federal government to look at: the Department of Defense (DoD) and the Civilian Agencies. As we mentioned earlier, the DoD is the largest buyer, but you may not fit there. Don't worry if you don't; remember that "green is green."

A list of the major government buying offices, both military and civilian, is included in Appendix 2.

GET TO KNOW THE GSA

If a product or service is a commercial-type or general-purpose item, there is a good chance that the General Services Administration (GSA) buys it for all government agencies.

GSA, one of the largest agencies of the federal government, helps other federal agencies acquire the products, services, consulting advice, space, real estate, and vehicles they need from federal and commercial sources. It acts as a catalyst for approximately $66 billion in federal spending annually, which accounts for more than one-fourth of the U.S. government's total procurement dollars.

GSA simplifies government buying and reduces government costs by negotiating large multi-user contracts and by leveraging the volume of the federal market to drive down prices. Federal agencies then place orders against these contracts. Orders are placed in a variety of ways— through GSA customer representatives or catalogs, phone or fax, charge cards, electronic requisitioning, auctions, the Internet, or by contacting suppliers directly. GSA contracts are awarded for a period of five years, with three- to five-year options clauses. Most GSA contracts are for standard services and "commercial off-the-shelf" (COTS) products and equipment in three major areas:

- general-purpose supplies, equipment, and services

- building construction, repair, maintenance and architectural services

- information technology and professional services

GSA contracts are available to both large and small businesses able to provide nationwide or local services and products. GSA contracts are advertised, awarded, and managed by GSA headquarters and regional offices. All GSA contracting opportunities over $25,000 are advertised on the FedBizOpps web site.

So, as you can see, if your business provides commercial products or services, GSA is a potential customer that you want to get to know and learn how to do business with. And, as you can also see, it is easy to understand why GSA is sometimes referred to as the "Sears, Roebuck" for the government.

GSA Service Organizations

The GSA has three service organizations:

- *Public Buildings Service (PBS)* — This is the largest public real estate organization in the U.S., maintaining more than 330 million square feet of workspace for more than one million federal employees in more than 2,000 cities, with an inventory of 8,300 government-owned buildings and leased properties.

- *Federal Technology Services (FTS)* — This provides federal agencies with information technology, network services and professional services.

- *Federal Supply Service (FSS)* — This provides federal and other customers with the products, services, and programs they need to meet their supply, service, procurement, vehicle purchasing and leasing, travel and transportation, and personal property management requirements. This is done by bringing hundreds of thousands of federal customers together with over 9,000 contractors through FSS's six primary business lines:

    — Commercial Acquisition

    — Transportation Programs

    — Travel Programs

    — Vehicle Acquisition & Leasing Services

    — Property Management

    — GSA Global Supply

Since the GSA's Federal Supply Service, with its business line Commercial Acquisition, is the area that presents the greatest opportunity for small businesses, this is where we will focus our discussion. (For further information on the Public Buildings Service, see http://www.gsa.gov/pbs/fps/fps.htm. To learn more about the Federal Technology Service, see http://fts.gsa.gov.)

Getting on Schedule

Like any business looking to sell its products or services to the government through the GSA, your goal is to get on a "GSA Schedule" and obtain your "GSA number." Here's what that means.

GSA manages what is called the Federal Supply Schedules Program, which has two parts: the Single Award Schedules (SAS) and the Multiple Awards Schedules (MAS).

Single Award Schedules are contracts made for a specific product at a stated price for delivery to a geographical area, as defined in the SAS. The distinguishing principle here is that these contracts are for a specific item only.

The more popular Multiple Award Schedules (MAS) are long-term, government-wide contracts with commercial firms that provide commercial services and products that can be ordered directly by government buyers from GSA Schedule contractors or through GSA Advantage!, GSA's online shopping and ordering system. GSA Schedules cover a vast array of brand name items from office supplies and copier paper to systems furniture and from computers to laboratory equipment as well as a wide range of services, such as accounting, engineering, management, graphic design, and landscaping.

To "get on schedule"—become a GSA Schedule contractor—you must first be awarded a contract. In order to obtain a GSA Schedule contract, you must submit an offer in response to the applicable Schedule solicitation. GSA uses practices similar to those found in the commercial buying arena and awards contracts to responsible companies that offer commercial items falling within the generic descriptions in the Schedules (these descriptions are referred to as Schedule Item Numbers or SINs). Contracting Officers determine that prices are fair and reasonable by comparing the prices or discounts that a company offers the GSA with the prices or discounts that the company offers to its own commercial customers (known as "most favored customer" pricing). In order to make this comparison, GSA requires companies to furnish commercial pricelists and disclose information regarding their pricing/discounting practices during the application process.

Why would government buyers prefer to order via GSA Multiple Award Schedules instead of procuring on the open market? There are some very good reasons. When government buyers place orders against a GSA MAS contract, they are considered to have met federal regulations regarding competition, pricing, and other socio-economic requirements. In addition, government buyers know that to be "on schedule," GSA Schedule contractors have already been screened for quality, responsibility, reliability, and other criteria during the application process; therefore government buying offices save the time, money, and trouble of having to go through that process themselves.

We assume that, at this point, you are seeing some benefits in getting your company "on schedule." Although the process can be somewhat long and complicated, it can be worth it to you and your company. The following discussions provide a step-by-step guide to help you move through the process easier and faster, as well as guidelines for marketing your GSA Schedule contract after you have been selected.

Work Smart

You can get other assistance with the GSA schedules application process. GSA offers Schedule Workshops for businesses looking to become GSA Schedule contractors. To find more information, see http://www.gsa.gov/Portal/gsa/ep/contentView.do?contentId=13321&contentType=GSA _OVERVIEW.

GSA now offers a free online training site for businesses that includes GSA Schedule information at https://fsstraining..gsa.gov/kc/Securelogin/login.asp?kc_ident=kc0001.

And, as always, you can consult your local PTAC for help and advice on working through the process.

Step-by-Step Guide for Multiple Award Schedules

The six steps in this guide will, among other things, help you determine the correct MAS and the correct Special Item Number (SIN), evaluate the competition's products and pricing, assess market potential, prepare a solicitation package, and handle negotiations with the GSA Contracting Officer. The end goal is that you "get on schedule" and receive that much-sought-after "GSA Contract" or "GSA Number," which many businesses work very hard to obtain.

Step 1 — Determine which GSA Schedule and which Special Item Number(s) [SIN(s)] apply to your company's product(s) and/or service(s). These are the numbers you will use throughout the application process and in dealing with GSA.

Note 1: There are more than 40 Schedules currently available through the MAS program. (See http://www.gsaelibrary.gsa.gov for the complete Schedule List. Use the Search command to find a brief description of the products and/or services that each schedule covers.)

Note 2: There is a rule that may affect the number of SIN categories you choose to use. In each SIN category, a contractor has to have sales of at least $25,000 in the first 24 months and for 12 months each following year or that SIN number can be cancelled for that contractor.

(a) Go to the GSA Schedules e-Library at http://www.gsaelibrary.gsa.gov and enter a keyword that best describes your company's product/service in the space under the line "What are you Searching for?". Then click the GO button. The search results will include a listing of the relative Schedule number(s) and the Special Item Number(s) (SIN) that best matches your keyword.

— Read the category description next to the SIN number and determine whether this SIN category is a good match for your product/service. If not, start a new search with a different keyword.

— Watch for the "Introduction of New Products" SIN categories, which could appear on most of the MAS Schedules.

(b) After finding a match on a SIN category, click on the highlighted SIN number itself. You will get a listing of all current contractors for that SIN category, their contract number, phone number, business indicators (large, small, woman-owned, disadvantaged, 8(a), veteran ownership, etc.), and details about their GSA Advantage! status. You will also get contact information, including name, phone, and email address.

— Review this information to learn details about possible GSA competitors.

— Print and save this information for later research on awards.

— Save the name, phone number, and e-mail address of the GSA Schedule contact person, which appears at the top of the first page. You may need answers to questions as you go through the process.

(c) Jot down your SIN number and the schedule number that corresponds with your desired SIN category (such as 75 Office Products/Services Schedule; or 03FAC Facilities Maintenance and Management Schedule). You will need your SIN and schedule numbers later in this process.

Step 2 — Determine whether your product or service is currently required to be purchased/contracted with so called "mandated" sources, such as the Federal Prison Industry or UNICOR, the National Institute of the Blind (NIB), or the National Industries for the Severely Handicapped (NISH).

It is difficult to win a GSA contract for products that GSA determines would compete with these mandatory product suppliers.

(a) Go to the GSA Advantage! web site at http://www.gsaadvantage.gov.

— Go to "Advanced Search."

— Login to the GSA Advantage! site. (You can use any zip code in place of the password when using the GSA Advantage! site.)

— Enter a product keyword, click in the box next to UNICOR Mandatory Items, and click Find It.

— Go BACK and repeat the process using the box next to NIB/NISH.

(b) If your product(s) does appear as a mandatory source item, further research is needed before proceeding. Do the following for each product shown as a Mandatory Source Item:

— Click on the highlighted UNICOR name button. This leads to its home page, which details its program, rules, and products.

— Click on the highlighted NIB/NISH name button. This leads to its home page, which details its program, rules, and products.

— For either UNICOR or NIB/NISH, contact the Schedule point of contact person listed in the GSA e-library research from Step 1. That person can advise you on whether to proceed with your own GSA solicitation or whether your product is too similar to a Mandatory Source Item.

Step 3 — Research your competition. Your competitors are those contractors that already have a GSA contract for the SIN category(ies) you are considering for your own product/service. There are two parts to this research. Both parts should be done for each prospective SIN category.

Part 1 — Determine who your competition is, including names, GSA-offered products, and prices for those products.

(a) Go to the GSA Library at http://www.gsaelibrary.gsa.gov. Enter the first SIN number you are considering in the search line at the top of the page to determine which companies already have a GSA contract. The results are a listing of all current GSA contractors, their GSA contract numbers, phone numbers, and business size standards. Also listed is a column called "View Catalog," which indicates the contractor's GSA Advantage! status. It will show the Advantage! Symbol or be blank. Note: GSA Advantage! is the site where government employees do their product research and online purchasing.

(b) Click on Yes...View/Order for each contractor. The results will take you directly to the GSA Advantage! web site listing for that contractor's products. The listing will show all of the contractor's products, item descriptions (including part numbers), and GSA contract prices. Note: In the case of services, pricing details may not be listed.

— Review this information to determine how your products compare to those already available.

— Consider whether the prices offered appear competitive.

— Consider whether your company's prices for similar products are competitive with those currently available on that MAS Schedule.

(c) While viewing a GSA contractor's product, notice the two lines under each product listing; one lists the product's manufacturer and the other lists the product's contractor (the GSA contract holder). This information will tell you whether the contractor is a dealer or the manufacturer of the product. Note: In some cases, a contractor is a dealer for multiple manufacturers.

Part 2 — In Part 1 of your research, you learned which possible competitors are currently on GSA Schedule, which products they offer, whether they are a dealer or the manufacturer, and their product prices. But there is more to learn about your potential competitors and the SIN(s) categories to help you determine your market potential. In order to determine this, your research in Part 2 is based on actual past sales from the GSA Schedules.

All GSA contractors are required to report on a quarterly basis their actual GSA sales. This reporting process is known as the "72A Quarterly Reporting." This data becomes part of the Schedule Sales Query (SSQ) Report that you will access in Part 2 of your competition research. The SSQ is the sales reported by contractors for specific report quarters from the current to the past five years.

The 72A Reports are GSA's way of determining the 0.75 percent Industrial Funding Fee (IFF) that all contractors must pay to GSA on a quarterly basis. (For more on the IFF, see Step 6.)

Note: Some contractors show $0 reported sales. There are two possible explanations for this: (1) they had $0 sales to report or (2) the contractor was only recently awarded its GSA contract, and enough time has not passed to file a 72A Quarterly Report.

To determine when a company was issued its GSA contract number: Go to the GSA e-library web site at http://www.gsaelibrary.gsa.gov, enter the contractor's name in the search line, and click GO. Click on the highlighted contractor's name. The results will provide useful research information, such as the contract number, expiration date, all contracted SIN(s) and GSA Advantage status, and the contractor's web site and e-mail address. Remember to subtract five years from the listed contract expiration date shown to get the actual GSA contract award (start) date (all MAS contracts are awarded for five years).

(a) Your research in Part 2 is based on actual past sales from the GSA Schedules. At http://ssq.gsa.gov/ReportSelection.cfm, there are 11 report formats to choose from. Some formats indicate sales by quarter, while others are for yearly totals. More options include reports by specific SIN, Schedule, and contractor name or contract number.

(b) Use SSQ Report format 7 (Total by Quarter & SIN by Contract Number and Fiscal Year) to find each contractor's *actual sales* by SIN number on a quarterly basis. You will need the information you printed and saved in Step 1 of your research to look up each contractor by its contract number.

(c) Next use SSQ Report format 8 (Total for Each Quarter for a Specific SIN by Fiscal Year) to get the *grand total* of each SIN category by quarter. There are two things to look for here: (1) whether one contractor is getting the majority of the awards, and (2) whether the *overall award amount* for that SIN category is on the low side. If either of these is true, you might want to re-evaluate the idea of getting your own GSA contract for your products that fall within that SIN category. Another issue to consider if overall award amount is low: if, say, eight contractors shared only $20,000 worth of sales during the past year in one SIN category and if you add your company's product to that SIN category, will you fare any better or make the awards be larger?

Step 4 — Locate the Schedule solicitation you have determined is best suited to your company's product(s)/service(s) and download all appropriate documents. The actual Schedule solicitations are updated at irregular intervals. In some cases the updates are known as "refreshed." In the case of refresh, they are numbered such as Refresh Number 5; always locate the solicitation with the most current "refresh" number.

Go to the site where solicitations are located at www.FedBizOpps.gov:

(a) Click on "Finding Business Opportunities" at the top-left of the page and click GO to get to the Find Business Opportunities page

(b) In the "Full Text Search" space, enter the Schedule number (generally 2 or 3 digits). Then scroll down to "Search by

Agency," highlight "General Services Administration," and click the "Start Search" button at the bottom of the page. The results will be a list of active GSA postings with that Schedule number. Note: You can enter the full solicitation number in the "Search by Solicitation" if known.

(c) View each synopsis and determine the correct solicitation. Often there is more than just the solicitation listed, there may be modifications and/or amendment documents. It is important to know whether there are additional documents.

(d) Download ALL documents, including the solicitation, any modifications, etc. Expect it to be many pages. Note: For the popular Schedule 084, be sure to download the appropriate attachment (there are over 11 different ones) for your product in addition to the master solicitation document itself.

(e) Click on the "Register to Receive Notification" line at the bottom of the solicitation announcement page and provide an e-mail address. This is a subscription to a mailing list for all future modifications or refreshed announcements for that solicitation.

Step 5 — Complete the solicitation package. Now that you know which MAS Schedule fits your product/service line and have downloaded all necessary documents, it's time to complete the solicitation package.

(a) Remove cover pages. The first pages of a solicitation are the cover pages. They contain general information and notices of significant changes made to the solicitation since its last issuance. These notices are informational and should be removed prior to submission of the solicitation package to GSA.

(b) Sign SF 1449. The first page of the actual solicitation is the Standard Form 1449 Solicitation/Contract, also known as the SF-1449 order for commercial items. Only complete blocks 12, 17, and 30a, b, c. The SF-1449 must be signed by someone able to bind the company into a legal contract with GSA.

(c) Read, understand and complete basic solicitation. All clauses that require responses must be completed; if they aren't, GSA will return your solicitation package as incomplete. Take the time to read the entire document, paragraph by paragraph, so everything is understood. Contact the POC (point of contact) with any questions or concerns you might have. An e-mail and phone number for the POC is listed on the cover pages.

(d) Include pricelist and catalog/brochure. An important document in the solicitation process is your commercial pricelist. Two copies of your dated commercial pricelist and catalog/brochure containing the products you plan to offer must be submitted with your offer. There are several acceptable forms of pricelists, including published or printed, computer-generated, and copies of internal pricelists. In the catalog/brochure and your pricelist, you must mark the Special Item Number (SIN) next to ALL the products/services you are "offering." All the other products/services must be lined or marked out and the word "excluded" written next to those items not being offered. Do not supply a pricelist just for the GSA items; the Contracting Officer needs to see your actual commercial pricelist, not one that was specially designed just for GSA purposes. Note: If you are a dealer or distributor, a copy of your manufacturer's pricelist must be submitted along with a letter on the manufacturer's letterhead stating it authorizes you, the dealer, to sell to GSA and that it, the manufacturer, will provide all the necessary inventory to support the dealer's GSA sales.

(e) Complete the Commercial Sales Practice Form (CSP-1). The CSP-1 form is a crucial part of any MAS solicitation. There are instructions on how to complete this form in the solicitation. In this form, you must state "whether the discounts and concessions which are being offered to the Government are equal to, or better than, the offeror's best price (discount and concessions in any combination) to any customer acquiring the same items offered under the SIN regardless of quantity or terms and conditions."

— If the answer is "yes," you must complete the chart for customer(s) who receive your best discount.

— If the answer is "no," you must complete the chart for all customers or categories of customers to which you sell at a price that is equal to or better than the prices being offered to the government. You must include an explanation of the situations that led to deviations from your standard practice.

— If the Contracting Officer is unable to determine that the prices offered are fair and reasonable because the deviations from your written policies or standard commercial sales practices are so significant, then the Contracting Officer may ask you to provide additional information. This may include current company invoices to your "most favored customer."

(f) Fill-in the Representations and Certifications. The Reps & Certs portion of the solicitation must be read and the appropriate boxes filled in. These cover such things as business size standards, small or large business, woman-owned, veteran-owned, etc.

(g) Include additional documents and data. There may be additional data or documents that need to be sent with the solicitation package. Carefully read all the paperwork (clauses) and follow directions to the letter since each MAS is different. (This gets back to our 3 Rs for success as a government contractor: Read, Read, Read.) For example, product warranty documentation may be requested. Here are some other common items that you need to include or consider:

— Registration in Central Contractor Registration (CCR Registration)

— A valid DUNS number

— Acceptance of credit cards as a form of payment

— A submitted VETS-100 form

Step 6 — Negotiate with the GSA Contracting Officer and finally "get on schedule." In some cases, the Contracting Officer may make an award without negotiations or discussions. Remember that the main reason for negotiations is to resolve major differences between the prospective contractor's proposal and the GSA's main negotiation objective: to always obtain the best price. Here are some tips for successful negotiations:

(a) You do not have to give in on all factors recommended by the Contracting Officer. You do have rights, and it is not worth losing money just to get a GSA Contract.

(b) A common point of negotiation is what is referred to as the "prompt payment discount." Do not feel pressured to give a discount in this area; stay with net 30 days.

(c) At the end of negotiations, the Contracting Officer may request a solicitation/proposal revision from you. The revision is GSA's way to confirm all the terms and conditions that you and the Contracting Officer agreed upon.

(d) If you are offering your best price and it is equal to or better than that of your best customer or group of customers, then you do not need to do better.

(e) Be aware of the 0.75 percent Industrial Funding Fee (IFF) that comes out of your product/service prices each quarter, so include this 0.75 percent in your GSA price.

(f) Be sure of the shipping points and FOB points when negotiating. If the proposal calls for FOB Destination, then you have to pay freight. However, try negotiating for FOB Origin under which the freight is pre-paid.

(g) Often the Contracting Officer will try to get quantity discounts. If your standard policy has been not to give these discounts, then decline this suggestion.

(h) GSA may want on-site warranty repair anywhere in the country. Watch out for such provisions; they can be costly.

(i) Generally provide domestic delivery only, not international.

Guidelines for Marketing a GSA Schedule Contract

Obtaining a Schedule contract can be a bit overwhelming and time-consuming. However, when you are finally awarded a contract, your hard work is definitely not over. If you want to really capitalize on your new opportunity and generate sales against your hard-earned contract, you will now have to actively market your contract to potential buyers. As many GSA Contracting Officers will tell you, getting "on schedule" and having a GSA contract is only a license to "hunt" for opportunities.

Here to help you in your hunt is a five-step approach to marketing your company to all the federal agencies that shop for suppliers through GSA. Note that the first two steps—the Federal Supply Schedule Price List and the GSA Advantage!—are not options; they are required by regulation to be included in every GSA Schedule contract.

Step 1 — Design your Authorized Federal Supply Schedule Price List and develop a distribution list. When you are awarded a GSA Schedule contract, you are required to prepare, print, and distribute a document called the Federal Supply Schedule Price List. Think of this price list as an important marketing piece for your new GSA Schedule contract. The price list, which is designed by each individual contractor, covers 26 specific points designated or negotiated in the contract itself, such as, F.O.B. Point, Discounts, Foreign Items, Warranty Provisions, Production Points, Delivery Times, SIN numbers, Minimum Order, and Maximum Order.

When designing your own Federal Supply Schedule price list, it is best to keep it simple and short. A one-page flyer covering only the required 26 points specified in your contract usually is best. (You can give details about your product details in your brochure or catalog.) It is very important to make sure that all the information in your price list is correct. Inclusion of incorrect information will require you to go to the time and trouble of correcting, reprinting, resubmitting, and redistributing your price list.

The price list must be distributed to a Customer Mailing List provided to you by the Contracting Officer. You can refer to the original Schedule itself for the approximate numbers of Customer Mailing List labels or contact the Contracting Officer for the count. The total number of customers on each mailing list can vary, depending on the product or service, from less than 500 for some service categories to over 10,000 for office supplies. Note: Some GSA Schedules are discontinuing the mailing.

When mailing the Federal Supply Scheduled Price List to your prospective customers, be sure to include your company brochure and other literature about your product or service. The mailing/distribution should be done within 30 days of the date your contract was awarded. For best timing, do your mailing/distribution after your company's contract is on the GSA Advantage! system.

Work Smart

Remember that you may also send your price list to agencies that are not included on the mailing list supplied by the Contracting Officer. Use the official mailing list as a base, but it is to your advantage to add agencies, as applicable, and develop your own mailing/distribution list.

Step 2 — Prepare your electronic company catalog and submit it to GSA Advantage! The GSA has a very sophisticated online shopping and ordering system known as GSA Advantage! Using this menu-driven database system, government buyers can search for the products they need, compare prices and product information (in cases where there is more than one supplier), and place their orders.

As a GSA Schedule contractor, you are required to submit your electronic company catalog to GSA Advantage! no later than six months after your contract award. However, it is best to do this within the first 30 days, if possible.

You can submit your electronic company catalog into the GSA Advantage! system by using the Schedule Input Program (SIP) software, available for downloading at the GSA Vendor Support Center (VSC) web site at http://vsc.fss.gsa.gov. The VSC staff is there to assist new contractors with the preparation and submission of their electronic catalog data and can be reached toll-free at 877-495-4849. Note: New Schedule contractors must first register at the

VSC web site in order to get a login and password to use with the SIP software.

When entering your information, be sure to:

- Use either the Option or the Accessory Tool when listing the sub-categories for each of your products (or services), such as color or style choices.

- Mark any special categories for each product, such as "recycled materials" or "energy efficient."

- At each product listing on GSA Advantage!, use the link option to your company's web site.

- Include a product photo.

Caution

 As you prepare your electronic catalog, it is critical to your success to keep in mind that GSA Advantage! is the principal marketing tool for a Schedule contractor to the buying agencies that will use it. There are some things you need do to maximize your marketing potential.

First, when entering your product data into the SIP software, don't use only two or three words to describe your product or service—take advantage of all the lines that you are allowed for this purpose. This allows you to do some marketing by including important or unique details about your product.

Second, make sure that the words and phrases you are using are the most effective possible. (The "most effective" are those that will lead government buyers to your catalog listing and convince them to buy your products over other similar items in the system.) The best way to do this is to do some research and searches of your own in GSA Advantage!. Experiment with various words and phrases to get a sense of what "works" in a listing and what does not. For example, which terms work best as search words? Do sentences or just phrases work best for your type of product? Which listings come up first? Look at how your competitors have their information in the system. How do they list product part numbers? How are names listed—e.g., HP or Hewlett Packard?

Lastly, make sure that all the information that you have entered is correct, including grammar and spelling. Your information will appear in the system exactly how you key it in, errors and all. After it is submitted, you will not be able to go back into the system to correct or improve your information. GSA is reluctant to allow any changes unless there is a modification or change to the contract itself.

We realize that the initial set-up on GSA Advantage! can be very time-consuming, especially if you have many products/services to enter. But because submitting your company's electronic catalog is basically a one-shot deal, your efforts to make it right—and to make it marketable—are worth it.

Step 3 — Place an ad in GSA's *MarkeTips Magazine*. GSA's *MarkeTips Magazine*, which is mailed to more than 100,000 federal and DoD buyers and end-users worldwide every two months, provides an opportunity for you, as a GSA contractor, to promote your products or services to the federal marketplace. Best of all, the advertising space in *MarkeTips* is free of charge for GSA contractors. But because space is limited, advertising space is offered on a first-come, first-served basis and vendors are limited to one ad per year per GSA contract. But, again, the ad is free.

To get started, visit the *MarkeTips* web site and download the latest advertising specifications and guidelines. Go to http://www.gsa.gov and enter the word *MarkeTips* in the Search command. At the *MarkeTips* home page, you can download past issues of the magazine as well as locate the *MarkeTips* field editor serving the GSA Acquisition Center that covers your contract. Be sure and read the ad specifications carefully as they change from time to time.

Make getting your free ad in GSA's *MarkeTips* a priority in your marketing efforts. It should be done within the first 30 days after award.

Step 4 — Use GSA logos on all your marketing materials. A great way to market a new GSA contract is by incorporating one of the "GSA Schedule" or "GSA Contract Holder" logos, along with your contract number(s), into your company's marketing materials and brochures. Be sure to also include a GSA logo on your company's home page. Simply go to http://www.gsa.gov, use the search term "logo" and this will link you to the logo site. Then download the logos you prefer.

Step 5 — Make your web site "GSA-friendly." Some companies have a separate web site for federal agencies via their link from the GSA Advantage! system. But an even easier approach is to make updates or changes to your company's web site to reflect your new GSA contract. Here are just a few possible changes to consider:

- Use one of the GSA logos with your contract number on your home page.

- Provide a link from your company's web site to your company's product listing on the GSA Advantage! web site. Contact the Vendor Support Center staff (see Step 2) for help, if needed.

- Establish a special company e-mail just for GSA Schedule inquires. Be consistent by also using this new e-mail address on the Federal Supply Schedule Price List form and on the GSA Advantage! web site.

- Use any of the special symbols (e.g., energy-efficient, recycled, environmental items) for which your company's products qualify on your company's web site. Again, be consistent and use the same symbols on products listed on the GSA Advantage! web site.

In addition, here are some more miscellaneous marketing ideas:

- Market your GSA contract to any local federal agencies in your area that might have a use for your product or service. Consider your local U.S. Post Office, IRS Office, VA Hospital, FAA Authority, National Guard facilities, etc., as possibilities.

- Subscribe to professional journals and industrial or trade magazines that cover your line of business. Run ads in the publications that government employees might read. Be sure to include the GSA logo with your company contract number in the ads.

- Participate in GSA's Small Business Outreach events. For more information, call the Office of Small Business Utilization (OSBU) at 202-501-1021 or email at small.business@gsa.gov.

Chapter 7

Get Registered

One of the most important things you need to do early in the process is to let the government know that you are ready and able to provide the products or services it needs. To do this, you must register your company with the Central Contractor Registration (CCR) at http://www.ccr.gov, the primary database of government vendors and suppliers. The CCR collects, validates, stores and disseminates data in support of federal projects and missions.

Both current and prospective government suppliers are required to complete a one-time registration to provide basic information relevant to procurement and financial transactions. In order to receive a federal contract, or grant for that matter, a company must be registered in CCR prior to the award. However, note that registration does not guarantee business with the government.

You are responsible for ensuring the accuracy of your registration and for updating all of your registration information as it changes. You must renew your registration once a year to maintain an active status. If you do not, your registration will expire and your ability to conduct business (i.e., receive contract awards and payments) with the government will be affected.

Did You Know?

CCR now provides one-stop registration in the federal acquisition process and allows businesses to take responsibility for the accuracy of their own business information by inputting it themselves directly into the central government database for contractor information.

Small businesses also can provide additional business data into a sub-database that captures this important information. This also provides a more dynamic search capability when people are looking for potential business support from the small business community.

One-stop registration in CCR will avoid administrative duplication and will allow contractors to take responsibility for the accuracy of their own business information by supplying it directly to the government through this single site.

However, this wasn't done overnight. While the mandate to streamline the procurement process was given in 1994, it took until October 2002 to get the job done.

In order to register, you must use a personal computer and have access to the Internet. If you don't have access, you may use a personal computer at a Procurement Technical Assistance Center, Small Business Administration office, Federal Procurement Office, or your local library. It is best if you have your own computer, because the federal government is quickly moving toward a computer-based acquisition format and you will be left behind if you don't get one soon.

As you prepare for registration, you'll no doubt be overwhelmed by the endless litany of codes used by government contractors. When so many goods and services change hands every year, some type of "shorthand" language is needed to keep track of it all. A complete understanding of these codes is absolutely necessary if you hope to successfully compete for the government's business, and we'll cover what you need to know.

- registering with the CCR

- using Online Representations and Certifications Applications (ORCA)

- deciphering government codes

REGISTERING WITH THE CCR

Any company, large or small, wishing to do business with the Federal government must register in the Central Contractor Registration (CCR), the central databank for government contractors.

To register, access the CCR database at http://www.ccr.gov and enter the required information about your company. CCR contains both mandatory and optional fields, and although your application will be considered complete if you fill out just the mandatory fields, we strongly recommend that you fill out *all* fields. Since government buying offices use the CCR database to help them identify companies that might be able to provide the goods and services they need, it is to your advantage to provide a complete picture of your company's capabilities and qualifications.

We also recommend that you gather all the required information and have it at hand before you go into the database. Having to go back in to change the information is a waste of your time.

Because proper CCR registration is so important, we are going to review some of the information that you will need to register, below. We also give you tips to help make sure that you enter the information correctly.

If you have questions regarding CCR registration, call the Registration Assistance Center at 1-888-227-2423 (1-269-961-4725 internationally).

Information You Will Need to Register in CCR

Please note that we are not going to review every piece of information included on the CCR form. Instead, we are going to discuss what we consider the essential information for small businesses.

We have organized the information that you will need into the following categories:

- Identification numbers
    - Data Universal Numbering System (DUNS) Number
    - DUNS +4 Number
    - CAGE Code
    - U.S. Federal TIN
    - A-T Number
- General information about your company
- Classification codes for your products and/or services
    - NAICS codes
    - SIC codes
- Information about electronic funds transfer
- Registration acknowledgment and point of contact information

For your convenience, we have provided a space next to each item so you can, if you wish, jot down the correct information for your company and have it handy when you fill out the electronic form.

We want to remind you that when you enter the information on the CCR web site, you must fill in all the fields designated as mandatory or your application will be considered incomplete and your registration will not be accepted. And, again, we encourage you to fill in the optional fields as well.

Identification Numbers

Data Universal Numbering System (DUNS) Number _____

The Data Universal Numbering System (DUNS) number is a unique nine-character identification number provided by The Dun & Bradstreet Corporation (D&B). If you do not have a DUNS number, call Dun and Bradstreet at 1-866-705-5711 or 610-882-7000 to request one. Be prepared to provide an address, telephone number, business start date, and type of business. The process takes about 10 minutes and is free of charge. The number will be issued within three working days. If you already have a DUNS number, the D&B representative will advise you over the phone.

If you have access to the Internet, you can also submit your business's request for a DUNS number through D&B's web site at https://eupdate.dnb.com/requestoptions.html?cmid=EOE100537.

If you do know your DUNS number, the CCR can perform DUNS validation online. After you enter your DUNS number and company information into the system, the CCR will run a background validation against the D&B Global database. You then select the Dun & Bradstreet data to pre-populate the CCR file.

Work Smart

When entering your DUNS number on the CCR Web site, enter only the numbers—do not enter the dashes.

DUNS +4 _____

The CCR process allows businesses to assign an additional 4 characters to their DUNS number to uniquely identify an affiliate or division at the same physical location. For example, a business might want to have two records for itself at the same physical location to identify two separate bank accounts. Either a DUNS or a DUNS +4 number can be used to successfully complete the registration process.

Vendors wishing to register their subsidiaries and other entities should make sure that each additional location obtains a separate DUNS number from Dun & Bradstreet at 1-866-705-5711. If you have questions regarding the use of DUNS +4, contact the CCR Assistance Center at 1-888-227-2423.

CAGE Code _____

The Commercial and Government Entity (CAGE) code is a five-character ID number used extensively within the Department of Defense to identify specific companies.

If you don't have a CAGE code and your company has a U.S. address, you may submit the CCR registration form without it and one will automatically be assigned and filled in for you as part of the CCR registration process.

However, if you are a foreign vendor (i.e., your company does not have a U.S. address), you must include an NCAGE code on the registration or it will be considered incomplete. Note: Per 31 U.S.C. 7701 (c) (3) Principle Purpose(s), the TIN may be used by the government to collect and report on delinquent amounts arising out of the offeror's relationships with the government

U.S. Federal TIN

The U.S. Federal TIN (Tax Identification Number) is the nine-digit number that companies use for income tax purposes. If you do not know your TIN, contact the Internal Revenue Service at 1-800-829-1040. If you operate as an individual sole proprietorship, you must enter your Social Security number in the provided space.

If your business is located in the United States and you do not fill in this field, your application will be considered incomplete and your registration will not be accepted. If you are located outside the United States, you are not required to provide a TIN.

Work Smart

When entering your TIN or SSN on the CCR web site, enter only the numbers—do not enter the dashes. (Example: 123456789, not 123-45-6789)

A-T Numbers

This is a new data element being added to the CCR database. Austin Tetra is providing the A-T Number on a quarterly basis. The A-T Number is being added to support an ongoing requirement to identify purchase card merchants socio-economic reporting information. It is a tracking method to monitor sales through credit and debit card purchases.

A-T Numbers are the key to linking corporate family relationships within the A-T database. Since each location of a business has its own unique A-T Number, a large organization has many different A-T Numbers within its corporate "family." The A-T Number is non-indicative so it remains with a business throughout its lifecycle and is never reused.

The A-T Number will only be displayed in CCR Tools. The A-T Number will be used by the Acquisition Information Reporting (AIR) systems within the Integrated Acquisition Environment (IAE).

Additional information about Austin Tetra can be found at: www.austintetra.com. The support telephone number is 972-756-8100. You must ask for Customer Support.

General Information about Your Company

Legal Business Name and Doing Business As _____
Your legal business name is the name under which you are incorporated and pay taxes. If you commonly use another name for normal operations, such as a franchise or licensee name, then include that in the space below the "Legal Business Name" field.

Work Smart

Your legal business name and street address, as entered on the CCR registration, must match the legal business name under which you are registered with Dun & Bradstreet. If the information does not match, your registration may be rejected during processing.

Street Address _____
You must provide a valid street address where your business is located. A Post Office Box or c/o may not be used in this space. If you use a P.O. Box for correspondence, you may include it in the space allocated under the tab "Address Info."

Street Address 2 _____
If necessary, use this space to continue your physical street address.

City, State, Zip _____
The nine-digit zip code is mandatory.

Work Smart

When entering the nine-digit zip code on the CCR web site, enter the numbers only—do not include the dash. (Example: 123456789, not 12345-6789)

Country _____
Choose the appropriate country code abbreviation from the list provided.

Date Business Started _____
Enter the date your business was started in its present form. This may be used to distinguish your business from others with similar names. Use the format mm/dd/yyyy. (Example: 01/01/1995)

Fiscal Year-End Close Date _____
This field calls for the month and day on which you close your fiscal year. For example, if you operate on the calendar year, enter 12/31. In any case, use the format mm/dd.

Average # of Employees and Average Annual Revenue _____
You must provide accurate information about the number of employees and three-year average annual receipts for your business since these values are used to determine your business size classification. These values cannot be zero.

Work Smart

When entering revenue information on the CCR web site, enter numbers only—do not enter dollar signs or commas.

Company Security Level _____
Choose the correct level of security for the facility, if your facility has a clearance.

Highest Employee Security Level _____
Choose the highest level of security for an employee located at that facility, if any of your employees carry a security clearance.

Corporate Web Page URL _____
If you have a company website, provide your company's homepage. Both upper and lower cases are acceptable. This is good marketing.

Corporate Information _____
Here is where you indicate what type of business relationship you are establishing with the U.S. federal government. If you plan to respond to government contracts, check "Contracts." Check "Grants," if you are looking for this option. The last choice, "Both Contracts and Grants," would be for those who plan to respond to both.

Corporate Status (check one):
You must choose one of the following boxes to indicate the corporate status of your business. If you are a Limited Liability Partners Company or S-Corporation, choose "Corporation." It is important to understand that you should select business types that reflect the current status of your business. The business types are not an indication of the business opportunities you hope to pursue.

☐ **Sole Proprietorship**

If you choose Sole Proprietorship as your status, you must provide the name and phone number of the owner of the business on the "Corporate Info" page.

- ☐ **Corporation (not tax exempt)**

    If you choose Corporation as your status, you must enter the state of incorporation if your business is incorporated in the United States. If you are incorporated outside of the United States, you must enter the country of incorporation and check "Foreign Supplier" under business types (see below).

- ☐ **Corporation (tax exempt)**

    If you choose Corporation as your status, you must enter the state of incorporation if your business is incorporated in the United States. If you are incorporated outside of the United States, you must enter the country of incorporation and check "Foreign Supplier" under business types (see below).

- ☐ **Partnership**

- ☐ **U.S. Government Entity (choose one below):**

    - ☐ **Federal**

    - ☐ **State**

    - ☐ **Local**

- ☐ **Foreign Government**

- ☐ **International Organization**

- ☐ **Other**

Business Types (check one or more)
Check all the descriptions that apply to your business—you must choose at least one for your application to be complete. If you are unsure as to whether you qualify under a category, contact your local Small Business Administration (SBA) office for the appropriate guidelines or visit their web site at www.sba.gov.

- ☐ Local Government

- ☐ Minority Institution

- ☐ Foreign Supplier

- ☐ Small Business

- ☐ Minority-Owned Business

- ☐ Small Disadvantaged Business

- ☐ State Government

- ☐ Federal Government

- ☐ Tribal Government
- ☐ Service Location
- ☐ Research Institution
- ☐ Women-Owned Business
- ☐ Labor Surplus Area Firm
- ☐ Veteran Owned Business
- ☐ 8(a) Program Participant (see below)
- ☐ Sheltered Workshop (JWOD Provider)
- ☐ Nonprofit Organization
- ☐ Construction Firm
- ☐ Emerging Small Business
- ☐ Large Business
- ☐ Municipality
- ☐ Historically Black College or University
- ☐ Limited Liability Company
- ☐ Educational Institution
- ☐ Manufacturer of Goods
- ☐ American Indian Owned
- ☐ Service-Related Disabled Veteran Owned
- ☐ S Corporation
- ☐ Historically Underutilized Business Zone (HUB Zone) Firm

If you answer Minority Owned Business, then you must choose one of the following:

- ☐ Native American Owned
- ☐ Black American Owned
- ☐ Hispanic American Owned
- ☐ Asian-Pacific American Owned
- ☐ Subcontinent Asian (Asian-Indian) American Owned
- ☐ No Representation/None of the Above

If you check 8(a) Program Participant, you will be required to complete name and address of certifying party.

- ☐ SBA Certified Small Disadvantaged Business
- ☐ SBA Certified 8(a) Program Participant
- ☐ SBA Certified HUBZone Business
- ☐ DoT Certified Disadvantaged Business Enterprise

Classification Codes for Your Products/Services

The Department of Commerce identifies the economic base of the country (i.e., products and services) by types of industry, such as manufacturing, construction, agricultural, service group, etc., through a coding system. This system enables the government to obtain the data it needs to analyze economic trends and similar information.

North American Industry Classification System (NAICS) Codes
___ NAICS codes (pronounced "nakes") are used for classifying business establishments and industries doing business with the government. You must supply at least one for your registration to be complete. If you do not know your NAICS codes, you may search on the Internet at http://www.census.gov/epcd/naics02 or you may go to http://www.wingovcon.com for links to the NAICS search site. You must use six-digit NAICS Codes in your registration.

Although you have to enter only one valid code for your registration to be complete, *be sure to list all codes that apply to your products and services.* This could help government buying offices identify your company as one that provides needed goods or services. When entering your codes, don't get carried away by putting in a lot of different ones. Be realistic and use those NAICS that are best for you.

Work Smart

Effective October 1, 2002, the Small Business Administration is using the NAICS 2002 version of the codes for their size standards. They apply to all SBA programs and to all other federal government programs and actions where eligibility as a small business is a factor or a consideration.

Standard Industrial Classification (SIC) Codes _____
Formerly, the government had used these codes for classification of businesses and industries, but is still a mandatory field for registering in

CCR. You must supply at least one valid SIC code for your registration to be complete. If you do not know your SIC codes, you may search on the Internet at http://www.osha.gov/oshstats/sicser.html. Some agency or buyer may still be using the system, and you should be aware of what your numbers are and/or how to find them. SIC codes can be four or eight digits.

You can access the SIC manual on the Internet through the Small Business Administration's home page at http://www.sba.gov or in hard copy through your public library. If you are using a print copy of the manual, you can find your SIC Code by looking for your industry and then going down the list to see where you fit.

Note: When you set up your company, particularly if you incorporated, chances are that it was classified with a SIC code because that's one of the things that's asked for in the incorporation papers.

Work Smart

When entering your NAICS, SIC or FSC codes on the CCR web site, separate the codes with a comma and a space, not just a space. (Example: 1234, 5231, 9012)

Electronic Funds Transfer

Under recent law, the government is legally mandated to use Electronic Funds Transfer (EFT) for all contract payments. Therefore, all registrants must complete this section. (There are exceptions: foreign vendors doing business outside the United States, utility companies, and government agencies do not have to supply this information.)

If you need help with the required information, your bank or financial institution should be able to help you. Or you can call the CCR Registration Assistance Center at (888) 227-2423 or (269) 961-4725 internationally.

Work Smart

Effective Fall 2003, payments by all federal agencies to government contractors will be made on the basis of electronic funds transfer (EFT) information contained in CCR. This means that all firms doing business with the federal government will have to be registered in CCR in order to be paid. If you let your registration lapse (i.e., fail to renew it) or if you cancel your registration, all payments, if ones are being made, will cease. A company must remain active in CCR until all payments are made to avoid discontinuation.

Financial Institution _____

Provide the name of the bank that you use for business banking purposes.

ABA Routing Number _____

The ABA Routing Number is the American Banking Association's 9-digit routing transit number for your financial institution. You can obtain the routing number by contacting your financial institution or you may find it on one of your checks. It usually appears as the first nine digits in the lower left-hand corner.

Account Number, Type, & Lock Box Number _____

Enter the account number to which you want your EFT payments deposited and check the proper box to indicate whether checking or savings account. If you prefer to use a lock box service, enter the appropriate account number in the space provided. If you use a lock box for your banking purposes, you must also check "checking" under account type.

Work Smart

When entering the date on the CCR web site, you must enter it as mm/dd/yyyy. No date earlier than the date of registration may be entered.

Automated Clearing House _____

Enter the appropriate contact information for your bank's Automated Clearing House (ACH) coordinator. The ACH will serve as the contact if problems occur with your EFT transfer. Note that e-mail addresses requested under the contact entries refer to Internet e-mail addresses, not local area network e-mail addresses within your office.

Work Smart

When entering the phone numbers on the CCR web site, enter the numbers only, not dashes or parentheses. (Example: 9995551212, not (999) 555-1212)

Remittance Information _____

Enter the address where you would like a paper check mailed in the event that an EFT transfer does not work. On the name line, enter to whom the check should be mailed and fill in the appropriate information. If you use a lock box and want checks mailed directly to the bank, enter the bank name and address here.

Credit Card Information _____

Does your company accept credit cards for payment? This is a yes or no question.

Registration Acknowledgment and Point of Contact Information

Registrant Name _____

Enter the name of the person that acknowledges that the information provided in the registration is current, accurate, and complete. The person named here will be the *only* person within the registering company to receive the Trading Partner Identification Number (TPIN). (The TPIN is a password to protect access to your registration and banking information on the CCR.)

Work Smart

Never give your TPIN to anyone you don't know. This information should always be protected. CCR personnel will never ask you for your TPIN. To avoid becoming a victim of a fraudulent scheme to compromise your TPIN and damaging your company, keep your TPIN strictly confidential.

The Registrant and the Alternate Contact (see below) are the only people authorized to share information with CCR Assistance Center personnel. It is important that the person named here have knowledge about the CCR registration.

Correspondence Check Boxes _____

_____ US Mail _____ FAX _____ E-mail

To promote prompt receipt of information, e-mail or faxes are definitely the preferred modes of communication. Recently, CCR has replaced mailings with secure e-mail. The TPIN and Welcome letter information will now be e-mailed to the primary point of contact (POC) listed on the CCR registration. If there is no e-mail address listed, these letters will be mailed via US mail. The 30-day renewal notification and expiration notice are sent via e-mail if an e-mail address has been provided for the primary POC.

Alternate Contact _____

Enter the name and phone number for another person at your company in case questions arise when the primary contact is not available.

Accounts Receivable _____

Provide contact information for the accounts receivable person at your company. This is the contact provided to the Defense Finance and Accounting Service regarding EFT payments on your government contracts. Note that this contact is not authorized to receive and/or release information regarding the CCR registration to any Registration Assistance Center personnel. It may be beneficial to have the accounts receivable contact also act as the alternate contact for the registration.

Owner Information

If you have checked "Sole Proprietorship" as your business type, you must provide the name and phone number of the owner of the business.

Government Business POC

This POC is that person in the company responsible for marketing and sales with the government. An email address is required. Both upper and lower cases are acceptable for all e-mail addresses. This POC and contact information, if entered, will be publicly displayed on the CCR Search Page. All contact methods are mandatory. The Alternate Government Business POC also is mandatory.

Past Performance POC

This POC is that person in the company responsible for administering the company's government past performance reports and response efforts. An email address is required. Both upper and lower cases are acceptable for all e-mail addresses. This POC and contact information is mandatory and, when entered, will be publicly displayed on the CCR Inquiry web site. All contact methods are mandatory. This person will be your watchdog over the performance ratings given by the government. It is very important that you monitor these ratings continuously.

Electronic Business POC

The EBPOC is the person in the company responsible for authorizing individual company personnel access into government electronic business systems (e.g., Electronic Document Access (EDA), Wide Area Workflow (WAWF)). POC and contact information is mandatory. This information will be publicly displayed on the CCR Inquiry web site. All contact methods are mandatory. Visit https://rmb.ogden.disa.mil/vreg.htm#Step2 to view detailed information on EBPOC responsibilities for WAWF.

Marketing Partner ID Number (MPIN)

This is a self-defined access code that will be shared with authorized partner applications (e.g., Past Performance Information Retrieval System (PPIRS), Federal Technical Data Solutions (FedTeDS) etc.). The MPIN acts as your password in these other systems, and you should guard it as such. The MPIN must be nine characters and contain at least one alpha character, one number and no spaces or special characters.

Caution

About three years ago, the CCR and SBA's PRO-Net databases were merged so that small businesses only need to register their information at one site. While this is good news, there is a downside to it. Many small businesses do not take the time to complete the additional company information required for the SBA database. Once a small business completes the basic CCR registration successfully, they are asked if you want to input additional information into SBA/PRO-Net. If you don't, buyers and others using the "Dynamic Small Business Search" will not find you and that may cost you business!

One more thing to remember, when you update your data, the small businesses also must change data in the SBA/PRO-Net database. The databases are not totally integrated yet. Just remember, CCR is a work in progress.

ONLINE REPRESENTATIONS AND CERTIFICATIONS APPLICATION (ORCA)

Effective January 1, 2005, the Federal Acquisition Regulation (FAR) requires the use of the Online Representations and Certifications Application (ORCA) in federal solicitations as a part of the proposal submission process. ORCA is an e-government initiative to replace the paper-based Representations & Certifications (Reps & Certs) process. ORCA is a web-based system that centralizes and standardizes the collection, storage and viewing of many of the FAR-required representations and certifications previously found in solicitations. Registration in ORCA is required if the solicitation being responded to requires an active registration in CCR.

With ORCA, you now have the ability to enter and maintain your representation and certification information, at your convenience, via the Internet at http://orca.bpn.gov. You will no longer have to submit representations and certifications completed in ORCA with each offer. Instead, a solicitation will contain a single provision allowing you to either certify that all of your representations and certifications in ORCA are current, complete and accurate as of the date of your signature, or list any changes. If registrants need help, they can contact the Procurement Technical Assistance Center (PTAC) (www.dla.mil/db/procurem.htm) closest to them.

In addition, rather than receiving and reviewing paper submissions, government contracting officials can access ORCA and review your information online as a part of the proposal evaluation process.

ORCA records are considered public information. Anyone with access to the Internet, and knows a registrant's DUNS number, can search the archives to view an ORCA record. More information can be found in the ORCA Handbook: http://orca.bpn.gov/ORCA_Handbook9_04ver.pdf

1. Go to www.bpn.gov to obtain the ORCA Handbook

2. Click on "Vendor" listed under Online Representations and Certifications Application (ORCA)

3. Click on "help" at the top of the page.

4. Click on "ORCA Handbook"

Note: Go to Appendix D in the ORCA Handbook to view ORCA letters.

Work Smart

 Firms interested in architect-engineer (A-E) contracts with the federal government also can enter their general qualifications required by Standard Form 330, Part II, into the ORCA database. Question #26 on the ORCA questionnaire collects all SF330 information. However, the registrant must answer all the other fields on the questionnaire, not just #26. In addition, the registrant must answer all the Reps and Certs information in order to provide any SF330 Part II information.

Note: For an A-E firm, submission of the SF330 Part II through ORCA is voluntary.

ORCA Registration Instruction

To register in ORCA, the vendor must have the following: (1) a DUNS Number, (2) a completed registration in CCR, and (3) a Marketing Partner Identification Number (MPIN) established in an active CCR registration.

The Marketing Personal Identification Number (MPIN) is a 9-digit code containing at least one alpha character and one number (no special characters or spaces). The MPIN is created by the registrant in their company's CCR registration and acts as a password for various other government systems. The MPIN is the last data field in the "Points of Contact" section of the registration and is mandatory.

Once the registrant has registered in CCR and entered their new MPIN, it will take 24 to 48 hours to become active. After that, they can begin their registration in ORCA. For more information on CCR registration and setting up an MPIN, the customer can go to www.ccr.gov.

Registrants can update or change their Reps and Certs information whenever necessary. Every registrant must update their ORCA and CCR registration at lease once a year to remain active. The clock will start over from the day of each update.

1. Go the Business Partner Network (BPN) home page at www.bpn.gov.

2. Click on "– Vendor" under "Online Representations and Certifications Applications (ORCA)" on the left margin of the home page.

3. Type your DUNS and MPIN into the appropriate fields.

4. Click on "Login to ORCA."

5. The first page is pre-populated with company information pulled from your CCR registration. You need to review the information.

    — If the information is correct, click on "Update your partially saved information" to complete a new ORCA registration.

    — If you have a completed registration, and want to update it, click on "Update your completed information."

    — If the information is not correct, you need to update your CCR registration at www.ccr.gov. Once you have updated your CCR registration, it will take 24 to 48 hours to become active. After that, you can resume your ORCA registration.

6. Fill in ORCA Primary Contact Information.

7. Click on "Continue."

8. Fill in the ORCA Questionnaire. Note: Registrants must answer all questions by filling in the appropriate fields, and then click "Add" or click the appropriate radio button.

9. Click on "Continue." Note: If you get the message "Review your questionnaire you are missing information," you must fill in missing information before you can continue.

10. Review and certify the Reps and Certs.

11. Click "Submit Certification" to activate the ORCA record. You will receive email confirmation when registration is active.

Because ORCA information is public, the database is available for anyone to search. Here are some instructions for doing some good old-fashioned market research:

1. Go to www.bpn.gov.

2. Click on "Public" listed under Online Representations and Certifications Application (ORCA).

3. Type the DUNS Number of the company you researching into the appropriate field.

4. Click "Search."

DECIPHERING GOVERNMENT CODES

Anyone who does business with the government can't help but be confused at times by the different types of codes that the government uses to identify, classify and inventory the products and services that it uses. However, it is important for you to understand the importance and purpose of each type.

Federal Supply/Service Code

The FSC (Federal Supply/Service Code) is a four-digit code used by government buying offices to classify and identify the products, supplies, and services that the government uses and buys. An understanding of which FSCs apply to your products or services is crucial to finding opportunities. For instance, you will need to know the FSCs that apply to your products in order to register to do business with the government. Moreover, since buying offices have responsibility for specific products, you can also use your FSCs to identify potential buying offices.

And since government buyers often use the registration databases to identify the companies that can meet their needs for products and services, it is important that you know all of the FSCs that apply to your company's end products so buyers can find you. Knowing the appropriate FSCs will also help you identify which buying offices issue contracts for the item.

In addition, you can do marketing research based on the FSC when reviewing the buying forecasts that the buying office issues. All four digits of a product code are numeric, for example 1015. In this example, 10 designates a weapon item. The second two numbers, 15, identify the size of the weapon item—in this instance, 75mm through 125mm.

Product service codes (PSC) are alpha/numeric, from "A" to "Z," with "I" and "O" not used. Three numbers are added to the alpha to further define what type of service is needed. For example, in the service code D308, the D3 indicates that the general type of service is Automatic Data Processing and Telecommunication Services, and the 08 indicates that the specific service is Programming Services. In another example—R608—the R means that the general type of service is Professional, Administrative and Management Support Services, and the 608 means that the specific service is Translation and Interpreting Services (including sign language).

Need help finding the FSC codes that apply to your products and services? The government issues a manual called the "Product and Services Codes Manual" that lists all the service and product codes. Look up your end product(s) in the manual and make a note of the code(s). Knowing the codes that apply to your capabilities will not only help you identify the government buying offices that have a need for your product or service, but will also help you register and search for bid opportunities.

The Product and Services Codes Manual is free. Just call the Federal Procurement Data Center at 202-219-3416 to request a copy.

You may also search for applicable FSC codes by keyword on the Internet at the Defense Logistics Information Service web site at http://www.dla.mil.

National Stock Number

The NSN (National Stock Number) is the 13-digit number that the federal government assigns, for purposes of identification and inventory control, to every piece of supply, equipment and material that it uses and buys. You can think of the NSNs as a federal cataloging system based on the concept of one NSN for any one item and one single item manager for each particular class of product. (Note that, because services are not inventoried, services don't fit this model. For services, only the first four digits are used—see discussion of FSCs, above.)

In a typical NSN—for example, 4720-00-101-9817—the first four numbers are the Federal Supply Code (FSC), which places the item in a specific category. In this example, 4720 is Pipe, Tubing, Hose, and Fittings because it starts with 47. The second two numbers, 20, identify the item as Hose and Flexible Tubing, which includes air duct, metallic, nonmetallic, and textile fiber hoses and their assemblies, etc. The next two numbers—in our example, 00—identify the country that buys the item; 00 or 01 is the code for the U.S. The remaining numbers of the NSN—101-9817—are referred to as the National Item Identification Number (NIIN) and are used to index NSNs.

How does all of this help you? Understanding the NSN, while at first somewhat of a challenge, is one of the keys that will open up some doors of opportunity for you. The NSN classification system helps to identify the offices and agencies that have control over the item and/or buy that item. Remember, for this to be useful, you must know the complete NSN.

If you know the NSN, searching on the NIIN can assist you in finding previous buying trends, previous supplies, and procurement history. Also, if the NSN "gets lost," you can sometimes use the NIIN to locate where it was reassigned since the NIIN tends to remain with an item over time.

You can do an Internet search based on NSNs at http://www.dscc.dla.mil/search/NSN.

NAICS and SIC

The NAICS (North American Industry Classification System) and the SIC (Standard Industrial Class) codes identify products and services by type of industry and are used by the government to evaluate economic performance. The NAICS codes, which replaced the SICs in October 2000 as the codes the government uses to classify businesses and industries, were developed jointly by the U.S., Canada, and Mexico to provide new comparability in statistics about business activity across North America.

You will need to know the NAICS codes that apply to your business in order to register with the government. You should also be able to identify all the NAICS and SIC codes that apply to your capabilities in order to help ensure your chances of success in doing business with the government. For example, government buyers looking for contractors use the codes of the products and services they wish to buy when searching for businesses profiled on the CCR and Pro-*Net* systems.

You can access the NAICS/SIC manual at the Small Business Administration's web site (http://www.sba.gov). Or you can search for your products and services by keyword at the NAICS web site at http://www.census.gov/epcd/www/naics.html.

Although NAICS codes are now the official codes being used by the government, SIC codes may continue to be used by some agencies for some time during the transition.

Solicitation Numbers

The Solicitation Number for a specific bid opportunity is a wonderful source of information that can help you identify a procurement office. Using the Defense Logistics Agency (DLA) buying centers, let's look at what the number means and the type of contract that is contemplated.

Sample Solicitation Number: SPO450-05-Q-1234

SPO450 is the alpha/numeric identifying the buying office that issued the solicitation as the Defense Supply Center Richmond. DLA has used the facility location to designate which center is the buying office (i.e., DSCC is in Columbus, Ohio; DSCP is in Philadelphia; and DSCR is located in Richmond, Va.). Here are the alpha/numeric designations for the three centers, note that Philadelphia has four major commodity areas:

SPO100 – DSCP (Philadelphia) – Clothing and Textile

SPO200 – DSCP (Philadelphia) – Medical

SPO300 – DSCP (Philadelphia) – Subsistence

SPO400 – DSCR (Richmond) – Industrial and aerospace equipment and supplies, misc.

SPO500 – DSCP (Philadelphia) – General and Industrial

SPO700 – DSCC (Columbus) – Electronics

Sometimes you will see that the last two digits of the six-digit number are different, as in our sample solicitation number: the DSCR identification is SPO450, not SPO400. This indicates that the solicitation comes from the same buying office, DSCR, but a different commodity area within that buying office.

The next two digits (character position seven and eight) designate the fiscal year that the solicitation was issued, so 05 is 2005, 02 was 2002, 03 was 2003, etc.

The next digit (in the ninth location) is an alpha character that identifies the type of solicitation and contract. This is important. In our sample solicitation number, that letter is a "Q," SPO450-05-**Q**-1234. Here are the explanations for the various letters that are used:

- **T** – Indicates that the item meets the criteria for award by computer. The computer will determine what terms would apply and attempts to award the solicitation two days after the closing under the PACE (Procurement Automated Contract Evaluation) System. The value of these awards is usually below $2,500 and just for fun, no human is involved.

- **Q** – Represents a solicitation generally more complex then a T bid. It might have a higher level of inspection, restricted drawing, first article or long-term contract terms. A "buyer" is involved who can answer questions, review/evaluate offers and award contracts. An offeror can submit quotes up to the point of award.

- **U** – Signifies a manual bid, similar to a Q, but designated as a PACE award candidate by the buyer. The terms and conditions of PACE will apply; the same as for T bid solicitations.

- **X** – Belongs to an express quote or award. It is usually issued orally by the buyer because of the need for quick award, therefore, time is shortened by a few days and the purchase is not posted on the Procurement Gateway. The buyer will usually only go to known sources and the value will be under $25,000.

- **R** – Identifies a large buy solicitation over $100,000 through negotiated procurement. Offers must be mailed in on the original solicitation format and must be received prior to the closing date of the bid. These bids are posted on FedBizOpps. If you're late on these, you're out of luck.

- **B** – Reveals that the solicitation is "Invitation for Bid" or "Sealed Bid," which are less frequently used. The requirements are clear and the technical data complete. All offers received are opened at a public meeting at a specific time and date. The apparent low offeror is known by the conclusion of the opening.

The last series of numbers, **1234** in our sample solicitation number are nothing more than a sequential number series in a log that keeps track of the number of solicitations issued.

Chapter 8

Find Bid Leads

OK, let's get down to the nitty gritty. How do you go about finding leads on all those millions of contracts that the federal government awards each year? We discuss several ways:

- Monitor FedBizOpps

- Get included on Solicitation Mailing Lists

- Search SUB-*Net*

- Use electronic bulletin boards

- Check agency bid boards

- Submit an unsolicited proposal

- Get registered on qualification lists

Monitor FedBizOpps

One way to find bid leads is through FedBizOpps (http://www.fedbizopps.gov), the official web site listing of all federal government contracting opportunities and awards over $25,000. Federal agencies are required by law to post their contracting opportunities over $25,000 here.

Through this single point of entry, government buyers can post bids soliciting the products and services they need directly to FedBizOpps via the Internet, while commercial vendors seeking to sell their products and services to the government can search, monitor, and retrieve these bids.

Work Smart

The FedBizOpps system includes an e-mail notification service that lets companies looking for government business fill out a subscription form in order to receive e-mail notification of new bids that match the criteria they have selected. Companies can specify the agency, buying office, location, supply or service codes, etc. that they are interested in.

While the General Services Administration (GSA) is responsible for the operation and maintenance of the system, the content of the notices is the sole responsibility of the agency that has issued the notice.

All federal procurement offices are required to announce in FedBizOpps virtually all proposed procurement actions over $25,000. Government agencies are also required to publish information on subcontracting opportunities, including the names and addresses of firms awarded contracts over $25,000 that are likely to result in subcontracts.

There are exceptions to the notice requirements. For example, FedBizOpps usually does not list procurement notices when the supplies or services are classified or are required immediately due to an emergency.

Many procurement announcements are reserved for, or "set aside," for small businesses, minority-owned businesses, women-owned firms, and veteran-owned businesses and they are listed as such.

FedBizOpps postings cover both services and supplies that the federal government wants to purchase, plus the information you need to make an informed offer, including:

- the specific service or product wanted

- the buying agency

- the due date for offers

- the phone number of the agency contact

- the addresses for obtaining complete specifications

- links to related sites

Think of FedBizOpps as a classified ad section for the government. Since FedBizOpps is updated every business day with new notices, it is to your advantage to look for new "ads" everyday, just like you would in a newspaper. You don't want to miss a new opportunity.

Caution

One of the common misconceptions that some small business owners have about FedBizOpps is that it posts every buying opportunity that the government has.

However, nothing could be further from the truth. Remember that the only bids listed on FedBizOpps are those for $25,000 or more, and those account for only a small fraction of the total amount of bids that the government puts out.

To find bids in all ranges, consider registering with a PTAC or a commercial bid service.

Get To Know FedBizOpps

While the government continues to enhance the capabilities of FedBizOpps and to make it easier and faster to use, finding your way around the site can be tricky and sometimes confusing.

The official manual explaining and illustrating the system can be found at the FedBizOpps Vendors Guide index page at http://www.eps.gov/EPSVendorsManual/VG1-Index.htm. You can view the manual onscreen or download it from that site. Make sure you go over the entire manual carefully and check each web page, as you go, so that you know where you are and what you are looking at.

It may take some time and effort to get to really know the FedBizOpps system, but it is worth it in the long run. The site contains lots of useful information, including synopses of government solicitations for products or services, actual solicitations, Requests for Proposals and Quotations, sources being sought, market surveys for government planning purposes, amendments/modifications, and award notices.

The search system has many useful options, allowing you to refine your searches, with just a click of your mouse, to a particular date range, classification code, place of performance, agency, etc. Once again, the time you spend trying out and learning about the search features will be time well spent.

Remember that finding what you need on any search system is always easier if you feed it "good" keywords—in the case of FedBizOpps, words that describe the products/services that you provide (or are capable of providing) and the correct product/service codes. If you find that your searches and/or the e-mail notification service are not retrieving bids that relate to the types of products and/or services your company provides, don't just give up. Go in and change your search criteria, trying different keywords and product/service codes.

If you are looking for subcontracting work, try searching FedBizOpps for awards. Use criteria similar to what you would use when searching for prime contracting opportunities. You can find out the award winner, dollar amount and point of contact. You then can search CCR for more details about the company receiving the award. This is a great marketing tool.

Caution

The look and functionality of the FedBizOpps site can change without notice, so it's in your best interest to keep up with any enhancements or changes in how the site works, what information you have to provide, etc.

As of early 2002, online bidding through FedBizOpps is becoming more commonplace. Soon it will be considered "regular business" to use FedBizOpps to complete your bid information, fill in your prices, and send in your offer to the buying location by simply clicking on the "Submit" button. (This feature first began to appear on some Requests for Quotes.) Bids are usually reviewed in the order in which they are received. If you are the successful bidder, you will be notified.

Classification Codes

Notices of contract opportunities that appear in FedBizOpps are arranged by Federal Supply Groups (FSG). These classification codes are divided into two groups:

1. service and product codes (alpha or alpha/numeric)

2. supplies, equipment and material codes (numeric)

While the General Services Administration (GSA) is responsible for the operation and maintenance of FedBizOpps, it is the contracting officer, not GSA, who determines the appropriate classification code for a particular notice. Therefore, the contracting officer is the one held responsible if a notice of a contract is misclassified and, as a result, fails to effectively notify the firms most likely to respond.

To search for opportunities using classification codes, go to http://www.FedBizOpps.gov and click the "go" button next to "Find Business Opportunity" on the home page. Scroll down to "Search by Procurement Classification Code" where you will find a list of codes. Scroll through the list and highlight the code of interest to you. Scroll to the bottom of page and click the "Start Search" button. This will bring up a listing of leads.

There are two manuals available that can give you information to better identify your areas of interest. The Federal Supply Classification Cataloging Handbook and Handbook H2 can both be found by going to http://www.wingovcon.com and clicking on the FSC/PSC Tab.

Numbered Notes

When you read a notice in FedBizOpps, you will often see references to numbered notes within the text. (For example, you may see such phrases as "Notes 12 and 26 apply" or "See Note(s) 22 and 23.")

The purpose of these numbered notes, which are similar to footnotes, is to avoid the unnecessary repetition of information in various announcements. Whenever a numbered note is included in a notice, the note referred to must be read as part of the item or section in which it appears. (A complete listing of numbered notes and their meaning is included in Appendix 6.)

Work Smart

Remember as you look through synopses in FedBizOpps that each one identifies a buying office and a personal contact. What a great marketing tool! If the item or service isn't exactly what you sell, you still have a contact to call to learn more about the buyer's needs.

Potential Sources Sought

You can use FedBizOpps to find special advance notices of procurement opportunities by searching for "potential sources sought" in the system. At the FedBizOpps home page, click "go," scroll down to "Full Text Search" and enter the search term: potential sources sought. Scroll down and click the Start Search button to get the list.

These synopses provide you with an opportunity to submit information that will permit your capabilities to be evaluated while allowing the government to gauge interest in possible contracts. Responding is very important if a particular community (e.g., small businesses, minority-owned small businesses, women-owned small businesses, or historically black colleges and universities/minority institutions, etc.) desires a set-aside. The decision to set a project aside is often made on the basis of responses received to these Potential Sources Sought synopses.

Business News

You can also use FedBizOpps to find out about important upcoming meetings and conferences dealing with federal procurement activities, including pre-proposal and bidders' conferences. These meetings are great places to market your capabilities, identify the competition, and structure potential teaming arrangements.

At the FedBizOpps home page, click "go," scroll down to "Full Text Search," and enter the search term: special notice. Scroll down and click the Start Search button at the bottom of the page. Check the "Title" area to locate the notices of interest.

GET INCLUDED ON SOLICITATION MAILING LISTS

Another way of receiving bid leads is to get your company included on the Solicitation Mailing List (SML) of the specific buying offices likely to have a need for your product or service. The SML database lists the capabilities of businesses interested in selling to the government, and thus enables a buying office to find potential sources to meet its needs for products and services.

Recently, we've learned that some offices dealing with actions under $25,000 will still use the Standard Form 129, "Solicitation Mailing List," because many are not yet automated. So make sure you ask them if they still use the SF 129. With the federal government quickly moving into e-business processes, this method of finding bid leads will, most likely, eventually go away.

Once again, using the target list of prospective customers that you put together in Chapter 6, make an effort to contact them. Be sure to contact the small business specialist at each agency to make sure you do what is necessary to be listed on the appropriate SML.

When the SML is extremely long, the purchasing agency may use only a portion of it for a particular acquisition and rotate the other segments of the list for other acquisitions. In such situations, the regulations require that a prorated number of small businesses be solicited.

Work Smart

Contracting for architect-engineering (A-E) and construction services follows a special procedure and does not use SMLs. For government contracts, A-E firms are selected on the basis of the professional qualifications necessary to perform the required services satisfactorily. Construction companies are selected in a similar manner. Firms interested in such work should file Form SF 330, "Architect-Engineer Qualifications" (attainable from any federal government buying office or PTAC), with the agency responsible for the geographic area(s) or specialized area of construction in which the firm desires to work.

You can get SF 330 by going to www.gsa.gov. Use the drop-down menu under "About GSA" and click on "Forms." Change the default to "Standard Forms" and then look for SF 330. Or you can go to the CCH Business Owner's Toolkit (www.toolkit.cch.com) for the latest downloads.

Remember that sometimes there is a geographical limit on who will be considered for an award.

SEARCH SUB-*NET*

SUB-*Net* is a part of the Small Business Administration web site on which large businesses, government agencies, and other prime contractors post solicitations and bid opportunities.

This is a good place for small businesses to search and view bid opportunities. Small businesses may also register in this area to post a bid opportunity, but only if they are seeking teaming partners or subcontractors for a specific procurement that they would not be able to perform alone.

To access SUB-*Net*, go to http://web.sba.gov/subnet. When searching, again remember to think like the government. Choose search terms that have to do with your end products, not your process.

USE ELECTRONIC BULLETIN BOARDS

The Departments of the Army, Navy and Air Force, as well as various other Department of Defense (DoD) organizations and agencies, use electronic bulletin boards (EBBs) to inform the public about contracting opportunities, provide details of government solicitations, and respond to questions about solicitations. EBBs also permit electronic submission of bids and proposals.

Unfortunately, to use EBBs, you will have to register at each particular site. So bear with the redundancy for now. As the government gets the Central Contractor Registration (CCR) running up to speed, the need to register again and again hopefully will fade. (Note: For now, you will need your tax ID, DUNS and CAGE numbers, as well as other information to register at DoD sites.)

In a typical bulletin board, the government posts a Request for Quote. Interested businesses can submit standard paper quotes or, in some cases, electronic quotes for the buyer to review. Most of the remaining documentation is still on paper.

When this book went to press, there were still some agencies that were using electronic bulletin boards, but except for smaller buying offices, we believe that they will eventually become a thing of the past and will be replaced with an Internet version.

Example

The EBB was the original system for transmitting information via computer and modem connecting to a special network through the use of telephone lines. The use of EBBs was largely the result of the Federal Acquisition Streamlining Act of 1994, which required the government to convert from an acquisition process driven by paperwork to an expedited process based on electronic data interchange (EDI).

CHECK AGENCY BID BOARDS

Bid boards, while still used by some buying agencies to post bid opportunities, are becoming a thing of the past, as the Internet becomes more a part of business life.

In the "old days," every DoD buying office maintained, in a public place, a bid board on which it displayed a copy of each small purchase solicitation it issued for contracts valued at less than $25,000. Every notice was posted on the bid board for seven calendar days. If it was impractical to post a copy of the entire solicitation, the bid board notice offered a brief description and the location of the full text version.

There are still agencies that use bid boards, and you can hire an individual in the area to visit the bid board and monitor it for you. That individual can either send you everything on the board or pick and choose for you. At one time, we had twelve of these prospectors getting bids for our clients. It worked, but was expensive and time-consuming.

SUBMIT AN UNSOLICITED PROPOSAL

Sometimes you can create your own contracting opportunities by submitting an unsolicited proposal. Such a proposal is a written offer to the government to perform a task or effort that you initiate. To be considered, an unsolicited proposal must offer a unique and innovative concept to the government. You can learn about an agency's research and development (R&D) needs from advance notices on www.fedbizopps.gov and from informal contacts with agency personnel.

The FAR provides general guidance for submitting an unsolicited proposal. The proposal should contain an abstract of the proposed effort, the method of approach, and the extent of the effort. It should also include a proposed price or estimated cost. You should clearly mark any proprietary data you wish to protect from possible release to others.

These regulations allow the government to use other-than-competitive procurement procedures when they receive a favorably evaluated unsolicited proposal. They also require that the prospective contractors be notified of government's intentions regarding the proposal.

If you're not sure what specific buying office might be really interested in the item or service, then send it to the headquarters operation in Washington, D.C. For example, for the Department of Army, instead of sending a proposal to the electronics command, send it to headquarters, U.S. Army in Washington. For the civilian side, it would be similar. For example, instead of sending a proposal to the Chicago regional area of the FAA, send it to FAA Operations in Washington, D.C.

Remember you are sending in a proposal that is supposed to help the government agency accomplish its mission. They want a well thought-out and clear description of what you are proposing as a solution.

GET REGISTERED ON QUALIFICATION LISTS

A less common way to receive bid leads is by getting registered on a qualified product list (QPL), a qualified manufacturers list (QML), or a qualified bidders list. Qualification lists are used only for products that require lengthy or costly testing to determine whether they meet the government's requirements. The lists identify the specifications and the manufacturers or distributors of each qualified item. When the government wishes to procure a product for which a qualification list exists, bids or proposals are usually accepted only for specific products or from companies on the list.

To have your product or your company included on a qualification list, contact the small business specialist responsible for qualification at the buying office identified in the product specification.

If all else fails, you can always get help from a bid-matching service or your local PTAC office. These methods are discussed in detail in Chapter 20.

Chapter 9

Get the Bid Package

Once you have found a bid that you are interested in, the next step is to get the bid package (it is also sometimes referred to as a solicitation package). Getting the bid package is often as easy as downloading it off the Internet.

GETTING THE SPECIFICS

To get the package, you can do one of the following:

- Contact the buyer and request the bid package. The buyer's name, address, phone number, and e-mail address are listed on the bid notice. When you request the bid package, also ask for any amendments that might have been issued.

- Locate the web page address in the bid notice and download the bid package off the Internet. A word of caution: Before you start downloading, double-check the number of the bid contract you have selected for download to make sure it's the right one. (The solicitation number will be something like: DAA123-00-R-1234. Or it may say: SOL: or SOL Number.) Proceed carefully; all of the numbers sometimes start to look the same.

CONTRACTS AND PRICING ARRANGEMENTS

When requesting a bid package, you need to be familiar with the types of contracts—or pricing arrangements—that the government uses in buying a product or service. The type of contract used is determined by the circumstances of the acquisition and the extent to which the government wishes to accept the cost risks. The contract type used will have an important effect on the way you price out the contract (see Chapter 12). These pricing arrangements reflect the risk involved in contract performance.

There are three basic categories of contracts:

1. fixed-price

2. cost-reimbursement

3. special situation

Fixed-Price Contracts

These are the types of contracts that small businesses will, for the most part, be dealing with. Under the fixed-price arrangement, the final price is basically determined before the work is performed. There are various types of fixed-price contracts:

- **Firm fixed-price:** The price is not subject to adjustment. The contractor is obligated to perform the contract at the awarded price and accepts 100 percent of the profit or loss of performing the contract within that price. (See FAR 16.202)

- **Fixed-price with economic price adjustment:** The price may be adjusted upward or downward based upon the occurrence of contractually specified economic contingencies that are clearly outside the contractor's control. (See FAR 16.203)

- **Fixed-price incentive:** The profit is adjusted and the final price is established by a formula based on the relationship of the final negotiated cost to the target cost. (See FAR 16.204)

- **Firm fixed-price, level-of-effort:** A fixed price is established for a specified level of effort over a stated time frame. If the level varies beyond specified thresholds, the price may be adjusted. (See FAR 16.207)

Cost-Reimbursement Contracts

Cost-reimbursement contracts provide for the final price to be determined either when the work is finished or at some interim point during contract performance. If a contract is cost-reimbursable, the contractor can legally stop work when all contract funds are spent. Thus, the cost risk is essentially shifted to the government. There are various types of cost-reimbursement contracts:

- **Cost:** Reimbursement consists of allowable cost; there is no fee provision. (See FAR 16.302)

- **Cost-sharing:** An agreed portion of allowable cost is reimbursed. (See FAR 16.303)

- **Cost-plus-fixed-fee:** Reimbursement is based on allowable cost plus a fixed fee. (See FAR 16.306)

- **Cost-plus-incentive-fee:** Reimbursement consists of allowable cost incurred and a fee adjusted by a formula based on the relationship of the allowable cost to the target cost. (See FAR 16.304)

- **Cost-plus-award fee:** Reimbursement consists of allowable cost incurred and a two-part fee—a fixed amount and an award amount based on an evaluation of the quality of contract performance. (See FAR 16.305)

Special Situation Contracts

There are also special types of contracts, including:

- **Time and material:** Direct labor hours expended are reimbursed at fixed hourly rates, which usually include direct labor costs, indirect expenses and profit. Material costs are reimbursed at actual cost plus a handling charge, if applicable. (See FAR 16.601)

- **Labor hour:** Direct labor hours expended are reimbursed at a fixed hourly rate, usually including all cost and profit. (See FAR 16.602)

- **Definite-quantity:** The contract quantity is defined, but the delivery schedule is flexible. Payment is made on some form of fixed-price basis. (See FAR 16.502)

- **Requirements:** Actual delivery schedules and quantities are flexible during the contract period. Payment is based on a predetermined fixed-price basis. (See FAR 16.503)

SPECIAL BIDDING TECHNIQUES

There are two new bidding techniques that the government is using that the small business needs to be aware of:

- **Auction** — A government buying technique where the bidding continues until no competitor is willing to submit a better (i.e., lower) bid. The technique is often referred to as "reverse auction" because the government is looking for the lowest price, not the highest price.

- **Bundling** — A technique where the government consolidates two or more requirements that were normally bought separately into a single contract. The support contracts of many military bases, which require a variety of work disciplines to keep the base operating, are being bid this way.

Both can present potential problems for small businesses.

If you decide to compete for a bid using the auction method, you need to spend time and effort researching and preparing so that you are sure that you can do what is required at the price you offer. You also need to protect yourself from the auction mentality that can take over. This is a fast-pace environment, and it is easy to get caught up in the moment. In an effort to win, you could end up bidding too low, receiving the contract, and not being able to cover your costs.

In bundling, there may be requirements included in the solicitation that cover areas that a small business cannot perform or manage. If you are considering making a bid, make sure you carefully read every provision of the bid to make sure you have the capability to perform all that is required, including project management.

A word to the wise: Be very cautious if you choose to participate in these bidding techniques.

BUYING OFFICES' TERMINOLOGY

The following information is from the Defense Supply Center Richmond, illustrating procurement processes at a DoD buying office. DSCR is part of the larger DoD buying organization, and if you understand better what DSCR is doing, you will be better prepared to work with the other Supply Centers and federal buying offices.

DSCR, like many other buying offices, issues many long-term contracts. These contracts are more than just fixed-price, fixed-quantity awards. Generally, they contain a range of annual estimated quantities, a separate ordering quantity and a small guaranteed quantity. These quantities will be utilized over a period of a year or years with option terms. For long-term contracts over $100,000, the most common type is referred to as an Indefinite Quantity Contract (IQC). Long-term contracts under $100,000 are identified as Indefinite Delivery Purchase Orders (IDPOs).

- **Indefinite Quantity Contract (IQC)** — An IQC is a contract issued for an estimated but indefinite quantity of supply to be ordered via delivery orders during a specified period of contract performance. This is the government's preferred method of long-term contracting. Total value of an IQC, including all option years, is anticipated to exceed $100,000. The limitation of the contract is based on the maximum estimated annual demand quantity for each contract period. Typically, contracts are issued with a base year and up to four option years. Each option year must be exercised via a modification to make the option effective. The determination to exercise the option is made solely by the government.

- **Indefinite Delivery Purchase Order (IDPO)** — An IDPO is a purchase order (not a contract) issued for an estimated but indefinite quantity of supply to be ordered via delivery orders during a specified period of contract performance. Like the indefinite quantity contract, it sets minimum and maximum delivery order sizes and an estimated annual demand. Its term is based on the maximum contract value of $100,000. The contract expires whenever the threshold of $100,000 is attained, with a maximum of 5 years allowed.

Long-Term Contract Clauses

If you hope to compete for a long-term contract, there are a number of features that are unique to these kinds of arrangements. Be sure you understand these various elements before committing yourself to a project.

- **Guaranteed Minimum** — This is the minimum quantity the government agrees to buy during the contract period. The government is not obligated to buy any quantity beyond the guaranteed minimum quantity and may, if justified, buy elsewhere after that quantity has been procured (though that is not the intent and is not a common occurrence). The guaranteed minimum provides a vendor assurance of some sales and delineates where vendor risk in pricing begins.

- **Estimated Annual Demand/Quantity** — This spells out the actual quantity the government estimates that it will order during the contract period. Estimates are based on prior demand history but not assured. A check with contract history will reflect the consistency pattern of prior demand history.

- **Contract Maximum Quantity** — This is the maximum cumulative quantity the government can procure during the period of contract performance. If a contract period runs from January to December and in September the full quantity is reached, no further orders will be issued until the new contract period (option) is exercised.

- **Minimum Order Quantity** — This shows the minimum quantity that will be ordered at one time in a delivery order. It is usually based on average demand quantity ordered by requisitions. Consideration of this quantity is critical in pricing and considering the size of a production run.

- **Maximum Order Quantity** — This sets the maximum quantity that will be ordered at one time in a delivery order. The Government may order a larger quantity but vendors have the right to decline the order or request a modification to the delivery schedule to meet the increased demand. At no time can the order quantity exceed the (accumulated) maximum contract quantity.

- **Flexible Option** — This clause allows the government to exercise an option earlier than the expiration of the contract term. If a contract covers a period from January to December, and the full contract quantity is utilized in September, the contracting officer will not have to wait until December to exercise the option. With the flexible option, the option can be exercised in September and the new contract period would then run from September to August of the next year. While this process may shorten the ultimate contract period, the quantities are not altered and both vendor and government are unharmed by the action.

- **Paperless Order Processing System (POPS)** — This requires the use of special software and a Value Added Network (VAN) when electronically sending delivery orders via Electronic Data Interchange (EDI). Failure to comply with POPS during award performance may result in a termination for default. While a vendor does not need to have the system in place at the time of solicitation, it must be in place within 30 days after award. Your local PTAC can help you identify potential VANs.

Blanket Purchase Agreements

Some buying offices refer to "purchase agreements," which are pre-arranged agreements signed prior to doing business with the agency. DSCR requires no such agreements, only that you are registered on the CCR. These purchase agreements are often confused with Blanket Purchase Agreements.

DSCR does have a Blanket Purchase Agreement (BPA) program, which is utilized to make awards below $25,000 (See FAR 13.303 and FAR 16.7). A Blanket Purchase Agreement is a negotiated set of terms under which awards can be made. Once in the BPA program, vendors compete for solicitations, with delivery orders issued against the terms of the BPA. These agreements have a number of features:

1. A wide variety of items in a broad class of supplies or services are generally purchased, but the exact items, quantities, and delivery requirements are not known in advance and may vary considerably.

2. Commercial sources of supplies are needed for one or more offices or projects in a given area that do not have or need authority to purchase otherwise.

3. Numerous purchase orders do not need to be written.

4. No current contract exists for the required supply or service.

If you want to be considered as a supplier under the BPA program, you are evaluated on these criteria:

*   A dependable past performance

*   A history of quality services and supplies at lower prices

*   Numerous purchases have been provided at or below the simplified acquisition threshold

*   A letter certifying status as an authorized distributor for a manufacturer

*   Access to electronic commerce/electronic data interchange capability (EDI Standard ANSI X12)

Solicitations issued under the BPA system will have a "Z" in the ninth position of the solicitation number. Award numbers will contain an AA or AB in the ninth position of the basic agreement. Once the BPA number is issued, it will remain in effect until the vendor requests removal of the BPA. The BPA award number is automatically updated every year with a new fiscal year in the seventh and eighth position. No formal notice is sent to confirm this.

Surge Requirements

In order to cover emergency situations, many DoD long-term contracts now specify surge quantities. Surge requirements are excess requirements (above the basic quantity) that must be available with an accelerated delivery. These would typically be utilized during times of war or unforeseen surges in demand. *Vendors must be capable of supplying any normal contract quantities at the same time as any surge requirement.*

Surge items are listed as a separate line item, allowing vendors to reflect a premium price (if justified) to compensate for any overtime shifts, stock rotations/storage, equipment, shipping costs required to supply the surge quantity. The government determines the quantity and delivery desired for the surge requirements. The vendor provides the price necessary to meet the demand.

Due to the critical nature of availability, vendors are generally asked to provide the government with a surge and sustainability plan that details how the vendor will meet the requirements (See DFARS 217.208-70 and DFARS 252.217-7001). Look for the surge clause in section I of the solicitation.

Marketbaskets

Marketbaskets are long-term contracts for large groupings of multiple items with National Stock Numbers (NSN) that are lumped together based on manufacturing processes. Due to the variety and size of these buys, they are evaluated on a line-item basis, enabling a vendor to respond to one, few or all of the items needed. Most of these buys contain competitive item descriptions and are solicited as some type of set-aside (SB, HUBZone or 8(a)).

Vendors interested in these buys must be careful to consider the volume of items they quote, the impact on their production lines, the ability to meet delivery of multiple items at the same time, the impact of surge requirements as well as the normal impact of packaging and delivery order requirements. Careful attention must be paid to detail in the solicitation. Marketbaskets are highlighted on the DSCR Business Opportunities page, under Corporate Contracting/Special Acquisitions and Small Business Acquisitions.

Hopefully this has provided you with a better understanding of the variety of contract situations the government uses to assure its needs are met.

Chapter 10

Review the Bid

Here is where you get to look at your first bid package. And here is where we let you in on the secret to winning and making a profit on the contract you are bidding on:

Read the bid. Then read it again. And after you think you're finished, read it again.

Why is this so important? In most cases, when you submit your bid, all you have to do is fill in some of the blanks on the forms contained in the package and send the package back to the government. But here's the catch: Even though the government itself generated and provided the package, when you send it back to the government, it becomes *your* offer, and the government will look at it as if you had put the entire package together yourself and as if they had never seen it before.

Therefore, you need to understand what's in the bid package because it is more than a solicitation for a bid—if and when the government signs it, it is also your *binding contract*. That means that you must carefully check out *all* portions of the contract, not just the description and specification portion. That also means that you can't just gloss over parts that you do not completely understand—you need to take notes as you go so you can address those parts later on.

The package contains all the information you need in order to bid intelligently—all you need to do is read it.

Example

A small safety equipment company had been doing government work for the military and doing quite well at it. When the owner died unexpectedly, the owner's widow and son continued running the business. Later, they received a bid package for a stretcher for the Navy, and since this was an item that they supplied, they submitted a bid and won the small dollar purchase order.

When the inspector came out to check the stretchers before shipment, the owners discovered that they had made a very serious error. The requirement in the contract called for more than a stretcher—it also called for the stretcher to be enclosed in a hanging unit for use on the wall of a ship—a requirement that they had missed because they didn't read the bid carefully. And since their bid reflected the cost of the stretcher, not the added cost of the hanging unit, completion of the contract at the price quoted would have broken their company.

We recommended that they try to plead their case to the commander at the buying office and ask to be let out of the contract. Luckily for them, the commander must have been having a good day and cancelled the contract—a very rare occurrence for the government.

So, not reading the bid carefully could have cost the owners their business. They were lucky, but you may not be if you fail to carefully review the contract.

TYPES OF BIDS/SOLICITATIONS

Solicitation packages usually range anywhere from 10 to 50 or more pages, depending on dollar value, the Statement of Work and other requirements. They will include clauses and instructions and other information that will tell you the who, what, where and how of the contract.

The first six positions of a solicitation number (e.g., DAA123-00-R-1234) identify the department or agency issuing the document, the next two positions (e.g., 00) are the last two digits of the fiscal year issued, and the single alpha character (e.g., R) identifies the type of solicitation. For example, B= Invitation for Bid, P= Purchase Order, C= Contract, Q= Request for Quote, R= Request for Proposal, etc. The last four positions identify the sequential order for a particular solicitation.

Bids with an alpha of Q or T are for requirements under $100,000. Usually T bids do not have technical data packages included with them, so if you want to bid on them you are looking at reverse engineering a product or trying to go to the original manufacturer and getting the technical data from them . . . lots of luck!

Note: There is a new character, Z, which is used by at least two agencies for special evaluation and approval. You must first receive approval from and, in most cases, the local DCMO which will visit you and see if you are a "regular" dealer/manufacturer in the goods you are trying to sell to the government. These types of contracts will most likely result in using Electronic Data Interchange as a condition of the contract. So if you see a "Z" bid, be aware that it is a special contract where you will be expected to have your EDI up and running.

The bid package you receive will most likely come in one of three forms:

- **Invitation for Bid (IFB)** — An IFB is an advertised contract, also referred to as a "Sealed bid." There are no discussions, and the bid package is considered complete for bidding purposes. The price is a major consideration, and the signing of the solicitation form—Standard Form 33 (SF 33)—by the bidder and by the government creates a binding document. The solicitation number will look something like DAAE20-00-B-1234, with the "B" in the number indicating it is a sealed bid. It is competitive and the low bid will get it. Also, it is probably worth more than $100,000 in value.

- **Request for Proposal (RFP)** — An RFP is a negotiated contract. There will be discussions, and the bidder may get the opportunity to change bid pricing, technical requirements, etc. As with the IFB, above, the SF 33 is the form that will be used and, again, becomes a binding contract when both the bidder and the government sign. The solicitation number will look something like N00023-00-R-1234, with the "R" in the number indicating it is a negotiated solicitation. Price and other factors will determine the winner. Here again the value is probably more than $100,000.

- **Request for Quote (RFQ)** — An RFQ is a request for information that may include price, but is not a binding contract or document. This is also considered a negotiated bid because the government will want to talk over the information obtained. The number will look something like F62509-00-Q-1234, with the "Q" indicating the solicitation is for information and prices. It is negotiated and may be valued at greater than $100,000. If a contract is made, the government will use a Standard Form 26, Award/Contract.

Common Government Forms

Here are some of the more common forms that you may encounter in bidding on government work. (In Chapter 13, we'll help you fill out some of these forms.)

DD Form 1707, **Information to Offerors or Quoters**, *is a form used by the Defense Department along with the SF 33. It is used by bidders to indicate no response to the solicitation and provides the buying office with various pieces of information such as why you are not bidding.*

Standard Form 33, **Solicitation, Offer and Award***, is a solicitation/contract form used by the federal government not only to solicit offers but also to award a contract since it is a bi-lateral (i.e., two-signature) document. This means that the bidder signs the document and submits it to the government and, upon acceptance of the bid, the government signs the same document and a binding contract is established. This form is used for either sealed bids or negotiated contracts valued at $100,000 or more.*

Standard Form 26, **Award/Contract***, is a form used by the federal government to award a contract, usually as the result of a* Request for Quotation. *Both parties sign, but it requires references to the basic solicitation and/or other documents. In general, the SF 26 and SF 33 ask for similar information to be filled in, but the SF 26 requires some certification information that is not required on the SF 33.*

Standard Form 30, **Amendment of Solicitation/Modification of Contract***, is a form used to do what its title implies: amend a solicitation before it closes or modify a contract that has been awarded. Normally this form is filled out by the government and is then sent to the bidder or contractor for signature.*

Standard Form 18, **Request for Quotation***, is used to obtain information and quotations, but the responses are not considered offers. A SF 26 is sometimes used to award a contract resulting from the use of a SF 18.*

Standard Form 1449, **Solicitation /Contract/Order for Commercial Items***, is used to buy commercial items when the simplified acquisition procedures are used. It can also be used to ship and receive product.*

HOW TO READ A TYPICAL BID

Let's take a closer look at a typical bid using a common form as an example—Standard Form 33 (SF 33)—and we'll show you how to look for what is important.

The SF 33 is divided into four major parts:

- **Blocks 1-8** — The first part contains basic information about the solicitation and is filled in by the government buying office. (Block 2, the contract number, is not filled in by the government until award is made.)

- **Blocks 9-11** — The second part is the Solicitation area. Block 11, Table of Contents, is very important. The sections of Block 11, *when taken together*, make up the whole solicitation and resulting contract. For example, it contains specific information about the solicitation and also the place where you will enter your bid price.

- **Blocks 12-18** — The third part is the Offer area and is filled in and signed by the bidder before returning the offer to the buying office.

- **Blocks 19-28** — The fourth part is the Award area and is completed and signed by the government when it makes the award.

Caution

We strongly recommend that, when reading a bid, you read it in a particular order. Certain sections are related to each other, and it will be much more efficient and understandable if you read them together.

Here is the order we recommend for reading SF 33:

Identify which sections of the form apply to the particular bid. We begin our reading of the bid by first taking a careful look at Block 11, Table of Contents. We begin here because the Table of Contents identifies all the applicable sections that will make up the contents of the subsequent contract. For instance, Section B (see below) of Block 11 tells you what is being bought and provides the place where you will put your bid price.

Note that the Table of Contents is divided into the following four parts:

Part I	The Schedule
Part II	Contract Clauses
Part III	List of Documents, Exhibits, and Other Attachments
Part IV	Representations and Instructions

Each Part is further broken out into several sections. Here is a sample Table of Contents for Part I. *Note that all the various sections may or may not apply; a check mark or "x" in the left column will let you know which do.*

Section A	Solicitation/Contract Form
Section B	Supplies or Services and Prices/Costs
Section C	Description/Specification/Work Statement
Section E	Inspection and Acceptance
Section F	Deliveries or Performance
Section G	Contract Administration Data
Section H	Special Contract Requirements
Section I	Contract Clauses
Section K	Representations, Certifications and Other Statements of Offerors
Section L	Instructions, Conditions and Notices to Offerors
Section M	Evaluation Factors for Award

Note that the majority of pages consist of the Part I The Schedule, Table of Contents; and Part II Contract Clauses. Part III List of

Documents itemizes all the attachments included with the solicitation. Part IV Representations and Instructions contains the solicitation provisions that require completion by the bidder, and the information and instructions to guide bidders in preparing proposals, such as evaluation factors for award.

Find out the government's needs and specs. The first—and most important—sections you should review are Part I Section B (Supplies or Services and Prices/Costs) and Part IV Section L (Instructions, Conditions and Notices to Offerors). These sections are crucial, so read them together carefully and check out the information to see whether this is a product or service that you can provide, and whether you comply with the requirements. Take notes!

Assess the evaluation factors. Next, read Part IV, Section L (Instructions, Conditions and Notices to Offerors) and Section M (Evaluation Factors for Award). (Note that you just read Section L in the preceding step, but you need to read it a second time in conjunction with Section M.) These sections tell you which factors the government is going to use in evaluating the bids and making its decision for award, such as key personnel, technical capability, or financial or transportation resources. Check the factors carefully to see whether your company is deficient in any area. If it is, correct the problem before you send in the bid or do not bid on the solicitation. Remember that you must consider all the factors in the contract, not just some. Take notes!

Determine the general and specific requirements of the contract. The next areas to review are Part I, Section C (Description, Specifications and Work Statement), and Part I, Section J (List of Attachments). Section C gives you the general specifications of what the government is looking for. Check the specs carefully; you must be able to comply with all of them. Note that sometimes you may find some inconsistencies between the requirements in Section C and the requirements in Section J. That's because Section J contains the attachments to the bid, which could include changes that affect the work statement in Section C. In general, Section C contains the general requirements for the contract, while Section J contains the specific requirements. It is imperative that you read *both* sections carefully! Be sure to take notes!

Caution

If you have any questions, you must address them before award of the contract or, if issued under sealed bid procedures, before the bid opening. If you sign the contract in the hopes that the government will accept something else afterward, you are betting on a really dead horse.

Check out the technical and special requirements. Now read Part II Section I (Contract Clauses); and Part I Section H (Special Contract Requirements), Section D (Packaging and Marking), Section E (Inspection and Acceptance), Section F (Deliveries or Performance) and Section G (Contract Administration Data). These sections provide all the technical requirements on which you will need to perform. Check the packaging requirements in Section D carefully and, if necessary, work with someone knowledgeable in government packaging and marking. Some of the requirements might sound extreme, but remember (especially if the part, product or assembly is for the military) that the item may have to withstand extreme conditions (e.g., battlefield, being dropped out of a plane, hitting a beach at 30 miles per hour, etc).

In some cases, both the military and civilian offices have recently loosened up on some of their special packaging and packing requirements. Packaging standards in the commercial market are often just as good or better than government standards, so commercial items are now often accepted as they come from the supplier. Also, the government is moving toward an "as needed basis" mentality – in other words, the government no longer stocks items as it did in the past, which permits less stringent packaging requirements.

Read the certification provisions. Currently, you don't have to answer these reps and certs in each solicitation you respond to (see Chapter 7 on Online Representations and Certifications Application). You only need to certify that the data you put into ORCA is current or to indicate any changes necessary for the specific solicitation. However, read Part IV, Section K (Representations, Certifications and Other Statements of Offerors). Here is where you certify that you are a small, minority, or women-owned business; that you have not been debarred by the government; that you are an Equal Employment Opportunity business; and that you agree to certain other policies or programs of the government.

Remember that you must read each and every applicable section of each and every Part, word for word, and understand the information contained in each in order to be able to bid intelligently on the solicitation.

RFID AND UID

Currently, the use of UID (unique identification) and RFID (radio frequency identification) is just emerging within the government acquisition arena. This information would be included in Section D of the solicitation, if applicable, and possibly Section A, as well. The use of special product IDs dates back to the Vietnam War era, when containerized shipments were not well identified as to content.

Moreover, because of the tremendous number of shipments coming in, this method of inventory tracking often made it quicker to reorder, instead of wasting time going through the containers for the supply item. There are many cost-saving reasons to use UID and RFID.

Unique Identification (UID)

UID is something you will hear more and more about. The current rule requires all contractors to uniquely identify, through the use of Item Identification Marketing, all items to be delivered to the federal government. The policy was issued on July 29, 2003 and became effective January 1, 2004. UID has been established to identify tangible items, using all practical international standards and commercial item markings.

It will facilitate item tracking in DoD business systems and will give the government reliable and accurate information for management, financial, accountability and asset management purposes. (DoD will be using Commercial ISO/IEC SC31 as its standard along with MIL-STD-130L, go to http://www.ide.wpafb.af.mil/engdat/pubnews.htm; you also can find more information at http://www.uniqueid.org and http://www.acq.osd.mil/uid, or through your local PTAC.)

The benefits to the government are many: It will integrate item data; improve data quality and global interoperability; facilitate management and accountability of items; enhance asset visibility and lifecycle management through traceable and more accurate audit opinions on the property, plant, and equipment, operating materials and supplies portions of financial statements.

In fact, Wal-Mart is using the same type of system to track its entire inventory in all its stores all over the country. They can tell every time someone buys an item, takes it out of inventory or moves it in the system.

Work Smart

The bottom line for small businesses is: "How does this affect me?" The answer: If you hope to supply the government with an item, you had best get up to speed on these new inventory tracking systems.

What is an item? According to the DoD, "An item is a single hardware article or a unit formed by a grouping of subassemblies, components or constituent parts. In the Department, an item is any article produced, stocked, stored, issued, or used or any product, including system, material, parts, subassemblies, sets, and accessories."

Needless to say, that covers just about everything over $5,000. Use the nearby flow chart to help you determine your needs.

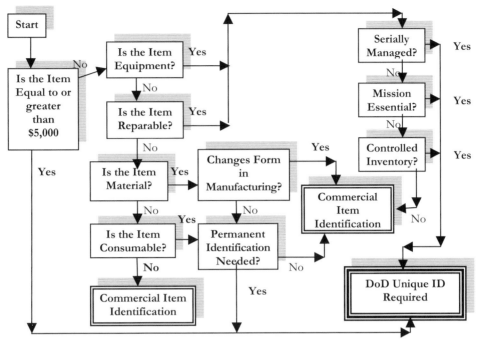

Commercial Item Identification examples are the Universal Product Code (UPC) and Health Industry Bar Code (HIBC).

If you think that the government is just doing this to you personally, please remember that the rest of the world is also switching over, and this is the price of doing business with just about anyone nowadays. Also, if you think you will get out of this situation by being a subcontractor, think again. The primes will just flow down the requirements to you.

Radio Frequency Identification Devices (RFID)

Another way to track items involves RFID (radio frequency identification) tags, which use low-level RF signals to transmit stored information from a tag to an electronic reader. The RFID tags are simply microchips that transmit without the use of hand-held scanners, eliminating all manual labor associated with bar codes.

Currently, a few large retailers mandate the use of this technology, including Wal-Mart, Albertson's and Target. In fact, some large businesses have issued a mandate that use of RFID will start as early as January of 2005 with its top largest suppliers, and a year later with its next largest suppliers. These suppliers must apply RFID tags to all cases and pallets sent, eventually expanding to include all receivables within the company.

Basically, RFID technology means that business easily and quickly can track when the goods arrive at a specific location. In fact, when items are placed on conveyer belts, the goods can move at 600 feet per minute and the radio frequency readers will recognize the items as they move by. Not only will the business know when the goods arrive, they will also be able to track the empty boxes so that they know when the goods have been stocked on the shelves. And of course, when goods are sold, they will be tracked again.

As it is now, businesses spend **billions** of dollars per year on labor to manually scan bar code labels. This cost will be reduced to almost nothing with the use of RFID, which means better prices or more profit.

Other benefits of RFID over bar codes include allowing goods to move more rapidly both at loading docks and point-of-sale stations. Inventory can be tracked without manual stock counts, and there is an expectation of reduced losses from theft because every item can be tracked as it leaves the premises. The retail industry is expected to benefit tremendously from the use of RFID by managing its inventory at every stage of the supply chain.

However, instead of labor costs there will be costs associated with the technology itself. Knowing where each item is at any time provides a tremendous source of information, but unless this information is managed it does not help the enterprise. Thus, companies will need to spend additional financial resources on data management and integration tools.

The immediate short-term impact on the small business is probably negligible. However, in the long run, small businesses also will need to embrace RFID and include tags on all their items; on the flip side, small businesses receiving raw materials from suppliers would benefit by learning how to manage their own inventory issues through RFID. Currently, an RFID tag still costs about 30 cents per item. It is expected that this cost will be reduced to about a penny in the next few years.

Outside of the retail industry, there are other implementations of RFID. For example, some gas stations use RFID in their SpeedPass system, allowing customers to pay for purchases. Meanwhile the Food and Drug Administration is looking at adding RFID to prescription drugs to ensure proper distribution, and to ensure correct dosage based upon prescriptions issued.

Right now most of the work is currently limited to Fortune 1000 companies, and the reason is primarily due to the high cost of the RFID tags, the readers and the subsequent integration of data with the inventory systems. The cost of implementing and operating this RFID technology is to be considered a normal cost of transportation and logistics.

Chapter 11

Get Technical Data

Now that you have reviewed and understand the contents of the bid package, it's time to start gathering information needed to complete the offer, including the technical data related to a particular bid.

Technical data is comprised of the specifications and standards, such as engineering design and manufacturing documents and drawings, that describe the requirements for a material, product or service. It also includes the criteria for determining whether those requirements are met.

Under federal regulations, the specs cover only the government's actual minimum needs in a manner to encourage maximum practicable competition. The government uses a spec only when it knows exactly what it wants and needs.

With recent changes in acquisition policy, more requirements will be based on commercial specifications and standards. Therefore, if the requirement is being purchased under Part 12 of the Federal Acquisition Regulation (Acquisition of Commercial Items), then the item/service is being bought against performance criteria citing commercial specs and standards.

TYPES OF GOVERNMENT SPECS

There are two categories of government specifications:

- **Federal Specifications** — These cover materials, products or services used by more then two federal agencies. They are issued by the General Services Administration (GSA) and must be used by all federal agencies. Federal specifications can be obtained at http://apps.fss.gsa.gov/pub/fedspecs/ or from your local PTAC.

- **Military Specifications** — These cover items or services that are intrinsically military in character or commercial items modified to meet special requirements of the military. They are distributed by Naval Publications and Forms Center (NPFC), located in Philadelphia, PA. NPFC stocks and issues Department of Defense printed and digital matter without charge to federal agencies and the general public. Documents distributed by NPFC include military specifications and standards, federal specifications and standards, Qualified Product Lists (QPLs), Military Handbooks, and Departmental Documents. Here again, many PTACs offer military specifications and standards as a part of their services to their clients.

GETTING CORRECT SPECS

These days, finding specs and standards can be as easy as logging onto a subscription service on the Internet. Subscription services can get you the specs quickly and easily, but at a hefty price tag. On the other hand, your local Procurement Technical Assistance Center (PTAC) can provide you with the specs you need and, in most cases, will either charge only a small fee or provide them for free. Either way, it ensures that you get the specs required by the solicitation.

Caution

If there appears to be a conflict or question about what specs are required, get it resolved immediately. Whatever you do, don't try to second-guess the government. We can cite case after case where a contractor made a wrong assumption about a spec and it ended up costing the contractor big money.

Normally when you order the solicitation from the buying office, it will send the necessary technical data package with it unless the documents are considered common and are only referenced. If the buying office doesn't send the tech information, then you will have to contact the resource identified in the solicitation. Because of the government's shift to the Internet and e-commerce environment, the solicitation may include a web site where you can download the necessary documents and the appropriate readers for the drawings.

Work Smart

You may also want to think about developing your own library of the specs and standards that you use most often, either in hard copy or electronic format. When you find a good site on the Internet for specs and standards, remember to bookmark it for later visits. Government specifications are required on a large number of items. Check out what is required on the bids that interest you and start to build your library. It will be very helpful to you in the long run.

Technical Data Web Sites

The federal government continues to move more and more acquisition processes to the Internet and e-business environment. To secure technical data, the government has developed a new web site, Federal Technical Data Solutions (FedTeDS). It is an online dissemination solution designed to safeguard sensitive acquisition-related information for use by all federal agencies and their approved business partners (https://www.fedteds.gov/). This now means that there are more controls in place to keep track of who is asking for the information.

These sites should help you locate the data you will need. The Technical Data Packages (TDPs) found on these sites have the engineering design and manufacturing drawings related to the items found in FedTeDS solicitations.

- **Automated Bidsets Interface Web Server** (http://abiweb.dscp.dla.mil/abi/) — The ABIWeb Server is a system that allows Engineering Data Lists (EDLs) and digitized drawings for open procurements to be electronically retrieved by the public. The ABIWeb Server allows the identification and retrieval of drawing lists and digitized drawings for solicitations currently open at DLA Supply Centers. Drawings that are not in electronic format, are classified, or have restrictions on dissemination will not be available from ABIWeb

- **Naval Logisitics Library Virtual Bidroom** (http://logtool.net/) — This site offers engineering drawings for the Naval Supply Systems Command bid-sets only. Instructions for using this site are available at the site.

- **Army Corps of Engineers Electronic Bid Solicitation (EBS)** (http://tsn.wes.army.mil/Default.asp) — The USACE corporate EBS process implements a standard DoD business process for the electronic delivery and distribution of contract solicitation documents. Prospective bidders are provided a CD-ROM containing all contract documents and the royalty-free software that enables complete utilization of the documents from any Windows-based personal computer. Internet access is also required for the solicitation announcement and for accessing entire bid packages for small projects that do not require contract drawings.

- **Defense Standardization Program (DSP)** (http://www.dsp.dla.mil/) — Customers now have immediate and free access to Defense specifications and standards through this greatly improved site. Users simply click on 'SPECS and STDS', and they are led to a DTIC document search screen, on which they enter the document information (e.g., number or title). The results are then displayed, and the user selects the desired document. If it's a Defense Spec or Std, the ASSIST-Enterprise screen is then displayed, allowing the user to click on the selected document's icon. The user then views a full text version of the document in Adobe PDF, which can be downloaded and printed.

- **Government Industry Data Mart (GIDM)** (http://www.dlis.dla.mil/GIDM/) — Through this site you have access to the following:

  — CCR system, which is a repository of all companies and agencies registered to do business with the federal government

  — Universal Directory of Commercial Items (UDCI), which is a global catalog of items based on Commercial bar code (Universal Product Code (UPC) or European Article Number (EAN)

  — The U.S./Canada Joint Certification Program System, which assists in the identification of companies that have been assigned a Certification Number under the Joint Certification Program

  — The Business Identification Number Cross-reference System (BINCS), which identifies foreign and domestic government/commercial contractors, manufacturers and suppliers

  — Government Industry Reference Data Edit and Review (GIRDER) program, which works with government manufacturers and suppliers to maintain the correct relationship between the CAGE code, manufacturer part number and National Stock Number (NSN)

Web Tools

The following tools and links can assist you in viewing solicitations and technical drawings.

- **Adobe Acrobat Viewer** — The Adobe Acrobat Viewer allows you to view the solicitations that are offered by the many sources contributing to DoDBusOpps.com. You can download a free copy of Adobe Acrobat Viewer at http://www.adobe.com/prodindex/acrobat/readstep.html.

- **CALS Raster Format Viewer** — The CALS Raster Format Viewer is required to view technical drawings. DoDBusOpps is aware of two viewers that support this format:

  — ImageR is an image viewer for viewing and manipulating various types of raster and vector files. You must register with the JEDMICS web site to download ImageR from http://jtshelp.redstone.army.mil/index.asp.

  — SwiftView's Plug-In is a free trial download from http://www.ndg.com/plug1.htm. After a several week trial, there is a 30-second time delay before each document is viewed. Information on licensing is available from this site.

Chapter 12

Price It Out

This is the one step in the contracting process where you are the expert and we are not. Given that there are so many different types of businesses out there and so many different ways of pricing, our best advice is to be as competitive as possible.

The old stories of $200 toilet seats and $300 hammers are simply that—old history—and you better believe that you have to sharpen your pencil as much as possible in order to be competitive.

COMMON PRICING FACTORS

At the same time, however, you also need to make sure that you cover all of your costs and protect your profit. Here are some things to consider in determining your price:

- **Consider Pricing History** — You can often get pricing history from the buying office by asking the Point of Contact identified in the contract (Block 10 if you are using Form SF 33). You can also contact a Procurement Technical Assistance Center and ask it to run a computer review of pricing history for an item. If you are bidding on a service, it becomes more difficult to get good pricing history. Ask the contracting officer to provide you with the previous contract number so you can obtain the contract. Make sure the statement of work is the same as yours so you can make a fair price comparison.

- **Cost Out All Special Requirements** — The buyer may ask for many costly extras. Especially watch out for packaging requirements—they can be expensive. Don't just stick on a percentage of the cost of the item to cover packaging.

- **Think Carefully about Quality Requirements** — Will any of the certifications and acknowledgments add on extra costs? (See our discussion of quality assurance standards in Chapter 16.)

- **Factor in Bidding Costs** — Some offers are rather simple and straightforward, but as the value of the contract increases, more time and labor are usually required. As a general rule of thumb, you can estimate that the cost of putting together an offer will run 3 to 4 percent of the value of the proposed contract. Make sure current finances can handle that cost.

- **Don't Forget Overhead and Profit** — Make sure your profit is reasonable. Remember that the bidding process is very competitive. You are free to figure in as high a profit as you wish, but you must win the contract to enjoy it. Never bid if it doesn't make good business sense. And while making sure that your price covers your overhead costs may seem very basic and obvious, it is the pricing factor that small businesses most often get wrong, to the detriment of the company: If your cost information is not correct, you can't accurately bid a contract, be competitive, or make good decisions for your company.

DETERMINE YOUR TRUE COSTS

Why do we say that small businesses tend to get their cost information wrong? Simply because many, if not most, small businesses don't really know what their overhead costs are.

Often, when pricing out a project, businesses will simply take their prime costs (labor and materials) and mark that figure up by some arbitrary percentage that they believe is sufficient to cover all indirect costs and give them some profit. Or they will use a single, company-wide rate applied on only one type of base, such as direct labor hours or engineering hours, for assigning indirect costs to the product or service provided. In either case, if this estimated percentage is higher than what their overhead really is, it affects their ability to be competitive. If their estimate is lower than what their costs really are, it affects their ability to be profitable.

If your business falls into one of these categories, we strongly recommend that, before you bid on a contract (or on any other project for that matter), you take the time and the steps necessary to determine your actual costs.

You might consider using some form of activity-based costing (ABC) to accomplish this. ABC, in its simplest terms, is a cost management method that allows a business to determine the actual cost associated with each product and service. With this method, you look at every item and activity in your business associated with putting out your product or service (e.g., heats, light, administrative help, sending out an invoice, doing payroll, etc.) and then attach a cost to it. In other words, you break your costs down to their least common denominator so you know what they really are.

Without knowing your true costs, you can never be sure where money is being made or lost, you can't identify moneymakers and losers (an increase in sales does not necessarily mean an increase in profit), and you can't make good strategic decisions and plans for your company.

Although ABC is geared toward a large business, a small business can adapt this philosophy and utilize a more simplified form of it. For more information on ABC, try searching the Internet or check out some of the books on the topic in your bookstore or online.

Caution

Federal Acquisition Regulation (FAR) Part 15 discusses negotiations and costs for contracts of $100,000 or more and looks at allowable and allocable costs. If you are going to be submitting a proposal over $100,000, either bone up on the FAR in this area or get an accountant who is familiar with government contracting.

Again, we want to remind you to carefully read the solicitation and make notes on points you don't understand. Then go ask the questions. Go to the buyer or Point of Contact identified in the contract, the small business specialist at the buying office, or a Procurement Technical Assistance Center. But please ask someone! The answers could significantly affect your price—and your profit.

Chapter 13

Write Your Proposal

Once you have reviewed the bid, received the specs, gotten pricing history, and priced out the items or services, you are ready to put it all together and write your proposal.

There are two situations that you should be prepared for:

- Writing a proposal when the solicitation is an Invitation for Bid

- Writing a proposal when the solicitation is a negotiated bid, such as a Request for Proposal.

WRITING A PROPOSAL FOR AN IFB

When the solicitation is an Invitation for Bid, which is the case most of the time for small businesses, writing your proposal will consist of filling out the forms that you received from the government in the bid package and sending them in.

But it's not as simple as it sounds. Even though all you basically have to do is fill in some blanks on forms that the government has provided and send back the bid package, you must still be very careful. As we pointed out earlier, *when you send back the bid package, the government will look at it as if you had put it together yourself and as if they are seeing it for the first time.*

To give you a first-hand look at some of the standard forms that you can expect to see with an IFB, we are reproducing some of the more common ones, along with a line-by-line explanation of how to fill them in.

Filling out DD Form 1707

The first form that we will look at is DD Form 1707, *Information to Offerors or Quoters*. This is the cover sheet that accompanies the solicitation itself and is mainly informational. One of its main purposes is to gather information on why a company does not want to bid. This form is used for most Department of Defense (DoD) large dollar solicitations, which are those over $100,000. Let's start with the cover page and proceed block by block.

Block 1: Solicitation Number — We are using the example number **SP0700-00-Q-HE22**. This is the number that will identify this specific solicitation throughout the life of the buying action. Any amendments to the solicitation will use this number plus the amendment number as the identifier. SP0700, the first six alpha/numeric sequence, identifies the buying office where the order originates. The second grouping—00—is the fiscal year the solicitation was issued. The single alpha character Q indicates what type of solicitation it is:

- B = Invitation for Bid (IFB)   C= Contract
- R = Request for Proposal (RFP)   P= Purchase Order
- Q= Request for Quote (RFQ)

The last alpha/numeric sequence—HE22—is the sequential order number for that solicitation.

Block 2: Type of Solicitation — As previously mentioned, there are three types of bid packages:

- *Invitation for Bid (IFB)* — This is a method of contracting that consists of competitive bids, public opening of bids (yes, you can be there when they are opened), and award. Most of these bids are for buys over $100,000. With this type of bid, the government knows specifically what it wants, how many it wants, and where it wants them sent. The award is based on price and price-related factors.

- *Request for Proposal (RFP)* — The government uses this type of contracting when it is not sure of what it wants and is looking for a way to talk to you on how you plan to fulfill their need for the item or service. This type of bid may be competitive or non-competitive.

- *Request for Quote (RFQ)* — This method is often used to solicit prices or market information. The quote submitted does not constitute an offer. Therefore, it cannot be accepted by the government to form a binding contract. An SF 26, which is a two-signature document, would have to be used.

Form DD 1707

INFORMATION TO OFFERORS OR QUOTERS SECTION A – COVER SHEET	Form Approved OMB No. 9000-0002 Expires Oct 31, 2004

The public reporting burden for this collection of information is estimated to average 25 minutes per response, including the time for reviewing instructions, searching existing data sources, gathering and maintaining the data needed, and completing and reviewing the collection of information. Send comments regarding this burden estimate or any other aspect of this collection of information, including suggestions for reducing the burden, to Department of Defense, Washington Headquarters Services, Directorate for Information Operations and Reports (9000-0002), 1215 Jefferson Davis Highway, Suite 1204, Arlington, VA 22202-4302. Respondents should be aware that notwithstanding any other provision of law, no person shall be subject to any penalty for failing to comply with a collection of information if it does not display a currently valid OMB control number.
PLEASE DO NOT RETURN YOUR FORM TO THE ABOVE ADDRESS. RETURN COMPLETED FORM TO THE ADDRESS IN BLOCK 4 BELOW.

1. SOLICITATION NUMBER SP0600-03-R-0114	2. *(X one)* ☐ a. INVITATION FOR BID (IFB) ☒ b. REQUEST FOR PROPOSAL (RFP) ☐ c. REQUEST FOR QUOTATION (RFQ)	3. DATE/TIME RESPONSE DUE 25 November 2002/3:00 PM Eastern Standard Time

INSTRUCTIONS

NOTE: The provision entitled "Required Central Contractor Registration" applies to most solicitations.
1. If you are not submitting a response, complete the information in Blocks 9 through 11 and return to the issuing office in Block 4 unless a different return address is indicated in Block 7.
2. Offerors or quoters must include full, accurate, and complete information in their responses as required by this solicitation (including attachments). "Fill-ins" are provided on Standard Form 18, Standard Form 33, and other solicitation documents. Examine the entire solicitation carefully. The penalty for making false statements is prescribed in 18 U.S.C. 1001.
3. Offerors or quoters must plainly mark their responses with the Solicitation Number and the date and local time for bid opening or receipt of proposals that is in the solicitation document.
4. Information regarding the timeliness of response is addressed in the provision of this solicitation entitled either "Late Submissions, Modifications, and Withdrawals of Bids," or "Instructions to Offerors – Competitive Acquisition."

4. ISSUING OFFICE *(Complete mailing address, including ZIP Code)* SEE BLOCK 8B	5. ITEMS TO BE PURCHASED *(Brief description)*		
	Marine Gas Oil	NSN: 9140-01-313-7776	31,668,300 GL
	Fuel Oil, Intermediate 180	NSN: 9140-01-271-5280	1,043,000 GL
	Fuel Oil, Intermediate 380	NSN: 9140-01-235-2832	2,482,000 GL
	DIESEL FUEL, GRADE #2	NSN: 9140-01-456-9443	1,410,000 GL

6. PROCUREMENT INFORMATION *(X and complete as applicable.)*

☒	a. THIS PROCUREMENT IS UNRESTRICTED.	
☐	b. THIS PROCUREMENT IS ____ % SET-ASIDE FOR SMALL BUSINESS. THE APPLICABLE NAICS CODE IS:	
☐	c. THIS PROCUREMENT IS ____ % SET-ASIDE FOR HUB ZONE CONCERNS. THE APPLICABLE NAICS CODE IS:	
☐	d. THIS PROCUREMENT IS RESTRICTED TO FIRMS ELIGIBLE UNDER SECTION 8(a) OF THE SMALL BUSINESS ACT.	

7. ADDITIONAL INFORMATION:
THE NOTES ON THIS DD FORM 1707 PROVIDE INFORMATION THAT WARRANT YOUR SPECIAL ATTENTION PRIOR TO PREPARATION OF YOUR PROPOSAL. ADDRESS YOUR PROPOSAL TO:

ATTN: BID CUSTODIAN
DESC-CPC ROOM 3815
8725 JOHN J. KINGMAN RD. SUITE 4950
FORT BELVOIR, VA 22060-6222

8. POINT OF CONTACT FOR INFORMATION

a. NAME *(Last, First, Middle Initial)* ARMSTRONG, GARRELL L.	b. ADDRESS *(Include ZIP Code)* DESC-PHB ROOM 3815 8725 JOHN J. KINGMAN RD. SUITE 4950 FORT BELVOIR, VA 22060-6222
c. TELEPHONE NUMBER *(Include Area Code and Extension)* -703-767-8457	d. E-MAIL ADDRESS garmstrong@desc.dla.mil

9. REASONS FOR NO RESPONSE *(X all that apply)*

☐ a. CANNOT COMPLY WITH SPECIFICATIONS ☐ b. UNABLE TO IDENTIFY THE ITEMS(S) ☐ c. CANNOT MEET DELIVERY REQUIREMENT	☐ d. DO NOT REGULARLY MANUFACTURE OR SELL THE TYPE OF ITEMS INVOLVED ☐ e. OTHER

10. MAILING LIST INFORMATION *(X one)*
WE ☐ DO ☐ DO NOT DESIRE TO BE RETAINED ON THE MAILING LIST FOR FUTURE PROCUREMENT OF THE TYPE INVOLVED.

11a. COMPANY NAME	b. ADDRESS
c. ACTION OFFICER	
(1) TYPED OR PRINTED NAME *(Last, First, Middle Initial)*	(2) TITLE
(3) SIGNATURE	(4) DATE SIGNED *(YYYYMMDD)*

DD FORM 1707, FEB 2002   PREVIOUS EDITION IS OBSOLETE.

Block 3: Date/Time Response Due — This information, supplied by the buying office, tells you when you need to have your offer into the buying office.

The next section titled "Instructions" contains information about responding.

Block 4: Issuing Office — This is the office that issued the solicitation.

Block 5: Item To Be Purchased — This is a brief description of what is needed.

Block 6: Procurement Information — This is where you will find out which, if any, restrictions or set-asides apply to this solicitation. It will be marked either "restricted" or "unrestricted." If it is marked "unrestricted," that means that any business—large, small, or in between—can bid on it. If it is marked "restricted," that means it is earmarked as a set-aside for either Small Business or Hub Zone Concerns, or restricted to 8(a) firms.

Block 7: Additional Information — In this block you will usually find any additional information needed to bid on the contract, such as where to send the bid, when it has to be received, who to contact or what web site to visit.

Block 8: Point of Contact Information — Here will be listed the buyer's name, address and telephone number. We should also add that, these days, you may only get an e-mail address for the buyer, and it's likely that the buyer might accept inquiries only in that form.

Block 9: Reason for No Response — As previously mentioned, if you are not going to bid on the solicitation, for whatever reason, be sure to fill out this block and send the form back to the buyer. This is very important! If you don't, you will probably be dropped from the buyer's bidders list and have to start all over again.

Caution

Most forms include a "Reason for No Response" section or block. (For example, in the case of DD Form 1707, this section is in Block 9.) If you decide not to bid on a solicitation, for whatever reason, be sure to fill out the "Reason for No Response" section of the form and send the form in anyway. The government buyer will thank you and, better yet, you will not be dropped off the bidders' list the next time an opportunity comes up. Some buyers give you only one chance. If you don't send in the form to indicate that you are not responding to a bid, you go back to "Go" and start over.

If the buyer gives you an e-mail address, you may send in your response that way, but remember to identify your company with your name, the company name, and your CAGE Code.

Block 10: Mailing List Information — Here you indicate whether you want to be left on future mailing lists for an item. Respond either yes or no.

Block 11: Responding Firm — This is you! This is where you fill in your information, including your bid price. (If necessary, review the discussion of Block 11 in Chapter 10: Review the Bid. You need to read and understand all the applicable sections.) Remember that the sections of Block 11, when taken *together*, make up the whole solicitation and resulting contract.

Back Side of Form — The back side of the form is set up as a fold-over mailer. Just address it, put your stamp on it, and drop it in the mail.

Filling out Standard Form 33 (SF 33)

Next, let's look at the Standard Form 33: *Solicitation, Offer and Award*. This is the form that is used to solicit offers and award contracts. It is referred to as a bi-lateral or two-signature document. You sign the form in Block 17, and the government signs the same form in Block 27. That establishes a binding contract.

Before you start going through our line-by-line explanation, this may be a good time to go back to Chapter 10, where we showed you how to read a contract and included an explanation of the general layout of the SF 33. The top portion, Blocks 1-11, is the Solicitation area and is filled in by the government with information about the solicitation. Blocks 12-18, the Offer area, are filled in by you before returning the offer to the buying office. The last portion, Blocks 19-28, is the Award area and is completed by the government and sent back to you, if and when you are awarded the contract.

Work Smart

Note the paging format "Page 1 of ##." Check your page numbers and if there are any missing, call the buying office immediately. You can't submit an accurate bid if there is information missing. More than one company has been caught in this situation. When sending out millions of bids a year, as the government does, these things can happen.

Solicitation Section (filled in by the government)

Block 1: Contract is a Rated Order — A rated contract is one that has a specific classification for how "hot" the need is. Although these days you will hardly ever see activation of rated procedures, it is there in case the need arises. About the only time you might see a rated bid is during time of national emergency or war.

Block 2: Contract Number — The government will not fill in this number until it awards the contract. The numbering will be similar to the number in Block 3, the Solicitation Number, but it will have a "C" instead of an "R" in the number sequence.

Block 3: Solicitation Number — This is the number we discussed in the DD Form 1707 explanation (Block 1), above.

Block 4: Type of Solicitation — This block will identify whether this is a Sealed Bid IFB (Invitation for Bid) or an RFP (Request for Proposal).

Block 5: Date Issued — This is the date that this contract "hit the street" and became a live requirement.

Block 6: Requisition/Purchase Number — This number is an internal document number used by the requisition people for tracking the item or service to be purchased. This is the original number for that "need," and there might be multiple requisition numbers against a solicitation number.

Block 7: Issued By — This block identifies the government office that is doing the buying. Make special note of the information here. Remember that you might be dealing with a "buying agency" that is physically located very far from the actual end user. You can spend a lot of time with the end user, convincing the user that you are the answer to all their problems, and still lose the whole deal by not checking out where the buy is going to be made.

Example

We dealt with a company that was talking to the end user every week, had developed a one-on-one relationship, but never thought to ask where the buying office was located. The company missed the issue date and only found out that the bid had gone out when it came through a distributor. The company did not lose the contract, but by going through the distributor, it had to pay a commission it wouldn't have had to pay if it had gotten the contract directly.

Block 8: Address Offer To — This block gives you information on where to submit your offer.

Block 9: Additional Info — This block will tell you whether the buying office wants additional copies of the offer for evaluation purposes and where to bring the offer if you hand-carry it to the buying office. This block also tells you the time and date when you need to have the offer in.

Standard Form 33

| SOLICITATION, OFFER AND AWARD | 1. THIS CONTRACT IS A RATED ORDER UNDER DPAS (15 CFR 700) | RATING | PAGE | OF | PAGES |

| 2. CONTRACT NUMBER | 3. SOLICITATION NUMBER | 4. TYPE OF SOLICITATION | 5. DATE ISSUED | 6. REQUISITION/PURCHASE NUMBER |
| | | ☐ SEALED BID (IFB) ☐ NEGOTIATED (RFP) | | |

| 7. ISSUED BY | CODE | 8. ADDRESS OFFER TO (If other than Item 7) |

NOTE: In sealed bid solicitations "offer" and "offeror" mean "bid" and "bidder".

SOLICITATION

9. Sealed offers in original and _____ copies for furnishing the supplies or services in the Schedule will be received at the place specified in Item 8, or if handcarried, in the depository located in _____ until _____ local time _____
(Hour)   (Date)

CAUTION - LATE Submissions, Modifications, and Withdrawals: See Section L, Provision No. 52.214-7 or 52.215-1. All offers are subject to all terms and conditions contained in this solicitation.

| 10. FOR INFORMATION CALL: | A. NAME | B. TELEPHONE (NO COLLECT CALLS) | | | C. E-MAIL ADDRESS |
| | | AREA CODE | NUMBER | EXT. | |

11. TABLE OF CONTENTS

(X)	SEC.	DESCRIPTION	PAGE(S)	(X)	SEC.	DESCRIPTION	PAGE(S)
		PART I - THE SCHEDULE				PART II - CONTRACT CLAUSES	
	A	SOLICITATION/CONTRACT FORM			I	CONTRACT CLAUSES	
	B	SUPPLIES OR SERVICES AND PRICES/COSTS				PART III - LIST OF DOCUMENTS, EXHIBITS AND OTHER ATTACH.	
	C	DESCRIPTION/SPECS./WORK STATEMENT			J	LIST OF ATTACHMENTS	
	D	PACKAGING AND MARKING				PART IV - REPRESENTATIONS AND INSTRUCTIONS	
	E	INSPECTION AND ACCEPTANCE			K	REPRESENTATIONS, CERTIFICATIONS AND OTHER STATEMENTS OF OFFERORS	
	F	DELIVERIES OR PERFORMANCE					
	G	CONTRACT ADMINISTRATION DATA			L	INSTRS., CONDS., AND NOTICES TO OFFERORS	
	H	SPECIAL CONTRACT REQUIREMENTS			M	EVALUATION FACTORS FOR AWARD	

OFFER (Must be fully completed by offeror)

NOTE: Item 12 does not apply if the solicitation includes the provisions at 52.214-16, Minimum Bid Acceptance Period.

12. In compliance with the above, the undersigned agrees, if this offer is accepted within _____ calendar days (60 calendar days unless a different period is inserted by the offeror) from the date for receipt of offers specified above, to furnish any or all items upon which prices are offered at the price set opposite each item, delivered at the designated point(s), within the time specified in the schedule.

| 13. DISCOUNT FOR PROMPT PAYMENT (See Section I, Clause No. 52.232-8) | 10 CALENDAR DAYS (%) | 20 CALENDAR DAYS (%) | 30 CALENDAR DAYS (%) | CALENDAR DAYS (%) |

| 14. ACKNOWLEDGMENT OF AMEND-MENTS (The offeror acknowledges receipt of amendments to the SOLICITATION for offerors and related documents numbered and dated): | AMENDMENT NO. | DATE | AMENDMENT NO. | DATE |

| 15A. NAME AND ADDRESS OF OFFER-OR | CODE | FACILITY | 16. NAME AND TITLE OF PERSON AUTHORIZED TO SIGN OFFER (Type or print) |

| 15B. TELEPHONE NUMBER | | | 15C. CHECK IF REMITTANCE ADDRESS IS DIFFERENT FROM ABOVE - ENTER SUCH ADDRESS IN SCHEDULE. | 17. SIGNATURE | 18. OFFER DATE |
| AREA CODE | NUMBER | EXT. | ☐ | | |

AWARD (To be completed by Government)

| 19. ACCEPTED AS TO ITEMS NUMBERED | 20. AMOUNT | 21. ACCOUNTING AND APPROPRIATION |

| 22. AUTHORITY FOR USING OTHER THAN FULL AND OPEN COMPETITION: ☐ 10 U.S.C. 2304(c) ( ) ☐ 41 U.S.C. 253(c) ( ) | 23. SUBMIT INVOICES TO ADDRESS SHOWN IN (4 copies unless otherwise specified) | ITEM |

| 24. ADMINISTERED BY (If other than Item 7) | CODE | 25. PAYMENT WILL BE MADE BY | CODE |

| 26. NAME OF CONTRACTING OFFICER (Type or print) | 27. UNITED STATES OF AMERICA (Signature of Contracting Officer) | 28. AWARD DATE |

IMPORTANT - Award will be made on this Form, or on Standard Form 26, or by other authorized official written notice.

AUTHORIZED FOR LOCAL REPRODUCTION
Previous edition is unusable

STANDARD FORM 33 (REV. 9-97)
Prescribed by GSA - FAR (48 CFR) 53.214(c)

Work Smart

If the solicitation says that an offer needs to be in by 10:00 p.m. on a particular day and you show up at 10:01 p.m., you are out of luck! It's your responsibility to be there on time.

Block 10: For Information Call — This block identifies the person that you will contact for information on this specific bid, including phone number and e-mail address, if available.

Block 11: Table of Contents — This should be the same as the "TOC" page, but without the "Appendices." Some buying offices will do both, some will not. Make sure they match. This section will also give you the page counts for each section. If it says that there are 25 pages in Section C: Description/specs/work statement and you have only 23 pages, you had better call the buyer and find out what's missing. Don't assume that you will automatically be sent the missing material. And, again, keep in mind that the sections of Block 11, when taken *together*, make up the whole solicitation and resulting contract.

Offer Section (completed by the bidder)

Block 12: Acceptance Period — This block will give you the opportunity to mark how long your bid will be good for. If you don't put in a specific number, it will default to 60 days.

Work Smart

If you give the government too long an acceptance period, prices can change and so can your costs. Make sure you don't get bitten: Be competitive, but set your limits.

Block 13: Discounts for Prompt Payment — This block is where you will put the size of the discount, if any, that you will give the government if it pays you promptly.

Work Smart

The government passed the Prompt Payment Act in the mid-1980s, which requires the government to pay small businesses within 30 days if the business completes its end of the contract! Check to see whether your competitors are offering a discount. If they are, then you should do so as well in order to be competitive. If they aren't . . . why leave money on the table?

One important catch with the Prompt Payment Act: The clock on this Act starts only if your invoice, when received, is correct. If your invoice is not correct, it gets kicked back until it is corrected and received by the government. Therefore, the definition of "prompt" under this Act is directly tied to the accuracy of your invoice.

Block 14: Acknowledgments of Amendments — In this block you will let the buyer know that you have received all the amendments that it sent out. If the buyer mailed out four and you list only three, the buyer will throw out your bid as non-responsive if the omitted amendment impacts on the material aspects of the solicitation.

Block 15a: Name and Address of Offeror — Here is where you will enter your company name, address and, in the little box marked "code," your Cage Code and your facility code, if you have one.

Block 15b: Telephone Number — Enter the appropriate phone number.

Block 15c: Remittance Address — If you want the government to send the check for payment to an address different from the one you provided in Block 15a, mark this box and enter the address on the schedule.

Block 16: Name and Title of Person Authorized To Sign Offer — In this block enter the name and title of the person "authorized" to sign the contracts. Please don't have someone sign the contract if they are not listed in CCR (Central Contractor Registration) as the "authorized signor." You will lose the award.

Block 17: Signature — This is where the authorized person must sign the contract.

Caution

More than a few companies that carefully prepared their bid lost out just because the contract was not signed. Don't forget to sign the contract.

Block 18: Offer Date — Enter the date on which you are sending the contract.

Award Section (completed by the government)

After you fill in Block 18, above, you have completed your portion of Form 33. If you see the SF 33 coming back in the mail with the Award section filled in by the government, guess what? You won the contract! You are now a prime contractor!

Block 19: Accepted as to Items Numbered — Government will identify which specific items have been awarded to you.

Block 20: Amount — This is the dollar amount of the contract. The cash!

Block 21: Accounting and Appropriation — The government will fill in the appropriate accounting and appropriation codes. (In general, you don't have to concern yourself with this information.)

Block 22: Authority for Using Other Than Full and Open Competition — This field is informational only.

Block 23: Submit Invoice to Address Shown in — The government will tell you where to look in the contract for the appropriate address.

Block 24: Administered By — This is the office that will administer the contract. Note that the office listed here may be different than the one putting out the bid.

Block 25: Payment Will Be Made By — This is the paying office, the office from which you will receive your money.

Block 26: Name of the Contracting Officer — The name of the Contracting Officer is typed here. You will see this person's name only if you win the contract.

Block 27: United States of America — This is the block where the Contracting Officer will sign that you have an active, actual, real government contract.

Block 28: Award Date — This is the date the government contracting officer signs the award.

Work Smart

Award can be made on the SF 33; on another form, such as the SF 26; or by any other authorized official written notice. Be watching for it, check on who won, for how much, and what the details of the award were. Ask questions . . . that's how you find out what you did right or wrong. There are two ways to do this: Either call the buyer and ask for the information or get award notices from FedBizOpps.

Amendments to Solicitation — Standard Form 30

When there is a need to change or modify the quantity, specifications, delivery or any other part of a solicitation, or if there is some part of the solicitation that is defective or incorrect, those changes will be made by an amendment to the solicitation using Form SF 30, *Amendment of Solicitation/Modification of Contract*. The form itself is completed by the government and sent to prospective bidders.

If the solicitation is an Invitation for Bid, you must bid the requirement as presented. To do otherwise will probably result in your bid being "kicked out." If you think a change is necessary, call the buyer before the bid opening date and explain why it needs to be changed. If the buyer agrees, the bid will be modified or cancelled and re-bid with the changes. Of course, everyone else will get to bid the change also.

If the solicitation is negotiated, you may be able to bid the changes explaining why this is in the best interest of the government. Read the solicitation carefully to make sure that this approach is allowed. If you are not sure, talk to the buyer to get the answer.

As we mentioned above, you will be asked to list any and all amendments that you have received on the bid form before you send it in. If you fail to do this or if you omit an amendment, your bid will be considered non-responsive. That means that your bid could be thrown out, even if you are the low bidder. Therefore, if you received Amendment number 0001 and 0003 and you have not received 0002, you need to call the buyer and find out what the missing amendment is.

If there is a change that will affect the bid opening, the government will extend the bid opening date (BOD) and send a notice to all prospective bidders. And, again, you must acknowledge this amendment in your bid.

WRITING A PROPOSAL FOR AN RFP OR RFQ

As we discussed above, when the solicitation you are responding to is an Invitation for Bid, writing your proposal will basically consist of filling out the forms that the government provides. However, when the solicitation is a negotiated solicitation, such as a Request for Proposal or Request for Quote, things are different.

A Request for Proposal (RFP) is a solicitation or bid document that outlines a problem or requirement and asks companies to propose methods for solving the problem and to calculate what the costs might be.

Therefore, in addition to filling out any required forms, you will have to create your own proposal explaining your plan for meeting the government's particular need and provide your own documentation. You may be required to work up your own drawings, biographies on personnel, management plans, and other types of documents that demonstrate the company's capabilities to fulfill the requirements. The proposal must, at the same time, be simple, straightforward, concise, complete, and correct.

As you can see, an RFP can take a significant amount of time, effort, and money to create. (You definitely won't be able to get it done over the weekend between watching the kids play soccer and running errands.) So, before you even start, take some time to evaluate whether it is in your best interests to proceed with the proposal. To make your efforts worthwhile, the proposal should present a real opportunity for your company.

Decision Time: Respond or Not?

How can you decide whether to respond to the RFP or RFQ that you are considering? Here are some questions to help you make a decision:

- **Is the Request you are considering an RFP or an RFI?** In other words, is the government looking to buy or is it just taking a look at the product market? If the government is just taking a look, it will put out what is known as a Request for Information (RFI), as opposed to a request for products or services that it is looking to buy (RFP). Some people look at a request for information and think it's a bid. Take a close look and make sure you are considering the right one. In some cases, an RFI also may be a request that could end up becoming an actual contract. Respond to the RFI if you really have something to offer, giving the government any information they may need to use to put together a solicitation. But, don't give away the farm! Make sure you mark all information that might be considered private as "proprietary." Once you give it to the government, if it is not properly marked, it's theirs to use as they see fit.

- **Does the product or service required under the RFP fit your company?** Some companies try to respond to every RFP that comes their way, hoping that, like the lottery, sooner or later they will win. Although this is great practice for when you find one that really fits you, it's not reasonable to respond to all of them. It is best to first qualify the RFP. See whether the requirements in the RFP are a match for your capabilities and whether the scope of work is within your technical abilities. If your company does not provide, or is not capable of providing, the needed product or service, you may do best to pass it up. On the other hand, don't fail to respond to an RFP that is a good match for your capabilities just because the RFP seems to be written to a specific company or specific technology or product. If you can demonstrate that you can make or do the same thing—and possibly even better (perhaps you can offer additional benefits, a lower price, etc.)—you still have a possibility of winning. So long as you meet the specs (that is the key), consider it as an opportunity for you.

In one instance that we know of, the contracting agency actually used a particular company's brochure as the basis for the scope of work in its RFP. Although it certainly looked like the RFP was written to that particular company, that was not the case. The brochure happened to describe best what the agency wanted, but it in no way meant to exclude other companies that could match—or exceed—the features outlined in the scope of work.

- **What are the marketing considerations?** Is this request something considered a new product for you? And, if so, can you leverage this into more business by selling to other customers? Also consider whether winning will cost you an existing account or be at the expense of your other lines and services.

- **What about the customer?** Is the government buyer someone you want to do business with? In other words, do you already have some kind of relationship with the buyer? Is it good or is it strained?

- **Is the project funded?** It may be a good idea to find out whether the project is funded. (All you have to do is ask.) If there are no funds, the buying agency can't go to contract and you may end up putting a lot of effort into a proposal without a chance of getting a contract out of it. If you are told that there are reserve funds for the project, you could still end up without a contract because the government has the right to reallocate reserve funds if it needs the money for other priorities. You could meet all the requirements and even be low bidder, but the project is going no farther without funds.

If, after consideration of all the factors, you decide not to respond to an RFP, but you have had contact or discussions with the contracting officer prior to the RFP being issued, you should, out of courtesy, let the contracting officer know, in writing, that you are not bidding and the reasons why.

Keep in mind that the worse that could happen in taking a chance and doing a proposal for the government is that you win the bid but that the government cannot fund it and it won't go to contract. The most you will ever lose is the time and cost of preparing the proposal. If a project goes to contract, that means it is funded. Unlike a commercial contract, you never have to worry about not getting paid for work done under a contract with the government.

What To Do Before You Start Writing

OK, you've made the decision to bid the RFP or RFQ from the government. What should you do next?

Anyone that will be involved in writing the proposal (that may be just you) should do the following before you write the proposal:

- Read the RFP again.

- Make an outline of the RFP by section and decide who is responsible for responding to each one (if it is just you, note on each section anything you need to do to gather and prepare the required information).

- Create a proposal calendar with timelines, milestones, and due dates clearly spelled out.

- Review the evaluation criteria that the buying office will use to measure the proposals. Ask the buyer or contracting officer if there is anything else that you need to know and to clarify any criteria that you don't understand. Make sure that you understand all points so that you can address each and every one in your proposal. Do this before you begin to write. Here are just some of the common criteria that evaluators might use in evaluating a proposal and some of the points you should cover:

  — Is the proposal formatted according to instructions?

  — Is the project solution presented in the proposal plausible?

  — Is the proposal organized and is it responsive to the basic requirement?

  — Are the basic requirements in the RFP followed?

  — Is the company's delivery schedule acceptable?

  — Does the company demonstrate the capability to perform?

  — Does the company have related experience?

  — Has the company had past performance history?

  — Is the company financially stable?

  — Is the cost reasonable?

— Is the costing method credible?

— Are the company's personnel resources adequate?

— Has a bill of materials been created?

Caution

Don't make the mistake of many small businesses and just focus on the Scope of Work section in their proposal. Give as much study and attention to the evaluation section and write to that as well. While the Scope of Work may state the requirement for 100,000 rubber bands, it is the Evaluation section that will contain the requirement that they have to be delivered within 24 hours. You have to address both requirements. If you aren't familiar with the evaluation factors, you will have lost the game before you begin.

- Gather and review any information (including marketing materials) about your competition. It is easier to communicate the superiority of your products/services if you are very familiar with the features and benefits your competition offers.

- Gather information on any subcontractors you will need and use.

- Create an outline for your proposal. Below are sample categories that you may want to consider for your outline. They will give you a general idea of the areas that need to be covered and how to organize them. (The outline is more applicable to contracts over $100,000, but can be a user tool for smaller contracts as well.)

Outline of Proposal

Executive Summary

Introduction

Benefits of the Proposed Solutions

Your Organization and Experience

Company's Project Management

Technical Methods

    (a) Explanation of the proposed project

        1. Project overview

        2. Proposed project configuration

   (b) Project requirement

   1. Standard products/services

   2. Maintenance

   3. Project characteristics

   4. Bill of Materials

   (c) Future enhancements

   1. Project growth

Cost Proposal

   (a) Cost basis

   1. Project procurement costs

   2. Operating costs

   3. Maintenance costs

Delivery and Acceptance

Qualification

Pre-Award Considerations

Organization

Financial Status

Work Smart

 If, in responding to an RFP, you will be sharing proprietary technical information, you should include a Proprietary Notice in your proposal. The notice should appear on a separate sheet at the beginning of the proposal and should read something like the following:

"This proposal contains confidential information on ABC Company which is provided for the sole purpose of permitting the holder of this document to evaluate the proposal submitted to {fill in the blank}. In consideration of the receipt of this proposal, the buyer agrees to maintain the enclosed information in confidence and to not reproduce or otherwise disclose any information to any person outside the group or team directly responsible for evaluation of its contents."

It is best to get legal advice on the best wording for your situation.

Tips on Writing a Proposal

Your proposal should, at the same time, adequately address the government's requirements, be clearly written, and be persuasive. Here are some pointers:

- **Write your proposal like a sales document.** Your proposal must sell your company's ability to meet the requirements, to fulfill all of the stated conditions, and to deliver on time. Be specific and direct—being vague will only demonstrate that you do not understand the requirement and will create questions in the minds of the evaluators. Substantiate your promises and assertions with facts and details. Your goal is to persuade evaluators that your offer is superior to those of competing companies and to prove that your company can do the job.

- **Demonstrate a complete understanding of the stated requirement or problem.** This may sometimes be a challenge. While, in some cases, the government buying office will know exactly what it needs, in other cases, it may not know or may use conflicting or vague terminology. In either event, it is *your* responsibility to demonstrate your understanding of the requirement; it is not the responsibility of the buying officer to interpret your understanding. If your proposal does not respond to the stated requirement or responds to only part of the requirement, it will not be considered for a contract award and may not even receive a complete evaluation.

- **Demonstrate that you are qualified.** This means that not only must you demonstrate your understanding of the problem or requirement, you must also demonstrate your ability to solve or meet it. Include your staff's qualifications, relevant facilities and equipment, as well as any other qualifications that are specific to the project you are bidding on. Your proposal should clearly communicate your ability to successfully perform the contract. Documentation of successful fulfillment of past contracts may also help prove your point.

- **Respond to the stated evaluation criteria.** Section M of the solicitation identifies the factors that the buying office will look at when evaluating your proposal. Cost is but one factor. If your proposal does not respond to these criteria, it will be judged to be technically unacceptable and will not be considered for contract award.

- **Follow the required proposal format.** Section L of the solicitation specifies which topics should be covered in your proposal as well as the order in which they should be presented. If you do not follow the required content format and organization, you risk neglecting or omitting important information, which will result in rejection of your proposal.

- **Provide adequate management and cost information.** Demonstrate your ability to manage the work and account for all of the costs involved in performing the contract. Also provide adequate cost and pricing data.

- **Proofread and critique your proposal.** Writing an effective proposal requires time, patience, and care. Be prepared to write, evaluate, and rewrite, as necessary. Rewriting gives you the chance to improve the quality and responsiveness of your proposal. Pay attention to detail. Good grammar and spelling count. If necessary, ask another person with those skills to proofread the final draft for you.

- **Provide clear explanations.** If you use abbreviations, acronyms, or in-house or trade terms, make sure that you spell them out or define them, at least the first time they are used. You might refer to something like "ASC II" and assume that all those who read your proposal will know what you mean. They may not. It could end up costing you some points, since you are not being clear on what you are trying to say.

- **Attend a proposal-writing workshop.** There are a number of good ones offered through Procurement Technical Assistance Centers. (For more information on PTACs, see Part IV.)

- **Keep a database of all your project proposals.** This can end up saving you time and money down the road. The next time you have to write a proposal, you can go back and perhaps use all or part of a proposal that you did in the past.

- **Make Plans for an Oral Presentation.** The government may require prospective offerors to give an oral presentation as part of the selection process. In the GSA, they record this on video for later review. When they request the officers to come in and do a presentation, that does not mean the sales manager; it usually means the president, and the vice-president of marketing if the company is big enough. If you're a woman-owned business, that means the "woman" not the male sales manager or husband. If you represent yourself as a certain business type, be sure that comes out at the presentation. This could mean the difference between being the winner or requesting a post-award debriefing. This is your opportunity to demonstrate why your company is the answer to their requirement.

Chapter 14

Submit Your Bid

Congratulations, you have arrived at the last step—submitting your bid. You can do this via the U.S. mail, UPS, RIP, or another carrier. However, it is important to keep in mind that if your bid is late, the U.S. mail is the only carrier that the government will recognize for consideration of a late bid.

But before you seal up that envelope and send it in, take a few minutes to go through our final checklist to help make sure that you have done everything you need to do.

Final Bid Checklist

☐ *Have you placed your name on the bidder's list for supplies and/or services that you are qualified to provide? This means going to the CCR web page and filling out all the fields (see Chapter 7).*

☐ *Have you read the solicitation carefully? If you wait to read it until after you get an award, you might be in for some severe shocks. For example, you may find out that the packaging costs are greater than the unit cost. How are you going to handle that? (See Chapter 9.)*

☐ *Have you carefully read the specifications and standards that apply to this contract? Remember: It's your responsibility to find and get the specs before you bid. Where applicable, you must also get the tech package, which contains the drawings. More than a few companies that have bid on contracts without seeing a print have been in for a sad awakening when the inspector refused to sign off because they didn't meet contract requirements. (See Chapter 10.)*

☐ *Did you bid on the exact parts that the buyer is looking for and do you propose to furnish material in exact accordance with the specifications, drawings, and description as are in the contract solicitation? If not, you better tell the government how you propose to deviate and make sure that you will still be furnishing what they want. If you plan on bidding with an exception, then you need to explain why as well as how the government will benefit. Be careful because you can only do this on a negotiated solicitation. If the solicitation is a sealed bid you must bid the requirement first, then an alternative. The government can only consider the alternative if your offer is the low one.*

☐ *If the product that you bid on requires qualification approval (i.e., a QPL), have you made sure that the approval number that you have entered is correct, and current and was issued to the plant location where the product will be produced?*

☐ *Have you checked out all packaging and marking requirements? The government has some special packaging requirements that the commercial market does not have. Sometimes the packaging costs can exceed the unit product cost.*

☐ *Have you checked and verified the unit prices for the contract? Check your math carefully— you don't want to lose the bid or lose money because of a simple arithmetic error.*

☐ *Is your bid for delivery in exact accordance with the delivery requirements specified in the solicitation? If the buyer is looking for delivery in 45 days or less, do your proposed dates fall within their requirements?*

☐ *Does your acceptance time conform to the requirements in the solicitation?*

☐ *Have you requested any information or clarification on points that are not clear to you? Have you gotten them in writing? (If you don't have them in writing, then you don't have them.)*

☐ *Have you properly completed the "Representations, certifications and acknowledgments" portion of the bid? Remember that if you are a Women-Owned Small Business, you are not a Small Disadvantaged Owned Business. Or if you are owned by a large business, you are not a small business just because you have only 40 workers at your location.*

☐ *Have you entered your discounts correctly? (Note: You don't have to offer a discount.)*

☐ *Have you signed the contract? We are serious here! Go back and make sure. Is the person who signed the contract authorized to do so? Your assistant cannot sign for you unless he or she is authorized.*

☐ Have you read the whole contract . . . *a second and even a third time?*

☐ *Have you acknowledged all amendments on the bid? The buyer will automatically kick your bid out if you haven't.*

☐ *Did you include any condition that would modify the requirements? In this regard, be careful of any transmittal or cover letters. If your normal company letterhead contains any statement about terms, price, time of delivery, or anything else that goes to the substance of the bid, it will negate your offer as "nonresponsive" because you have taken exception to the terms and conditions of the solicitation and your bid will be thrown out. All the government wants you to do is provide accurate and complete information on the forms that have been provided to you. But, if you are responding to an RFP, you may have exceptions and need to use a transmittal letter. However, make sure it doesn't have special terms and conditions on it.*

☐ *Did you include the correct number of copies? Make sure all of the copies are collated correctly, with no pages missing or out of order.* Also make sure you keep a copy for yourself.

☐ *Did you put enough postage on the bid?*

☐ *If you are submitting a sealed bid, did you put the "Sealed Bid" label on the envelope and not on the bid itself?*

☐ *Have you given yourself enough time to mail or overnight the bid to the purchasing office? UPS and RIP are not the U.S. mail. Bids sent by these methods, if they are received late, do not qualify for consideration under the "late bid procedures" regulation. Isn't it nice to be able to blame it on the mailman?*

O.K., that's it! Run down to the post office and get your bid in the mail!

Part III

After the Bid

Well done! You have completed the work, gone through the steps and submitted your first bid. Now what happens?

Basically, once you are finished with your part of the process, it is time for the government buyer to take over and do its part. Once all of the bids are in, the buyer will begin evaluating all of the offers and ultimately make a final decision on which company will be awarded the contract.

And what if your company is the one that is awarded the contract? What should you be doing and thinking about?

In this Part, we will try to answer some of these questions and look at what comes next. We will first look at how the evaluation process works and the factors that could influence who will win the award. We will also offer some pointers on what to do immediately upon receiving a contract.

We will then discuss the importance of quality assurance standards and provide a checklist for getting you started on setting up an effective quality assurance program for your company. Finally, we will discuss contract terminations and one of the most important and interesting things of all . . . getting paid.

Chapter 15, Bid Evaluation and Award: We tell you what government buyers look for when they evaluate your bid against others and how they decide on the winner. If you are being considered for award, the government may want to perform a pre-award survey to make sure you are capable—we tell you how to prepare. Finally, we provide a checklist of things you need to do right away if you are the winner.

Chapter 16, Quality Assurance Standards: Quality assurance is a crucial part of doing business with the government. How can you assure buyers that you will provide a quality product? We explain the different levels of quality standards and tell you what you need to do to develop a good quality control program for your company.

Chapter 17, What To Know When Things Go Wrong: What happens when problems and issues arise that can't be easily resolved? We tell you what to expect and cover everything from contract terminations to simple protests and disputes to court action.

Chapter 18, Getting Paid: Find out how you can help ensure prompt payment and what constitutes a "proper invoice." Also learn about the forms of payment: electronic funds transfer and the government credit card.

Chapter 15

Bid Evaluation and Award

Once the government buyer receives all the bids, the evaluation and award process begins. Here is an outline of what happens.

Non-Negotiated Bids (IFBs). If the solicitation is an Invitation for Bid (IFB)—a non-negotiated, sealed bid situation where best valued bidder wins—the bid is opened and the information is recorded on what is referred to as a "bid abstract." This will be used as the bid history database. The abstract contains, in order of opening, the names of the bidding companies, the items being bid, the prices quoted, and any other information that the bidding officer deems relevant.

This is important information that could prove to be very useful to you, whether you get the bid or not. And since the information contained in the bid abstract is considered public information, you can get it just by asking. The government buying office will send you a copy of the abstract if you enclose a self-addressed stamped envelope along with your bid. You should also include a letter stating that you are requesting the bid abstract under the Freedom of Information Act. (See now, isn't the government helpful? You probably won't be able to get similar information from the private business sector at any time in the near future.)

With this information in hand, you can see where you stand in the bidding process. If your price quote is in the upper third of the price ranking, you are outside the competitive range. If you find yourself in the middle third, you're getting there. If you are in the lower third, you are in the right place.

Remember that you will not win all bids. Figure that after you become an old hand at bidding, your rate will be, on average, about three out of ten. Take a look at the investment in time and money you put in going after a commercial contract. It's the same plan of action with the government.

Negotiated Bids (RFPs or RFQs). If the solicitation is negotiated—in other words, if it is a Request for Proposal or Request for Quote—the information on bidding companies, pricing, etc. is not public information. When the award is made, the name of the successful bidder and the contract price become public information.

FACTORS INFLUENCING BID OUTCOME

Which factors do government buyers consider in looking at your bid and finally awarding the contract? Here are some of the most important:

Does Your Bid Meet All Essential Requirements?

One of the first things that government buyers will do is make sure that your bid conforms to all essential requirements of the solicitation. This includes exact conformance to all the specifications, drawings, descriptions, and standards specified in the contract solicitation, as well as materials, delivery dates, packaging and marking requirements, past performance history, etc. Often, these factors are referred to as "Best Value."

Are You Capable?

Buyers will also consider whether you are capable of performing and delivering on the contract. Just because you know in your heart that you can do the work is not enough for buyers. They will be looking at your technical capability and trying to make sure that you have the experience and know-how to do the work.

Do you have the production capability? If the contract calls for 100,000 widgets and you have one drill press and a milling machine and a part-time retired guy . . . well, they might see a problem and you probably won't get the contract. Do you have a real place of operation? If you are manufacturing items out of your garage, then that could also be a handicap in getting a contract.

Here's a major consideration: financial capability. For some reason, reasonable business people think if they are in financial trouble, a government contract will be able to fix the situation and get them financially healthy again. Sorry, but if your business is in trouble, the last thing you want is a contract where the margins are tight and you might have trouble getting financial help to do the work. The government buying offices are not in the business of starting and financing a private company!

What's Your Performance Record?

Another important consideration for buyers is your past performance record. If you didn't meet a deadline on your first contract or if you have a history of late deliveries on contracts, the government will not want to work with you. The government operates on strict schedules and when you don't meet one, the government tends to get very upset and never forget. Even in cases where price is a deciding factor, the government now factors in past performance in figuring out the real cost for an item.

You now can check your company's delivery status by going to the Business Partner Network (www.bpn.gov) web site—the single source for vendor data for the federal government. The BPN search mechanism provides unprecedented access into several key databases across federal agencies (see Chapter 19, "Help from the Government" for more complete coverage on BPN). When you go to the BPN site, check out your past performance record.

The Past Performance Information Retrieval System (PPIRS) contains report cards assessing a vendor's past performance in doing business with the government. It is made available to government source selection officials who use the information as one of several factors in determining which company should be awarded a new contract. Contractors are encouraged to validate their own past performance information and to refer to records in PPIRS when preparing proposals.

To access PPIRS, the contractor must register a past performance point of contact in the Central Contractor Registration profile and generate a Marketing Partner Identification Number (MPIN). Your CCR POC is the only person with access to your company's active registration, therefore you need to contact your CCR POC to establish the MPIN. Contractors may then log onto PPIRS using their DUNS number as a user ID and their MPIN number as a password. It takes about a week to update PPIRS with newly activated MPIN numbers. New information is made available every Thursday morning.

Contractors who have successfully obtained an MPIN may find that there are no records available on them in PPIRS. This is either because the contractor has no contracts meeting the thresholds for report cards (in DoD, $1 million for services and information technology and $5 million for systems and operations support; $100,000 for federal agencies) or because the reports have not yet been written. Contractors are encouraged to contact their buyers to ensure that the reports are written.

Do You Have Adequate Quality Control?

Government buyers want assurance that you will provide a quality product. You may not need to go all out and get certified under strict international quality standards, but you should have a good, well-documented quality control program that tells all of your customers, including the government, how you guarantee that you will provide quality products and services.

(Quality assurance is such a crucial part of any government contract that we are going to expand on this topic in a separate chapter later in this Part.)

PRE-AWARD SURVEY

The government's responsibility in evaluating a bid is to determine, first of all, the responsiveness of an offer to the solicitation. This is more of a technical process and consists of checking all the paperwork and making sure there are no unacceptable deviations. The government must then determine whether the proposed winner is responsible and capable enough to handle the contract.

To help make this determination, the government might perform what is called a Pre-Award Survey (PAS). The PAS is made in sufficient depth to assure that the proposed award winner has the ability to meet the requirements of the solicitation. It may involve a full government team coming out to check a company's capabilities first-hand, or it may entail nothing more than taking a look at the pertinent information about the company to determine if it is able to go ahead with the contract.

How to Prepare for the Pre-Award Survey

If you are the proposed winner of a government contract, there are certain things you can do to prepare for the Pre-Award Survey to help ensure a favorable outcome for your company:

- Select the person who will meet with the government survey team. This person should be empowered to speak for the company and should be completely familiar with the details of the solicitation and of your company's offer.

- If relevant, make available one or more technicians to answer questions.

- Identify any disparities that may exist between the solicitation and your company's offer that should be resolved during the initial meeting with the survey team.

- Think about how you can demonstrate actual technical capability, or the development of technical capability, on the proposed contract.

- Get your production plan ready and available for review by the survey team.

- Make sure your plant facilities and equipment are available and operable. If they are not, be prepared to demonstrate that they can be developed or acquired in time to meet proposed contract requirements.

- Be prepared to show that you can meet the transportation, packaging, packing and preservation conditions of the solicitation.

- If industrial security clearance is required under the proposed contract, be prepared to show it.

- Make sure that your labor resources have the proper skills or that personnel with the needed skills can be hired expeditiously.

- Gather and make available to the survey team documentation, such as previous government contracts or subcontracts or commercial orders, to demonstrate a past satisfactory performance record with regard to delivery, quality and finances.

- Look over your production plan and make sure that you can demonstrate a capability to meet contract schedules.

- Gather financial documentation for the team financial analyst, including the company's current profit and loss summary, balance sheet, cash flow chart and other pertinent financial information.

- Prepare a listing of available tools and equipment for the team production specialist.

- Make sure that plans are in place for vendor supplies and materials or subcontracts to assure that the final delivery schedule can be met. Make sure that these plans are verifiable.

- Review any technical data and publications that may be required under the proposed contract and make sure you understand them.

- If the contract is a type other than a firm-fixed price or if you have requested progress payments, prepare adequate accounting documentation for review by the audit agency representative of the team.

- Review your quality control program and make sure that it is workable and consistent with the quality requirements stated in the contract. Be prepared to go over the details with the survey team.

- If government-furnished equipment, property or material is involved in the proposed contract, make sure you have established procedures in accord with the regulation stated in the contract.

- Prepare any other information or data that might be pertinent in assisting the government team.

As you become more experienced in the government market, you will find that all this takes less and less time. As with anything new, there's a learning curve.

Work Smart

What if you get turned down? There may be a "second bite of the apple" for you if your company is a small business and gets turned down on the Pre-Award Survey. If you can convince the Small Business Administration that you can do the work, the SBA could decide to back you and issue you another pre-award, known as a Certificate of Competency. The Certificate of Competency is like a bond and will allow you to receive the contract.

YOU WON IT! NOW WHAT?

Now, to the big question: What happens next if your company is the one that is awarded the contract? After you have congratulated yourself, what should you be doing and thinking about? Simply put, it is now up to you to fulfill the requirements of the contract, whether it's to produce a product, provide a service or build a structure.

Although it is impossible to cover the infinite variety of situations that might be involved in any given contract, we can offer a checklist of the actions you need to take immediately upon receiving a contract. The items on the checklist may seem obvious to you, but most companies get into trouble simply because they fail to do the obvious.

Contract Performance Checklist

☐ ***Reread the Contract.*** *You probably hoped that you had heard the last of this, but here we go again. The first thing you should do upon being awarded a contract is to read, read, read the provisions. Recheck your delivery dates, packaging requirements, reports you may be required to submit, and delivery destination. Make sure you haven't missed something—let's hope you are not surprised at what you may find.*

☐ ***Record Important Contacts.*** *Look on the face of the contract and jot down the name, address, telephone number, and e-mail address of the following contacts so you will have the information handy for on-going reference:*

— *Procuring Contracting Officer (PCO)*

— *Administrative Contracting Officer (ACO)*

— *Paying Office*

— *Government Inspector (You should be contacted by this individual. This might be a local person who will work with you to get the contract completed. If it is a military contract, the local Defense Contract Management Agency (DCMA) should be a big help to you. Think of these people as part of your management team to help complete the contract.)*

☐ ***Don't Take Unnecessary Actions.*** *If the PCO or the ACO directs you to take a specific action, you must do so. But don't act on anyone else's direction! If you do, you will be liable for any costs or consequences that may result. Only the PCO, ACO, Contracting Officer's Representative (COR) or the contract itself can authorize you to take any action.*

☐ ***Resolve Any Questions.*** *If you have any questions about what a specific provision means or if you find any inconsistencies in your contract, contact the Contracting Officer (CO) immediately and ask for a meeting or "post-award conference." Open the lines of communication and develop a good working relationship right away. If you are really new to the process, ask for all the assistance that the CO is willing to give you. There is no question that is too "dumb" or "embarrassing"; what is really embarrassing is not performing on the contract. Address any problem right away before it gets out of hand.*

☐ ***Keep accurate, timely and well documented records.*** *Even in this paperless society, a paper trail is important. You have no case if you can't prove what was said and done. We have found that simple misunderstandings can easily degenerate into a "he said, she said" sort of situation where no one wins and the relationship with the government people becomes, shall we say, "touchy."*

☐ ***Determine internal responsibilities.*** *Make sure your people understand what is to be done and in what time frame. This will help ensure that everything goes smoothly and that delivery is made in accordance with the terms of the contract.*

☐ ***Issue orders and plan production.*** *Place any long lead items on contract immediately to ensure that there will be no holdup with production.*

☐ ***Produce/provide the service.*** *If everything was planned out properly, this part should go relatively smoothly. If not, don't forget to keep the Contracting Officer informed. If you see that delivery under the contract may be affected, seek an extension before the due date to avoid being delinquent.*

☐ ***Review your quality control program.*** *Make sure procedures are in place and are adequate to guarantee that the quality of the item will meet government requirements. If necessary, update your procedures and your manual.*

Copy this checklist, and then put it and all other information in the work order or folder. If you miss something, this will make it easier to go back and make changes.

Chapter 16

Quality Assurance Standards

Every customer wants a quality product, and the government is no exception.

When the government purchases products or services from your company, you will be subjected to a very definite standard of quality as specified in your contract. The level and type of quality standard that you will be required to meet will depend on the product or service being purchased. For example, an extensive quality requirement would probably not be imposed if you are producing a non-complex item, since simple measurement or testing would be able to determine whether it conforms to contract requirements.

To assure the government, as well as other prospective customers, that you will provide a quality product, you need to have a well documented quality assurance (QA) program in place. Your program should provide a systematic approach for evaluation, inspection, testing, calibration or whatever is needed to monitor and assure the quality of your product. And, most importantly, that approach should be written down. (See the "Sample Quality Assurance Manual" in the Appendices.)

From the government's point of view, the purpose of a quality program is to provide a way to assure that an item complies with contract specifications. From your point of view, the purpose is twofold: It will attract and assure government buyers, and perhaps even more importantly, it will also save you money by providing you with the necessary indicators and tools to identify problem areas and the means for correcting those areas. It will make you look at every aspect and phase of your manufacturing and operating processes as well as the results of those processes. If a process results in a bad output, you will be able to identify where changes need to be made to produce an acceptable product.

Example

The owners of a small company in the Midwest that manufactured items for the government had no quality control system, but they did have a 100-percent acceptance rate with the government inspectors. However, they were losing money and couldn't figure out why.

Their approach was to scrap all the items that didn't meet government specs, let the government see only the "good" items, and simply buy enough materials to accommodate the high scrap rate. While this approach resulted in a high acceptance rate, the high cost of materials ate into their profits and hurt the company financially. A good quality control system would have helped them identify the real problem, reduce the amount of scrap, and cut the cost of materials.

Set up a good quality control system and it will pay for itself by reducing material and operational costs, and will make your company more attractive to prospective customers. Remember that the government, like any customer, wants a quality product, on time and at a reasonable price. No more, no less. And these days, ISO certification becomes a marketing tool to help sell your company.

A high-quality QA program will also assure that the reliability and quality of the product are maintained throughout the life of the product. Companies that do business with the government need reliability assurance, since the government now requires guarantees on some of their purchases. Also, an aggressive quality control program will prevent product degradation below some minimum requirement that you set.

The government assures quality by reviewing a contractor's inspection system, quality program, or any method used by the contractor to assure compliance with the contract requirements. But, regardless of the government's quality assurance actions, the contractor is responsible for inspecting and controlling product quality, and for offering to the government only materials that conform to contract requirements, either as an individual item or in conjunction with any other item.

Caution

All government quality assurance requirements are spelled out in Part 46 of the Federal Acquisition Regulation (FAR). Any language that you will see in a bid or contract related to quality control consists of clauses extracted from this Part.

CONTRACT QUALITY REQUIREMENTS

When the contracting officer issues a sealed bid (IFB) or a request for proposal (RFP), the solicitation will specify the quality provisions that will be required by the government. Every solicitation or bid will include one of four basic categories of QA coverage for assuring conformance of products and services to contract requirements:

1. **Contractor's existing quality assurance system (applicable to contracts for commercial items).** When the government buys commercial items, it may rely on the contractor's existing quality assurance system, without government inspection and testing. However, if customary market practices for the commercial item being bought include in-process inspection, then the government may do some inspection and testing by its own personnel. Any in-process inspection conducted by the government must be conducted in a manner consistent with commercial practice.

2. **Inspection by the contractor (applicable to contracts for non-commercial items $100,000 or less).** When a contract for non-commercial items (i.e., items built to government specs) is expected not to exceed the simplified acquisition threshold of $100,000 or less, the government may specify that the contractor is responsible for performing all inspections and tests necessary to substantiate that supplies or services furnished conform to contract quality requirements. However, the government may impose stricter requirements if it has special needs that require a greater degree of quality assurance.

3. **Standard inspection requirements (applicable to contracts for non-commercial items over $100,000).** When a contract for non-commercial items is expected to exceed $100,000, the government may require the contractor to provide and maintain an inspection system that is acceptable to the government. The government also has the right to conduct inspections and tests while work is in progress and to require the contractor to keep and make available to the government complete records of its inspection work. Here we are talking about more complex items, such as sub-assemblies, minor components, or items critical to function or safety.

4. **Higher-level quality standards (applicable to complex or critical items—contacts may be for less than $100,000).** When a contract is for complex or critical items, higher-level requirements are applicable. The contracting officer is responsible for identifying the higher-level standard(s) that will satisfy the government's requirement. Examples of higher-level standards that the contracting officer may cite are ISO 9001, 9002, or 9003; ANSI/ASQC Q9001, Q9002, or Q9003; QS-9000; AS-9000; ANSI/ASQC E4; and ANSI/ASME NQA-1. (We discuss some of these standards in more detail, below.) This quality level would be required when it is important for control of work operations, in-process controls, and inspection

or attention to such factors as organization, planning, work instructions, documentation control, etc.

HIGHER-LEVEL INTERNATIONAL STANDARDS

ISO international standards, developed by the International Organization for Standardization (ISO) based in Geneva, Switzerland, are considered among the world's strictest and highest quality standards. The ISO, a non-governmental organization established in 1947, comprises a worldwide federation of national standards bodies from each of 100 countries. The organization aims to facilitate the international exchange of goods and services by establishing international standards and reconciling regulatory differences between countries.

ISO standards contain precise criteria for the features and characteristics of products and services to ensure that these products and services are fit for their purpose. For example, the format of credit cards is derived from an ISO international standard. Complying with an international standard, which defines such features as the optimal thickness (0.76 mm) of each card, means that the cards can be used worldwide.

International standards thus contribute to making life simpler and to increasing the reliability and effectiveness of the goods and services that we use. Coordinated standards for similar technologies in different countries or regions can also effectively remove so-called "technical barriers to trade."

The scope of ISO covers all technical fields, except electrical and electronic engineering, which is the responsibility of the International Electrotechnical Commission (IEC). The IEC is the international standards and conformity assessment body for all fields of electrotechnology. The work in the field of information technology is carried out by a joint ISO/IEC technical committee.

The ISO issues the certifications and certifies individuals that work with companies in setting up ISO standards in their business. ISO certification is very pricey—on average, it runs between $20,000-$35,000 per year. A company can't say that it is ISO unless a certified ISO auditor has declared it so. Because of the cost of ISO, some contracts will specify ISO *compliant*. While this doesn't require certification, it does mean you are taking steps in that direction.

ISO 9000

ISO 9000 is a set of five universal standards for a Quality Assurance system that is accepted around the world. Ninety countries have adopted ISO 9000 as national standards, and the federal government is moving closer to having ISO as the one, so to speak, standard to replace its major systems standard, MIL-Q-9858.

When a customer, such as the government, purchases a product or service from a company that is registered to the appropriate ISO 9000 standard, the customer has important assurances that the quality of what it receives will be as it expects.

ISO 9000 registration is rapidly becoming a must for any company that does business with the government or overseas involving complex or critical items. Many industrial companies require registration by their own subcontractors, so there is a growing trend toward universal acceptance of ISO 9000 as an international standard.

The most comprehensive of the 9000 set of standards is ISO 9001. It applies to industries involved in the design and development, manufacturing, installation and servicing of products or services. The standards apply uniformly to companies in any industry and of any size.

Many companies require their suppliers to become registered to ISO 9001, and because of this, registered companies have found that their market opportunities have increased. Registered companies have also had dramatic reductions in customer complaints, significant reductions in operating costs and increased demand for their products and services.

A company in compliance with ISO 9001 ensures that it has a sound Quality Assurance system, and that's good business. ISO 9002 is almost identical to ISO 9001, except that the provisions on "Design Control" are only applicable to 9001. Therefore, ISO 9001 is the appropriate standard if your organization carries out the innovative design of products or services; otherwise ISO 9002 is applicable.

ISO 9001 or ISO 9002?

ISO 9001, entitled "Quality System — Model for quality assurance in design/development, production, installation and servicing," applies in situations when:

1. design is required and the product requirements are stated principally in performance terms, or they need to be established, and

2. confidence in product conformance can be attained by adequate demonstration of a supplier's capabilities in design, development, production, installation and servicing.

ISO 9002, entitled "Quality System — Model for quality assurance in production, installation and servicing," applies in situations when:

1. the specified requirements for the product are stated in terms of an established design or specification, and

2. confidence in product conformance can be attained by adequate demonstration of a supplier's capabilities in production, installation, and servicing.

ISO 14001

Before we end our discussion of ISO standards, we want to mention ISO 14001, an emerging international standard for environmental management systems (EMS). The ISO 14000 series is a voluntary set of standards intended to encourage organizations to systematically address the environmental impacts of their activities. The goal is to establish a common approach to environmental management systems that is internationally recognized, leading to improved environmental protection and reducing barriers to international trade.

ISO 14000 is a management system standard, not a performance standard. It is intended to be applicable to firms of all shapes and sizes around the world. The standard does not require specific environmental goals.

Instead, it provides a general framework for organizing the tasks necessary for effective environmental management, including planning, implementation and operations, checking and corrective action, and management review. The series of documents that encompasses ISO 14000 includes components such as environmental management systems, environmental auditing, environmental labeling and product life cycle assessment.

The ISO 14001 standard, which lays out requirements for establishing an EMS, is the centerpiece of the series. In order to qualify for ISO certification, firms must meet the requirements laid out in the ISO 14001. All of the other standards in the ISO 14000 series provide supporting guidance.

ISO 14001 is currently the subject of heated debate. Proponents of ISO 14001 argue that the new standard will be an effective tool for improving industrial environmental performance and help to ease burdens on environmental regulators. At the same time, many in the environmental community worry that compliance with ISO 14000 does not guarantee environmental improvements.

Work Smart

There are several web cites that offer information about ISO standards—search for "ISO" or "ISO standards" to get a list. You can also receive information by contacting:

American National Standards Institute
11 East 42nd St.
New York, NY 10036
Phone: 1-212-642-4900 Fax: 1-212-302-1286

HIGHER-LEVEL U.S. STANDARDS

In the previous discussion, we mentioned that the U.S. government is moving closer to having ISO as the one, so to speak, standard to replace its major quality assurance standard for complex military systems and hardware, MIL-Q-9858. But a funny thing about the government, particularly the military, is that old habits die hard. Two quality assurance standards, MIL-I-45208 (An Inspection System) and MIL-Q-9858A (A Quality Program), have been cancelled, but live on in contract terminology.

MIL-I-45208

Entitled "An Inspection System," this quality specification pertaining to military items sets forth the objectives and essential elements of an inspection system, and was referenced in a contract whenever an inspection system was required for the item. This system was used when technical requirements required in-process as well as final end item inspection, including control of measuring and testing equipment, drawing and changes, and documentation and records.

This requirement impacted both large and small businesses alike. In simple terms, it meant that you had to document your inspection system to assure continuity.

This spec was cancelled a few years ago, along with MIL-STD-45662 (calibration standard), but there are many contracting officers and contracts that still require it, but don't use the name. (See the "Sample Quality Assurance Manual" in the Appendices.)

MIL-Q-9858A

Entitled "A Quality Program," these requirements are sometimes still referenced whenever the technical requirements of a contract require such things as control of work operations, in-process control, inspection, organization, work instructions, documentation control and advanced metrology. This specification is intended for use in contracts that involve complex types of military hardware and systems.

Folks, this is not for the faint of heart. Don't try to put one of these together yourself. Our best advice is to get an expert to help you. By the way, this standard has also been cancelled and mostly replaced by the ISO series

CERTIFICATE OF CONFORMANCE

A Certificate of Conformance may be used in certain instances instead of source inspection at the discretion of the contracting officer. When a Certificate of Conformance is provided for in the contract, it gives the Contract Administration Office an option to allow material to be accepted and shipped without being inspected.

However, this option is exercised only when product quality history is excellent. When it is exercised, contractors are notified in writing by the inspector that the Certificate of Conformance procedure is applicable and the company can ship. Without this written notification, the contractor must expect regular inspection of product before shipment. Remember that the Certificate of Conformance is for the convenience of the government, not the contractor.

How to Read Specs and Standards

Federal specifications — The titles of federal specifications begin with a series of letters, followed by another letter and a serial number, and possibly a letter indicating the latest revision of the specification. The letter A represents the first revision, B represents the second revision, and so on. For example, A-A-104 is a federal spec for toothpaste. A-A-104B is the second revision of this spec.

Military specifications — The titles of military specifications begin with the letters MIL, MS, or DOD, followed by the first letter in the first word of the title, a serial number, and possibly a letter indicating the latest revision of the specification. It may also be followed by a number in parentheses indicating the last amendment to the specification.

"Revisions" represent major changes to a specification, and a revised specification supersedes all of the earlier versions. The letter A represents the first revision, B represents the second revision, and so on. "Amendments" represent minor changes to a specification, and an amended specification supplements, but does not replace, the latest revision and all earlier amendments.

For example, MIL-C-85322 is a military spec for "Coating, Elastomere, Polyurethane, Rain Erosion Resistant, For Exterior Aircraft Use." DOD-L-85336 is a military spec for "Lubricant, All Weather (Automatic Weapons)." DOD-L-85336A represents the first revision of DOD-L-85336. MIL-L-85314A (1) is a military spec for "Light Systems, Aircraft, Anti-Collision, Strobe." MIL-L-85314A represents the first revision of MIL-L-85314. This first revision has been amended one time [indicated by the (1)].

Industry-wide standards — The titles of industry-wide standards begin with the letters in the abbreviation of the appropriate association, institute or society, followed by identifying letters and/or numbers. For example AWS A6.1-66 is an industry-wide safety standard for "Gas Shielded Arc Welding" from the American Welding Society (AWS). ANSI B4.1-67 is an industry-wide standard for "Cylindrical Parts, Preferred Limits and Fits for" from the American National Standards Institute (ANSI).

Quality Requirements for Subcontractors

Right about now, you may be thinking to yourself, "If I am just a subcontractor, I won't have to do all this quality stuff, will I?" Guess again.

In many instances, a prime contractor will find it necessary or desirable to pass along the quality requirements to the subcontractor. Why? The prime contractor is responsible for the quality of materials supplied by the subcontractors or suppliers, and it is in its best interest to assure that all suppliers are capable of providing the materials and meeting the quality requirements of the prime contract.

The only way that the prime can assure itself that you can do quality work, on time and within budget, is to inspect your systems and get them approved. The day of the "pal" or "buddy" at the prime level that will issue a contract just on an owner's assurance that the company can deliver the required product is becoming a thing of the past. Many a small business that had this type of relationship has found, to their woe, that it must still have some kind of quality control system in place. So you must market your company in ways that you might not have had to before.

To the surprise of many contractors and subcontractors, government contract quality assurance at the subcontractor level does not relieve the prime contractor of any responsibilities under the contract nor does it establish a contractual relationship between the government and the subcontractor. So, if you think that you are getting out of some of the quality "stuff" by being a sub, think again.

The prime might, under a special exception or for a particular job, let you slide by without a QA program for a while, but it will eventually want to see a formal program in place or it won't want to work with you. Therefore, you may as well start creating your own program now, and do it to your satisfaction, without having the pressure of having to create one on the eve of a bid contract that you really want.

Assuring Measuring and Testing Requirements

Some years ago, there was a really nice spec, MIL-STD-45662, that thoroughly explained the how and why of what you needed to do to establish and maintain a system of all measurement and test equipment used in the contract. Now you must use Calibration Systems Requirements (ISO 10012-1, ANSI/NCSL Z540-1), which replaced the old 45662 standard.

Although the new spec is shorter, we miss the way that the 45662 explained what was needed. It was a great help for new contractors that had never had a calibration system and, for the most part, was easy to follow.

You may be able to get a copy of the old 45662 standard by contacting the Information Handling Services Group Inc. at www.ihs.com or www.usainfo.com, and ordering the historical files from them. They will charge a fee, but you might find it a good first step in creating your QA system. Contact your local PTAC because they may be able to get the information specs and standards at less cost to you than through a commercial source.

Assuring Packaging and Shipping Requirements

As we have already mentioned, packaging requirements are a big deal when you do business with the government. They need to be carefully considered and analyzed, not only in pricing out a bid, but also in implementing a QA program. To aid your understanding, we think it would be helpful to define the terms "packaging" and "packing" the way the government defines them.

"Packaging," as defined in the Governments Contract Dictionary, is:

1. "an all-inclusive term covering cleaning, preserving, packaging, packing, and marking required to protect items during every phase of shipment, handling, and storage.

2. "The methods and materials used to protect material from deterioration or damage. This includes cleaning, drying, preserving, packing, marking and unitization." (Unitization is a government term that defines the "unit" of shipment and refers to a grouping of items for shipment.)

"Packing" is:

1. "the assembling of items into a unit, intermediate, or exterior pack with necessary blocking, bracing, cushioning, weatherproofing and reinforcement."

The reason that we defined these terms is that some companies might think that if they produce a quality part, all they need to do when they ship is drop it in a box with some of those "peanuts" and send for UPS. As the definitions imply, there is more to it—a lot more. To further illustrate, let's look at what might be required in the packaging of a part that might be used by the Army.

Assume that your company was contracted by the Army to manufacture a simple, inexpensive item, specifically a "block" consisting of a metal piece approximately 2x4 inches made of a specified material that will withstand high pressure.

So how would you have to package this little block? Under typical government packaging requirements for such a product, the block must first be packed into a plastic package. The plastic package must then be put into another pack that is cushioned and reinforced. A water/vapor seal is then put over the entire package. The sealed package is then packed into a shipping container.

Sounds like a lot for just one item, right? Well, that little block is part of a 155 mm howitzer cannon and is used to fire rounds (those big pointy things that explode when they land). And although this may seem a somewhat roundabout and melodramatic way to show the importance of packaging, the typical civilian usually does not realize how the part he or she is working on will be used or delivered to its ultimate destination. The little block might be headed for a 10,000-mile flight, dropped out of a plane at 5,000 feet, and must be ready to work the first time, and every time, when it lands.

In addition, as electronic technology becomes more complex, expensive and sensitive to damage, protecting electronic products and the work environment is a key government goal. And one place this is reflected is in packaging standards.

So although packaging requirements on a government contract can sometimes seem complex and difficult, if you're smart and do your homework, you can be successful at meeting the challenge.

Packaging Levels and Specs

The government uses 3 levels of packing and protection:

1. *Level A, Maximum Protection, is used for the most severe shipment, handling or storage conditions, or for unknown transportation or storage conditions. Examples: All-wood boxes, sheathed crates, plastic or metal specialty containers.*

2. *Level B, Intermediate Protection, is used for known and favorable shipment, handling and storage conditions. Examples: Single-, double-, or triple-walled, weather-resistant fiberboard, sealed at all openings.*

3. *Level C, Minimum Protection, is used for known and most favorable shipment, handling and storage conditions. Example: Domestic fiberboard or paperboard.*

To give you an overview of what is involved in "packaging," we are listing three packaging specifications, below. But because this area is so complex, we recommend that you get an expert to help you.

You can contact the government office administering your contract and request help from a government packaging specialist. Or, better yet, you can find a packager that has experience in working with the government and form a partnership with that company. Then you, the packager, and the government will all come out fine.

Number:	MIL-STD-2073-1
Title:	DOD MATERIEL PROCEDURES FOR DEVELOPMENT AND APPLICATION OF PACKAGING REQUIREMENTS
Price:	$94.00
Revision/Edition:	D
Date1:	12/15/1999
# Pages:	212

Number:	MIL-STD-2073-2
Title:	PACKAGING REQUIREMENT CODES
Price:	$48.00
Revision/Edition:	C
Date1:	10/01/1996
# Pages:	85

Number:	MIL-STD-726
Title:	PACKAGING REQUIREMENT CODES
Price:	$93.00
Revision/Edition:	H
Date1:	06/23/1993
# Pages:	208

HOW TO DEVELOP YOUR OWN QA PROGRAM

These days, if you don't have a good, well-documented quality control program in place, you are really limiting your business. We can't emphasize its importance enough, not just in the government market, but in the commercial market as well.

The goal of your quality assurance initiative is to create written procedures that will assure full compliance with all contract requirements. Formal, written documentation provides the government and your other customers better assurance that there will be consistency in the process and that, if a mistake is made, the cause can be traced to a specific spot and then corrected. The government wants the who, what, where, when and how of your quality control, so you need to specify the details: Who is responsible, for what specific function, at what stage of the process, etc.

Begin creating your program by first assessing where you are in your company with regard to quality control. There is a good chance that you already have effective procedures in place, but that they are not formally written. You don't have to reinvent the wheel; just document the way you do your work and then organize the material into a manual or handbook.

Tips on Establishing QA Procedures

Here are some things to consider as you start planning and developing your own Quality Assurance program—whether you are looking to set up a full system to fulfill high-level military or international standards or to establish quality standards for a non-complex item.

As you establish quality assurance procedures and policies, be sure to write them down. This documentation will form the basis of your company's quality assurance manual.

- ☐ *Review the work rules and quality control policies and procedures that you and/or your employees already follow, but that up to now have just been verbalized. Start writing them down. Also write down any "defect prevention" rules that your company may have.*

- ☐ *Take a fresh look at your operation end to end, and identify every function and activity that affects the quality of your product or services. Look for possible quality trouble spots in every phase of the production, inspection and shipping cycle.*

- ☐ *If you don't already have them, set acceptance/rejection standards, procedures for controlling products that have been accepted/rejected, and a means of using failure information to improve the quality of your product or service.*

- ☐ *Establish procedures to ensure supplier product quality control. Watch purchases to make sure that the people you buy from know and observe your quality requirements, as well as any technical specifications.*

- ☐ *Set up procedures to ensure that any necessary measurement and test equipment is properly calibrated to the proper standard.*

- ☐ *Create procedures to spot defects as early in production as possible—for example, nonconforming material control.*

- ☐ *Decide which records and reports will be required to track all steps of the production, inspection and shipping cycles to identify existing and potential problem areas.*

- ☐ *Assign responsibility for administration and supervision of the various stages of your quality control program.*

- ☐ *Let your government inspector provide some assistance. Contact the office administering your contract and ask for help.*

Tips on Creating Your QA Manual

It is easier than you think to create your own quality assurance manual. We can't write it for you, but we can offer some tips:

- Please don't go out and copy a generic manual word for word from "Quality Control for Dummies"or get a manual from your Uncle Ned. It will not work for the government, and, more importantly, it will not work for you. Many community colleges offer courses on quality assurance and show you how to build your own documentation. Plus, the purpose of preparing written procedures and instructions is to establish a quality system that is effective for *your* company.

- Create your manual in a loose-leaf format so it will be easy to correct and update.

- Organize your manual by process. In other words, create separate sections for each operation, such as materials purchased, manufacturing, inspection, packing and shipping, etc.

- Include a Table of Contents to make it easier for you, your employees, and your customers to find what they need.

- Include an Introduction page briefly describing the purpose of the manual and the person(s) responsible for administering and supervising the QA program. Also clearly state the procedure that must be followed if and when any changes to your quality program and the manual are made. Finally, include the date the manual was prepared or last revised.

- Include any charts, forms, etc. that may be relevant to quality control.

Remember that the best manual in the world won't do any good unless all your employees, not just those responsible for quality assurance, know that producing quality products is your company's prime goal. (See our "Sample Quality Assurance Manual" in the Appendices.)

Chapter 17

What To Know When Things Go Wrong

For 95 percent of the companies doing business with the government, things run quite smoothly, contracts are successfully completed, and any issues or problems that do arise are resolved by the contracting officer to everyone's satisfaction. However, for the rare few, problems and issues arise that can't be resolved and require more formal action—all the way from contract termination to simple protests and disputes to court action.

It is these instances that we want to address here. Let's look at what recourses are available to the contracting parties (you and the government), and the procedures and requirements that must be followed when things go wrong.

CONTRACT TERMINATIONS

Almost every federal contract contains a clause allowing the government to terminate a contract for the convenience of the government. In addition, most contracts in excess of $25,000 contain a clause covering terminations for default when the government believes that a contractor failed to perform in accordance with the provisions of the contract.

Termination for Convenience

A termination for convenience (T for C) allows the federal government to terminate all or part of a contract for its convenience. This type of termination protects the government's interests by allowing cancellation of contracts for products that become obsolete or unneeded. The termination does not arise from any fault on the part of the contractor.

If the federal government terminates your contract for its convenience, it must notify you in writing. The notice of termination must contain the effective date of the termination, the extent of the termination, and any special instructions.

The contract termination notice and clause generally require a contractor to stop work immediately on the terminated portion, to terminate all affected subcontracts, to perform any specified unterminated portions of the contract, and to proceed promptly to settle termination claims, both its own and those of its subcontractors.

If you receive a termination notice and fail to follow these directions, you do so at your own risk and expense. You should also receive detailed instructions as to the protection and preservation of all property that is, or may become, government-owned.

After termination, the government is required to make a fair and prompt settlement with you. Generally speaking, settlement takes the form of a negotiated agreement between the parties. The idea is to agree on an amount that will compensate you fully and fairly for the work you have done and for any preparation you have made for the terminated portion of the contract. A reasonable allowance for profit is also included. Settlement of cost-reimbursement contracts is somewhat simpler than that of fixed-price contracts, since you will have been reimbursed on a cost basis from the beginning of the contract.

You are entitled to recover all allowable costs incurred in settling a termination for convenience. Those costs may include the following:

- Preparation and presentation of claims

- Termination and settlement of subcontracts

- Storage, transportation, protection and disposition of property acquired or produced for the contract

- Other termination activities

The federal government retains the right to approve or ratify any settlements made with subcontractors. When you and the government agree to all or part of your claim for compensation as a result of the termination, a written amendment (known as a settlement agreement) is made to the contract.

Generally, termination halts regular payments to you under the contract. However, since you may have money tied up in finished and unfinished products, materials and labor, most termination clauses provide you with interim financing through partial payments.

Termination for Default

A termination for default (T for D) means that the government believes that you, the contractor, have not performed in accordance with the terms of the contract.

The government may terminate all or part of a contract for anything that was done that was not in the interest of the government, including:

- Attempted fraud

- Failure to meet quality requirements

- Failure to deliver the supplies or perform the services within the time specified in the contract

- Failure to make progress and that failure endangers performance of the contract

- Failure to perform any other provisions of the contract

Cure Notice

Before terminating a contract for default because of your failure to make progress or to perform, the contracting officer will usually give you a written notice, called a "cure notice." That notice allows you at least 10 days to cure any defects. Unless the failure to perform is cured within the 10 days, the contracting officer may issue a notice of termination for default.

Show-Cause Notice

If there is not sufficient time for a cure, the contracting officer will usually send a show-cause notice. That notice directs you to show why your contract should not be terminated for default. It ensures that you understand your predicament, and your answer can be used in evaluating whether circumstances justify default action.

Upon termination for default, you are entitled to payment on the contract only for items accepted by the government. *Under a default clause, the government has the right to repurchase the item elsewhere and charge any excess re-procurement costs to the contractor.*

Excusable Failure to Perform

If you can show that your failure to perform the contract is excusable, your contract cannot be terminated for default. To be excusable, the failure must be beyond your control and not caused by your fault or negligence.

Examples of excusable failure include:

- Acts of God

- Acts of a public enemy

- Acts of government

- Fires

- Floods

- Epidemics

- Quarantine restrictions

- Strikes

- Freight embargoes

- Unusually severe weather

Here is a happy thought! If, after termination, you are found not to be in default or the default is found to be excusable, the termination will be treated as one for the convenience of the government. This means that not only will you have removed the tarnished image that a T for D gives a contractor, but you will also get some of your money back as well!

YOUR RIGHT TO PROTEST AND DISPUTE

What if the contracting officer or buying agency makes a decision that you (the contractor) don't agree with or that you believe is incorrect? Government contracting regulations provide contractors with several remedies, all the way from filing a simple protest or dispute to taking the government to court.

To begin our discussion, we need to distinguish terminology. Under government contract law, you have the right to "protest" and also the right to "dispute." While these terms seem very similar and are often used interchangeably in everyday language, government contracting regulations treat them differently.

Generally speaking, these rules give you the right to "protest" a defective bid or the award of a contract to another bidder. They also give you the right to "dispute" an issue or disagreement with the contracting officer that arises after you have won and been awarded a contract. In addition, you may have other options as well.

Protesting a Bid or Award

By law, a protest must be filed by an "interested party," which means an actual or prospective bidder whose direct economic interest would be affected by the award of a contract or by the failure to award a contract. In challenges to the government's evaluation of proposals and the award of contracts, this generally means a bidder that would potentially be in line for award if the protest were sustained.

Although most protests challenge the acceptance or rejection of a bid or proposal, and the award or proposed award of a contract, defective solicitations or bids may also be the basis for a protest. Such bid defects include allegedly restrictive specifications, omission of a required provision, and ambiguous or indefinite evaluation factors. In addition, the termination of a contract may be protested if the protest alleges that the termination was based on improprieties in the award of the contract.

Therefore, in doing business with the government, you have a right to protest a bid or an award both before and after the award of a contract: You can protest the bid, you can protest an award, and you can protest termination of a contract.

Protest Procedures

Reflecting the government's goal to ensure effective and efficient expenditure of public funds, and fair and expeditious resolution of protests to a solicitation or award of federal procurement contracts, as well as reduce cases outside the agency, the regulations direct that, prior to submission of a protest to the contracting agency, all parties use their best efforts to resolve concerns with agency contracting officers through open and frank discussions.

In cases where concerns cannot be resolved at this level and a protest is submitted to the agency, the agency is directed to provide for inexpensive, informal, procedurally simple, and expeditious resolution of protests and to use, where appropriate, alternative dispute resolution techniques, third-party neutrals, or even another agency's personnel.

If a protest is received before the award of the contract, the contract will not be awarded, pending a decision on the protest, unless the items or services are urgently needed, delivery or the performance will be unduly delayed, or the prompt award will otherwise be in the best interests of the government. If the protest is received within 10 days after the contract was award, performance of the contract will be suspended, pending resolution of the protest. The contracting officer must notify all other eligible offerors of the protest especially when the award will be suspended pending resolution of the protest. If a protest is received 10 days after award of the contract, the individual agency procedures will determine how the protest will be handled. The contract performance might not be suspended or terminated in these cases unless it is likely that the award will be invalidated and the delay will not be prejudicial to the government's interest.

Although the regulations encourage companies wishing to protest to seek resolution within the contracting agency before filing a protest with the General Accountability Office (GAO), the regulations do allow the party to file with GAO for resolution.

Caution

If you decide to bypass the contracting officer and buying agency and file your protest directly with the GAO, keep in mind that this is the end of the line for your protest. The GAO's decision is final, and you cannot appeal it anywhere.

In addition to keeping your avenues of protest and appeal open, protesting to the contracting officer or contracting agency instead of directly to the GAO has other advantages. The company protesting can often gain additional time to gather more information that will assist it if it later protests to another forum.

Protests to GAO

There are some matters that cannot be protested to GAO. Among these are:

- *Contract administration* — The administration of an existing contract is within the discretion of the contracting agency. Disputes between a contractor and the agency are resolved pursuant to the disputes clause of the contract and the Contract Disputes Act of 1978. 41 U.S.C. 601-613. In the same vein, GAO will not make decisions relative to 8(a) awards to minority or socially and economically disadvantages firms unless there is a possibility of bad faith on the part of the government or violation of the regulations.

- *Small Business Administration issues* — Among these issues are challenges of small business size standards and standard industrial classification, and issues relative to 8(a) awards to minority or socially and economically disadvantages firms, unless there is a showing of possible bad faith on the part of government officials or violation of the regulations.

- *Affirmative determination of responsibility by the contracting officer* — A determination that a bidder is capable of performing a contract will not be reviewed unless there is a showing of possible bad faith on the part of government officials or that definitive responsibility criteria in the solicitation were not met.

- *Procurement integrity* — GAO will not review a protest for a procurement integrity violation unless the interested party has reported the information it believed constituted evidence of the offense to the contracting agency responsible for the procurement within 14 days after it first discovered the possible violation.

- *Protests not filed within the required time limits*

- *Protests that lack a detailed statement of the legal and factual grounds of protest or that fail to clearly state legally sufficient grounds of protest as required under the regulations*

- *Procurements by agencies not under the jurisdiction of the Federal Property and Administrative Services Act of 1949, 40 U.S.C. 472, such as the U.S. Postal Service and the Federal Deposit Insurance Corporation*

- *Subcontract protests* — GAO will not consider subcontractor issues unless the agency has agreed in writing and the award is made by or for the government, such as when a contractor acts as a purchasing agent for the government.

Although many parties retain an attorney in order to benefit from the attorney's familiarity with GAO's bid protest process and with procurement statutes and regulations, an attorney is not required for purposes of filing a protest. Under current regulations, if you win your protest, the contracting agency will pay your attorney's fees, but there is a cap (currently $150 per hour). If fees exceed that amount, you will have to show special circumstances to justify a higher amount.

A protest to GAO must be filed within 10 working days of the protestor's learning of the initial adverse agency action. The GAO can then take up to 60 days to respond. If there is an adverse decision by GAO, the contractor can file a Notice of Appeal, which can add another 90 days, or file suit in the Court of Federal Claims, which can take up to another 12 months. Appeal by either party to the Court of Appeals for the Federal Circuit can take another 60 to 120 days. All in all, it may take up to four years to get a hearing on claims over $50,000, although trial stage has been reached within two years in the Court of Federal Claims.

Protest or Not?

What's our conclusion about protesting? Think very carefully before you protest. In the past, some companies would protest every contract that they lost, which can create an adversarial relationship that can work against you on current or future contracts. If you are going to protest, you must have a "real" reason (vs. just sour grapes) and you must have evidence to back up your claim.

If you do decide to protest, it is probably best to get some advice before you do anything. Consult with your local PTAC to get started in the process and/or seek legal counsel. You also should familiarize yourself with all requirements and procedures as well as your rights under Part 33.1 of the FAR.

Disputing Contract Issues

Now we turn our attention to the matter of "disputes," which are very different from protests. As a government contractor, you have the right to "dispute" all material disagreements or issues in controversy that relate to a contract and to file a claim.

According to the regulations, a "claim" means a written demand or assertion by one of the contracting parties seeking, as a matter of right, the payment of money; the adjustment or interpretation of contract terms, including the period of performance; or other relief arising under or relating to the contract. A voucher, invoice, or other routine request for payment or equitable adjustment that is not in dispute when submitted is not considered a claim. The submission may be converted to a claim, by written notice to the contracting officer if it is disputed either as to liability or amount, or is not acted upon in a reasonable time.

Caution

Only a contractor, as a party to a federal government contract, is allowed to file a dispute claim. This intentionally excludes a subcontractor from being able to enter into the disputes process.

What kinds of issues do contractors typically dispute? Contractors dispute any number of things, including defective specifications, changing delivery dates, failure by the government to supply a contractor with what he/she needs to fulfill a contract, or any other "event" that would keep a contractor from completing the contract or from being able to perform the contract. The dispute is triggered when one of these events occurs and all informal attempts to resolve the issue fail.

Dispute Procedures

A contractor who wants to dispute an action or issue is required to submit the claim in writing to the contracting officer. In it, the contractor should describe the situation, state what action it is asking for, and request a final decision. After the contracting officer receives the contractor's written notice, he/she will have up to 60 days to respond. If the contractor does not hear from the contracting officer within that 60-day period, the contractor may consider its request denied.

If the contracting officer denies the action, the contractor can file a written "Notice of Appeal" with the Contracts Appeals Board and send a copy to the contracting officer. The contractor has only 90 days to do this.

Caution

If your claim is denied by the Contracting Officer and you decide to pursue your claim with the Contracts Appeals Board, carefully consider all the facts and document everything. Do not try to overstate or exaggerate the facts to win your case. If you are found to have misrepresented a fact with intent to deceive or mislead, your claim will be found to be fraudulent and you might have to pay a civil penalty. Whatever else happens, your days of doing business with the government will be over forever.

If the contracting officer denies your action, you also have the option of applying directly to the Court of Federal Claims instead of going through the Notice of Appeal process. This court is authorized by the Contracts Disputes Act to hear and decide an appeal of a contracting officer's final decision, but it can take up to a year before you receive a decision.

One major consideration is time. Claims under $100,000 tend to move through the system faster then a claim over that amount. This is because the Board of Contract Appeals is mandated to make a decision within 60 to 120 days, respectively. The smaller claims will take priority and the board will postpone an appeal concerning a larger dollar contract. The Court of Federal Claims could take up to a year or more just to reach the trial stage. If the dollar amount of the contract is large enough, the dispute could conceivably go to the U.S. Supreme Court.

Work Smart

If you decide to go through the dispute process, you can probably do most of the work yourself in the early stages if you read the FAR, follow the rules, and/or get help from a PTAC. However, if your claim is denied by the Contracting Officer and you want to appeal the adverse decision, you will need legal assistance in these later appeals. For information, check out http://www.gao.gov/decisions/bidpro/new.reg/regulation.htm.

Conflict Resolution: Other Options

While we want to let you know about your right to dispute and appeal, we also want to make you aware that the government's stated policy is to try to resolve all contractual issues in controversy by mutual agreement at the contracting officer's level. Government rules state that reasonable efforts should be made to resolve controversies, prior to the submission of a claim. And where appropriate, agencies are encouraged to use ADR procedures to the maximum extent.

Traditionally, contracting parties have relied on claims and litigation to resolve disputes. In the interest of economy and efficiency and achieving a "win/win" situation for both agencies and contractors, less confrontational resolution procedures are being utilized more and more often. Communication and openness throughout the procurement process greatly reduce conflicts. The Office of Federal Procurement Policy has recognized the value of such procedures by including an agency commitment to institute an informal, timely conflict resolution mechanism for resolving pre- and post-award issues. Here are three techniques that are being used.

Partnering

This is a technique for preventing disputes from occurring. Under this concept, the agency and contractor, perhaps along with a facilitator, meet after a contract is awarded to discuss their mutual expectations. The parties mutually develop performance goals, identify potential sources of conflict, and establish cooperative ways to resolve any problems that may arise during contract performance.

Creating a partnership agreement signed by all parties (i.e., contracting officer, quality assurance evaluator, program office, and contractor) creates a "buy in" to the overall goal of satisfactory performance on time, within budget, and without claims.

Both contractors and contracting agencies, including DOD's Army Corps of Engineers, that have participated in partnering have experienced positive results: more timely performance, better cost control, significant reductions in paperwork, professional vs. adversarial relationship/attitude, and fewer disputes.

Ombudsman

This procedure can be used at any stage of the contracting process. Some agencies have established an ombudsman to help resolve concerns or disputes that arise during the acquisition process. Typically, an ombudsman investigates selected complaints and issues nonbinding reports, with recommendations addressing problems and future improvements.

The Army Materiel Command (AMC), including all of the subordinate AMC buying commands, has an agency ombudsman that helps companies resolve problems they encounter on existing AMC contracts. The ombudsman, which can cut through any government "red tape," investigates reported complaints or requests for assistance from business/industry and ensures that proper action is taken.

The AMC-wide ombudsman program has been a positive force in the timely resolution of problems presented by contractors. It results in the solution of most problems presented without the need for expensive and time-consuming litigation.

NASA also established an ombudsman program to improve communication between the agency and interested parties. The NASA ombudsman hears and works to resolve concerns from actual and potential offerors, as well as contractors, during the pre- and post-award acquisition phases.

Alternative Dispute Resolution (ADR)

This means any procedure, or combination of procedures, used voluntarily to resolve controversies without resorting to litigation. Examples of ADR include conciliation, facilitation, mediation, and mini-trials.

ADR can provide an effective and less expensive method for resolving contract disputes, and many agencies include an agreement to utilize ADR in their contracts.

The Navy, which has used ADR techniques since 1982, has been able to resolve issues and controversies in almost 99 percent of the cases in which ADR was used. Recently, the Navy used ADR to resolve a $1.1 million dispute. The hearing on this matter was completed within six hours, and a decision was rendered the next day.

There is no single correct method for conducting ADR. Each situation is different, and the ADR technique and procedures must be tailored to a particular situation and the needs of the parties.

Case Study: From Dispute to Court Action

For a deeper understanding of the complete disputes process, we provide a description of a protest undertaken by a company under a solicitation issued by a contracting agency, in this case the United States Army's Tank-automotive and Armaments Command (TACOM), a contracting agency for the United States Army.

This study will not only present the facts of what occurred in this particular protest, but will also include the reasoning why the company chose the venue it did.

A protesting company may choose one of three venues in which to pursue its dispute with the contracting agency. In this case, the company chose an "agency" protest, for reasons discussed below. An agency protest is a protest filed with the same agency that issued the solicitation or contract. In choosing to file an agency protest, the company had to follow the procedural guidelines set forth by the agency unit that handled the protest on behalf of the Army, which in this case was Headquarters, Army Material Command (AMC) in Washington, D.C. The company also had to follow the Federal Acquisition Regulations (FAR).

Background

The protesting company is a mid-sized machine and tool shop that has been working for the Department of Defense and other private-industry customers for many years. The subject device of this protest was a part for a military vehicle, and the company was the exclusive supplier to TACOM for a number of years because of price and quality. Therefore, for years, the company became very familiar with the solicitation, bidding, and performance routines under government procurement agency contracts.

The supply network for the particular part is as follows: The castings were procured from overseas providers. Once received in the United States, the castings were then sent to subcontractors to be machined and painted. One of the sub-component parts of this device was procured from a vendor in the Ohio. The final assembly work and shipment to the Army's depots was accomplished from the company's facility in Illinois.

Although the part was not necessarily a sophisticated part piece of hardware, the solicitation, bidding, and performance time frames would span over a year's time. This particular part was located on the exterior of a military vehicle and was subject to wear. Therefore, the Army had to have a constant supply of these parts in their depots and in the field. The part performed a critical function on this vehicle and therefore the contract was "DX" rated. "DX"-rated contracts are for supplies and materials the Army needs in time of national crisis. Although the DX rating was canceled several years ago, it is still being used by buying agencies.

The contracting cycle worked as follows: At the same time the company was supplying the same part under a pre-existing contract, the contracting office (TACOM) in Warren, Michigan would release a solicitation to prospective bidders for the next series of parts it needed. The company would respond to that solicitation and, upon contract award, would begin the engineering, pre-production planning, and procurement process. Therefore, at the approximate time that the pre-existing contract terminated and all parts from that contract had been delivered, the new contract was in place and the company would continue to supply the part under a new contract. The contract term for this part was for three years.

The subject solicitation that caused all the trouble was released by TACOM in the normal fashion. The company responded to the solicitation, but was denied the contract. After consulting with the local PTAC (Procurement Technical Assistance Center) representative, the law firm was immediately contacted, and a review of the solicitation and award proceeded.

Being that this was a negotiated solicitation, the Contracting Office made its decision based upon price and past performance, with price being slightly more important that past performance, as set forth in the solicitation. The Contracting Office had a rating system to help it categorize the performance capabilities of bidders. When the company received notice that it had not won the award, after a quick analysis of the situation, it found it disagreed with the Contracting Office's rating relative to the company's past performance and price. It also disagreed with the rating the awardee company received. Rather than just fire off a letter to the Army complaining about what happened, the company decided to take another route.

Post-Award Debriefing of Offerors

The company determined that it was important to find out more about the decision-making process of the Contracting Office. The FAR provides for this option under section 15.506, Postaward Debriefing of Offerors.

a.

1. An Offeror, upon its written request received by the agency within three days after the date on which that Offeror has received notification of contract award in accordance with 15.503(b), shall be debriefed and furnished the basis for the selection decision and contract award.

2. To the maximum extent practicable, the briefing should occur within five days after receipt of the written request.

b. Debriefings of successful and unsuccessful Offerors may be done orally, in writing, or by any other method acceptable to the contracting officer.

c. The contracting officer should normally chair any debriefing session held. Individuals who conducted the evaluations shall provide support.

d. At a minimum, the debriefing information shall include:

1. The Governments evaluation of the significant weaknesses or deficiencies in the Offeror's proposal, if applicable;

2. The overall evaluated cost or price (including unit prices) and technical rating, if applicable, of the successful Offeror and the Debriefed Offeror, and past performance information on the Debriefed Offeror;

3. The overall ranking of all Offerors, when any ranking was developed by the agency during the source selection;

4. A summary of the rational for award;

5. Reasonable responses to relevant questions about whether source selection procedures contained in the solicitation, applicable regulations, and other applicable authorities were followed.

e. The Debriefing shall not include point-by-point comparisons of the Debriefed Offeror's proposal with those of other Offerors. The outcome of the debriefing shall not reveal any information prohibited from disclosure or exempt from release under the Freedom of Information Act***

Within the three day period, the company e-mailed the Contracting Office requesting a post-award debriefing. The Contracting Office responded and a date for a telephonic debriefing was set for the fifth (business) day after the request had been made.

Because the FAR did not detail any procedures beyond those set forth above, the company checked with the Contracting Office to see if it had its own procedural guidelines explaining how it would conduct the postaward debriefing. (Although postaward debriefings are informal, the company didn't want to drop the ball on any procedural rules.) TACOM complied and e-mailed an outline of how they were going to proceed through the debriefing.

1. *Participants*

2. *Ground rules*

3. *What cannot be discussed*

4. *Source selection authority*

5. *Evaluation procedures — In this part of its outline, TACOM explained how it evaluated the company's past performance and price under prior contracts for the same article; it also said it would assess the risk of each offeror and proposal and assign a rating to each offeror*

6. *Other pertinent information and an opportunity for feedback*

The outline further said that the participants for the Government in the debriefing would be the Contracting Officer, Contracting Specialist, and an attorney for TACOM. The outline included ground rules:

1. *To instill confidence in the offeror that it was fairly treated*

2. *To assure the offeror that its proposal was evaluated in accordance with the solicitation and applicable laws and regulations*

3. *To give the offeror an opportunity to provide feedback regarding the evaluation of the solicitation*

The ground rules went on to state that the debriefing is not a debate or defense of the Government's award decision or evaluation results. The document further warned that if the company intended to debate TACOM's decision, the debriefing would be terminated. Finally, any discussion of proposals submitted by the competition would be disallowed.

The company and TACOM conducted their post-award telephonic debriefing. The company's concern centered on whether the awardee had recent, relevant contracts, and thus had sufficient demonstrative past performance upon which the Agency could determine that the awardee would be a better supplier than the incumbent company. Because the company could not ask questions about how TACOM rated the competition, it was only able to inquire about the rating it received.

After the debriefing, the company's management huddled with its attorney. With information from the session with the Contracting Office, and with knowledge of other facts, the company decided to file a protest. But it had only ten days in which to determine in which venue to file its protest and to prepare the protest document.

Venue for Filing Protest

The company had three choices of venues in which to file its protest. One option was to file in Federal District Court, but that option was discarded because of the lengthy time frames and expenses involved.

The second option was to file with the General Accounting Office (GAO). For many years the GAO has provided a forum for dispute resolution concerning federal contract awards. A body of law has developed from decisions of the Comptroller General of the United States, upon which protestors may rely to shape arguments for their own protests.

The Office of General Counsel, in publication GAO\OGC-96-24, published a descriptive guide for bid protest at GAO. This is an informative set of materials on which a protestor may partially rely if it chooses the GAO venue. However, being merely a guide, the protestor would have to refer to the GAO bid protest regulations that, of course, are far more detailed and are the law concerning where and how to file a protest. Since the GAO does change its regulations from time to time, protestors should check the Federal Register and the Code of Federal Regulations (Title 4 of the Code of Federal Regulations) (C.F.R., Part 21). Even though the GAO bid protest descriptive guide states that an attorney is not necessary when filing a protest within the GAO venue, there are many procedural requirements that, if not followed precisely, could foreclose a protestor from proceeding with its protest.

The company also looked at filing a protest within the agency itself. The Army Material Command does have a protest program and publishes its program procedures at www.amc.army.mil\amc\cc\protest.html. The company reviewed the AMC program and it did other research relative to whether this venue would meet its needs. In comparing the agency-level versus the GAO protest, the company determined to proceed with the agency-level protest. Its reasoning was that the agency-level protest was significantly less complex in its procedures and requirements. In reviewing the AMC protest program procedures, the company determined that it would likely receive fair and expedited treatment in this venue. Going with an agency-level protest would also be less expensive. Not only does the FAR itself suggest agency-level protests, Executive Order 12979 encourages agency-level protests and other alternative dispute resolution options instead of using the GAO as the protest forum. But GAO or federal district court may make more sense under different circumstances.

Part 33 of FAR is where the protest process is explained. In Section 33.103, it instructs agencies to set up "inexpensive, informal, procedurally simple, and expeditious resolution of protests."

AMC established protest procedures that required the following to be included in the protest documents:

1. *protestor's identity and contact information*

2. *solicitation contract number and identity of the contracting activity and contracting officers names*

3. *a detailed statement of all legal and factual grounds for protest, with the warning that a protestor's mere disagreement with the decisions of the contracting officer does not constitute grounds for protest*

4. *copies of all relevant documents*

5. *request for ruling and request for relief*

Since the company had only ten days after the debriefing to file its protest, it began immediately to prepare its protest under the rules of the AMC agency-level protest guidelines.

Preparation of Protest

Before the company sent its protest to AMC, it filed a Freedom Of Information Act (FOIA) request with TACOM for documents, because it felt there was more information available to it with which it could further develop its arguments. Because FOIA responses did not have to be replied to before twenty days after the agency received the request, the company knew it would not have the documents in time to meet the ten-day filing deadline of the protest. So when the company filed the protest, which it did within the ten-day deadline, it also notified AMC that it may file supplemental protest documents. Being an informal protest process, AMC granted an extension, and waited for the further information.

While it was waiting, AMC sent the company's protest to TACOM, which, by AMC procedures, had to provide an Administrative Report back to AMC. But the company did not have the chance to see TACOM's report to AMC. (This is one thing the company gave up when it decided to go with an agency-level protest. The GAO protest format allows this, but it takes longer to get a decision back. Plus, the company believed it could meet its burden of proof without the need to contradict TACOM's report.) Also interesting is that the awardee in such situations can get a copy of the protest documents, albeit in redacted form. Although the awardee may file papers of its own in support of the decision of the Contracting Office, the awardee in this case chose not to do so in this case, ostensibly preferring to stay on the sidelines.

The company's protest filing was based on a dispute it had with the Contracting Office's determination that the awardee's past performance and relevant experience justified a better rating than the incumbent; further, the company disagreed with the Contracting Office's assessment that the incumbent company had a less than favorable rating. The solicitation said the contract would be given to the company that had the best past performance.

To support its argument that the awardee did not deserve the favorable rating it received, the company performed research on government web sites. The company was able to show that although the awardee had, years before, produced the same part, the quantities were small and its contract was never renewed. (The protesting company had received all subsequent awards for this part following awardee's end of performance on that old contract). Awardee had little else in recent or relevant contracts with the government or private sector, and the company highlighted that fact in its protest.

Basing its argument on facts and the solicitation's guidelines, the company argued that the Contracting Office erred in assigning a favorable rating to the awardee, where there was scant past performance history to evaluate.

The second component of the company's protest consisted of a detailed analysis of its past performance on prior contracts for the same part. Some initial deliveries of the part to the Army depots had been late, and the company knew those late deliveries were counted against it when TACOM evaluated its past performance. Not only were the delays explained, but they argued they were aggressive in meeting and exceeding delivery schedules.

As an example, although this company had been making these parts for many years, the contract solicitation required a first article test (FAT). The company requested that the Government waive that FAT requirement or perform a FAT on parts that were already in production or on pieces produced in earlier runs. The company argued that had this FAT been waived, there would have been no delay on that particular contract.

Coincidentally, at about the same time the company received its denial on this contract, the same contracting agency let contracts to the company for other parts for this same vehicle. The company then questioned whether or not the evaluation criteria used by the agency had changed from one contract to another, when the solicitation criteria for the different parts were essentially the same.

Supplemental Protest

The agency-level protest is flexible and allows for extensions and the filing of supplemental pleadings. In this case, because the company had not received the FOIA responses in time for the deadline in which to file the initial protest, the company was allowed to file a supplemental protest.

When it received the FOIA response, the company felt it had another argument that should be developed in the supplemental protest. The gist of its argument in the supplemental protest is that the agency may not have treated offerors equally during the evaluation process. This situation presented the company with a strategic decision, that being whether to delve into the area of bias. Company management thought long and hard about this, because it didn't want its relationship with a good customer, TACOM, to be affected.

The company knew also that once it ventured into alleging bias, it would be dealing with a body of federal case law where the burden of proof is difficult to meet. The burden of proof a protestor must meet to succeed in its allegation of bias is stated as follows:

"we will not attribute bias in the evaluation of proposals on the basis of inference and supposition without strong evidence to support such a conclusion, we will not assume that Agency employees acted in bad faith. Furthermore, in addition to producing credible evidence showing bias, the protestor must demonstrate that the Agency bias translated into action which unfairly affected the protestor's competitive position." *(Comptroller General decisions from GAO protests).*

However, because of the importance of this contract to the company and because of its long-standing history as a quality supplier of parts to the military, the decision was made to proceed with the supplemental protest.

The solicitation in question did require a FAT. The FOIA response contained e-mails between TACOM and the awardee, which showed that the awardee convinced the agency to waive the FAT, even though the awardee hadn't made the part in over seven years. The result of receiving such a waiver allowed the awardee to significantly improve upon its delivery schedule.

As stated before, in one of the prior contracts for the same part under which the company was performing, the TACOM refused to waive the first article test. The result of that denial of the FAT to the company created a slight delay in performance.

The agency reviews past performance on similar relevant contracts and assigns a risk rating to an offeror. Of course, the agency downgraded the company's rating for past performance because of the delay. But the company argued the delay in delivery was caused by the agency's own refusal to waive the FAT. From that, the company argued that it was receiving disparate treatment by the agency, especially since the agency waived the FAT for the awardee.

Because federal case law says "the protestor must demonstrate that the Agency bias translated into action which unfairly affected the protestor's competitive position," the company had to argue the connection between the agency's conduct and the loss of the contract. In its protest, the company said it not only lost this particular contract but that the company's future opportunities to supply parts to this Agency were negatively affected.

The AMC protest procedure guidelines require a request for relief and the company complied. Relief can be asked for in the alternative, such as the following:

1. *Terminate the subject awarded contract to the awardee*

2. *Award the contract to the company*

3. *Re-compete the contract*

4. *Issue a new solicitation*

5. *Provide the company with additional or alternative relief that the Agency deemed appropriate*

This type of request for relief pretty much leaves it up to the agency attorneys to decide what to do, if they find that the protestor deserves relief.

Result

Although the company did win this protest, its relief was not complete because, in the company's opinion, the agency struck a compromise. This particular solicitation allowed the agency to award the single contract to two sources. Therefore, the form of relief chosen by AMC attorneys was to modify the contract it originally awarded solely to awardee. The contract was modified so the company would produce half of the items and the awardee would produce the other half. The Army came out a winner because it now has two suppliers of that same part, guaranteeing future competition.

Although the company could have pressed the issue forward and tried to recover the entirety of the contract (believing that it had strong enough arguments to do so), it took that result as a victory. It could have decided to file a protest with the GAO (expensive and time-consuming) or in federal court (even worse).

In conclusion, the company was satisfied with its result and felt that its decision to proceed with an agency-level protest was the right decision. AMC has a number of attorneys tasked to handle such protests, some with many years of experience. The company felt it received fair treatment by AMC protest attorneys. The company was able to successfully prosecute this protest without the expense of sending representatives to hearings in Washington, D.C.; this protest was handled by telephone, e-mail, and facsimile.

Chapter **18**

Getting Paid

Now we turn to every business owner's favorite topic: getting paid. After you have delivered, and the government has accepted, the contracted product or service, all you have to do is submit a proper invoice to the billing office specified in your contract. Under law, the government is required to pay you within 30 days.

Caution

For all of the conditions and requirements for payment, refer to Federal Acquisition Regulation (FAR) 52.232-25.

PROMPT PAYMENT AND A "PROPER" INVOICE

The Prompt Payment Act, which was enacted in the mid-'80s, requires the government to pay a small business within 30 days after receipt of the invoice, if the business completes its end of the contract. However, as you might expect, there is an important catch. The clock on this Act starts only if your invoice, as received, is deemed "proper" under the law.

If your invoice is not deemed "proper," it will get sent back to you within seven days after the billing office received it, with a statement of the reasons why it is not considered proper. You will then have to correct it, resubmit it to the government, and restart the 30-day wait. Therefore, "prompt payment" by the government is directly tied to the "properness" of your invoice.

To make sure that your invoice is correct and proper the first time around, include the following items:

- The name and address of your company.

- Invoice date. You are encouraged to date invoices as close as possible to the date of mailing or transmitting the invoice.

- Contract number or other authorization for supplies delivered or services performed. Be sure to also include the order number and contract line item number.

- Description, quantity, unit of measure, unit price and extended price of supplies delivered or services performed.

- Shipping and payment terms, such as shipment number and date of shipment, prompt payment discount terms, etc. Bill of lading number and weight of shipment will be shown for shipments on government bills of lading.

- The name and address of the person at your company to whom payment is to be sent. This must be the same person specified in the contract or in a proper notice of assignment.

- Name, title, phone number and mailing address of the person to be notified in the event of a defective invoice.

- Any other information or documentation required by the contract, such as evidence of shipment.

- While not required, you are strongly encouraged to assign an identification number to each invoice.

In addition, your invoice may be deemed not proper, for purposes of prompt payment, if the information you furnished in the CCR (Central Contractor Registration) database regarding EFT (electronic funds transfer) is incorrect or not current. (For details on CCR, see Chapter 7: Get Registered.)

INTEREST PENALTY

The law requires the government to pay a small business within 30 days after receipt of a proper invoice. Payment is considered as being made on the day a check is dated or on the date of an electronic funds transfer. An interest penalty will automatically be paid to the contractor if payment is not made by the due date and if the following conditions are met:

- A proper invoice was received by the designated billing office.

- A receiving report or other government documentation authorizing payment was processed, and there was no disagreement over quantity, quality or compliance by the contractor with any contract term or condition.

- The amount due was not subject to further contract settlement actions between the government and the contractor.

GOVERNMENT INVOICE FORM

You may use your own invoice to bill the government, but you must make sure that it meets all of the requirements previously discussed. If it doesn't, you will only slow up payment. Sometimes you might find it easier to use a government form. One common form that is used with military contracts is the DD Form 250, *Material Inspection and Receiving Report* (see the Appendices for a copy of the form.

The DD Form 250 is basically a material inspection and receiving report (MIRR) that can be used by the government to document contract compliance and by the contractor to submit an invoice. The contractor is responsible for preparing the MIRR, except for entries that an authorized government representative is required to complete. You should contact the office that is administering your contract to get specific help with this form. The appropriate office is identified in the contract. A handy guide for contractors now is available at http://www.dfas.mil/index.htm, in the "Commercial Pay" section.

Specifically, this multi-purpose report is used for the following:

- Evidence of government contract quality assurance at origin or destination

- Evidence of acceptance at origin or destination

- Packing lists

- Receiving

- Shipping

- Contractor invoice

- Commercial invoice support

Work Smart

The DD Form 250 applies to supplies or services acquired by the Department of Defense when the clause at DFARS 252.246-7000, Material Inspection and Receiving Report, is included in the contract.

Subcontractors do not use the DD Form 250 for shipments to their primes unless specified in their subcontract.

ELECTRONIC FUNDS TRANSFER

It is now government policy to pay all contractors by EFT, electronic funds transfer, whenever feasible. In making EFT payments, the government uses the information contained in the Central Contractor Registration (CCR) database.

This policy underscores the need to get your company registered in the CCR database, and to make sure that the information that you have entered is correct and current (for details, see Chapter 7: Get Registered in Part II). If the EFT information in the CCR database is incorrect, then the government may suspend payment until correct information is entered. Remember that if your EFT information changes, *you* are responsible for seeing that the information in the CCR database is updated.

If you have more than one remittance address and/or EFT information set in the CCR database, you must remember to notify the government of the payment receiving point applicable to the contract you are working on. Otherwise, the government will automatically make payment to the first address.

If an incomplete or erroneous transfer occurs because the government used a contractor's EFT information incorrectly, the government is responsible for making a correct payment, paying any prompt payment penalty and recovering any erroneously directed funds.

The government has two mechanisms for making EFT payment: the Automated Clearing House (ACH) network or the Fedwire Transfer System. If the government is unable to release one or more payments by EFT, you will be paid by check or some other mutually agreeable method of payment, or you may request the government to extend the payment due date until such time as the government can make payment by EFT.

Under certain specific circumstances, payment by electronic funds transfer may be made through other than the CCR database. In this case, the contractor will be required to provide the EFT information directly to the office(s) and by the date designated in the contract. And, again, if the EFT information changes, the contractor is responsible for providing the updated information to the designated office(s).

The EFT information that the contractor must provide to the designated office(s) includes:

- The contract number (or other procurement identification number).

- The contractor's name and remittance address, as stated in the contract(s).

- The signature (manual or electronic, as appropriate), title, and telephone number of the contractor official authorized to provide this information.

- The name, address, and 9-digit Routing Transit Number of the contractor's financial agent.

- The contractor's account number and the type of account (checking, saving or lockbox).

- If applicable, the Fedwire Transfer System telegraphic abbreviation of the contractor's financial agent.

Caution

All government requirements pertaining to electronic funds transfer are spelled out in the Federal Acquisition Regulation (FAR 32.1110 and FAR 52.232-33 and –34). Any language that you will see in a bid or contract related to EFT consists of clauses extracted from these sections.

Note that the government is required to protect against improper disclosure of all contractors' EFT information.

EFT Includes Government Credit Card

Under recent legislative requirements, the term "electronic funds transfer" now includes a government-wide commercial purchase card. Under the law, the government purchase may be used as a means to meet the requirement to pay by EFT.

A government-wide commercial purchase card is similar in nature to a commercial credit card and is used by the government to make financing and delivery payments for supplies and services. A government purchase card charge authorizes the third party (e.g., financial institution) that issued the purchase card to make immediate payment to the contractor.

The contract will identify the third party and the particular purchase card to be used, but will not include the purchase card account number. The purchase card account number is provided separately to the contractor.

The provisions related to EFT payment will be specified in your contract. Complete details on electronic funds transfer are included in FAR 32.1110 and FAR 52.232-33 and -34.

Part IV

Who Will Help Me?

Firms, both large and small, interested in doing business with the federal government must help themselves by learning how the federal government conducts its business and by identifying and seeking out those purchasing offices that buy the products and services they can supply.

However, additional help and advice are available to you as you work through this maze called government contracting. In this Part, we will describe the general areas from which you can get assistance as you go through the contracting process:

- Directly from the government

- From government-sponsored and commercial counseling services

- From professional associations

Each one has its strengths and weaknesses. Depending on your situation and circumstances, you will have to determine which one or which combination works best for you.

We also describe another area of assistance that is available to you: the special federal programs and initiatives designed to benefit small businesses.

Chapter 19, Help from the Government: The government stands ready to help you during the contracting process. Learn about the different types of small business specialists that have been hired to work with, and advocate for, small businesses during the contracting process. We also tell you which government web sites and publications are most helpful for small businesses and where to find out about procurement conferences, which provide a great way to network with government buyers and large prime contractors.

Chapter 20, Help from Counseling Services: Personalized assistance and advice are available to you through both government-sponsored and commercial counseling services and from professional associations. We explain the services they offer and tell you how to find them.

Chapter 21, Special Small Business Programs: There are several federal programs that are designed to encourage participation by small businesses in the government contracting process, including small businesses owned by certain minority and disadvantaged groups. Find out what benefits they offer and what you need to do to qualify.

Chapter 19

Help from the Government

There are several ways in which the federal government tries to assist you in finding opportunities and doing business with it:

- Government web sites

- Specialized government personnel

- Government procurement conferences

- Government publications

GOVERNMENT WEB SITES

The federal government has more than 4,300 web sites, according to a recent GAO report. Fortunately, if you're looking for contract opportunities, you don't have to cover all of those sites.

In order to help companies identify government opportunities and buyers, the government is making a strong effort to reduce the number of locations and to create a more uniform format to simplify the process. The government is looking to establish "gateways" (i.e., web sites with multiple links) to make your search easier. There are several already in existence that are being used more and more to post and find opportunities.

Following is a list of the better ones (as of the time this book went to press). Remember that these sites will help you find the opportunities, but once you do, you—not the government—will have to do the work.

- **FedBizOpps (Federal Business Opportunities)** — All

government procurement opportunities of $25,000 or more are posted here. Here, government buyers are able to publicize their business opportunities by posting information directly to FedBizOpps via the Internet, and commercial companies looking to do business with the government are able to search, monitor, and retrieve opportunities solicited by the entire federal contracting community. (http://www.FedBizOpps.gov)

- **Small Business Administration (SBA)** — This site has a wide range of information pertaining to small businesses as well as SBA-*Net*, a gateway to resources, opportunities, and networking. Most importantly, it has a direct connect to PRO-*Net*, which is fast becoming the sole database used by government buyers to locate potential small business contractors. (http://www.sba.gov)

- **Procurement Gateway** — This is the Defense Logistics Agency site for all opportunities from its buying offices. (http://progate.daps.dla.mil)

- **Federal Acquisition Jumpstation** — Although not a place where opportunities are posted, it has most links to the federal sites that small business owners would have an interest in. (http://prod.nais.nasa.gov/pub/fedproc/home.html)

SPECIALIZED GOVERNMENT PERSONNEL

There are several types of government employees whose main job is to help you do business with the government.

- **Small Business Specialists (SBS)** — By law, every government buying location must have a Small Business Specialist to work with small businesses trying to do business with that office. Major government buying offices have a full-time staff, while smaller offices have a part-time person assigned to that task. These specialists can be a valuable resource for you on the inside. Get to know them.

- **Competition Advocate** — This individual is assigned at a high management level at major buying offices and is responsible for promoting the acquisition of commercial items and for promoting full and open competition. To that end, Competition Advocates challenge barriers to the acquisition of commercial items and to full and open competition, such as unnecessarily restrictive statements of work, unnecessarily detailed specifications, and unnecessarily burdensome contract clauses. They also look at requirements for a specific item to see what can be done to expand competition for the item, challenging any requirements that are not stated in terms of required performance or essential physical characteristics.

- **SBA Procurement Center Representative (PCR)** — Procurement Center Representatives work for the Small Business Administration, but are often located at a major government buying office. Their job is to identify items and services that could be produced or provided by small businesses and try to get them "set aside" for small businesses (i.e., only small businesses can bid on them). If the buying office is small, the PCR may work out of an SBA District office and travel to the buying office.

- **SBA Commercial Marketing Representative (CMR)** — Commercial Marketing Representatives monitor the performance of large companies under their large government contracts and can help you get subcontract work from large prime contractors.

PROCUREMENT CONFERENCES

The government, as well as other non-government sponsors, hold conferences to help you in your quest. Procurement conferences are a good way to meet and speak with government buyers and large prime contractors. Some areas of the country have several conferences per year; other parts have only a few.

Usually you won't get a contract at one, but you can make valuable contacts. The "FedBizOpps News" area of the FedBizOpps web site will often announce these events and tell you whom to contact. Other government web sites post these conferences on their calendars as well. You also can learn about upcoming conferences and events from your local PTAC.

GOVERNMENT PUBLICATIONS

The government issues a large number of publications to assist small businesses, but we're only going to mention the most useful ones. You can order these from the Government Printing Office for a fee or you can go to a government web site and read or print it. If you go to a web site, try looking under "publications" or "helps" to see what they have to offer.

- *Selling to the Military* — This publication covers general information about items purchased by the military. It also gives locations of the buying offices and a phone number for the Small Business Office. You can download this publication by going to http://www.acq.osd.mil/sadbu/publications/selling.

- *Small Business Specialists for DoD* — Here is a listing of names, addresses, and phone numbers for all the resources you need to do business with the Department of Defense. See above for web address.

- *Doing Business with the General Services Administration* — This publication covers general information about items purchased by GSA and tells you where the buying offices are located. To get this publication, log onto the web site http://www.pueblo.gsa.gov/cic_text/smbuss/business-gsa/business-gsa.pdf. This site has other interesting information as well. Take some time to browse it.

- *Participating in VA Acquisition Program* — Here is a fact sheet that covers general information about how and what the Veterans Administration buys. Check it out at http://www.va.gov/OSDBU/factsheets/participate.htm.

Chapter 20

Help from Counseling Services

If you need more personalized, ongoing assistance and advice, you can get it through government-sponsored or commercial counseling services. You can also get answers to questions and problems your business may be facing by joining a professional association.

PROCUREMENT TECHNICAL ASSISTANCE CENTERS

The Procurement Technical Assistance Program started in 1985 to help the Department of Defense place contracts in areas of the country that needed an influx of federal dollars. Although it has never been called an economic development program, it works like one to some extent.

Through cooperative agreements, the federal government enters into a cost-sharing arrangement with a state or local government or not-for-profit organization to provide general counseling services to businesses seeking government contracts. Its original purpose was only to help with military contracting and with areas of high unemployment, but over the years it has expanded to provide assistance to businesses wanting to do or doing business at the federal, state or local level.

It is a well-run and very cost-effective program with counselors with a high level of expertise. The Procurement Technical Assistance Center (PTAC) will help you identify contractual opportunities with the government; help locate potential marketing opportunities; help prepare proposals, financial, and contractual forms; and provide guidance with regard to quality assurance, production, and/or the resolution of engineering, financial, quality or production problems. It will also provide you with assistance on e-commerce issues.

While most services are free, some PTACs may charge a nominal fee for certain services such as electronic bid matching or for getting copies of specifications and standards. You can contact one of the regional directors at the Association of Procurement Technical Assistance Centers at http://www.aptac-us.org, and the director will put you in contact with the appropriate local center. In addition, the web sites www.sellingtothegovernment.net, www.wingovcon.com and www.ilflexnet.com could help you to locate a PTAC near you. PTAC's are the lead information source for RFID/UID and WAWF.

COMMERCIAL COUNSELING SERVICES

Hiring a private commercial counseling service is another way to get help in doing business with the government. The good ones can offer great personalized assistance, but will cost you some kind of money, flat fee, percentage of contract, retainer plus costs, or some combination.

If you decide to use this method, try to find a service that is accustomed to working with small companies. And remember: Buyer beware. If a service tells you that it can guarantee you contracts, keep looking. Check references and talk to some of the government people that the service has worked with.

You can find a commercial counseling service through word of mouth or by searching on the Internet. Sometimes a Small Business Specialist will be able to recommend a good one.

NATIONAL CONTRACTS MANAGEMENT ASSOCIATION

The National Contracts Management Association (NCMA) is a government-supported organization that was started years ago (1959) because of the lack of good help for companies doing business with the federal government.

Over the years, it has grown in numbers and effectiveness. It is recognized for its member certification program, educational seminars, and monthly magazine, "Contract Management," which alone is worth the price of membership. The new membership fee is about $120; the annual renewal fee thereafter is about $100.

Membership also entitles you access to its members-only site on the Internet, where you can get answers and advice on contract-related questions and problems, read and download "Contract Management" magazine articles all the way back to January 1980, and get a list of web sites that are helpful to contractors.

Besides the national organization, there are local chapters in many parts of the country. To find out more about the organization, visit its web site at http://www.ncmahq.org.

Chapter 21

Special Small Business Programs

Traditionally, the government has used the federal acquisition process as a tool to implement and further its programs and initiatives for social and economic change, and this trend continues.

There are several important initiatives that are intended to benefit businesses, particularly small business. These programs, which include incentive, set-aside, and preference programs, give small businesses and small businesses owned by special minority and disadvantaged groups advantages in bidding on federal contracts. Following are some of the more important federal programs that are designed to benefit small businesses.

Caution

Under federal law (15 U.S.C. 645(d)), any person who misrepresents a firm's status as a small, small disadvantaged, or women-owned small business concern in order to obtain a contract to be awarded under the small business preference programs established under federal law is subject to:

- *the imposition of fines, imprisonment, or both*

- *administrative remedies, including suspension and debarment*

- *ineligibility for participation in programs conducted under the authority of the Small Business Act.*

SMALL BUSINESS SET-ASIDE PROGRAM

This first program is probably one of the oldest, if not the original, program set up to help small businesses win government contracts. The Small Business Set-Aside Program (SBSA) helps assure that small businesses are awarded a fair proportion of government contracts by reserving (i.e., "setting aside") certain government purchases exclusively for participation by small business concerns.

The determination to make a small business set-aside is usually made unilaterally by the Contracting Officer. However, this determination may also be joint. In this case, it is recommended by the Small Business Administration procurement center representative (PCR) and agreed to by the Contracting Officer. The regulations specify that, to the extent practicable, unilateral determinations initiated by a Contracting Officer, rather than joint determinations, should be used as the basis for small business set-asides.

- **Contracts of $1 to $2,500** — No set-asides available.

- **Contracts of $2,500-$100,000** — Under the set-aside program, every acquisition of supplies or services that has an anticipated dollar value between $2,500 and $100,000 (except for those acquisitions set aside for very small business concerns, as described below) is automatically reserved exclusively for small businesses. However, every set-aside must meet the "Rule of Two," which requires that there must be a reasonable expectation that offers will be obtained from two or more small business concerns that are competitive in terms of market prices, quality, and delivery. If only one acceptable offer is received from a responsible small business concern in response to a set-aside, the Contracting Officer is required to make an award to that firm. If no acceptable offers are received from responsible small business concerns, the set-aside will be withdrawn and the product or service, if still valid, will be solicited on an unrestricted basis.

- **Contracts over $100,000** — In addition, the Contracting Officer is required to set aside any contract over $100,000 for small businesses when there is a reasonable expectation that offers will be obtained from at least two responsible small business concerns offering the products of different small business concerns and that award will be made at fair market prices.

- **Partial Set-Asides** — A small business set-aside of a single acquisition or a class of acquisitions may be total or partial. The Contracting Officer is required to set aside a portion of an acquisition, except for construction, for exclusive small business participation when:

— A total set-aside is not appropriate.

— The government's purchase requirement is severable into two or more economic production runs or reasonable lots.

— One or more small business concerns are expected to have the technical competence and productive capacity to satisfy the set-aside portion of the requirement at a fair market price.

— The acquisition is not subject to simplified acquisition procedures.

- **Qualified Products List (QPL)** — Any products on a QPL are not set-aside for small business.

Set-Aside or 8(a) Contract Program Requirements

To get this type of contract, a business must perform at least a given percentage of the contract. This provision limits the amount of subcontracting a concern may enter into with other firms when performing these types of contracts. The provisions are as follow:

- **Construction** — For general and heavy construction contractors, at least 15 percent of the cost of the contract, not including the cost of materials, must be performed by the prime contractor with its own employees. For special trade construction, such as plumbing, electrical, or tile work, this requirement is 25 percent.

- **Manufacturing** — At least 50 percent of the cost of manufacturing, not including the cost of materials, must be done by the prime contractor.

- **Services** — At least 50 percent of the contract cost for personnel must be performed by the prime contractor's own employees.

VERY SMALL BUSINESS PILOT PROGRAM

The purpose of the Very Small Business (VSB) Pilot Program is to improve access to government contract opportunities for "very small business concerns" by reserving certain acquisitions for competition among such concerns. (Unless this currently expired initiative is extended by Congress, VSB contracts under this program must have been awarded before September 30, 2003.)

A "very small business concern" is defined as a business that has no more than 15 employees and average annual receipts of less than $1 million and that has headquarters located within one of the following ten designated SBA districts:

1. Albuquerque, NM (serving New Mexico)

2. Los Angeles, CA (serving the following counties in California: Los Angeles, Santa Barbara, and Ventura)

3. Boston, MA (serving Massachusetts)

4. Louisville, KY (serving Kentucky)

5. Columbus, OH (serving the following counties in Ohio: Adams, Allen, Ashland, Athens, Auglaize, Belmont, Brown, Butler, Champaign, Clark, Clermont, Clinton, Coshocton, Crawford, Darke, Delaware, Fairfield, Fayette, Franklin, Gallia, Greene, Guernsey, Hamilton, Hancock, Hardin, Highland, Hocking, Holmes, Jackson, Knox, Lawrence, Licking, Logan, Madison, Marion, Meigs, Mercer, Miami, Monroe, Montgomery, Morgan, Morrow, Muskingum, Noble, Paulding, Perry, Pickaway, Pike, Preble, Putnam, Richland, Ross, Scioto, Shelby, Union, Van Wert, Vinton, Warren, Washington, and Wyandot)

6. New Orleans, LA (serving Louisiana)

7. Detroit, MI (serving Michigan)

8. Philadelphia, PA (serving the State of Delaware and the following counties in Pennsylvania: Adams, Berks, Bradford, Bucks, Carbon, Chester, Clinton, Columbia, Cumberland, Dauphin, Delaware, Franklin, Fulton, Huntington, Juniata, Lackawanna, Lancaster, Lebanon, Lehigh, Luzern, Lyocming, Mifflin, Monroe, Montgomery, Montour, Northampton, Northumberland, Philadelphia, Perry, Pike, Potter, Schuylkill, Snyder, Sullivan, Susquehanna, Tioga, Union, Wayne, Wyoming, and York)

9. El Paso, TX (serving the following counties in Texas: Brewster, Culberson, El Paso, Hudspeth, Jeff Davis, Pecos, Presidio, Reeves, and Terrell)

10. Santa Ana, CA (serving the following counties in California: Orange, Riverside, and San Bernadino)

Under the VSB program, a Contracting Officer must set aside for very small business concerns any acquisition that has an anticipated value exceeding $2,500 but not greater than $50,000 if there is a reasonable expectation of obtaining offers from two or more responsible very small business concerns that are competitive in terms of market prices, quality, and delivery. In addition, the businesses must be headquartered within the geographical area served by the designated SBA district.

If only one acceptable offer is received from a responsible very small business concern in response to a very small business set-aside, the Contracting Officer is required to make an award to that firm. If no acceptable offers are received from responsible very small business concerns, the Contracting Officer is authorized to cancel the "very small business set-aside" and proceed with the acquisition as a "small business set-aside."

The VSB program does not apply to contracts awarded pursuant to the 8(a) Program (see below), which pertains to small disadvantaged business concerns (see below). It also does not apply to any government purchase requirement that is subject to the Small Business Competitiveness Demonstration Program.

SMALL BUSINESS R&D FUNDING PROGRAMS

The government sponsors two programs, the Small Business Innovation Research (SBIR) Program and the Small Business Technical Transfer (STTR) Program, which have proven very effective in releasing the "innovative juices" of the research and development minds of the small business community. Although they were resisted at first by government buying offices, they are now very popular with both the buying offices and Congress. If you watch late-night TV, these initiatives are usually the source of the "Grants" that you hear about. . .and they are certainly not free!

Small Business Innovation Research Program

The SBIR program is a highly competitive program that encourages small businesses to explore their technological potential while providing the incentive to profit from its commercialization. SBIR funds the critical startup and development phases of R&D projects that serve a government need and have the potential for commercialization in private sector and/or government markets. Although the risk and expense of conducting serious R&D efforts are often beyond the means of many small businesses, by reserving a specific percentage of federal R&D funds for small business, SBIR protects the small business and enables it to compete on the same level as larger businesses.

The program, which was funded at $1.2 billion in Fiscal Year 2000, is administered by the following ten federal agencies:

1.   Department of Agriculture

2. Department of Homeland Security

3. Department of Defense

4. Department of Education

5. Department of Energy

6. Department of Health and Human Services

7. Department of Transportation

8. Environmental Protection Agency

9. National Aeronautics and Space Administration

10. National Science Foundation

The government agencies issue a SBIR solicitation once or twice a year, depending on the size of the agency's budget, describing its R&D needs and inviting R&D proposals. Only small, for-profit, American-owned, independently operated businesses can apply under the program. (To be considered "small" under SBIR, the business must have 500 or fewer employees, including all affiliates and/or subsidiaries.) In addition, the principal researcher must be employed by the business.

Companies apply first for a six-month Phase I award of $50,000 to $100,000 to test the scientific, technical and commercial merit and feasibility of a particular concept. If Phase I proves successful, the company may be invited to apply for a two-year Phase II award of $500,000 to $750,000 to further develop the concept, usually to the prototype stage. Proposals are judged competitively on the basis of scientific, technical and commercial merit. Following completion of Phase II, small companies are expected to obtain funding from the private sector and/or non-SBIR government sources for Phase III, which is to develop the concept into a product for sale in private sector and/or government markets.

Since its enactment in 1982, as part of the Small Business Innovation Development Act, SBIR has helped thousands of small businesses to compete for federal research and development awards. Their contributions have enhanced the nation's defense, protected the environment, advanced health care, and improved the management and manipulation of information and data.

Small Business Technical Transfer Program

Although similar in structure to SBIR, the Small Business Technical Transfer Program (STTR) funds cooperative R&D projects involving a small business and a non-profit research institution (i.e., a university, federally funded R&D center, or non-profit research institution). Established by Congress in 1992, the purpose of STTR was to create an effective vehicle for moving ideas from the nation's research institutions to the market, where they can benefit both private sector and government customers. The government STTR program was funded for $62 million in Fiscal Year 2000.

The STTR program is administered by the following five federal agencies:

1. Department of Defense

2. Department of Energy

3. National Aeronautics and Space Administration

4. Department of Health and Human Services

5. National Science Foundation

Just like the SBIR, there are three phases to the program. Phase I is the startup phase for the exploration of the scientific, technical and commercial feasibility of an idea or technology. Awards for Phase I are for up to one year and up to $100,000. Phase II is the expansion phase of Phase I results. During this period, the R&D work is performed and the developer begins to consider commercialization potential. Awards for Phase II are for up to two years and up to $500,000. Phase III is the period during which Phase II innovation moves from the laboratory into the marketplace; there is no STTR funding of this phase.

Example

Historically, about 15 percent of SBIR and STTR proposals are awarded a Phase I contract, and approximately 40 percent of Phase I projects are subsequently awarded a Phase II contract. However, in recent solicitations, a much higher percentage of STTR Phase I proposals was awarded a Phase I contract.

The qualifications for companies applying for STTR are similar to those for STIR. Only small for-profit businesses can apply under the program. In addition, the business must be American-owned and independently operated, with size limited to 500 employees. Although a company does not have to be an established business when it bids, *it must be an established business when the award is made.*

There is no size limit for the research institution partner. In other words, small businesses can team up with some rather large operations to work along with them to get an idea to market.

Since this program consists of developing and bringing a new idea or technology to market, it is important that the future rights to projects are determined at an early stage. The small business and the research institution must develop a written agreement prior to a Phase I award. This agreement must then be submitted to the awarding agency if requested.

For more information on the SBIR and STTR programs, contact your local PTAC office or:

> Small Business Administration Office of Technology
> 409 Third Street, SW
> Washington, DC 20416
> (202) 205-6450

Getting Started in SBIR and STTR

To get started in the SBIR or STTR programs, you must first obtain the current solicitation, which lists all the research topics under which government agency is seeking Phase I proposals and contains detailed information on how to submit a proposal.

The DoD issues two SBIR solicitations and one STTR solicitation each year. The first SBIR solicitation is issued in May and closed in August. The second SBIR solicitation is issued in October and closed in January of the following year. The STTR solicitation is issued in January and closed in April.

To receive hard copies of current and future SBIR and STTR solicitations, place your name and address on the SBIR/STTR mailing list by calling 800-382-4634 or by registering online at http://www.acq.osd.mil/sadbu/sbir. You can also access the SBIR and STTR solicitations electronically through this web site. In addition, this site (http://www.acq.osd.mil/sadbu/sbir/othersites/index.htm) identifies all federal agencies in the SBIR/STTP program.

After receiving the solicitation, resolve any questions you may have. If you have a technical question about a specific research topic listed in the solicitation, you can talk by telephone with the Topic Author, whose name and phone number will be listed in the solicitation topic. (Keep in mind that Topic Authors will be listed, and telephone questions will be accepted, only during the two months following public release of the solicitation on the web site and before the government begins accepting proposals.) Or you can submit a written question through the SBIR/STTR Interactive Topic Information System (SITIS), in which the questioner and respondent remain anonymous and all questions and answers are posted electronically for general viewing until the solicitation closes.

If you have a general question about the SBIR or STTR programs, contact the government agency SBIR/STTR Help Desk by e-mail at SBIRHELP@us.teltech.com or by telephone at 800-382-4634.

DoD SBIR/STTR "Fast Track"

The "Fast Track" is a special program for the Department of Defense SBIR and STTP programs that offers a significantly higher chance of

SBIR/STTR award, and continuous funding, to small companies that can attract outside investors. Small companies retain the intellectual property rights to technologies that they develop under these programs. Funding is awarded competitively, but the process is more streamlined and easier.

Projects that obtain such outside investments and thereby qualify for the Fast Track will, subject to qualifications described in the solicitation, be evaluated for Phase II award under a separate, expedited process and be eligible to receive interim funding of $30,000 to $50,000 between Phases I and II. They will be selected for Phase II award provided they meet or exceed a threshold of "technically sufficient" and have substantially met their Phase I technical goals.

Caution

To qualify for Fast Track, small companies and outside investors must follow the procedures and rules detailed in section 4.5 of the SBIR/STTR solicitation. This discussion only summarizes the most important requirements.

Many small companies have found the Fast Track policy to be an effective tool for leveraging their SBIR (or STTR) funds to obtain additional funds from outside investors. This is because, under the Fast Track, a small company can offer an investor the opportunity to obtain a match of between $1 and $4 in DoD SBIR (or STTR) funds for every $1 the investor puts in.

Toward the end of a small company's Phase I SBIR or STTR project, the company and its investor must submit a Fast Track application stating, among other things, that the investor will match both interim and Phase II SBIR or STTR funding, in cash, contingent on the company's selection for Phase II award. The matching rates needed to qualify for the Fast Track are as follows:

- For small companies that have never before received a Phase II SBIR or STTR award from DoD or any other federal agency, the matching rate is 25 cents for every SBIR or STTR dollar. (For example, if such a company receives interim and Phase II SBIR funding that totals $750,000, it must obtain matching funds from the investor of $187,500.)

- For all other companies, the matching rate is $1 for every SBIR or STTR dollar. (For example, if such a company receives interim and Phase II SBIR funding that totals $750,000, it must obtain matching funds from the investor of $750,000.)

The matching funds may pay for additional R&D on the company's SBIR or STTR project or, alternatively, they may pay for other activities (e.g., marketing) that further the development and/or commercialization of the technology.

In the application, the company and its investor must certify that the outside funding qualifies as a "Fast Track investment," and that the investor qualifies as an "outside investor." Outside investors may include such entities as another company, a venture capital firm, an individual "angel" investor, or a non-SBIR or non-STTR government program. Outside investors may not include the owners of the small business, their family members, and/or affiliates of the small business.

DoD will notify each Fast Track company, no later than 10 weeks after the end of Phase I, whether it has been selected for Phase II award. Once notified, the company and investor must certify, within 45 days, that the entire amount of the matching funds from the outside investor has been transferred to the company.

If you need assistance regarding Fast Track, you can visit DoD's STIR/STTR web site at http://www.acq.osd.mil/sadbu/sbir/homepg.htm for complete details on the program. The site also contains a list of private-sector sources of early-stage technology financing as well as a list of ongoing Phase I SBIR and STTR projects.

You can also contact the SBIR/STTR Help Desk by e-mail at SBIRHELP@us.teltech.com or by telephone at 800-382-4634.

SBA PROGRAMS

The Small Business Administration administers several programs that are designed to help small businesses market to both large business and government procurements:

- **The Small Disadvantaged Business (SDB) Certification Program** is designed to treat small companies equitably and empower them to pursue business in both the private and public sector contract arenas by providing them specific advantages in the procurement process.

- **The 8(a) Business Development Program** provides on-going personalized business assistance and counseling to certified 8(a) small disadvantaged businesses in expanding their business, fostering profitable business relationships and becoming more effective in both the large business and government sectors.

- **The HUBZone Empowerment Contracting Program** is designed to stimulate economic development and create jobs in urban and rural communities. The program provides contracting opportunities to small businesses located in, and hiring employees from, Historically Underutilized Business Zones.

- **The 8(a) BD Mentor-Protégé Program** is a public-private partnership sponsored by the SBA that seeks to grow disadvantaged startup businesses with the help of experienced ones.

- **The Veterans Entrepreneurship Program** is another recently launched program that provides assistance to veterans owning small businesses, especially those who are service-disabled.

Small businesses cannot receive benefits from these programs unless the SBA certifies that they meet the specific criteria applicable for the particular program and that they qualify to participate.

SDB Certification Program

The Small Disadvantaged Business Certification Program (SBD Program) is administered by SBA and designed to help small disadvantaged businesses compete in the American economy by providing specific advantages and benefits in the federal procurement process.

(Note that companies that are certified as 8(a) firms automatically qualify for SDB certification. The 8(a) program is explained below.)

Benefits of SDB Program

If you can qualify as a small disadvantaged business (SBD), then you are entitled to participate in special preference programs aimed at encouraging participation by SBDs in government business.

SDB certified companies may benefit in two main ways. First, SDBs are eligible for special bidding benefits. An SDB can qualify for a price evaluation adjustment of up to 10 percent when bidding on federal contracts in certain industries or services where the U.S. Department of Commerce has determined that SDBs are underrepresented because of the effects of ongoing discrimination.

Work Smart

As of October 1, 1998, SDBs are eligible to receive the price credit when competing in the following industry categories:

Industries	Industries	Services	Services
Agriculture	Mining	Electric	Retail trade
Fishing	Manufacturing	Gas	Finance
Forestry	Transportation	Sanitary services	Insurance
Construction	Communications	Wholesale trade	Real estate services

Second, the program also provides evaluation credits to prime contractors who achieve SDB subcontracting targets, which in turn boosts subcontracting opportunities for SDBs. All prime contractors are encouraged to use certified SDBs as subcontractors through mandated evaluation factors and optional monetary incentives. The program is intended to help federal agencies achieve the government-wide goal of 5 percent SDB participation in prime contracting.

To receive this credit, a contractor must confirm that a joint venture partner, team member, or subcontractor representing itself as a small disadvantaged business concern is, in fact, identified as a certified small disadvantaged business. Confirmation may be made by checking the database maintained by the Small Business Administration (PRO-*Net*) or by contacting the SBA's Office of Small Disadvantaged Business Certification and Eligibility.

The extent of participation of SDB concerns is evaluated in competitive, negotiated acquisitions expected to exceed $500,000 ($1,000,000 for construction). The SDB preference program does not apply in small business set-asides, 8(a) acquisitions, negotiated acquisitions where the lowest price technically acceptable source selection process is used, or contract actions that will be performed entirely outside of the United States.

Note that this price credit does not apply to government procurements that are below the simplified acquisition threshold of $100,000, procurements that are set aside for small business (i.e., small business set asides, HUBZone set asides and procurements under the SBA 8(a) program).

We also want to mention a new benefit. Under recent federal procurement regulations, the SBA certifies SDBs for participation in federal procurements aimed at overcoming the effects of discrimination.

Eligibility Requirements

Any small business wanting to take advantage of the SDB Program must be certified by the SBA that it meets specific social, economic, ownership, and control eligibility criteria. To qualify as a Small Disadvantaged Business (SDB), the business must be a small business concern that is at least 51 percent owned and controlled by one or more individuals who are both socially and economically disadvantaged.

Social disadvantage. Socially disadvantaged individuals are those who have been subjected to racial or ethnic prejudice or cultural bias within American society because of their identities as members of groups and without regard to their individual qualities. The social disadvantage must stem from circumstances beyond their control.

Caution

To receive the benefits of the SBD Program, a small business must be certified by SBA that it meets all of the requirements.

The U.S. population is broken down into two groups: designated groups and non-designated groups. For designated groups, the law allows for a presumption of discrimination. However, keep in mind that the presumption of discrimination may be rebutted.

Businesses whose owners are members of one of the following groups are presumed to qualify:

- African American

- Hispanic American

- Native American (American Indians, Eskimos, Aleuts, or Native Hawaiians)

- Asian-Pacific American (persons with origins from Burma, Thailand, Malaysia, Indonesia, Singapore, Brunei, Japan, China, Taiwan, Laos, Cambodia (Kampuchea), Vietnam, Korea, The Philippines, U.S. Trust Territory of the Pacific Islands (Republic of Palau), Republic of the Marshall Islands, Federated States of Micronesia, the Commonwealth of the Northern Mariana Islands, Guam, Samoa, Macao, Hong Kong, Fiji, Tonga, Kiribati, Tuvalu, or Nauru)

- Subcontinent Asian (Asian-Indian) (American persons with origins from India, Pakistan, Bangladesh, Sri Lanka, Bhutan, the Maldives Islands, or Nepal)

Individuals in non-designated groups can qualify if they can successfully make an argument for discrimination based on certain types of evidence, which include all of the following:

- At least one objective distinguishing feature that has contributed to social disadvantage such as gender disability, sexual orientation, or living in an economically isolated community

- Personal experiences of substantial and chronic social disadvantage

- Negative impact on one's education, employment entry, and advancement in the business world.

Economic disadvantage. Economically disadvantaged individuals are socially disadvantaged individuals whose ability to compete in the free enterprise system has been impaired due to diminished capital and credit opportunities as compared to others in the same or similar line of business who are not socially disadvantaged.

In assessing the personal financial condition of an individual claiming economic disadvantage, his or her net worth may not exceed the limit set by law. All individuals must have a net worth of less than $750,000, excluding the equity of the business and primary residence.

Successful applicants must also meet applicable size standards for small businesses in their industry.

Once certified, the firm is added to an online registry of SDB-certified firms maintained in the PRO-*Net* database (see Part II, Chapter 7 for details). Certified firms remain on the list for three years. Contracting Officers and large business prime contractors may search this online registry for potential suppliers.

Application and Certification

Prior to applying for certification, the SBA highly recommends that you take their online training course on SBA certification eligibility available at http://www.sba.gov/training/courses.html. Look under the topic "Government Contracting" and click on "Certification Programs." It would be nice to be certain you meet the criteria before investing your time.

Recently, the SBA has automated the 8(a)/SDB process to speed it up and eliminate bottlenecks. The SBA hopes this process will revolutionize the way the Business Development Program Office oversees 8(a) and Small Disadvantaged Business certification, resulting in a more streamlined, user-friendly, and an easier method for the applicant to apply for certification. You can now apply online at the SBA web site (https://sba8a.symplicity.com/applicants/guide), but there are some details you must do first.

1. To do business with the Federal government and to be certified under the 8(a) Program or as an SDB, you *must* register in the Central Contractor Registration (CCR) database, and complete the Small Business Supplemental Page within CCR. This Supplemental Page is identified at the completion of your CCR registration and before you close out of the site. As a government-wide single point of vendor registration, CCR is a key aspect of streamlining and integrating electronic commerce into the federal procurement process

2. You must register for an account in the SBA's General Log-in System (GLS), the single log-in point for all of its services

(https://eweb.sba.gov/gls/dsp_publicaccount.cfm). This assists SBA in improving its service delivery to their clients.

3. You must download, sign and submit your notarized Authorization form, also referred to as a "signature" authorization (https://sba8a.symplicity.com/applicants/certification.pdf). This authorization is sent separately to the SBA. Upon the receipt of this document, the SBA will begin the time frame for screening and reviewing of the entire electronic application.

4. Log-in to the 8(a)/SDB Application via SBA General Log-in System (https://eweb.sba.gov/gls/dsp_login.cfm?).

5. Complete and submit your application form. Make sure you use the help screens designed to guide you along when you submit your application.

The length of time needed to review your application will depend on its complexity. For example, a sole-proprietorship 100-percent-owned by a designated group member will not take as long as a multi-owned corporation located in a community property state. The regulatory time frames are 90 days for a response from an 8(a) application and 75 days for a response from an SDB application. There are two parts to reviewing any application. First, the SBA makes certain they have all the information required to process the application, and then the information is reviewed and analyzed.

Your electronic application information is protected by a username/password-based authentication system for all interactions. The process uses secure, 128-bit encrypted communications to ensure that system passwords cannot be detected by network intruders. For further information regarding SBA's Internet Privacy Policy, see http://www.sba.gov/privacy.html.

Please make sure that your submitted answers are truthful and accurate, as there are serious legal consequences for falsifying information in an 8(a)/SDB application that may include fines, imprisonment or both. Should you have questions, e-mail the SBA at 8ABD@sba.gov or call (415) 744-6784.

Help Getting Certified

You can work directly with SBA in completing your application and providing the required documentation, but if there is something wrong with your paperwork, you will be denied certification and given 45 days in which to respond to the rejection. If you don't satisfactorily address the deficiencies within that time frame, you will have to wait a year to reapply.

Don't forget that PTACs and Small Business Development Centers may be of help with your application, so be sure check if your local office can assist you.

Keep in mind that, no matter how you choose to complete your paperwork and application, *you* are the one ultimately responsible for making sure that all questions are accurately addressed and all required information is provided.

For further information on the SDB program, call 415-744-6784 or e-mail the SBA at 8ADB@sba.gov.

8(a) Business Development Program

The 8(a) Business Development Program, like the Small Disadvantaged Business Certification Program described above, is administered by SBA and designed to help small disadvantaged businesses compete in the American economy. Note that companies that are certified as 8(a) firms automatically qualify for SDB certification.

Example

The 8(a) Business Development Program was named for a section of the Small Business Act. In fiscal year 1998, more than 6,100 firms participated in the 8(a) program and were awarded $6.4 billion in federal contract awards.

In addition to the federal procurement benefits available through the SDB Program, for which 8(a) firms automatically qualify, 8(a) firms receive a broad scope of assistance, including one-on-one assistance and coaching from a Business Opportunity Specialist to help them grow and expand their businesses. Under this program, 8(a) businesses enter into a nine-year partnering relationship with the SBA—a four-year developmental stage and a five-year transition stage.

During the developmental stage, businesses are offered help in expanding their business and fostering meaningful business relationships. During the transitional stage, businesses are helped to become more effective in both the large business and government sector market in dealing with complex business deals and to prepare for post-8(a) program expansion and development.

The overall goal of the program goal is to graduate firms that will go on to thrive in a competitive business environment. To achieve this end, SBA district offices monitor and measure the progress of participants through annual reviews, business planning, and systematic evaluations.

At any time during a firm's term, the SBA may terminate a firm's participation in the 8(a) program for non-compliance with program requirements and regulations.

For requirements on the amount of work that must be performed by the prime contractor in order to be awarded an 8(a) contract, see our discussion about the Small Business Set-Aside Program at the beginning of this chapter.

Benefits of 8(a) Program

In addition to the on-going personal counseling services, the program offers specialized business training, marketing assistance, and high-level executive development provided by the SBA and its resource partners. Businesses may also be eligible for assistance in obtaining access to surplus government property and supplies, SBA-guaranteed loans and bonding assistance.

Moreover, recent regulations permit 8(a) companies to form beneficial teaming partnerships and allow federal agencies to streamline the contracting process. In addition, the recent rules make it easier for non-minority firms to participate by proving their social disadvantage. Specifically:

- Participants can receive sole-source contracts, up to a ceiling of $3 million for goods and services and $5 million for manufacturing. There is also a limit on the total dollar value of sole-source contracts that an individual participant can receive while in the program: $100 million or five times the value of its primary NAICS code (NAICS codes are explained in Part II).

- Federal acquisition policies encourage federal agencies to award a certain percentage of their contracts to SDBs. To speed up the award process, the SBA has signed Memorandums of Understanding with 25 federal agencies allowing them to contract directly with certified 8(a) firms.

- Recent changes permit 8(a) firms to form joint ventures and teams to bid on contracts. This enhances the ability of 8(a) firms to perform larger prime contracts and overcome the effects of contract bundling (the combining of two or more contracts together into one large contract).

Eligibility Requirements

To qualify for the 8(a) program, a small business must be owned and controlled by a socially *and* economically disadvantaged individual; in other words, a disadvantaged owner must be involved on a full-time basis. Certain minority groups are presumed to qualify as socially disadvantaged and include African Americans, Hispanic Americans, Asian Pacific Americans, and Subcontinent Asian Americans.

However, an individual does not qualify automatically as socially disadvantaged just because he or she belongs to one of the named groups. SBA may challenge an individual's claim of social disadvantage if there is substantial evidence that the individual has not experienced, or has overcome, the traditional discriminatory social attitudes, racial prejudice and stereotyping that have created serious obstacles for many members of these groups when they attempt to obtain equal access to financing, markets and resources necessary to establish, maintain or expand small businesses.

Individuals who are not members of the named minority groups can be admitted to the program if they can show through a "preponderance of the evidence" that they are disadvantaged because of race, ethnic origin, gender, physical handicap, or geographic environment isolated from the mainstream of American society. The individual must demonstrate personal suffering and not merely claim membership in a non-designated group.

To qualify for the 8(a) program, a socially disadvantaged applicant must also be economically disadvantaged. In order to meet the economic disadvantage test, individuals must have a net worth of less than $250,000 for initial 8(a) eligibility, excluding the value of the business and personal residence. For continued 8(a) eligibility after admission to the program, net worth must be less than $750,000. This determination is made on the individuals and not jointly if spouses are involved. Separate personal financial statements on spouses are required.

Caution

To receive the benefits of the 8(a) Program, a small business must be certified by SBA that it meets all of the requirements.

In determining economic disadvantage, the SBA will determine whether the applicant has suffered diminished credit and capital opportunities, based on the following: personal and business assets; personal and business net worth; personal and business income and profits; success in obtaining adequate financing, adequate bonding and outside equity credit; and other economic disadvantages.

Successful applicants must also meet applicable size standards for small business concerns, be in business for at least two years, display reasonable success potential and display good character. Although the two-year requirement may be waived, firms must continue to comply with various requirements while in the program.

Application and Certification

To start the application process, contact the local SBA district office serving your area. An SBA representative will answer general questions over the telephone. Most district offices have regularly scheduled 8(a) orientation workshops designed to explain the 8(a) Business Development Program, the eligibility requirements and to review various SBA forms. An application will be provided at the informational session, along with filing instructions.

The 8(a) application process has been automated with the Small Disadvantaged Business program, as previously explained in this chapter. For further information, call the SBA Division of Program Certification & Eligibility at (202) 205-6417.

Women-Owned Small Businesses

Federal regulations require that women-owned small businesses (WOSB) have the maximum practicable opportunity to participate in performing contracts awarded by any federal agency. The regulations direct federal agencies to reach out to women-owned small businesses and make sure that they understand the process and are offered contract opportunities. As of this writing, there were no specific preference programs in this area and no requirements for formal certification. The system still recognizes self-certification.

However, if you are a women-owned small business and feel that you have been hindered in your efforts to do business, you can apply for certification as a socially and economically disadvantaged business under the SBA 8(a) program. See your local SBA office to discuss this issue.

One word of caution: If you are a male-owned business and you make your wife or another woman owner of 51 percent of the stock in order to qualify for 8(a) benefits, you are spinning your wheels. The SBA auditor will know what you are doing—51 percent ownership is a red flag. Similarly, if the auditor comes to your office and sees that the male office is bigger than the female's, you are not going to be certified. You must be able to show that the business is managed and controlled on a daily basis by a woman, and that the woman is the person who makes the life and death decisions of the company.

Work Smart

If you are looking for information about opportunities for women-owned small businesses, a good place to start is at http://www.womenbiz.gov.

HUBZone Program

The Historically Underutilized Business Zone (HUBZone) Empowerment Contracting program, which was enacted into law as part of the Small Business Reauthorization Act of 1997, provides federal contracting assistance and opportunities for qualified small businesses located in distressed historically underutilized business zones, known as "HUBZones." Among other things, it allows small firms located in many urban or rural areas to qualify for sole-source and other types of federal contract benefits. The underlying purpose of the program is to encourage economic development and increase employment opportunities.

The HUBZone program falls under the auspices of the Small Business Administration (SBA), which is responsible for implementing the program and determining which businesses are eligible to receive HUBZone contracts. SBA maintains a listing of qualified HUBZone small businesses that federal agencies can use to locate vendors and also adjudicates protests of eligibility to receive HUBZone contracts. In addition, SBA is responsible for reporting to Congress on the program's impact on employment and investment in HUBZone areas.

While the Small Business Reauthorization Act of 1997 increased the overall government-wide procurement goal for small business from 20 to 23 percent, the statute sets the goal for HUBZone contracts at 1½ percent for 2000, 2 percent for 2001, 2½ percent for 2002, and 3 percent for 2003 and each year thereafter.

Benefits of HUBZone Program

There are four types of contract benefits that a HUBZone-certified business can qualify for:

- **A competitive HUBZone contract** can be awarded if the Contracting Officer has a reasonable expectation that at least two qualified HUBZone small businesses will submit offers and that the contract can be awarded at a fair market price.

- **A sole source HUBZone contract** can be awarded if the Contracting Officer does not have a reasonable expectation that two or more qualified HUBZone small businesses will submit offers, determines that the qualified HUBZone small business is responsible, and determines that the contract can be awarded at a fair price. The government estimate cannot exceed $5 million for manufacturing purchases or $3 million for all other requirements.

- **A full and open competition contract** can be awarded with a price evaluation preference. The offer of the HUBZone small business will be considered lower than the offer of a non-HUBZone/non-small business, providing that the offer of the HUBZone small business is not more than 10 percent higher than that of the non-HUBZone business.

- **A subcontract** could be awarded by a large prime contractor. Federal rules require these contractors to include HUBZone contracting goals.

In addition to the contract benefits, certified HUBZone firms can qualify for higher SBA-guaranteed surety bonds on construction and service contract bids. Firms in Empowerment Zones and Enterprise Communities (EZ/EC) can also benefit from employer tax credits, tax-free facility bonds, and investment tax deductions.

Eligibility and Certification

To qualify for the HUBZone program, a business must meet four requirements:

1. It must be a small business.

2. It must be owned and controlled *only* by U.S. citizens.

3. The principal office of the business must be located in a "historically underutilized business zone."

4. At least 35 percent of its employees must reside in a HUBZone. Existing businesses that choose to move to qualified areas are eligible. To fulfill the 35 percent requirement, employees must live in a primary residence within that area for at least 180 days or be a currently registered voter in that area.

Caution

If you are a one-person business and your office is located in a HUBZone, but you don't reside in the HUBZone, you do not qualify!

To be designated a "HUBZone," an area must also meet certain criteria. It must be located in one or more of the following three areas:

1. a qualified census tract (as defined in the Internal Revenue Code of 1986)

2. a qualified "non-metropolitan county" (as defined in the Internal Revenue Code of 1986) with a median household income of less than 80 percent of the State median household

income or with an unemployment rate of not less than 140 percent of the statewide unemployment rate, based on U.S. Department of Labor recent data

3. a federally recognized Indian reservation

The certification process is fully electronic, Internet-based, and integrated with CCR (see Part II for details on CCR). The SBA will verify eligibility and make sure that ownership, location, and employment percentage requirements are satisfied. The average time for processing is approximately 30 days, and SBA's decision will be in writing.

To apply, companies are encouraged to use the electronic application directly on the HUBZone web site at http://www.sba.gov/hubzone/. Applicants can also submit a paper copy to SBA headquarters in Washington, D.C. Applicants can download the paper version from the web site or obtain it from any local SBA district office.

Computer mapping software available on SBA's web site allows firms to search a database to determine whether or not they are located in a qualified HUBZone. The system allows searches by address, county or town and displays metropolitan areas, Indian reservations and areas that qualify by income, unemployment rate, or both.

For further information and to find out if your location is in a HUBZone, you can visit the SBA web site at https://eweb1.sba.gov/hubzone/internet/.

SDB, 8(a) and HUBZone Compared

The SBA administers three core certification programs for small businesses: the Small Disadvantaged Business Program (SDB), the 8(a) Business Development Program, and the HUBZone Program. All three are designed to help small businesses market themselves to both large business and government procurements. However, not every small business can participate in these programs. To participate, a business must meet specific criteria and must be certified by SBA that these criteria have been met.

Benefits Compared

There are some major differences in the benefits of the SDB, 8(a), and HUBZone programs. SDB and HUBZone are essentially contractor programs designed to expand economic opportunity for disadvantaged businesses. In contrast, 8(a) is a business development program that provides a broad scope of assistance to disadvantaged firms, including personalized business counseling. Under the program, each 8(a) certified company is assigned a Business Opportunity Specialist (BOS) who advises and coaches the company in business matters. There is no such benefit in SDB and HUBZone.

Only the HUBZone Program specifically promotes business opportunities in distressed communities. Small businesses not located within these areas may be eligible for certification in the SDB or 8(a) BD Programs.

Certification Requirements Compared

To be certified for the SDB, 8(a), or HUBZone programs, a business must demonstrate that it meets the basic requirements for admission. Although there are differences in the requirements for each, there is one universal requirement for all of these programs: the business must be classified as small.

For SDB and 8(a) certification, a business must generally show that it is unconditionally owned and controlled by one or more socially and economically disadvantaged individuals who are of good character and citizens of the United States. In addition, the net worth of the individual claiming economic disadvantage may not exceed the limit set by law. For SDB eligibility, net worth must be less than $750,000, excluding the value of the business and personal residence. For initial 8(a) eligibility, the net worth of an individual claiming disadvantage must be less than $250,000, excluding the value of the business and personal residence. For continued 8(a) eligibility after admission to the program, net worth must be less than $750,000. (Note that companies that are 8(a) firms automatically qualify for SDB certification.)

For HUBZone certification, your business must be located in a qualified HUBZone area. A predetermined percentage of employees who work for the company must also live in a HUBZone.

Application Process Compared

You can apply to all three certification programs and, under the right circumstances, you could conceivably qualify for all three—for example, if you were an 8(a) eligible business located in an Historically Underutilized Business Zone.

Although you can apply to all three programs, there is no universal application. Each core program has its own application form and specific process for certification. However, all three certification programs require similar information along with your application, including such items as personal financial statements, previous tax returns, SBA forms, and IRS forms.

8(a) Mentor-Protégé Program

The SBA has implemented the Mentor-Protégé Program (MPP) to help starting 8(a) companies learn the ropes from experienced businesses. The program is offered under SBA's 8(a) Business Development program serving disadvantaged firms.

The MPP seeks to encourage major federal prime contractors (mentors) to help develop the technical and business capabilities of small disadvantaged businesses and other eligible protégés in order to enable the protégé to expand its business base within the federal government. Through credit toward subcontracting goals or some direct reimbursement of costs, the MPP provides incentives for these mentors to establish and implement a developmental assistance plan that enables the protégé to compete more successfully for government prime contracts and subcontract awards.

The mentor firms represented in the MPP encompass a broad range of industries, including environmental remediation, manufacturing, telecommunications, and health care. Mentors provide technical and management assistance, financial assistance in the form of equity investments and/or loans, subcontract support, and assistance in performing prime contracts through joint venture arrangements with 8(a) firms.

Protégés have only one mentor at a time. Generally, a mentor will not have more than one protégé at a time without SBA authorization.

Work Smart

The information presented regarding the Mentor-Protégé Program is general in nature. Be sure to review specific agencies' MPPs to find out if unique criteria apply. In the DoD MPP, for example, eligible companies include qualified organizations employing disabled persons or enterprises owned by women.

Protégé Requirements

To participate in the program, the protégé must be in good standing in the 8(a) program and must be current with all reporting requirements. In addition, the protégé must also meet *one* of the following requirements:

- It must be in the developmental stage of the 8(a) program.

- It must have never received an 8(a) contract.

- It must have a size of less than half the size standard for a small business based on its primary NAICS/SIC code.

MPP Certification for Non-8(a) Firms

Federal regulations require that any firm that is not an 8(a) certified firm but is seeking to be eligible as a Small Disadvantaged Business for participation as a Protégé under the Mentor-Protégé Program must be certified as an SDB by the Small Business Administration. Self-certifications are no longer sufficient.

Contact the local SBA District Office (http://www.sba.gov) for an application package. Submit the completed application to SBA's Assistant Administrator for Small Disadvantaged Business Certification and Eligibility (AA/SDBCE). No firm will be recognized as an SDB without certification by the SBA for any of the purchasing programs that give an SDB preference for award.

Mentor Requirements

The mentor can be a business that has graduated from the 8(a) program, a firm in the transitional stage of the program, or a small or large business. A mentor must have the capability to assist the protégé and must make a commitment for at least a year. In addition, the mentor must meet *all* of the following requirements:

- It must be financially healthy and must have been profitable for at least the last two years.

- It must be a federal contractor in good standing.

- It must be able to provide support to a protégé through lessons learned and practical experience gained from the 8(a) program or through its general knowledge of government contracting.

Entering the Program

Mentor and protégé firms enter the program by entering into an SBA-approved written agreement outlining the protégé's needs and describing the assistance the mentor has committed to providing. The protégé's servicing district office evaluates the agreement according to the provisions contained in the regulations (13 CFR 124.520). SBA conducts annual reviews to determine the success of the mentor-protégé relationship. We have included a Sample Agreement in the Appendices.

For additional information on the program, contact your SBA District Office or:

> 8(a) BD—Mentor-Protégé Program
> U.S. Small Business Administration
> 409 Third Street, SW
> Washington, DC 20416
> Phone: (800) 827-5722

The SBA also provides details on the program at its web site (http://www.sba.gov).

Veterans Entrepreneurship Program

The Veterans Entrepreneurship and Small Business Development Act of 1999 and the Benefits Act of 2003: Procurement Program for Small Business Concerns Owned and Controlled by Service-Disabled Veterans provides for set-aside and sole-source procurement authority for service-disabled veteran-owned small business (SDVOSB) concerns.

The contracting officer may:

- award contracts on the basis of competition restricted to SDVOSB concerns if there is a reasonable expectation that two or more SDVOSB concerns will submit offers for the contracting opportunity and that the award can be made at a fair market price

- award a sole-source contract to a responsible SDVOSB concern if there is not a reasonable expectation that two or more SDVOSB concerns will submit an offer, the anticipated contract price (including options) will not exceed $5 million (for manufacturing) or $3 million otherwise, and the contract award can be made at a fair and reasonable price

The laws limit use of SDVOSB procurement authority to procurements that would not otherwise be made from Federal Prison Industries or the Javits-Wagner-O'Day.

The laws are also designed to cushion the impact on small businesses when their owners or essential employees who are reservists are ordered to active duty during military conflicts by providing loans, loan payment deferrals, and technical and managerial assistance. Moreover, the laws provide for technical, financial and procurement assistance to veteran-owned small businesses under the auspices of the SBA.

There are federal contracting and subcontracting goals required for participation of small businesses owned and controlled by service-disabled veterans. The goals are 3 percent of the prime and subcontract opportunities available.

The Act also revises some common definitions for purposes of taking advantage of the new benefits, including the terms "veteran," "service-disabled veteran," "small business concern owned and operated by service-disabled veterans" and "small business concern owned and operated by veterans."

You can check the status of this program by contacting SBA Office of Veterans Affairs at http://www.sba.gov/vets. You also can find help at the Veterans' Affairs web site at www.vetbiz.gov.

OTHER ASSISTANCE MEASURES

There is other assistance that is available to small businesses to help them in the acquisition process.

Certificate of Competency

This program, sometimes referred to as the "second bite of the apple," comes into play when a government buyer determines that a small business is "not responsible" for a specific contract award. In other words, the buyer has determined that the business does not show certain elements of responsibility, such as capability, competency, capacity, credit, integrity, perseverance, or tenacity, for the purposes of receiving and performing that specific government contract. In such a case, the Contracting Officer is required to withhold the contract and refer action to the Small Business Administration for a possible Certificate of Competency (COC).

Once the matter is referred to the SBA, the SBA must, within 15 days, inform the company of the Contracting Officer's decision and offer it an opportunity to apply to the SBA for a COC. After receiving an acceptable application, the SBA conducts an independent pre-award survey to determine the company's ability to perform on the specific contract. If the SBA determines that the company is able to perform, the COC program authorizes the SBA to issue a Certificate of Competency. The COC certifies to government Contracting Officers as to all elements of responsibility of the small business concern to receive and perform on the specific government contract.

If the small business decides that it has bid too low or a better job comes along, it may want to ignore the COC involvement. If the COC is refused, the government buyer can then make the award to the next low responsive and responsible bidder.

DoD Regional Councils

The DoD Regional Councils for Small Business Education and Advocacy are a nationwide network of small business specialists organized to promote national small business programs to include minority and disadvantaged small business concerns and minority universities and institutions.

Additional objectives include promoting the exchange of ideas and experiences and general information among small business specialists and the contracting community; developing closer relationships and better communication among government entities and the small business community; and staying abreast of statutes, policies, regulations, directives, trends and technology affecting the small business program.

There are eight councils in all: Northeast, Mid-Atlantic, District of Columbia, Southeastern, North Central, South Central, Pacific

Northwest, and Western. They are sponsored by the DoD Office of Small and Disadvantaged Business Utilization (SADBU), but are governed by individual by-laws. Membership is open to small business advocates from the DoD and civilian agencies. The DoD Office of SADBU is an active participant and advisor to each Council; however, each Council establishes its own committee structure, meeting schedules and agendas.

Non-voting membership is extended to personnel representing small business interests such as Small Business Development Centers and Procurement Technical Assistance Centers. Some Councils invite the Small Business Liaison Officers representing prime contractors in an effort to promote small business subcontracting.

These councils offer small businesses a chance to "rub shoulders" with government and large contractors that may lead to contract opportunities.

You can visit the SADBU web site at http://www.acq.osd.mil/sadbu/ to get more information on the councils and a schedule of their various events.

Part V

Subcontracting: Another Huge Opportunity

OK, so maybe you tried several times to get a government contract and are not satisfied with the results. Or perhaps you don't feel quite ready to be a prime contractor and wish there were a way to ease into the government contracting business and learn gradually. Or maybe you are the type of person who finds dealing directly with government structure a bit daunting, but would still like to participate in the multi-billion dollar government market.

If you fit into any of these categories, then you are in luck because there is an excellent option: You can become a subcontractor to a prime that has a government contract. As a subcontractor, you would enter into an agreement with the prime to provide supplies and/or services that the prime needs to fulfill the requirements of its government contract. As such, your contractual agreement would be with the prime, not the government, and would provide an opportunity for you learn the ropes from someone who is familiar with all the rules, regulations, and what is required in dealing with the government.

In this Part, we'll give you a feel for the opportunity that exists for subcontractors to government primes. We'll also tell you what you need to know to succeed in your bid to be a sub, including how to lay the proper groundwork and the secrets that you need to know to tip the scales in your favor.

Chapter 23, What Are the Sub-Opportunities?: Find out about the magnitude of the market available to you as a subcontractor, get our top picks for the prime contractors that offer the best opportunity for subs, and weigh the advantages and disadvantages of being a sub. Did you know that prime government contractors must make a strong effort to hire small business subcontractors in order to win a government contract of their own? We'll explain why.

Chapter 24, Lay the Groundwork: Here you will learn what actions you should take to improve your chances of getting a subcontract with a government prime. Learn how to find the primes and the right people to talk to, and why getting to know all about the prime, your competition, and your capabilities is key to your success. We also tell you what you need to do to get on the Approved/Preferred Vendor Lists of primes you would like to work with as well as give you useful tips on preparing and delivering a winning presentation.

Chapter 25, Final Tips to Seal the Deal: Even when you are bidding against scores of other subcontractors, there are things you can do to tip the scales in your favor. We tell you how to improve your chances and what is really important to a prime in choosing a sub (and it's not always price). We also give you the bottom line for when you should bid and when you shouldn't. Finally, we give you a final review tip sheet for putting your best foot forward.

Chapter 22

What Are the Sub-Opportunities?

There is a huge market available to you as a subcontractor for a government prime. In FY 2003, for example, about 2,000 Department of Defense prime contractors awarded $86.5 billion in subcontracts, of which $32 billion (or 37 percent) was awarded to small businesses. Specific civilian statistics are more difficult to identify, but they are also impressive.

In this chapter, we'll identify the prime time players—those top 100 large contractors who do the most work for the federal government and, therefore, have the greatest need for subcontractors to help fulfill these obligations. Then we'll take it one step further and recommend the best 20 companies out of that top 100 that offer the best opportunities for small business subcontracting work.

Moreover, government rules regarding primes and subs have changed over the years, and current regulations are designed to assure sub-opportunities. Even so, a new practice known as contract bundling is changing the way small businesses get contracts from the government.

Finally, we'll discuss the advantages of subcontracting in comparison to being a prime contractor, and why being a sub may just be the best way for your small business to be involved in the federal procurement system.

PRIME-TIME PLAYERS

Following is a listing of some of the big players in government contracting and their area of interest. This data relates only to Supplies and Equipment and one service area, ADP (Automated Data Processing) Services and Equipment, but the data gives you some understanding of the amount of contract support that the large primes provide to the federal government.

Note that this is the most current data that we had available to us at the time of publication. For a current list of the 100 contractors that do the most business with the federal government, visit http://www.fpdc.gov/fpdc/fpr2003a.htm. A good commercial site that provides similar data is at http://www.govexec.com.

Top 10 Federal Contractors by Product/Service Category
Actions Reported Individually on SF279 Fiscal Year 2003 through Fourth Quarter

Supplier	Number of Actions	Dollars (000)
III. Supplies and Equipment		
Department of Defense		
Boeing Company The	2,474	11,344,572
Lockheed Martin Corporation	2,550	9,685,950
Raytheon Company	2,801	4,705,915
General Dynamics Corporation	2,575	4,231,756
United Technologies Corporation	2,755	4,020,115
Northrop Grumman Corporation	2,993	3,386,492
General Electric Company	2,663	1,931,080
L-3 Communications Holding Inc	1,196	1,197,544
Honeywell International Inc	2,318	837,866
Exxon Mobil Corporation	117	755,171
Civilian Agencies		
Amerisourcebergen Corporation	485	2,576,048
Boeing Company The	73	1,249,267
McDermott International Inc	63	593,201
General Motors Corporation	10,702	434,013
Integrated Coast Guard Systems	58	423,104
Alliant Techsystems Inc	438	408,214
Ford Motor Company	8,842	284,572
Lockheed Martin Corporation	29	282,471
Daimlerchrysler Ag	4,310	244,436
Archer Daniels Midland Company	297	206,696
IV. ADP Services And Equipment		
Department Of Defense		
General Dynamics Corporation	1,318	762,347
Northrop Grumman Corporation	2,216	866,298
Electronic Data Systems Corporation	4,354	667,060
Science Applications International Corp	812	650,805
Dell Inc	7,000	607,805
Computer Sciences Corporation	746	409,398
Worldcom Inc	2,659	365,215
GTSI Corp	2,865	325,222
Lockheed Martin Corporation	578	296,197
International Business Machine Corp	378	267,335
Civilian Agencies		
Science Applications International Corp	1,593	1,348,439
Lockheed Martin Corporation	472	1,262,402
Northrop Grumman Corporation	2,628	1,101,588
Computer Sciences Corporation	1,154	957,319
Electronic Data Systems Corporation	459	451,580
International Business Machine Corp	1,390	408,494
Booz Allen Hamilton Inc	658	331,115
Dell Inc	5,009	332,252
Accenture LLP	315	278,344
Anteon International Corporation	965	262,082

As of 04/12/2004

OUR TOP PICKS

Following are our picks of the 20 federal contractors out of the top 100 that we think small businesses stand the best chance of getting some work from. We eliminated foreign companies because they are not required to comply with laws protecting subcontractors. (We are not saying that they wouldn't, but it is an issue that you don't have to even think about when you subcontract with U.S. manufacturers.)

We also eliminated educational institutions when picking our top 20. While they may offer some service opportunities, they are generally looking for very specialized expertise, and opportunities are thus very limited for the general population of small businesses.

Our Top 20 Federal Contractors

Federal Contractor	Total $ Awards for 2001
Lockheed Martin Corporation	25,065,368
Boeing Company The	19,082,544
Northrop Grumman Corporation	11,911,412
Raytheon Company	8,284,449
General Dynamics Corporation	7,657,307
United Technologies Corporation	5,006,810
Science Applications International Corp	4,656,290
Bechtel Group Inc	4,597,221
Computer Sciences Corporation	4,245,606
Halliburton Company	3,155,042
Amerisourcebergen Corporation	3,067,429
L-3 Communications Holding Inc	2,849,637
General Electric Company	2,534,841
University of California	2,112,666
Humana Inc	1,820,294
Honeywell International Inc	1,804,708
B A E Systems PLC	1,801,730
United Space Alliance LLC	1,759,972
Westinghouse Electric Corporation	1,594,850
California Institute of Technology	1,539,102

GOVERNMENT RULES ASSURE SUB-OPPORTUNITIES

One of the government requirements that primes must meet in order to be awarded a federal contract really works to generate a significant market for small business subcontractors.

Major prime contractors and subcontractors receiving contracts valued over $500,000 ($1 million for construction) are required by federal regulations to develop plans and goals for subcontracting with small businesses, small disadvantaged businesses, women-owned small businesses, Historically Underutilized Business Zone (HUBZone) small businesses, and service-disabled veteran-owned small businesses. Under the law, if a prime contractor selected by the government fails to negotiate an acceptable subcontracting plan addressing all of these groups, it will not be awarded the contract.

It is easy to see why this requirement alone generates a significant and on-going subcontracting opportunity market. It is also easy to see why primes are always looking for "good" small business subcontractors. They need you in order to be able to do business with the government.

Note that if a prime has a federal contract that requires it to develop a subcontract plan and goals, only small disadvantaged [i.e., small disadvantaged owned and 8(a)] and HUBZone businesses that are officially certified at the federal level can be counted toward meeting plan and goal requirements. Currently, federal certification is not required for small businesses, women-owned small businesses, or veteran- or disabled veteran-owned small businesses; self-declaration is sufficient.

Work Smart

Since certification is required before a prime can count a small disadvantaged or HUBZone subcontractor toward meeting its subcontracting plan requirements, it is to your benefit to have your certification available when you meet with the prime contractor or other company representative for the first time. Being able to prove that you are officially certified could actually tip the scales in your favor over another sub that might still be in the process.

Another reason primes need good subcontractors is that most prime contracts are so big that the primes cannot do everything in-house, and they have needs that only small businesses can fulfill. Because of the size of the contracts, the economic situation, and the fact that one company is buying out another company that's buying out another company, and so on and so on, many of the big primes can't manufacture the end product like they used to. Instead they just get the parts from other sources and then become the assembler for the product. All the manufacturing expertise that was originally in the company that did all the work is often dissipated, so it now has to farm that out to subcontractors.

So, if you can make a prime's life easier by helping it do its job well and fulfill on its government contract efficiently, on time, and with quality products/services, you have a great chance of creating a long, rewarding relationship.

Primes Depend on Subs

- *AlliedSignal, consistently among the top prime contractors, depends on materials and components from 7,500 to 10,000 suppliers who accounted for 60 percent of its defense contract costs at one time.*

- *Sixty percent of the dollar value of Pratt & Whitney's military aircraft engines goes to suppliers.*

- *To build the inertial guidance system for the MX missile, Northrop relied on more than 500 subcontractors to make 19,000 parts.*

- *At Lockheed/Fort Worth, subcontracts consumed 75 percent of the cost of making the F-16 aircraft.*

BUNDLING INCREASES SUB-OPPORTUNITIES

Another factor that has increased subcontracting opportunities, while at the same time decreasing prime contracting opportunities, for small businesses is the recent (and controversial) trend by federal agencies of combining or bundling small contracts for different activities or requirements into large contract packages.

The government maintains that combining several smaller projects under one large umbrella contract is more efficient than managing several smaller contracts, allowing it to leverage its purchasing power to its advantage and to reduce its operating costs.

However, the umbrella contracts are too large for small and mid-size companies to realistically handle and often require project management capability that they usually don't have. The upshot is that thousands of small businesses have lost federal contracts in recent years because government agencies bundled contracts into large packages that were awarded to big businesses.

But there is a silver lining in all of this: Many big companies that get these awards are managers, not doers, and therefore must find capable subcontractors to help get the work done.

There is another boon to prospective small business subs. Under new SBA guidelines, if a bundled contract is seen as a necessity by the buying agency, the agency must establish a significant evaluation factor that will allow, to the maximum extent possible, subcontracting by small businesses. Part of this may include evaluating the prime contractor's past efforts in providing small firms with the chance to subcontract.

Effects of Bundling

The Small Business Reauthorization Act of 1997 stated that federal agencies are allowed to bundle contracts only to achieve "measurably substantial benefits" in terms of cost, shorter acquisition cycles, or better terms and conditions, among other benefits. Congress and the SBA, which have been tracking the increased use of this trend, have been concerned that if left unchecked the trend could lead to a decrease in prime federal contracting with small and mid-size businesses, which, according to 1998 statistics, averages about $40 billion per year of the $180 billion total.

Recently, the SBA has issued new rules that prohibit government buying agencies from combining contracts unless it is necessary and they can document "measurably substantial benefits" from doing so. In a move that may enable small businesses to compete for big umbrella contracts that, to date, only big companies could handle, the SBA also has established guidelines for small businesses that want to create joint ventures to go after bundled contracts. Under the former rules, small businesses banding together were sometimes disqualified because the resulting new employee count or combined revenues would exceed SBA's definition of a small business. However, the new SBA guidelines provide that, if the firms are small before they enter the arrangement, a joint venture won't change that status.

According to a study released by Congress, the number of federal contracts issued to small businesses fell 23 percent from 1997 to 1999. At the same time, however, the SBA says that the federal government met its goal of awarding small businesses 23 percent of its total contract dollars in 1998 and 1999. But because of bundling, fewer small businesses receive these contracts. The number of federal contractors dropped from 83,915 in 1992 to 70,755 in 1998, according to a study by Eagle Eye Publishers Inc. of Fairfax, Va.

ADVANTAGES OF SUBCONTRACTING

As we mentioned earlier, as a subcontractor, your agreement to provide supplies and/or services would be with the prime; you would have no contractual relationship with the government. Therefore, you have another entity—the prime, in this case—between you and the government.

This can work to your advantage since dealing with a prime is generally more straightforward, less complicated and less burdensome than dealing directly with the government. Administrative requirements are reduced. In addition, government rules offer more protection to subs when it's time to be paid, because the subs are required to get their money before the prime does.

Although the primes are looking for good suppliers, the key operative word is "good." You are not going to get a contract just because you're small, minority, woman-owned or some other defined category. You still have to supply them with good quality products on time and at a competitive price.

Less Administrative Burden

In general, there is less administrative burden for a subcontractor because many of the administrative requirements imposed by the government are borne by the prime. Some burdens might pass through or "flow down" to subcontractors, but there are relatively few. Also, the dollar value of a subcontract is often below the dollar threshold that must be reached before many of the government requirements kick in.

Have a problem while working on the job? If your contract is directly with the government, you would have to follow a certain prescribed procedure and chain of command, as would the government, for submitting your problem and getting it resolved.

If your contract is with a prime, you could probably get your problem resolved with a phone call. There will be structure in dealing with a prime, but it is not as rigid as the government structure. In addition, there is another advantage—payment protection.

More Protection

Traditionally, small businesses have dreamed of doing business with one of the "Big 3" auto makers. Associated with doing subcontracting work for any big player is the perception that you are part of a small, but "elite" group of small businesses that will always have work and will end up making lots and lots of money.

However, perception is not reality, and there are some definite disadvantages that you could experience in working for the Big 3 (or for any other big commercial company, for that matter) that you won't experience in working for a government prime. Some subcontractors to big players have found themselves dependent on these companies for 50 to 90 percent of their work and, because of that, having to work on slimmer and slimmer margins when "requested" to do so. It's easy to see why these small companies probably end up feeling more "stuck" than "elite."

Why won't you experience this same thing working for a government prime? Because just as the government is required, by law, to pay its contractors within 30 days after receiving a proper invoice, so are government primes required, by contract, to pay their subcontractors.

In fact, contractors do not get paid until they have shown proof that they have paid their subcontractors. This is called "flow down"—where the government requires specific prime contract requirements to flow down to subcontractors and be incorporated into their subcontracts.

Caution

However, there is a downside of "flow down." For example, if right now you are thinking, "Great! If I have no contractual relationship with the government, I won't have to deal with all that government paperwork and all those rules and requirements," you'd better think again. If the contract is complex, you could actually be required to put up with some of the same paperwork, rules, and obligations as the prime under a "flow down" clause in your subcontract.

Flow-down clauses are especially common in government and construction subcontracts. The government, recognizing the need to assure that important federal policies are followed throughout performance, sometimes will require specific prime contract requirements to flow down to subcontractors and be incorporated into their subcontracts.

The usual flow-down clause will incorporate, by reference, parts of the prime contract into the subcontract. Such clauses bind the subcontractor to the prime to the same extent that the prime is bound to the government. In effect, the prime contractor's duties and obligations "flow down" to the subcontractor. What was that about no paperwork?

However, if you have a problem with a prime contractor that involves a flow-down clause in the prime contract concerning subcontractors, such as paying for work performed or some technical issue, the government could possibly decide to step in on your side and help you fix it. (This depends on the nature and severity of the problem. There is no guarantee that the government will do anything.) However, if your problem does not involve a government flow-down requirement concerning subcontractors, you are on your own; the government will not help you.

Chapter 23

Lay the Groundwork

Before you even think about actually making a bid on subcontracting work, there are some things that you need to do to improve your chances for success. Finding the "right" prime (i.e., one whose products or services match your capabilities) and effectively presenting yourself and your company are going to take a little forethought and more than a little preparation.

To adequately prepare, you need to take action in each of the following areas for each prime that interests you:

- Find the right primes and the right people to talk to

- Do your homework and learn about the 3 Cs: your customer (i.e., each prime that interests you), your competition, and your own capabilities

- Learn how to sell yourself

- Get on Approved/Preferred Vendor Lists

FIND THE RIGHT PRIMES AND THE RIGHT PEOPLE

We have found that the most effective way to begin finding subcontracting work with a government prime is to:

1. identify the primes that have government contracts and regularly use small business subcontractors to satisfy their contract goals

2. get the name(s) of who to contact at each company

There are two main directories on the Internet that can help you get started.

First, you can find information about the prime contractors that have contracts with military government agencies at http://www.acq.osd.mil/sadbu/publications/subdir/index.html. Click on "Subcontracting Opportunities with DoD Major Prime Contractors" and then the state that interests you. This directory is issued annually by the Office of Small and Disadvantaged Business Utilization and lists, by state, the names and addresses of DoD prime contractors that have military contracts, the product or service line that the company provides to the DoD, and the name and telephone number of each prime contractor's Small Business Liaison Officer (SBLO).

An important part of the SBLO's job is to provide informational assistance to small businesses about subcontracting matters. They can tell you about past, present, and future purchases at their contractor locations.

In many companies, the small business liaison (or coordinator or director or similar title) is much like the government buyer: He or she is the person in the company who sources and/or works with subcontractors. Therefore, after you have done all your research and preparation work, this is more than likely the person (or one of the persons) that you have to market to.

A second directory that provides prime and contact information is at http://www.sba.gov/gopher/Government-Contracting/Subcontracting-Directory/. Here you will find a list of the names and addresses of the primes that have civilian contracts as well as the type of business and the name and phone number of the person you should contact for each prime. You can view or download the entire list of prime contractors or just the list for a particular state.

Think of these contacts as the front door to that company. Even if you don't fit into the plans for government-related work of the companies you contact, you might be able to get involved in their commercial work or, perhaps, both. After you prepare your presentation, you will want to call, visit, or write any contact whose business has products or services that might offer subcontracting opportunities for you.

But before you meet with a prime or its liaison person, you first have to do some homework. You have to learn more about each prime that interests you and take a closer look at the competition and your very own company.

Work Smart

Note that there are other directories on the Internet that might be able to help you find the right primes as well. For example, you can find one at http://www.ustreas.gov/sba/rfqlist.html that lists the prime contractors for the Department of the Treasury whose contracts require subcontracting plans as well as the names of their contact people. A search for "subcontracting directories" or other similar term might yield still others that interest you.

At this point, you may be thinking, "Wow, what a lot of work! Isn't there another approach I can use to find the primes with subcontracting opportunities?"

There is another approach to finding primes with subcontracting work using SUB-*Net* (http://web.sba.gov/subnet/), a government web site that is primarily used by primes with government contracts to post "live" solicitations for the products or services that they need from subcontractors. Here you can locate "live" subcontracting opportunities in your area of expertise. While the web site is designed primarily as a place for large businesses to post solicitations and notices, it is also used by federal agencies, state and local governments, nonprofit organizations, colleges and universities, and even foreign governments to post subcontracting opportunities.

You can identify subcontracting opportunities in one of two ways: You can search for opportunities that might be a fit for your capabilities, or you can fill out a profile about your company and have notices about opportunities that match your profile automatically sent to you. You can then decide whether to respond.

While this approach to finding primes requires less effort than researching, it will not get you the best results. And why not?

Because presenting yourself and your company's capabilities to the right primes and/or the right people within each company before a subcontract is awarded or, better yet, before bids are ever posted gives you an edge in the process.

By focusing on "live" bids as they come out, you are just part of a very large crowd. But by focusing on getting to know the right people first, you are ahead of the game. Primes get to know you and get to know all about what your company has to offer them. This could put you in the very favorable position of being part of the prime's planning process.

SUB-*Net* is a good resource that, when used in combination with seeking out the right people, will help you cover all bases.

Work Smart

There is no business in the world that is totally self-sufficient and does not depend on other businesses to create leverage, discuss issues and problems, and learn from one another. One of the most missed sources of leads, information, and advice is your peers.

You should go to business and chamber events (and any other event, for that matter, that relates to the improvement or advancement of your business) where you can meet with other businesses in your community. This is a rich source of information and you'd be surprised what you will find out.

However, as with any organization or group you join, you will only get out of it what you put in. If you only go to one or two meetings a year, don't expect much. Instead, become involved—better yet become a leader. Volunteer for events and functions. Join a committee; become its chairperson.

DO YOUR HOMEWORK

If you are serious about selling your company's products or services to a prime, it is going to take some work. Successful selling is knowing: your customer, your competition, and your capabilities.

Get To Know Your Customer

When we say, "get to know your customer," we mean that you need to learn everything you can about each prime that might offer some opportunity for you, including how it does business, what it needs, and what it doesn't need.

What does the prospective prime sell or produce? What product or service does it provide to its customers? What does the prime make in-house? What does it outsource? What products or services does it need to fulfill its manufacturing needs? And what's important to this particular prime? What are its hot buttons? Fast service? Quality parts? What does it need?

Identify your customers' needs and requirements and you'll always have work!

Work Smart

If you offer generic types of products—products that are used by almost every business no matter what product they manufacture or service they provide (for example, office supplies, janitorial services, or other products of a non-technical, consumer-like nature)—you don't need an intimate knowledge of a prime's products or services. But you do need to know how they buy the type of services that you can provide. Do they use corporate-wide contracts or can each location buy on its own?

As important as it is to know what each prospective prime needs, it is equally important to know what it doesn't need. For instance, you might have to look not only at what the prime buys, but also in what quantity.

Knowing the quantities of items can help you evaluate whether a prospective prime presents a good opportunity for your business. For example, if you need to sell 10,000 widgets per year to be profitable and a particular prime buys only 300 to 1,000 of that item over a year's time, you may want to re-evaluate whether you want to spend your time and effort trying to sell to a prime that buys such low quantities. In that case, the prime's needs and your needs may not be the good match you thought it was. And it is best to know this information before you walk in the door, so you don't waste precious time—both yours and the prime's. Remember, the average sales call costs your company about $250, so use your time wisely. Ask better questions!

Example

In general, small businesses that need long production-run items (usually in the tens or hundreds of thousands) and are looking in the government arena might be disappointed. The government and government primes usually need what some small businesses would consider short-run production (at the max, at the thousands level). There may be higher volume in certain products, such as ammunition, that are used up or worn out rapidly, but for the most part, it's going to be a low volume situation.

Where can you find this information? You can find much of it by doing research from the comfort of your own desk. Many, if not all, of the large prime businesses have web sites that should provide most of the information you need. The business section of your local newspaper or current or back issues of the *Wall Street Journal* may be of help. The Business Section of your local library could offer other helpful materials. A commercial web site that you may want to check out is www.govexec.com, which covers the federal government and usually has informative articles. It also publishes special editions on the top 100 or 200 federal contractors and on the IT business world.

Work Smart

A quick trip to your local PTAC (Procurement Technical Assistance Center) can also help you get information about the large government prime contractors in your area. PTACs participate regularly in meetings and conferences with large primes, both on a regional and national basis, to discuss contracting and government issues. Therefore, your PTAC is in a good position to help you make contact with the large primes in your area. It can tell you who the large primes in your area are, can advise you on which contractors might offer the best opportunity for your particular capability and what the issues might be, and can keep you informed about opportunities to present your capabilities to the group or attend a matchmaker conference (see www.wingovcon.com to find your local PTAC).

As a matter of fact, a trip to your local PTAC can help jump-start the subcontracting (or contracting) process for you at any stage and for free (for more information on PTACs, see "Part IV: Who Will Help Me?").

Since part of their job is to provide information to prospective small business subcontractors, you can also make a preliminary fact-finding call to the small business liaison or representative or the purchasing office of each prime you are interested in. Ask about their needs, the type of subcontractor they are looking for, the procedure required to become one of their subs, and the average size of an order.

Work Smart

Recently we had the good fortune of hearing a speaker at a government business conference who would be an inspiration to any small business working hard to succeed. She started as the sole employee/owner of a minority woman-owned business that today is doing millions of dollars in business with a prime contractor. What are the secrets to her success?

She came back to the same two "secrets" again and again: (1) She spent a great deal of time and effort identifying exactly what her targeted customer's needs and requirements were, and (2) she then set up her business to meet those needs and requirements to the letter.

She didn't try to get the prime to lower its expectations, or just give her a chance, or change the way it worked, or accommodate her on any level. Instead, she adapted to the prime's requirements and way of doing business. She got in step with the prime, instead of expecting or wishing that the prime would get in step with her. She didn't look for or take any shortcuts. She found out what was needed and simply did the work to make it happen.

If you want to be successful, you can't take any short cuts either. You have to do the work. You have to find out what they need and how they want it and then give it to them.

Get To Know Your Capabilities

After you have identified your prime's needs and requirements, you need to decide whether your company can provide them—i.e., whether your company and the prime are a possible match.

If, at first glance, you decide that you cannot fit into the prime's needs because you don't make the specific product the prime uses, take a moment to reconsider.

You probably spend lots of time thinking about what your company does, makes, etc., but how much time do you spend thinking about what your company *could* do, make, etc.?

Try thinking in terms of your capabilities. How can you use your same equipment, skills and processes to make other things—perhaps things you never even considered before (and perhaps things that the prime needs)? Changing the question from "Does my company make this?" to "Is my company capable of making this?" creates more possibility (and maybe more business).

However, in the end, unless you provide—or have the capability to provide—products or services that can be an integral part of what the prime needs, you will just end up spinning your wheels and being disappointed. If your capabilities are compatible with what the prime needs, you are a potential fit. If they are not, move on to the next prime.

Example

Re-thinking your process (be it welding or manufacturing or writing or whatever) in terms of the end product(s) that you are capable of producing can be good for your business, even if you never work for the government or a prime.

A few years ago, business was very slow for a small arc welding company that we know of. It did precision welding of industrial parts, but the economy had slowed down, none of its regular customers needed its normal services, and the company felt it had marketed to everybody in the area that might. Then at a meeting, someone had an idea: "We keep talking about working on the same kind of products. Let's not keep going in the same circles. Let's try to think about welding something we never tried before." When they began brainstorming about things they could make that were metal and that there might be a market for, it dawned on them that they could also make furniture out of metal.

Today, they are making lamps, chairs, and tables, among other things, out of steel and aluminum. In fact, they opened a showroom, and their furniture making could turn into a nice profit center for them.

What can you take away from this example? Don't get stuck on what you have always done or are doing now. Take the time to set a vision for what you can do.

Get To Know Your Competition

The third area you need to research is your competition.

Your goal here is to gather as much intelligence as you can about these companies, including the type of work they are doing for prime contractors, how much work they are getting, how they work with a particular prime, what they do best, etc.

However, getting this information is easier said than done. In your initial contact with the prime company, you can try asking about these issues. If the prime is not forthcoming with information, drop it and do some detective work on your own.

There's an element of practicality that needs to come into play here since all the answers about your competitors will probably require considerable time and effort. If you're looking at a big opportunity and it really does feel like there's a good fit in there, you might want to do as much as you possibly can. If it's not that type of a situation, we recommend you spend less time and effort. Do what you can, but consider rate of return on investment when you decide how to spend your time.

Are You Competitive?

As long as we're on the subject of competition, we'd like you to consider another important issue: How competitive are you in the marketplace? Are your products or services priced "right"? Are your prices competitive? Do they reflect your true overhead costs or do they just reflect some kind of average overhead rate that "seems" right? Could your prices be more competitive? Are you sure?

The hard fact is that unless you know what your true costs are, you can't control them. You can't ever know for sure what your overhead is, or whether your prices are "right," or whether you are being as competitive as possible.

If you don't really know what your costs are, we strongly recommend that you look into some type of activity-based costing, in which you look at everything—from your lights and heat and wages and unemployment, etc. to the costs of each activity, like sending out an invoice or preparing a proposal—and put a cost on it. Only then can you know your true costs and only then can you be sure about your pricing and about how competitive you can really be. (For more details on the ABC costing method, see chapter 12.)

You can look on the Internet for information on average rates, average salary information, etc. In addition, the U.S. Census Bureau has business statistics that you can use to gauge such things as whether you are salary-competitive with the industry. You can also obtain general average-rate information with regard to your industry from a consultant perspective from the SBA's Business Information Centers (BICs).

LEARN HOW TO SELL YOURSELF

Selling to large companies with government contracts is no different than selling to them in the commercial arena. Here are a few tips that may help you:

- Be courteous and considerate. Make an appointment and be on time.

- Be professional. Don't demand!

- Prepare your presentation. The research you have done earlier on the prime will pay off in creating your presentation. It should focus on one main point: How you can meet the prime's needs and fulfill all their requirements.

- Keep your presentation short, on point, and clear, and be sure to practice, practice, practice. Keep necessary supporting materials or documents out of the presentation in order to keep it short and focused; you can hand them out at the end. Don't just memorize the presentation (if someone asks a question in the middle of it, you may get lost.) Memorize just the important points you want to cover. Talk it; don't just read it and don't just wing it.

- Be ready to offer a 30-second summary/outline about your company. When you get to the point where you can tell your storyline in 30 seconds, you will find more people wanting to talk to you about what you do. Unfortunately, many companies adopt the opposite strategy, telling everything about the company: what they can do; how good they are; "just look at this;" how they can change the federal government if it would "just listen;" etc. If you don't talk about your core capabilities, you have lost their interest.

- Be yourself. Don't put on airs and don't try to make yourself something that you're not. Expressions like "I can do anything" or "I can do whatever you want me to do" are usually a turn-off. They make you sound desperate, not impressive. Be honest and realistic about your capabilities.

- Say it well and say it once. In other words, present the capabilities of your company in the best light possible and, when you have done that, stop speaking. If you continue, redundancy tends to set in and you start telling them again what you just told them. If you are uncomfortable with the silence after you have finished, you can throw it back to them and ask if they have any questions.

- An important fact that you have to deal with in today's market is that the moment that you stop being the best deal or best value for your customer, you are in trouble. But, like we explain in the next chapter, best value is not only price. You have to address a variety of other factors as well, including quality and performance. The best deal for one prime could be price; for another it could be something else. You stand a good chance of figuring out what that is for a particular prime if you have done your homework.

Five Things You Should Never Say During a Presentation

1. *Never just say: "We do good work." Instead prove to them that quality and delivery are central to your business. Explain your quality assurance procedures or, even better, show them your quality assurance manual.*

2. *Never just say: "You can't go wrong with us." Instead refer them to other customers that will attest to the quality and reliability of your work.*

3. *Never just say: "You'll really like us." In reality, the prime will "like" you only if you make him/her look good to the boss and to the government. Instead, emphasize that you always come through, as promised, on quality, delivery, and any other project requirements that you sign up for.*

4. *Never just say: "I know my trade. I've been in business for twenty years!" On its own, this statement probably won't impress the prime. But explaining how you have made your business more efficient over the years and producing a long list of satisfied customers over the 20-year span will. It will show your ability and willingness to keep up with new developments in your field as well as new ways of doing business.*

5. *Never just say: "We'll do anything and everything for you." Very unrealistic. Instead, let the prime know that you are ready and willing to abide by their protocols and procedures, and fulfill on their requirements.*

GET ON APPROVED/PREFERRED VENDOR LISTS

Almost every large business, including prime contractors, have an Approved/Preferred Vendor List, or something very similar, that lists the vendors and subcontractors that have been approved by the prime for quality, on-time delivery, and other factors. Many small businesses work very hard to get on these lists. And you should, as well, because being on the list means that you have passed the test that allows you to sell your products or services to that particular prime.

How do you get on these lists? Basically, you need to do two things: First, you need to fill out their Approved/Preferred Vendor evaluation form, and second, submit to an inspection.

Fill Out the Application Form

Each company has its own version of the Approved/Preferred Vendor Application Form, which you can obtain from the prime's small business liaison or purchasing department. The information that you will be asked to provide will vary from prime to prime, depending on the type of work you will be doing.

A few words of caution about filling out the form: Don't think of the vendor approval form as just another formality or just another piece of paper that you can quickly fill out and send in. You need to be concerned and careful about the information you enter. Submitting a vendor form with a set of numbers missing or filling in the wrong (or illegible) information could end your chances of winning a potentially lucrative contract. Therefore, before you return the form to the prime, make sure that it is complete, correct, and readable. Check it, and then check it again.

Are you on one or two lists already? Well, good for you, but in the long run it will be better for you to try to get on the lists of several different primes. One of the hidden dangers of focusing on doing business with just one or two large companies is that you become too dependent on them. Imagine the shock of losing 50 or 75 percent of your business in one day. And with all your eggs in only one or two baskets, so to speak, you are putting yourself in a position where this could happen. (Sadly, we have seen it more than once.)

This same principle of spreading your base applies to the industries with which you do business as well. It is worth the effort to try to generate business in different industries, if possible, or at least in different segments of an industry.

For your convenience, we have created a "Sample Approved/Preferred Vendor Application Form." It is a compilation of all the information that, in our experience, primes are looking for when they want to learn about a new vendor.

Although each prime has its own version of the application form, depending on its type of business, this is a good start and might help you fill out the real forms. As with most situations, if you have questions about the form, you can request help from your local PTAC.

Sample Approved/Preferred Vendor Application Form

Company Name _____

Address _____

City/State/Zip _____

Phone _____ Fax _____

CEO Name _____ CEO Title _____

CEO E-mail _____ CEO Phone _____

Marketing E-mail _____

Social Security Number _____ Name of SSN Owner _____

Federal Tax ID Number _____

Subcontracting: Another Huge Opportunity

---------------------- COMPANY INFORMATION ----------------------

Organization Type: Sole Owner ____ Corporation ____   S-Corp. ____

State of Incorporation? _____ Nonprofit? ____ Yes ____No

Other Socioeconomic Factor(s)? _____

Domestic/Foreign Owned? _____

Is your company owned by a parent company? ____Yes ____No

Parent Company Name _____

Parent Company Address _____

Parent Company Tax ID _____

Are you: Small Business? ____ Minority-Owned Business? ____ Veteran-Owned

Business? ____ Women-Owned Business? ____ Veteran Disabled-Owned Business? ___

Other Socioeconomic Factor(s)? _____

Certifications: 8a Certified? ____ Minority? ____ Women-Owned? ____ HUBZone? ____

Mentor Program: Mentor Company _____

Contact Information _____ Phone Number _____

Does your company accept credit cards? ____Yes ____No

Primary Standard Industrial Code _____

Additional SICs _____

Primary North American Industry Classification System Code (NAICS) _____

Additional NAICSs _____

Products/Services (short narrative): _____

_____

_____

Company's Web Site(s): _____

FSCM/Cage Code _____

Registered CCR?   ____Yes ____No

Did your company have a name change in the past 12 months?   ____Yes ____No

Name _____

Company Contact _____ Quality Assurance Contact _____

---------------------- GENERAL INFORMATION ----------------------

Area in Sq. Ft.: Manufacturing _____ Office _____ Total _____

Number of Personnel: Manufacturing _____ Quality Assurance _____ Engineering _____

Are clean room facilities used for manufacturing product? _____ Yes____ No

What percentage of present work is: Government _____ Commercial _____ Other _____

Describe any special processes that you perform (e.g., plating, painting, soldering, welding, wire wrap, etc.). _____

_____

Are you ISO-9000 certified? ____ Yes ____ No ISO Certificate Type _____

Registrar _____ Certificate Number _____

Expiration Date: ISO READY/Not Certified _____ Date of Certification _____

Registered or certified to any other Quality Management System or model?

_____ Mil-I-45208 _____ Mil-Q-9858 _____ Other

---------------------- QUALITY MANAGEMENT SYSTEM ----------------------

Do you maintain operation policies and procedures for your quality management system? ____ Yes ____ No

Is an internal audit program maintained that reviews compliance with all aspects of the quality program? ____ Yes ____ No

Does the organizational structure define quality responsibility and authority? ____ Yes ____ No

Does the organizational structure provide access to top management? ____ Yes ____ No

Is the health and status of your quality management system periodically reviewed with management? ____ Yes ____ No

Do you have a documented employee training program? ____ Yes ____ No

Is the quality organization responsible for acceptance of product and services? ____ Yes ____ No

Are records of inspections and tests maintained? ____ Yes ____ No

Are quality data used in reporting results and trends to management? ____ Yes ____ No

Are quality records available to support customer certifications? ____ Yes ____ No

---------------------- *DESIGN INFORMATION* ----------------------

Do procedures cover the release, change, and recall of design and manufacturing information, including correlation of customer specification? ____Yes ____No

Do records reflect the incorporation of changes? ____Yes ____No

Does quality control verify that changes are incorporated at the effective points? ____Yes ____No

Is the control of design and manufacturing information applied to the procurement activity? ____Yes ____No

Is there a formal deviation procedure? ____Yes ____No

---------------------- *PROCUREMENT CONTROL* ----------------------

Are procurement sources evaluated and monitored? ____Yes ____No

Are quality requirements and inspection procedures specified? ____Yes ____No

Is a documented system maintained for the evaluation of purchased materials? ____Yes ____No

Are incoming materials identified and segregated until acceptance? ____Yes ____No

---------------------- *MATERIAL CONTROL* ----------------------

Do procedures exist for storage, release, and movement of material? ____Yes ____No

Are materials in storage identified and controlled? ____Yes ____No

Are in-process materials identified and controlled? ____Yes ____No

Are materials inspections identified and controlled? ____Yes ____No

Do storage areas and facilities provide control to protect material from degradation? ____Yes ____No

Do you have an electrostatic sensitive device protection program? ____Yes ____No

Are nonconforming items identified, segregated, and controlled? ____Yes ____No

If required, do you have the ability to provide tractability? ____Yes ____No

Prepare for and Pass an Evaluation/Inspection

After you have submitted your application to the prime, the second thing that you need to do to get on the Approved/Preferred Vendor

List of a particular prime is to prepare for and pass some sort of evaluation or inspection. The prime wants to assure that you are qualified and can comply with the subcontracting requirements.

The evaluation can be anything from a desk review, in which the prime will examine your company's records, financial statements, and other documentation, to a full site inspection of your facility. The type of evaluation depends on the circumstances of the contract and/or on company policy.

If you are providing a critical part of the end product or there appears to be a potential for a long-term business arrangement, the prime will probably want to do a full site inspection, which can be done by one person or a whole team. If that is the case, in addition to having your documentation ready for examination, you will also need to be ready to address questions and look your best.

If, on the other hand, your work involves a requirement that is ancillary in nature, a desk review may suffice.

Caution

While the full-fledged evaluation/inspection we describe is basically an initial event that is part of getting on a prime's approved/preferred list, you can expect the prime to return, possibly multiple times, to inspect once you have won a subcontract and begun doing work. For example, the prime might want its quality or production people to watch a particular phase, to verify that a particular requirement is being fulfilled properly, or to just make sure that everything is on track. The type and frequency of inspections will depend on the terms of the particular contract and will occur as the need arises or as the situation or contract changes.

What type of information do you need to get ready for an evaluation? Following is a list of some general categories of data that you will be asked to provide (note that gathering this data will prepare you for an inspection by any prime that you may be interested in):

- **Manpower** — Include the availability of technical and supervisory personnel with special skills and know-how.

- **Facilities and equipment** — List your equipment and include the arrangements you have made for additional facilities and equipment, if needed.

- **Quality assurance** — Show the system(s) you use and indicate whether they have been approved by any government agency or other prime.

- **Production scheduling** — Have charts ready to show how you plan to meet the prime's schedules.

- **Schedule of total workload** — Include any anticipated and any repeat work as well as the dollar value of any remaining backlog.

- **Bill of materials** — Include a description of the product to be made in your plant and a list of materials you need to buy from the suppliers. Identify what you can do in-house and what, if anything, needs to be outsourced.

- **Inventory** — Check your existing inventory for usability on the proposed contract. Identify what steps you are taking to ensure that the parts and products you will need on the proposed subcontract will be on hand.

- **Materials, suppliers, and/or subcontractors** — Include written or other confirmations on delivery dates of major and critical items.

- **Cost breakdown and analysis** — Describe costs in sufficient detail to allow evaluation of cash flow spreadsheets.

- **Cash flow spreadsheets** — Include sheets for the proposed contract and for the company's total workload. Reconcile these with the production schedule and the company's commitments for materials as well as other financial commitments.

- **Financial statements** — Include, if necessary, your most recent profit and loss statement and balance.

Work Smart

Most primes will give you high marks for good documentation (as does the government). Therefore, as you gather this information, put it all in one place. Anything from a 3-ring binder to an electronic file will suffice—so long as you have covered the issues outlined above and the information is current and complete. It is nice to be able to just pull a book off the shelf or pull up a file on your computer and present information that is current, complete, and easy to interpret. This is a professional touch that will assure the prime that you are in control of the situation and that you have all your ducks in a row.

Chapter 24

Final Tips
To Seal the Deal

At this point, you've done all you can do to prepare to be a subcontractor to a prime government contractor. You've explored the numerous opportunities through various sources. The government is on your side—rules have been enacted to encourage small business participation in the process. You've laid the groundwork, by doing your homework on prospective primes and the competition. You may have even considered making changes to your operations to better position your company to compete.

All that's left is to sign a deal. To get that signature on the dotted line, we recommend that you follow this advice:

- Bid selectively and wisely

- Focus on providing "best value"

- Improve your chances as a sub

- Be what a prime looks for in a sub

- Put your best foot forward

BID WISELY AND SELECTIVELY

No business—large or small—is going to win all of the contracts they try for. Statistics show that, at best, you will win less than one-third of the contracts you bid on.

Our advice is to bid only when you are sure that you have a reasonable chance of success; in other words, only under the following conditions:

- when you have researched the product or service the prime is providing and you are sure that the prime's needs and your capabilities are a match

- when your qualifications are a near-perfect match with the requirements

- when your price is very competitive but still profitable for you

FOCUS ON PROVIDING "BEST VALUE"

The philosophical criteria that prime contractors use for awarding subcontracts has changed. It used to be that if you were qualified and were low bidder, you would probably win the subcontract. These days, that is no longer true. The prevailing philosophy that governs a prime's decision as to which company will win is no longer "lowest price," but rather "best value."

How, then, is "best value" defined? That's a tough question with no clear-cut answer. Often best value is some combination of quality, price, and performance. It also could be said to be what makes the best business sense. For example, the fact that a prospective subcontractor never missed a delivery schedule could be more important to a prime than the fact that it is a bit higher on price. Even if its price isn't the lowest, when you throw it all together, it is.

Other issues could also factor in, depending on the prime's specific needs or special requirements. For example, a prime looking for creative ways of improving production efficiencies would favor the sub that does a good job *and* offers that creativity over a sub that just does a good job. To another prime with special training needs, one sub's training experience would probably give that sub an advantage over another that didn't have that experience or didn't offer that added feature.

Therefore, we can say two things, for sure, about best value: (1) it varies from prime to prime, depending on their individual needs and requirements, and (2) lowest price alone just doesn't do it any more.

Note that the procurement philosophy for the government has also changed to best value. That's why doing your homework to find out what your customer's needs are (be it the government or a prime) and focusing on those needs is so important.

Work Smart

Quite often, prime companies have the need, but not the actual technical expertise, to do a job. If you are a top-notch engineer or technical person, you can do quite well as a subcontractor – and you get to create your own hours and vacation time!

IMPROVE YOUR CHANCES AS A SUB

As much as primes are looking for quality products at reasonable prices, they are also looking for subcontractors that can help them hold up their end of the bargain with the government and make the contract go smoothly.

Is there anything that could tip the scales in your favor? You can greatly improve your chances of getting the job if you can show that you are willing and able to learn the prime's protocols, do the required conferencing and follow-ups, and familiarize yourself with any required contract details and forms. As a sub, timing is crucial and communication is essential. Let the prime know that you are aware of this and are ready to satisfy their needs in these areas as well.

Lastly, all things being equal, most primes will choose the subcontractor that they think they can work with the easiest and the best.

BE WHAT A PRIME LOOKS FOR IN A SUB

Becoming a subcontractor takes hard work, persistence and a thick skin for rejection. Even when you do everything "right," you may still be passed over simply because you don't fit the profile of what the prime is looking for.

In deciding whether to use a sub, and which sub is right for the job, primes look at a variety of issues. Should they make or buy? Is it going to be less expensive for them to go out of plant to get the work done? Are there union issues? Is the technology such that they can only buy or use a sub? Does the potential subcontractor have the needed technical ability and qualifications to do the work? Are there socio-economic considerations in making a decision, like using small, minority-, women-, service-disabled-, and/or veteran-owned, businesses?

Our advice, then, is to prepare yourself and your company to look and function its best so you are ready to take advantage of an opportunity when it comes along. If you are serious about turning the opportunity into a subcontract, be prepared to burn the midnight oil.

PUT YOUR BEST FOOT FORWARD

Here is a review of the actions that will help prepare you to select the primes that match your capabilities and make the best first impression on your potential customer. This list does not include every possible action, nor will every action on the list be appropriate for your situation. But you can use it as a guide as you move through the process. Good luck!

- Identify what your company does best and what you are most competitive at. If you don't have one, make a list of your company's features and benefits. Think not only in terms of the products or services you provide, but also in terms of what you are capable of providing. Think in terms of possibilities!

- Check out the products the prime manufactures and the components and services they require to fulfill their mission. Determine which primes match your capabilities—not by guessing or assuming but by thoroughly researching. Select your target primes.

- Do your research and gather as much information as you can about your target primes. Check out their web sites, search the Internet, and check out the Business Reference Section of your local library for articles about the company in the *Wall Street Journal*, local newspapers, or trade magazines. You will make a better professional impression if you know the basics about these companies when you walk into your first meeting with them.

- Contact each of your target primes. Ask to speak to their small business liaison or representative or the purchasing office.

- In your initial contact, focus on getting the right information—i.e., information that will help you decide whether a particular prime offers some real opportunity. Ask about their needs, the type of subcontractor they are looking for, the procedure required to become one of their subs, and the average size of an order. Also ask about any required forms or documents that they may want you to fill out, including their Approved/Preferred Vendor application.

- Find out what your competition is doing. Your goal is to gather as much intelligence about how they're working with a particular prime as you can. In your initial contact with the prime, try asking about the type of work your competition is doing, how much work they are getting, the kind of relationship that exists, etc. If the prime is not forthcoming with information, drop it and do some detective work on your own.

- After contacting each target prime, weed out the primes that offer no real opportunity, and fill out any forms of those that seem promising. Make sure that all the information is complete and correct, and that you make a copy of the forms for your files.

- Preplan the sales call and presentation, and then practice, practice, practice. Never just read the presentation and never present completely off the cuff. Keep your presentation short, simple, and to the point—perhaps four or five slides with three or four bullets per slide. Hit only those points that address the prime's needs, such as the quality of your product or service, timeliness of delivery, related experience, and ability to be a team player. Include any unique ability or quality that singles you out from your competition and imply the competitiveness of your pricing.

- After the forms are complete and your presentation is ready, make an appointment to meet with the prime's small business liaison or representative. Be professional, friendly, and enthusiastic. Your goal is to convince the prime that working with you will be a good business arrangement for them. What is it that you do best? Emphasize that point again.

- No matter how the presentation ends—in a quote, in a request for more information, or up in the air—contact the prime again within 7-10 days to continue the relationship. Try to get a definite response if you didn't get one after your presentation.

- Create your own "good old boy" network. Try to establish some rapport with other personnel of the target prime company, including shop, technical, etc. Take advantage of every opportunity to network with primes and other vendors (yes, even your competition), particularly those vendors that augment your capabilities—you may be able to capitalize on that relationship to get work by partnering. Stay away from gifts and other gratuities. This may damage any relationship, even if offered out of kindness.

- If nothing happens, "pick up your tent" and move on to the next prospect.

Part **VI**

Appendices

Glossary

Following are the abbreviations and acronyms that you will be using when doing business with the federal government. Although not an exhaustive listing, it does contain the most commonly used abbreviations and acronyms that occur in conversations with government buying offices and in documents related to the contracting process.

A

Acceptance: The act of an authorized representative of the government by which the government, for itself or as agent of another, assumes ownership of existing identified supplies tendered, or approves specific services rendered as partial or complete performance of the contract.

Accounts payable: Amounts owed by you to others based on invoices or other evidence of receipt of goods or services, i.e., the amount due for goods or services that have been received but for which payment has not been made.

Accounts receivable: Amounts owed by others to you for goods furnished or services rendered. Reimbursements earned and refund receivables are included.

Accrual benefit cost method: An actuarial cost method where revenues and expenses are identified with specific periods of time and are recorded as incurred without regard to the date of receipt or payment of cash.

Accumulating costs: The collecting of cost data in an organized manner, such as through a system of accounts.

ACH: Automated Clearing House

ACMS: Advanced Cost Management Systems

ACO: Administrative Contracting Officer

Acquisition: The acquiring by contract with appropriated funds of supplies or services (including construction) by and for the use of the federal government through purchase or lease, whether the supplies or services are already in existence or must be created, developed, demonstrated, and evaluated. Acquisition begins at the point when agency needs are established.

Acquisition planning: The process by which the efforts of all personnel responsible for an acquisition are coordinated and integrated through a comprehensive plan for fulfilling the agency need in a timely manner and at a reasonable cost.

ACRS: Accelerated Cost Recovery System

Action program: A contractor's program that complies with Department of Labor regulations to assure equal opportunity in employment to minorities and women.

Actual cash value: The cost of replacing damaged property with other property of like kind and quality in the physical condition of the property immediately before the damage.

Actual costs: An amount sustained in fact on the basis of cost incurred, as distinguished from forecasted or estimated costs.

Adequate price competition: When two or more responsible offerors, competing independently, submit priced offers that satisfy the government's expressed requirements.

Administrative change: A unilateral contract change, in writing, that does not affect the substantive rights of the parties.

Administrative contracting officer (ACO): A contracting officer having responsibility for the administration of one or more particular contracts.

Advance agreement: An agreement negotiated in advance of the incurrence of a particular cost by a contractor specifying how that cost will be treated for purposes of determining its allowability (and thus its allocability) to government contracts. An advance agreement may be negotiated before or during a contract (but before the incurrence of the subject cost), and must be in writing. For a given contractor, advance agreements may be specific to a particular contract, a group of contracts, or all the contracts of a contracting office, an agency, or several agencies.

Advance payment: An advance of money made by the government to a contractor prior to, in anticipation of, and for the purpose of performance under a contract or contracts.

Advisory and assistance services: Those services provided under contract by nongovernmental sources to support or improve organizational policy development, decision-making, management and administration, program and/or project management and administration, or R&D activities.

ADR: Alternative Dispute Resolution

A&E or A/E: Architect-Engineer

AF: Air Force

AFAA: Air Force Audit Agency

Affiliates: Business concerns, organizations, or individuals are affiliates of each other if, directly or indirectly, (a) either one has the power to control the other, or (b) a third party controls or has the power to control both.

AFLC: Air Force Logistics Command

Agent: One employed to transact business for another. To the extent that the agent acts within the authority given, these acts are binding on the principal.

AICPA: American Institute of Certified Public Accountants

AID: Agency for International Development

Allocable cost: A cost that is assignable or chargeable to one or more cost objectives in accordance with the relative benefits received or other equitable relationships defined or agreed to between contractual parties.

Allocate: To assign an item of cost, or a group of items of cost, to one or more cost objectives. This term includes both direct assignment of cost and the reassignment of a share from an indirect cost pool.

Allowable cost: A cost that meets the tests of reasonableness and allocability, is in consonance with standards promulgated by the Cost Accounting Standards Board (if applicable), or otherwise conforms to generally accepted accounting principles, specific limitations or exclusions set forth in FAR 31.201-2, or agreed-to terms between contractual parties.

Alternative dispute resolution (ADR): Any type of procedure or combination of procedures voluntarily used to resolve issues in controversy quickly, creatively, and at less cost than established procedures.

AMC: Army Materiel Command

Amendment: A change to a solicitation before contract award.

AMIS: Agency Management Information System (DCAA)

AMP: Annual Management Plan

Announcement of opportunity (AO): A NASA broad agency announcement that does not specify the investigations to be proposed but solicits investigative ideas that contribute to broad objectives.

Annual funding: The current congressional practice of limiting authorizations and appropriations to one fiscal year at a time.

Anti-Deficiency Act: In accordance with the Act, no officer or employee of the government may create or authorize an obligation in excess of the funds available, or in advance of appropriations, unless otherwise authorized by law.

AO: Announcement of Opportunity

Applied research: The effort that (a) normally follows basic research, but may not be serviceable from the related basic research; (b) attempts to determine and exploit the potential of scientific discoveries or improvements in technology, materials, processes, methods, devices, or techniques; and (c) attempts to advance the state of the art.

Apportionment: Distribution by Office of Management and Budget of amounts available for obligation and outlay in an appropriation or fund account. The amounts may be available only for specified time periods, activities, functions, projects, objects, purposes, or combinations thereof. The specified amounts limit obligations to be incurred.

Appropriation: Statutory authority that allows federal agencies to incur obligations and to make payments out of the Treasury for specified purposes. An appropriation usually follows enactment of authorizing legislation.

AR: Army

Architect-engineer services: Professional services of an architectural or engineering nature, as defined by state law, if applicable, that are required to be performed or approved by a person licensed, registered, or certified to provide such services.

ASBCA: Armed Services Board of Contract Appeals

ASPR: Armed Services Procurement Regulation (changed to the DAR, which in turn was replaced by the FAR)

Assignment of claims: The transfer or making over by the contractor to a bank, trust company, or other financing institution, as security for a loan to the contractor, of its right to be paid by the government for contract performance.

Audit: The systematic examination of records and documents and the securing of other evidence by confirmation, physical inspection, or otherwise, for one or more of the following purposes: determining the propriety or legality of proposed or consummated transactions; ascertaining whether all transactions have been recorded and are reflected accurately in accounts; determining the existence of recorded assets and inclusiveness of recorded liabilities; determining the accuracy of financial or statistical statements or reports and the fairness of the facts they present; determining the degree of compliance with established policies and procedures relative to financial transactions and business management; and appraising an accounting system and making recommendations concerning it.

Automated Clearing House (ACH) Network: A national payment system that uses electronic means to transfer payment data and funds from an originator to a recipient's account at a receiving financial institution.

Award: Occurs when the CO has signed and distributed a contract to the contractor.

B

BAA: Broad Agency Announcement

Basic ordering agreement (BOA): A written instrument of understanding, negotiated between an agency, contracting activity, or contracting office and a contractor, that contains (1) terms and clauses applying to future contracts (orders) between the parties during its term; (2) a description, as specific as practicable, of supplies or services to be provided; and (3) methods for pricing, issuing, and delivering future orders under the BOA. A BOA is not a contract.

Basic research: Research directed toward increasing knowledge in science. The primary aim is a fuller knowledge or understanding of the subject under study rather than any practical application.

BCA: Board(s) of Contract Appeals

BDC: Business Development Center

BDE: Business Development Expense

Benefit-cost analysis: A systematic quantitative method of assessing the desirability of government projects or policies when it is important to take a long view of future effects and a broad view of possible side-effects.

Best value: The expected outcome of an acquisition that, in the government's estimation, provides the greatest overall benefit in response to the requirement.

Bid: A prospective contractor's (bidder's) reply to a formally advertised IFB. Needs only government acceptance to constitute a binding contract.

Bid and proposal (B&P) cost: The cost incurred in preparing, submitting, or supporting any bid or proposal, which effort is neither sponsored by a grant nor required in the performance of a contract.

Bid guarantee: A form of security assuring that the bidder (a) will not withdraw a bid within the period specified for acceptance and (b) will execute a written contract and furnish required bonds including any necessary coinsurance or reinsurance agreements, within the time specified in the bid, unless a longer time is allowed, after receipt of the specified forms.

Bid sample: A sample to be furnished by a bidder to show the characteristics of the product offered in a bid.

Bilateral contract: A contract between two parties and formed by a "promise for a promise," (offer and acceptance).

Billing rate: An indirect cost rate (a) established temporarily for interim reimbursement of incurred indirect costs and (b) adjusted as necessary pending establishment of final indirect cost rates.

Blanket purchase agreement (BPA): A simplified method of filling anticipated repetitive needs for supplies or services by establishing "charge accounts" with qualified sources of supply.

BML: Bidder's Mailing List

BOA: Basic Ordering Agreement

Boiler plate: The standard clauses, sections, and other repetitive language inserted in contracts and other legal documents..

Bond: A written instrument executed by a bidder or contractor and a second party to assure fulfillment of the principal's obligations to a third party.

Book value: Original capitalized value of an asset, adjusted for accumulated depreciation and modifications where appropriate.

BOPCR: Breakout Procurement Center Representative (SBA)

BOS: Business Opportunity Specialist

B&P: Bid and Proposal

BPA: Blanket Purchase Agreement

Breach of contract: A failure to perform any contractual duty of immediate performance. May include failure to perform acts promised, prevention or hindrance, or repudiation.

Breakeven point: The sales volume at which total revenue equals total costs. Profit is zero.

Broad agency announcement (BAA): A general announcement of an agency's research interest, including criteria for selecting proposals and soliciting the participation of all offerors capable of satisfying the government's needs.

Bulk funding: A system whereby a CO receives authorization from a fiscal and accounting officer to obligate funds on purchase documents against a specified lump sum of funds reserved for the purpose for a specified period of time rather than obtaining individual obligational authority on each purchase document.

Bundling: Consolidating two or more requirements for supplies or services, previously provided or performed under separate smaller contracts, into a solicitation for a single contract that is likely to be unsuitable for award to a small business concern.

Burn rate: The monthly rate at which a contractor's funds are expended during a contract.

Business Opportunity Specialist: An SBA employee working with an 8(a) company.

Business unit: Any part of an organization, or an entire business organization, that is divided into segments.

Buying-in: Submitting an offer below anticipated costs, expecting to (a) increase the contract amount after award; or (b) receive follow-on contracts at an artificially high price to recover losses incurred on the buy-in contract.

C

CA: Commercial Activities

CAA: Civilian Agency Acquisition

CAC: Contract Audit Coordinator (Defense Contract Audit Agency)

CACO: Corporate/Home Office Administrative Contracting Officer

CACS: Contract Audit Closing Statement(s) (DCAA)

CAD/CAM: Computer-Aided Design Manufacturing

CAGE Code (Commercial and Government Entity): A contractor identification code that is assigned and maintained by the Defense Logistics Service Center to identify commercial and government activities. They were known in the past as Federal Supply Codes for manufacturers and nonmanufacturers.

CAIG: Cost Analysis Improvement Group (DoD)

CAM: Contract Audit Manual (Defense Contract Audit Agency)

Cancellation: The cancellation, within a contractually specified time, of the total requirements of all remaining program years of a multi-year contract.

CAO: Contract Administration Office (or Officer).

Capital asset: Tangible property, including durable goods, equipment, buildings, installations, and land.

Capital stock: The shares in a corporation representing a percentage of ownership in the business.

Cardinal change: A change outside the scope of the contract. It occurs when the government effects an alteration in the work so drastic that it effectively requires the contractor to perform duties materially different from those originally bargained for.

CAS: Cost Accounting Standard(s)

CAS Board: Cost Accounting Standards Board

Cash basis of accounting: The accounting basis in which revenue and expenses are recorded in the period they are actually received or expended in cash. It generally is not considered to be in conformity with generally accepted accounting principles and is therefore used only in selected situations, such as for very small businesses and, when permitted, for income tax reporting.

CBD: Commerce Business Daily

CCDR: Contractor Cost Data Report(s)(-ing)

CCI: Consolidated Contract Initiative

CDR: Critical Design Review

CDRL: Contracts Data Requirements List

CECSR: Contractor Employee Compensation System Review

Certificate of Competency (COC): A document issued by the SBA stating that the holder is responsible (with respect to all elements of responsibility, including but not limited to capability, competency, capacity, credit, integrity, perseverance, and tenacity) for the purpose of receiving and performing a specific government contract.

Certificate of Current Cost and Pricing Data: A form of certification as set forth in FAR 15.406-2 that must be executed by a contractor certifying the contractor's current cost and pricing data when required to do so under the solicitation or contract.

CFR: Code of Federal Regulations

CFSR: Contract Funds Status Report(s)(-ing)

CFY: Contractor Fiscal Year

Change order: A unilateral written order, signed by the CO, directing the contractor to make a change that the Changes clause authorizes the CO to order, within the general scope of the contract, but without the contractor's consent.

CHOA: Corporate Home Office Auditor

CIPR: Contractor Insurance/Pension Review

Civilian Agency Acquisition (CAA) Council: A group composed of representatives of the Departments of Agriculture, Commerce, Energy, Health and Human Services, Interior, Labor, State, Transportation, Treasury, and Veterans Affairs; the Environmental Protection Agency; and the Small Business Administration that is charged with maintenance of the Federal Acquisition Regulation on a joint basis with the DAR Council.

Claim: A written demand or written assertion by one of the contracting parties seeking, as a matter of right, the payment of money in a sum certain, the adjustment or interpretation of contract terms, or other relief arising under or relating to the contract. A claim arising under a contract, unlike a claim relating to that contract, is a claim that can be resolved under a contract clause that provides for the relief sought by the claimant. However, a written demand or written assertion by the contractor seeking the payment of money exceeding $50,000 is not a claim under the Contract Disputes Act of 1978 until certified as required under the Act and FAR 33.207. A voucher, invoice, or other routine request for payment that is not in dispute when submitted is not a claim. The submission may be converted to a claim, by written notice to the CO as provided at FAR 33.206(a), if it is disputed either as to liability or amount or is not acted upon in a reasonable time.

Clarification: Limited exchanges, between the government and offerors, that may occur after receipt of proposals when award without discussion is contemplated.

Classified information: Any information or material, regardless of its physical form or characteristics, that is owned by the government and determined to require protection against unauthorized disclosure, and is so designated.

Clause: A term or condition used in contracts or in both solicitations and contracts and applying after contract award or both before and after award.

CLIN: Contract Line Item Number

CMO: Contract Management Office

CMS: Contract Management Services

CO: Contracting Officer

COC: Certificate of Competency

Code of Federal Regulations (CFR): A codification of the general and permanent rules published in the Federal Register by the Executive departments and agencies of the federal government.

COE: Corps of Engineers (Army)

Cognizant federal agency: The federal agency responsible for negotiating and approving indirect cost rates on behalf of all federal agencies. For contractors, other than educational institutions and nonprofit organizations, the agency with the largest dollar amount of negotiated contracts, including options.

Collection of information: Under the Paperwork Reduction Act, the obtaining or soliciting of facts or opinions by an agency through the use of written report forms, application forms, schedules, questionnaires, reporting or record-keeping requirement, or other similar methods (including requests for proposal or other procurement requirements). The collection of information by agencies requires OMB approval.

Commerce Business Daily (CBD): The public notification media by which U.S. Government agencies identified proposed contract actions and contract awards. The CBD was published in five or six daily editions weekly, as necessary. The CBD was replaced by the web site FedBizOpps.com.

Commercial advance payment: For a commercial item purchase, a payment made before any performance of work under the contract.

Commercial interim payment: For a commercial item purchase, any payment that is not a commercial advance payment or a delivery payment.

Commercial item/services: Any item, other than real property that is of a type customarily used for nongovernment purpose in accordance with FAR 2.101. Services of a type offered and sold competitively in substantial quantities in the commercial marketplace based on established catalog or market prices for specific tasks performed under standard commercial terms and conditions.

Commercial off-the-shelf (COTS) item: An item produced and placed in stock by a contractor, or stocked by a distributor, before receiving orders or contracts for its sale. They require no unique government modification to meet the needs of the government.

Commitment: Administrative reservations of allotments and resources authority based on approved requisitions, procurement requests, authorizations to execute contracts, or other written evidence that authorizes the creation of obligations without further recourse to the official responsible for certifying the availability of the allotment and resources authority.

Compensated personal absence: Any absence from work for any reason such as illness, vacation, holidays, jury duty, military training, or personal activities for which an employer pays compensation directly to an employee in accordance with a plan or custom of the employer.

Compensation: Wages, salaries, honoraria, commissions, professional fees, and any other form of payment, provided directly or indirectly for services rendered.

Competition: An environment of varying dimensions relating to buy-sell relationships in which the buyer induces, stimulates, or relies on conditions in the marketplace that cause independent sellers to contend confidently for the award of a contract.

Competition advocate: The person within each procurement activity who is responsible for challenging barriers to and promoting full and open competition.

Competitive range: A range appropriate to the post-evaluation, pre-award phase of competitive procurements. Determined by the CO on the basis of ratings of each proposal against all evaluation criteria.

Completion form: A cost-plus-fixed-fee contract that describes the scope of work by stating a definite goal or target and specifying an end product.

Component: Any item supplied to the federal government as part of an end item or of another component.

Component facility: A complex that is geographically separated from the NASA Center or institution to which it is assigned.

Configuration: A collection of an item's descriptive and governing characteristics that can be expressed in functional terms, i.e., what performance the item is expected to achieve, and also in physical terms, i.e., what the item should look like and consist of when it is built.

Consideration: Something of value exchanged by the parties when making changes to a contract, e.g., reducing the cost to allow extending delivery dates. Also, the inducement to a contract: the cause, motive, price, or impelling reason that induces a contracting party to enter into a contract.

Consolidated Contracting Initiative (CCI): NASA's commitment to progress towards developing, using, and sharing contract resources, whenever practicable, to meet agency needs. CCI aims at identifying and logically consolidating similar requirements whenever it makes sense.

Construction: Construction, alteration, or repair (including dredging, excavating, and painting) of buildings, structures, or other real property.

Constructive change: A contract change without formal written authority. During contract performance, an oral or written act or omission by the CO or other authorized government official that is of such a nature that it is construed to have the same effect as a written change order; e.g., when a contractor performs work beyond that required by the contract and it is perceived that such work was ordered by the government, or caused by government fault. The contractor is entitled to an equitable adjustment for a constructive change.

Constructive delivery: Concept under which costs are accrued as a contractor performs work on a contract, where goods are manufactured to Government specifications, since the Government takes title to goods as work progresses.

Contingent fee: Any commission, percentage, brokerage, or other fee that is contingent upon the success that a person or concern has in securing a government contract.

Contingent liability: Potential liability that may arise from presently known and existing conditions, the effects of which are foreseeable within reasonable limits of accuracy; e.g., anticipated costs of rejects or defective work.

Contract: A mutually binding legal relationship obligating the seller to furnish supplies or services (including construction) and the buyer to pay for them. Contracts do not include grants or cooperative agreements.

Contract administration: Costs incurred by the government in assuring that a contract is faithfully executed by both the government and contractor. Includes the cost of reviewing contractor performance and compliance with the contract terms (project surveillance plan), processing contract payments, negotiating change orders, and monitoring the closeout of contract operations.

Contract Administration Office (CAO): An office that performs (a) assigned post-award functions related to the administration of contracts and (b) assigned pre-award functions.

Contract financing payment: A government disbursement of monies to a contractor under a contract clause or other authorization prior to acceptance of supplies or services by the government.

Contract value: Total definitized cost (including fee) of all work to be performed under a contract, through the most recently executed modification.

Contracting: Purchasing, renting, leasing, or otherwise obtaining supplies or services from nonfederal sources. Contracting includes description of supplies and services required, selection and solicitation of sources, preparation and award of contracts, and all phases of contract administration. It does not include grants or cooperative agreements.

Contracting activity: An element of an agency designated by the agency head and delegated broad authority regarding acquisition functions.

Contracting officer (CO): A person with the authority to enter into, administer, and/or terminate contracts and make related determinations and findings. The term includes certain authorized representatives of the contracting officer acting within the limits of their authority as delegated by the contracting officer; e.g., "Administrative CO" and "Termination CO."

Contracting officer's technical representative (COTR): An individual possessing specialized technical expertise that has been designated and authorized in writing by the CO to assist in the technical monitoring or administration of a contract.

Contractor-acquired property: Property acquired or otherwise provided by the contractor for performing a contract and to which the government has title.

Contractor Purchasing System Review (CPSR): The complete evaluation of a contractor's purchasing of material and services, subcontracting, and subcontract management from development of the requirement through completion of subcontract performance.

Contractor team arrangement: An arrangement in which (a) two or more companies form a partnership or joint venture to act as potential prime contractor, or (b) a potential prime contractor agrees with one or more other companies to have them act as its subcontractors under a specified government contract or acquisition program.

CONUS: The continental United States, meaning the 48 contiguous states and the District of Columbia.

Cooperative agreement: A legal instrument to reflect a relationship between the government and a recipient to transfer a thing of value (money) to the recipient to accomplish a public purpose of support or stimulation authorized by federal statute. Also, substantial involvement is anticipated between the government and the recipient during performance.

Corporate Administrative Contracting Officer (CACO): A contracting officer having overall administrative contracting responsibility; i.e., on a corporate-wide basis, for certain contractors with two or more operational locations, each of which has a resident ACO assigned. Their purpose is for achieving consistency and efficiency in the contract administration function.

Cost Accounting Standards (CAS): Specific accounting policies prescribed by the CAS Board to ensure consistency in the application of cost accounting principles to government contracts. The cost accounting standards are enumerated in FAR 30, along with the criteria that dictate which contractors are subject to their application.

Cost Accounting Standards Board: Part of the OFPP, the board has exclusive statutory authority to achieve uniformity and consistency in the cost account practices governing the measurement, assignment, and allocation of costs to government contracts.

Cost analysis: The review and evaluation of the separate cost elements and proposed profit of (a) an offeror's or contractor's cost or pricing data, and (b) the judgmental factors applied in projecting from the data to the estimated costs in order to form an opinion on the degree to which the proposed costs represent what the cost of the contract should be, assuming reasonable economy and efficiency.

Cost and pricing data: All facts as of the date of price agreement that prudent buyers and sellers would reasonably expect to affect price negotiations significantly. It is factual, not judgmental, and is therefore verifiable. While it does not indicate the accuracy of the prospective contractor's judgment about estimated future costs or projections, it does include the data forming the basis for that judgment. Cost or pricing data are more than historical accounting data; they are all the facts that can be reasonably expected to contribute to the soundness of estimates of future costs and to the validity of determination of costs already incurred.

Cost breakdown structure: A system to provide for more effective management and control by subdividing a program into hardware elements and sub-elements, functions and sub-functions, and cost categories.

Cost input: The cost, except G&A expenses, that for contracting purposes is allocable to the production of goods and services during a cost accounting period.

Cost objective: A function, organizational subdivision, contract, or other work unit for which cost data are desired and for which provision is made to accumulate and measure the cost of processes, products, jobs, capitalized projects, etc.

Cost of capital committed to facilities: An imputed cost determined by applying a cost-of-money rate to individual facilities capital.

Cost of money: An imputed cost determined by applying a cost-of-money rate to facilities capital employed in contract performance, or to an investment in tangible and intangible assets while they are being constructed, fabricated, or developed for the contractor's own use. Although technically not a recovery of interest, as specifically expressed in FAR 31.205-10, cost of money is intended to compensate a contractor for the capital cost of employing certain facilities in the performance of contracts, and therefore has many of the characteristics of a reimbursement for interest. A cost-of-money provision is allowable only if the contractor's capital investment is accounted for in accordance with the relevant cost accounting standards and is specifically identified or proposed in the contractor's cost proposal for a given contract.

Cost-plus-award-fee (CPAF) contract: A cost-reimbursement contract that provides for a fee consisting of (1) a base amount fixed at inception of the contract, and (2) an award amount that the contractor may earn in whole or in part during performance and that is sufficient to provide motivation for excellence in such areas as quality, timeliness, technical ingenuity, and cost-effective management. The amount of the award fee to be paid is determined by the government's judgmental evaluation of the contractor's performance in terms of the criteria stated in the contract. This determination is made unilaterally by the government and is not subject to the disputes clause. (FAR 16.404-2)

Cost-plus-fixed-fee (CPFF) contract: A cost-reimbursement contract that provides payment to the contractor of a negotiated fee that is fixed at the inception of the contract. The fixed fee does not vary with actual cost, but may be adjusted as a result of changes in the work to be performed under the contract. This contract type permits contracting for efforts that might otherwise present too great a risk to contractors, but it provides the contractor only a minimum incentive to control costs. (FAR 16.306)

Cost-plus-incentive-fee (CPIF) contract: A cost-reimbursement contract that provides for the initially negotiated fee to be adjusted later by a formula based on the relationship of total allowable costs to total target costs. This contract type specifies a target cost, a target fee, minimum and maximum fees, and a fee adjustment formula. After contract performance, the fee payable to the contractor is determined in accordance with the formula. The formula provides, within limits, for increases in fee above target fee when total allowable costs are less than target costs, and decreases in fee below target fee when total allowable costs exceed target costs. This increase or decrease is intended to provide an incentive for the contractor to manage the contract effectively. When total allowable cost is greater than or less than the range of costs within which the fee adjustment formula operates, the contractor is paid total allowable costs, plus the minimum or maximum fee.

Cost realism: The costs in an offeror's proposal are realistic for the work to be performed, reflect a clear understanding of the requirements, and are consistent with the various elements of the offeror's technical proposal.

Cost-reimbursement contract: A type of contract that provides for payment of allowable incurred costs, to the extent prescribed in the contract. These contracts establish an estimate of total cost for the purpose of obligating funds and establishing a ceiling that the contractor may not exceed (except at its own risk) without the approval of the CO.

Cost-sharing: An explicit arrangement under which the contractor bears some of the burden of reasonable, allocable, and allowable contract cost.

COTR: Contracting Officer's Technical Representative

COTS: Commercial Off-the-Shelf Item

CPA: Certified Public Accountant

CPAF: Cost-Plus-Award Fee

CPFF: Cost-Plus-Fixed Fee

CPIF: Cost-Plus-Incentive Fee

CPR: Cost Performance Report(s)(-ing)

CPSR: Contractor Purchasing System Review

CPU: Central Processing Unit

CRAG: Contractor Risk Assessment Guide

Critical design review (CDR): A review conducted to determine that the detailed design satisfies the performance and engineering requirements of the development specification; to establish the detailed design compatibility among the item and other items of equipment, facilities, computer programs, and personnel; to assess producibility and risk areas; and to review the preliminary product baseline specifications.

Critical nonconformance: A nonconformance that is likely to result in hazardous or unsafe conditions for individuals using, maintaining, or depending upon the supplies or services or that is likely to prevent performance of a vital agency mission.

C/SCSC: Cost/Schedule Control System Criteria

CSRA: Civil Service Reform Act

CSSR: Cost/Schedule Status Report(s)(-ing)

Currently performing: A contractor has been awarded a contract, but has not yet received final notification of acceptance of all supplies, services, and data deliverable under this contract (including options).

CY: Calendar Year

D

DAC: Defense Acquisition Circular

DAR: Defense Acquisition Regulation (formerly the ASPR and now replaced by the FAR)

DCAA : Defense Contract Audit Agency

DCAAI: Defense Contract Audit Agency Instruction

DCAAM: Defense Contract Audit Agency Manual

DCAAP: Defense Contract Audit Agency Pamphlet

DCAAR: Defense Contract Audit Agency Regulation

DCAI: Defense Contract Audit Institute

DCMA: Defense Contract Management Agency

DCMAO: Defense Contract Management Area Operations

DCMC: Defense Contract Management Command

DCMD: Defense Contract Management District

DD: Designation of Department of Defense Forms

DDAS : HQ, DLA Office of Small and Disadvantaged Business Utilization

De facto standards: Standards set and accepted by the marketplace but lacking approval by recognized standards organizations.

Debarment: An action taken by a debarring official under FAR 9.406 to exclude a contractor from government contracting or government approved subcontracting for a reasonable specified period.

Decommitment: Downward adjustment of a previously recorded commitment.

Defective cost or pricing data: Certified cost or pricing data subsequently found to have been inaccurate, incomplete, or noncurrent as of the effective date of the certificate. In this case, the government is entitled to an adjustment of the negotiated price, including profit or fee, to exclude any significant sum by which the price was increased because of the defective data, provided the data were relied upon by the government.

Defense Acquisition Regulatory (DAR) Council: A group composed of representatives from each military department, the Defense Logistics Agency, and NASA that is charged with maintenance of the FAR on a joint basis with the CAA Council.

Defense Contract Audit Agency (DCAA): The DCAA has broad authority to perform a variety of contract audits as well as to assist in reviewing and evaluating contract cost, pricing, performance, and administration.

Defense Contract Management Agency (DCMA): An agency that provides contract management services in support of DoD, NASA, and other government agencies.

Deferred compensation: An award made by an employer to compensate an employee in a future cost accounting period or periods for services rendered in one or more cost accounting periods before the date of the receipt of compensation by the employee.

Definite quantity contract: A contract that provides for delivery of a definite quantity of specific supplies or services for a fixed period, with deliveries to be scheduled at designated locations upon order.

Delivery order: An order for supplies placed against an established contract or with government sources.

Delivery payment: A payment for accepted supplies or services, including payments for accepted partial deliveries.

Deobligation: Downward adjustment of a previously recorded obligation attributable to a contract termination or modification, price revision, or correction of amounts originally recorded.

Depreciation: A charge to current operations that distributes the cost of a tangible capital asset, less estimated residual value, over the estimated useful life of the asset in a systematic and logical manner.

Design-bid-build: The traditional delivery method where design and construction are sequential and contracted for separately with two contracts with two contractors.

Design-build: Combining design and construction in a single contract with one contractor.

Design-to-cost: A concept that establishes cost elements as management goals to achieve the best balance between life-cycle cost, acceptable performance, and schedule.

Designated payment office: The place designated in the contract to make invoice payments or contract financing payments.

Destination Inspection/Acceptance: Inspection at the point of receipt.

Determination and findings: A special form of written approval by an authorized official that is required by statute or regulation as a prerequisite to taking certain contract actions. The "determination" is a conclusion or decision supported by the "findings." The findings are statements of fact or rationale essential to support the determination and must cover each requirement of the statute or regulation.

DFARS: Defense Federal Acquisition Regulation Supplement

DFAS: Defense Finance & Accounting Service

DHHS: Department of Health & Human Services

DIIS: DCAA Integrated Information System

Direct cost: Any cost that can be identified specifically with a particular final cost objective.

Direct labor hours: Hours worked for labor or services that are directly assignable to a specific project, system, or task. Although hours representing labor or services of an overhead nature are directly attributable to a service output, these hours are not considered as direct in this context. However, where various categories of personnel such as cost analysts, budgeting and programming specialists, clerical employees, etc., have been assigned to facilitate the "total project management concept," the work performance should be classified as direct labor hours when the efforts can be directly related to specific projects.

Directly associated cost: Any cost that is generated solely as a result of the incurrence of another cost and that would not have been incurred had the other cost not been incurred.

Disbursement: Outlay of public moneys and the rendering of accounts in accordance with the laws and regulations governing the distribution of public moneys.

Disclosure statement: A statement in which persons or firms required to complete and submit a disclosure statement (Form CASB-DS-1) describe their contract cost accounting practices by providing data that are responsive to the form's requirements.

Discount for prompt payment: An invoice payment reduction voluntarily offered by the contractor if payment is made by the government prior to the due date.

Discussion: As used in FAR 15, any oral or written communication between the government and an offeror (other than communications conducted for the purpose of minor clarifications), whether or not initiated by the government, that (a) involves information essential for determining the acceptability of a proposal, or (b) provides the offeror an opportunity to revise or modify its proposal.

DLA: Defense Logistics Agency

DLAD: Defense Logistics Agency Acquisition Directive

DLAI: Defense Logistics Agency Instruction

DLAM: Defense Logistics Agency Manual

DLAR: Defense Logistics Acquisition Regulation

DLIS: Defense Logistics Information Service (formally DLSC)

DMS/DPS: Defense Materials System/Defense Priority System

DoC: Department of Commerce

DoD: Department of Defense

DoDD: Department of Defense Directive

DoDI: Department of Defense Instruction

DoDIG: Department of Defense Inspector General

DoE: Department of Energy

DoJ: Department of Justice

DoL: Department of Labor

DoT: Department of Transportation

Domestic end product: An unmanufactured end product mined or produced in the United States, or an end product manufactured in the United States, if the cost of its components mined, produced, or manufactured in the United States exceeds 50% of the cost of all its components.

Domestic offer: An offered price for a domestic end product, including transportation to destination.

Domestic services: Services performed in the United States. If services provided under a single contract are performed both inside and outside the United States, they shall be considered domestic if 25% or less of their total cost is attributable to services performed outside the United States.

Down selection: In a phased acquisition, the process of selecting contractors for later phases from among the preceding phase contractors.

DPRO: Defense Plant Representative Office

Draw-down: Used to indicate the federal funds that a grantee obtains from the federal government.

Drug-free workplace: The site(s) for the performance of work done by the contractor in connection with a specific contract at which employees of the contractor are prohibited from engaging in the unlawful manufacture, distribution, dispensing, possession, or use of a controlled substance.

DSC: Defense Supply Center

DTIC: Defense Technical Information Center

DWG: Drawings

E

EAC: Estimated at completion (cost)

Earned Value Management System (EVMS): Industry-developed standards, accepted by DoD and NASA, that ensure contractor management control systems that provide the contractor and the government with timely, accurate, auditable, and integrated contract cost, schedule, and technical performance data.

EC: Electronic commerce

Economic price adjustment (EPA): An alteration permitted and specified by contract provisions for the upward or downward revision of a stated contract price upon the occurrence of certain contingencies that are defined in the contract.

Economic purchase quantity: A quantity that produces economic benefit to the government.

ECP: Engineering change proposal

EDI: Electronic data interchange

EDP: Electronic data processing

Effective competition: A market condition that exists when two or more contractors, acting independently, actively contend for the government's business in a manner that ensures that the government will be offered the lowest cost or price alternative or best technical design meeting its minimum needs.

Effective date: The date agreed upon by the parties for beginning the period of performance under the contract.

EFT: Electronic funds transfer

Electronic commerce (EC): Electronic techniques for accomplishing business transactions, including electronic mail or messaging, World Wide Web technology, electronic bulletin boards, purchase cards, electronic funds transfer, and electronic data interchange.

Electronic data interchange (EDI): Transmission of information between computers using highly standardized electronic versions of common business documents.

Electronic funds transfer (EFT): Any transfer of funds, other than a transaction originated by cash, check, or similar paper instrument, that is initiated through an electronic terminal, telephone, computer, or magnetic tape for the purpose of ordering, instructing, or authorizing a financial institution to debit or credit an account.

Emerging small business: A small business concern whose size is no greater than 50% of the numerical size standard applicable to the NAICS code assigned to a contracting opportunity.

End product: Those articles, materials, and supplies to be acquired for public use under the contract.

Engineering change proposal (ECP): A proposal to the responsible authority recommending that a beneficial change to the specifications for an item of equipment be considered.

EPA: Economic price adjustment

Equitable adjustment: A corrective action and agreement where neither the government nor the contractor should secure a gain or suffer a loss as a result of an adjustment. Profitable contracts should remain equally profitable; losses should not be mitigated at the expense of the government.

Established catalog price: A price included in a catalog, price list, schedule, or other form that (a) is regularly maintained by a manufacturer or vendor, (b) is published or made available for inspection by customers, and (c) states prices at which sales are currently or were last made to a significant number of buyers constituting the general public.

Established market price: A current price, established in the usual and ordinary course of trade between buyers and sellers free to bargain, that can be substantiated from sources independent of the manufacturer or vendor, although such pricing data may have to come from the seller.

Estimated cost at completion (EAC): Actual direct costs, plus indirect costs or costs allocable to the contract, plus an estimate of costs (direct and indirect) for authorized work remaining.

Estimating costs: The process of forecasting a future result in terms of cost, based on information available at the time.

EVMS: Earned Value Management System

Excess personal property: Any personal property under the control of a federal agency that the agency head or a designee determines is not required for its needs and for the discharge of its responsibilities.

Executive agency: An executive department, a military department, or any independent establishment within the meaning of 5 U.S.C. 101, 102, and 104(1), respectively, and any wholly owned government corporation within the meaning of 31 U.S.C. 9101.

Expressly unallowable cost: A particular item or type of cost that, under the express provisions of an applicable law, regulation, or contract, is specifically named and stated to be unallowed.

F

F&A: Facilities and administrative (costs)

Facilities and administrative (F&A) costs: Costs for educational institutions that are incurred for common or joint objectives and, therefore, cannot be identified readily and specifically with a particular sponsored project, instructional activity, or any other institutional activity.

Facilities contract: A contract under which government facilities are provided to a contractor or subcontractor by the government for use in connection with performing one or more related contracts for supplies or services.

Fair and reasonable price: A price that is fair to both parties, considering the agreed-upon conditions, promised quality, and timeliness of contract performance. Although generally a fair and reasonable price is a function of the law of supply and demand, there are statutory, regulatory, and judgmental limits on the concept.

Fair market value: The price (cash or equivalent) that a buyer could reasonably be expected to pay and a seller could reasonably be expected to accept if the business were for sale on the open market for a reasonable period of time, both buyer and seller being in possession of all pertinent facts and neither being under any compulsion to act.

FAR: Federal Acquisition Regulation

Fast payment procedure: A procedure that allows payment under limited conditions to a contractor prior to the government's verification that supplies have been received and accepted.

FDP: Federal Demonstration Partnership

Federal Acquisition Regulation (FAR): The body of regulations that is the primary source of authority governing the government procurement process. The FAR, which is published as Chapter 1 of Title 48 of the Code of Federal Regulations, is prepared, issued, and maintained under the joint auspices of the Secretary of Defense, the Administrator of GSA, and the Administrator of NASA. Actual responsibility for maintenance and revision of the FAR is vested jointly in the DAR Council and the CAA Council. The FAR provisions are implemented and augmented by the various agency supplements, and are subject to interpretation by other entities, such as the federal courts, the Armed Services Board of Contract Appeals, the General Services Board of Contract Appeals, and others.

Federal Demonstration Partnership (FDP): A cooperative initiative among federal agencies (including NASA) and institutional recipients of federal funds. It was established to increase research productivity by streamlining the administrative process and minimizing the administrative burden on principal investigators while maintaining effective stewardship of federal funds.

Federal Register: The official daily publication for Rules, Proposed Rules, and Notices of federal agencies and organizations, as well as Executive Orders and other Presidential Documents.

Federal Supply Schedule (FSS): A GSA program that provides federal agencies with a simplified process of acquiring commonly used supplies and services in varying quantities at lower prices while obtaining discounts associated with volume buying.

Federally Funded Research and Development Centers (FFRDC): Research facilities, originally established to meet the special needs of World War II, that perform actual R&D or R&D management either upon direct request of the government or under a broad charter from the government, but in either case under the direct monitorship of the government; e.g., The Jet Propulsion Lab.

Fee: In specified cost-reimbursement pricing arrangements, fee represents an agreed-to amount beyond the initial estimate of costs. In most instances, fee reflects a variety of factors, including risk, and is subject to statutory limitations. Fee may be fixed at the outset of performance, as in a cost-plus-fixed-fee contract, or may vary (within a contractually specified minimum-maximum range) as in a cost-plus-incentive fee contract.

FFRDC: Federally Funded Research and Development Centers

FFP contract: Firm-fixed-price contract

FIFO: First in, first out

Final cost objective: A cost objective that has allocated to it both direct and indirect costs and, in the contractor's accumulation system, is one of the final accumulation points.

Final indirect cost rate: The indirect cost rate established and agreed upon by the government and the contractor as not subject to change. It is usually established after the close of the contractor's fiscal year (unless the parties decide upon a different period) to which it applies. In the case of cost-reimbursement R&D contracts with educational institutions, it may be predetermined; that is, established for a future period on the basis of cost experience with similar contracts, together with supporting data.

Firm-fixed-price (FFP) contract: A fixed-price contract that provides for a price that is not subject to any adjustment on the basis of the contractor's cost experience in performing the contract. This contract type places upon the contractor maximum risk and full responsibility for all costs and resulting profit or loss. It provides maximum incentive for the contractor to control costs and perform efficiently and imposes a minimum administrative burden upon the contracting parties.

Firm-fixed price, level-of-effort term contract (FFP-LOE): A contract that requires (a) the contractor to provide a specified level of effort, over a stated period of time, on work that can be stated only in general terms, and (b) the government to pay the contractor a fixed dollar amount.

First article: Pre-production models, initial production samples, test samples, first lots, pilot lots, and pilot models.

First in, first out (FIFO): An accounting term used to describe the inventory method that allocates cost on the assumption that the cost of the first goods purchased is the cost of the first goods sold.

First-tier subcontractor: A subcontractor holding a subcontract with a prime contractor.

Fiscal year: The accounting period for which annual financial statements are regularly prepared, generally a period of 12 months, 52 weeks, or 53 weeks. In the federal government, the period from October 1 through September 30.

Fixed assets: Assets of a permanent character having a continuing value such as land, buildings, and other structures and facilities including collateral equipment and noncollateral equipment.

Fixed-ceiling-price contract with retroactive price re-determination: A fixed-price contract that provides for (a) a fixed ceiling price, and (b) retroactive price re-determination within the ceiling after completion of the contract.

Fixed costs: Costs that do not vary with the volume of business during a given period, such as property taxes, insurance, depreciation, etc. In practice, some fixed costs are difficult to distinguish from variable costs. It has been said that all costs are fixed in the short run and variable in the long run.

Fixed-price (FP) contract: A contract type that provides for a price that is not subject to any adjustment on the basis of the contractor's cost experience in performing the contract.

Fixed-price contract with economic price adjustment: A fixed-price contract that provides for upward or downward revision of the stated contract price upon the occurrence of specified contingencies.

Fixed-price contract with prospective price re-determination: A fixed-price contract that provides for (a) a firm fixed price for an initial period of contract deliveries or performance, and (b) prospective re-determination, at a stated time or times during performance, of the price for subsequent periods of performance.

Fixed-price incentive (FPI) contract: A fixed-price contract that provides for adjusting profit and establishing the final contract price by application of a formula based on the relationship of total final negotiated cost to total target cost. The final price is subject to a price ceiling, negotiated at the outset.

Float: The time between the disbursement of funds and receipt of payment.

FOB: Free On Board

FOB destination: Shipping costs to cover freight to destination paid by supplier.

FOB origin: Shipping costs paid by the government.

FOIA: Freedom of Information Act

Forbearance: The act of refraining or abstaining from action. In negotiation, it allows both parties to agree to disagree and move on to the next issue without making a commitment one way or another.

Foreign offer: An offered price for a foreign end product, including transportation to destination and duty (whether or not a duty-free entry certificate is issued).

Form, fit, and function data: Technical data pertaining to items, components, or processes for the purpose of identifying source, size, configuration, mating, and attachment characteristics, functional characteristics, and performance requirements.

Forward funding: Carry-over of funding (budget authority) into the second year.

Forward pricing rate agreement (FPRA): A written agreement negotiated between a contractor and the government to make certain rates available during a specified period for use in pricing contracts or modifications.

FP contract: Fixed-price contract

FPI contract: Fixed-price incentive contract

FR: Federal Register

FPRA: Forward pricing rate agreement

Fraud: An action to gain some unfair or dishonest advantage that involves an intentional deceit or falsehood on the government by the contractor.

Free on board (F.O.B.) origin: The seller or consignor places the goods on the conveyance by which they are to be transported. Unless the contract provides otherwise, cost of shipping risk or loss is borne by the buyer or consignee.

Freedom of Information Act (FOIA): A public law established for the purpose of providing for the disclosure to the general public of government information not classified in accordance with national security or other confidentiality requirements.

FSS: Federal Supply Schedule

Full and open competition: With respect to a contract action, all responsible sources are permitted to compete.

Functional requirement: Contract requirement stated in terms of the objectives that must be achieved under the contract.

G

G&A: General and administrative

GAAP: Generally accepted accounting principles

GAGAS: Generally accepted government auditing standards

GAO: General Accountability Office

General Accountability Office (GAO): The audit agency of the United States Congress. GAO has broad authority to conduct investigations on behalf of the Congress and to review certain contract decisions, including protests of contract awards and decisions of COs with respect to the acquisition by the government of supplies and services related to automated data processing.

General and administrative (G&A) expense: Any management, financial, and other expense that is incurred by or allocated to a business unit and that is for the general management and administration of the business unit as a whole. G&A expense does not include those management expenses whose beneficial or casual relationship to cost objectives can be more directly measured by a base other than a cost input base representing the total activity of a business unit during a cost accounting period.

General wage determination: Contains prevailing wage rates for the types of construction designated in the determination and is used in contracts performed within a specific geographical area.

Generally accepted accounting principles (GAAP): Term used to describe broadly the body of principles, issued by the American Institute of Certified Public Accountants, that governs the accounting for financial transactions underlying the preparation of a set of financial statements.

Generally accepted government auditing standards (GAGAS): Auditing standards, issued by the Comptroller General of the United States, that are applicable to financial audits.

GFE: Government-furnished equipment

GFP: Government-furnished property

Government-furnished property (GFP), equipment (GFE): Property in the possession of, or directly acquired by, the Government and subsequently made available to the contractor.

Government property: All property owned by or leased to the government or acquired by the government under the terms of a contract.

Grant: A legal instrument to reflect a relationship between the government and a recipient to transfer a thing of value (money) to the recipient to accomplish a public purpose of support or stimulation authorized by federal statute.

H

Head of the contracting activity: The official who has overall responsibility for managing the contracting activity.

HBCU: Historically black colleges and universities

High-tech operations: Research and/or development efforts that are within or advance the state-of-the-art in a technology discipline and are performed primarily by professional engineers, scientists, and highly skilled and trained technicians or specialists.

Home office: An office responsible for directing or managing two or more, but not necessarily all, segments of an organization. It typically establishes policy for, and provides guidance to, the segments in their operations. It usually performs management, supervisory, or administrative functions, and may also perform service functions in support of the operations of the various segments. An organization that has intermediate levels, such as groups, may have several home offices that report to a common home office. An intermediate organization may be both a segment and a home office.

HQ: Headquarters

HUBZone small business: A small business concern that appears on the List of Qualified HUBZone Small Business Concerns maintained by the SBA.

I

IFB: Invitation for bid

IFMP: Integrated Financial Management Project

Improper influence: Any influence that induces or tends to induce a government employee or officer to give consideration or to act regarding a government contract on any basis other than the merits of the matter.

Incentive: Motivating the contractor in calculable monetary terms to turn out a product that meets significantly advance performance goals, to improve the contract schedule, to reduce costs, or a combination of these objectives.

Incremental funding: The obligation of funds to a contract in periodic installments as the work progresses, rather than in a lump sum. An act of increasing the funding ceiling of a contract in successive increments.

Indefinite quantity contract: A contract that provides for an indefinite quantity, within stated limits, of specific supplies or services to be furnished during a fixed period, with deliveries to be scheduled by placing orders with the contractors.

Independent research and development (IR&D) cost: The cost effort that is neither sponsored by a grant nor required in performing a contract and that falls within any of the four following areas: (a) basic research, (b) applied research, (c) development, and (d) systems and other concept formulation studies.

Indirect cost: Any cost not directly identified with a single, final cost objective, but identified with two or more final cost objectives or an intermediate cost objective.

Indirect cost pool: A grouping of indirect costs identified with two or more objectives but not identified specifically with any final cost objective.

Indirect cost rate: The percentage or dollar factor that expresses the ratio of indirect costs incurred in a given period to direct labor cost, manufacturing cost, or another appropriate base for the same period.

Ineligible: Excluded from government contract (and subcontracting, if appropriate) pursuant to statutory, Executive order, or regulatory authority other than the FAR and its implementing and supplementing regulations.

Information technology (IT): Any equipment, or interconnected system(s) or subsystem(s) of equipment, that is used in the automatic acquisition, storage, manipulation, management, movement, control, display, switching, interchange, transmission, or reception of data or information by the agency.

Inherently governmental function: As a matter of policy, a function that is so intimately related to the public interest as to mandate performance by government employees.

Insight: The process of gathering a minimum set of product or process data that provides adequate visibility into the integrity of the product or process. The data may be acquired from contractor records, usually in a nonintrusive parallel method.

Inspection: Examining and testing supplies or services to determine whether they conform to contract requirements.

Intangible capital asset: An asset that has no physical substance, has more than minimal value, and is expected to be held by the enterprise for continued use beyond the current accounting period for the benefits it yields.

Integrated Financial Management Project (IFMP): NASA's response to a mandate to all government agencies to re-design their current financial business processes, develop and maintain integrated financial management systems, issue audited financial statements, and develop a customer-driven approach to financial management, preferably using a commercial off-the-shelf software platform.

Intellectual property: Includes inventions, trademarks, patents, industrial designs, copyrights, and technical information, including software data design, technical know-how, manufacturing information and know-how, techniques, technical data packages, manufacturing data packages, and trade secrets.

Interagency acquisition: A procedure by which an agency needing supplies or services (the requesting agency) obtains them from another agency (the service agency).

Interested party: An actual or prospective bidder or offeror whose direct interest would be affected by the award of a contract or by the failure to award a contract.

Invitation for bid (IFB): A solicitation document used in sealed bidding. Responses to IFBs are offers called "bids" or "sealed bids."

Invoice: A contractor's bill, written document, or electronic transmission requesting payment for supplies delivered or services performed.

IR&D cost: Independent research and development cost.

ISO 9000: A series of standards and guidelines that define the minimum requirements for an effective quality system accepted internationally.

J

Just-in-time: A "pull" system driven by actual demand. The goal is to produce or provide one part just in time for the next operation. Reduces stock inventories, but leaves no room for schedule error.

Julian date: A way of identifying the specific calendar date, stating the year as the first two digits and the last three as a day (i.e., 04267).

K

Kickback: Any money, fee, commission, credit, gift, gratuity, thing of value, or compensation of any kind that is provided, directly or indirectly, to any prime contractor, prime contractor employee, subcontractor, or subcontractor employee for the purpose of improperly obtaining or rewarding favorable treatment in connection with a prime contract or in connection with a subcontract relating to a prime contract.

L

Labor cost at standard: A pre-established measure of the labor element of cost, computed by multiplying labor-rate standard by labor-time standard.

Labor-hour contract: A variation of a time and materials contract differing only in that materials are not supplied by the contractor.

Labor-rate standard: A pre-established measure, expressed in monetary terms, of the price of labor.

Labor-time standard: A pre-established measure, expressed in temporal terms, of the price of labor.

Last in, first out (LIFO): An accounting term used to describe the inventory method that allocates cost on the assumption that the cost of the last goods purchased is the cost of the first goods sold.

Latent defect: A defect that exists at the time of acceptance but cannot be discovered by a reasonable inspection. Failure to make the examination or test does not make a discoverable defect latent.

Lead agency: Term often used to describe, for a particular contractor (or a business unit or segment of a contractor), that federal government agency (or contract administration office) with primary responsibility for certain contract matters, such as negotiation of advance agreements and settlement of final indirect cost rates. In connection with the negotiation of advance agreements covering independent research and development costs, the term has the specific meaning attributed to it at FAR 42.1003 regarding the vesting of authority for such agreements within a single agency.

Lead time: The period of time between the determination of need for an item and the actual manufacture and delivery of the item.

Learning/improvement curve: A mathematical way to explain and analyze the rate of change of cost (in hours or dollars) as a function of quantity.

Lease: An instrument conveying an interest in land, buildings, or other structures and facilities for a specified term, revocable as specified by the terms of the instrument, in consideration of payment of a rental fee.

Letter contract: A written preliminary contractual instrument that authorizes the contractor to begin immediately manufacturing supplies or performing services.

Letter of credit: A commitment certified by an authorized official of a federal program agency, specifying a dollar limit available to a designated payee. A period of time of availability may also be specified.

Level of effort (LOE): The devotion of talent or capability to a predetermined level of activity, over a period of time, on the basis of a fixed-price or cost-reimbursement pricing arrangement. Payment is usually based on effort expended rather than results achieved; i.e., contract for man hours.

Leveraged buy-out: A mechanism under which a company is acquired by a person or entity using the value of the company's assets to finance its acquisition; this allows for the acquirer to minimize its outlay of cash in making the purchase.

Liabilities: Amounts owed by a business to its creditors.

Life-cycle cost: The total cost to the government of acquiring, operating, supporting, and (if applicable) disposing of the items being acquired over its planned lifespan.

LIFO: Last in, first out

Limitation-of-cost clause: A clause prescribed for inclusion in cost-reimbursement contracts that establishes requirements for notifying the government (a) at any point at which the contractor has reason to believe that the total cost for performance of the contract will be either greater or substantially less than had been previously estimated, or (b) when incurred costs as of a given date plus costs expected to be incurred over the subsequent 60-day period are expected to exceed 75 percent of the contract target cost. The notification provision is designed to allow the government an opportunity to assess the contract progress and to issue a stop-work order if it decides not to continue. The notification to be provided must be in writing. Failure to comply with this clause is one of the most common bars to recovery of cost overruns on cost-reimbursement type contracts.

Limitation-of-funds clause: A clause prescribed for inclusion in cost-reimbursement type contracts that establishes requirements for notifying the government when incurred costs as of a given date plus costs expected to be incurred over the subsequent 60-day period are expected to exceed 75 percent of the total amount so far allotted by the government (i.e., the funded amount). The notification provision is designed to allow the government to designate additional funding for the contract to proceed in a timely manner. The notification to be provided must be in writing.

Line item: An item of supply or service that must be separately priced in a quote, offer, or contract.

Liquidated damages: A stipulation in a contract on monetary amounts that must be paid by the contractor if the contractor fails to deliver supplies or perform services as specified in the contract or any modification. Payments are in lieu of actual damages related to the failure. The rate (e.g., dollars per day of delay) is fixed in the contract and must be reasonable considering probable actual damages related to any failure in contract performance.

Liquidity: The ability of a business to meet its obligations as they come due; the more liquid a business is (cash on hand), the better able it is to meet short-term financial obligations.

M

MADR: Maximum Allowable Defect Rate

Major nonconformance: A nonconformance, other than critical, that is likely to result in failure of the supplies or services, or to materially reduce the usability of the supplies or services for their intended purpose.

Major system: That combination of elements that will function together to produce the capabilities required to fulfill a mission need.

Management and operating contract: An agreement under which the government contracts for the operation, maintenance, or support, on its behalf, of a government-owned or controlled research, development, special production, or testing establishment wholly or principally devoted to one or more major programs of the contracting federal agency.

Market research: Collecting and analyzing information about capabilities within the market to satisfy agency needs.

Master solicitation: A document containing special clauses and provisions that have been identified as essential for the acquisition of a specific type of supply or service that is acquired repetitively.

Material-cost at standard: A pre-established measure of the material elements of cost, computed by multiplying material-price standard by material-quantity standard.

Material-price standard: A pre-established measure, expressed in monetary terms, of the price of material.

Material-quantity standard: A pre-established measure, expressed in physical terms, of the quantity of material.

Maximum allowable defect rate (MADR): The defect rate for the population above which the contractor's quality control for a particular work requirement is unsatisfactory.

Mentor-Protégé Program: A federal government program where approved prime contractors are given incentives to assist SDBs, HBCUs, minority institutions, and women-owned small business concerns in enhancing their capabilities to perform contracts and subcontracts, foster the establishment of long-term business relationships between these entities and prime contractors, and increase the overall number of these entities that receive contract and subcontract awards.

Micro-purchase: An acquisition of supplies or services (except construction), the aggregate amount of which does not exceed $2,500, except that, in the case of construction, the limit is $2,000.

Mid-range procurement: NASA's streamline acquisition process for "middle range" procurements; i.e., those greater than the simplified acquisition threshold and not more that $2,000,000 in basic value (not more than $10,000,000 with options) and for commercial items not more than $25,000,000, including options.

Modification: Any written change in the terms of a contract, such as the addition of new work or the extension of a contract (see also Change order, Administrative change, and Supplemental agreement).

Modular contracting: Use of one or more contracts to acquire information technology systems in successive, interoperable increments.

Moving average cost: An inventory costing method under which an average unit cost is computed after each acquisition by adding the cost of the newly acquired units to the cost of the units of inventory on hand and dividing this figure by the new total number of units.

Multi-year contract: Contracts covering more than one year, but no more than five program years. Each program year is annually budgeted and funded and, at the time of award, funds need only to have been appropriated for the first year.

N

NAICS: North American Industrial Classification System

NAIS: NASA Acquisition Internet Service

NASA: National Aeronautics and Space Administration

NASA Acquisition Internet Service (NAIS): The Internet service NASA uses to broadcast its business opportunities, solicitations, procurement regulations, and associated information.

NASA Centers: Field organizations that are led by a Center Director.

NASA component facility: Field organizations that are geographically separated from the NASA Centers to which they are assigned.

NASA FAR Supplement (NFS): An agency supplement issued by NASA for the purpose of implementing the basic Federal Acquisition Regulation in accordance with the specific policies of the agency.

NASA Online Directives Information System (NODIS): An Internet application used for creating NASA directives and for automating the coordination/clearance process.

NASA Research Announcement (NRA): A broad agency notice to announce research interest in support of NASA's programs.

Negotiated contract: A contract obtained by direct agreement with a contractor without sealed bids.

Negotiated subcontract: Any subcontract, except a firm fixed-price subcontract, made by a contractor or subcontractor after receiving offers from at least two persons not associated with each other or with such contractor or subcontractor, providing that (a) the solicitation to all competitors is identical, (b) price is the only consideration in selecting from among the competitors solicited, and (c) the lowest offer received in compliance with the solicitation from among those solicited is accepted.

Negotiations: Exchanges, in either a competitive or sole source environment, between the government and offerors, that are undertaken with the intent of allowing the offeror to revise its proposal.

Net income: The net return (earnings or profit) earned by a business after deducting all selling and administrative costs, depreciation, taxes, and any other adjustments prior to dividends and withdrawals.

NFS: NASA FAR Supplement

No cost extension: An extension of a cost-type contract that has "no increase" in the estimated cost.

No-setoff commitment: A contractual agreement that, to the extent permitted by the Assignment of Claims Act, payments by the designated agency to the assignee under an assignment of claims will not be reduced to liquidate the indebtedness of the contractor to the government.

NODIS: NASA Online Directives Information System

Non-fast pay: Payment made based on receipt of signed DD250, after government acceptance.

Nonmanufacturer rule: Provides that a contractor under a small business set-aside or 8(a) contract must be a small business under the applicable size standard and must provide either its own product or that of another domestic small business manufacturing or processing concern.

Nonrecurring costs: Those costs that are generally incurred on a one-time basis, e.g., preliminary design efforts.

Nonreimbursable agreement: Involves a government agency and one or more agreement partners in a mutually beneficial activity that furthers the agency's mission, where each side bears the cost of its participation and there is no exchange of funds between the partners. It permits the government to offer its facilities, personnel, expertise, or equipment as part of a collaborative arrangement.

North American Industrial Classification System (NAICS): Government codes that identify products and services by type of industry. Used by the government to evaluate economic performance in the United States, Canada, and Mexico and to find contractors. Used by contractors to register with the government and to identify bid leads.

NRA: NASA Research Announcement

O

Obligations: Amounts of orders placed, contracts awarded, services received, or other similar transactions that will require disbursement of money.

Offer: A response to a solicitation that, if accepted, would bind the offeror to perform the resultant contracts. It refers to responses for both IFBs and RFPs.

Office of Federal Procurement Policy (OFPP): An office within OMB that provides government-wide procurement policies that are to be followed by Executive agencies in their procurement activities.

Office of Management and Budget (OMB): OMB's predominant mission is to assist the President in overseeing the preparation of the federal budget and to supervise its administration in Executive Branch agencies. In addition, OMB oversees and coordinates the Administration's procurement, financial management, information, and regulatory policies.

OFPP: Office of Federal Procurement Policy

OMB: Office of Management and Budget

Ombudsman: The agency individual that is responsible for establishing a more open acquisition process by facilitating communication on an informal basis with outside parties. The program provides offerors, potential offerors, and contractors with a single point of contact to address their concerns if they are not able to achieve satisfaction under the standard process.

Option: A unilateral right in a contract by which, for a specified time, the government may elect to purchase additional supplies or services called for by the contract, or may elect to extend the term of the contract.

Organizational conflict of interest: Because of other activities or relations with other persons, a person is unable or potentially unable to render impartial assistance or advice to the government, or the person's objectivity in performing the contract work is or might be otherwise impaired, or a person has an unfair competitive advantage.

Overhead: Indirect costs other than those related to G&A expenses and selling expenses. A general term often used to identify any indirect cost.

Overhead rate: An indirect cost rate that expresses the relationship between costs accumulated in an overhead pool and the related base for allocating such costs, for a given period of time. A typical allocation base for an overhead pool is the related direct labor dollars.

Oversight: An intrusive process of gathering contractor product or process data through on-site, in-series involvement in the process. It entails very detailed monitoring of the process itself and is an in-line involvement in any activity through inspection, with review and approval authority implicit to the degree necessary to assure that a process's or product's key characteristics are stable and in control.

P

Paramount lien: A lien that is paramount to all liens and is effective immediately upon the first payment, without filing, notice, or other action by the United States.

Partial termination: The termination of a part, but not all, of the work that has not been completed and accepted under a contract.

Partnering: In construction and A/E contracts, a relationship of open communication and close cooperation that involves both government and contractor personnel working together for the purpose of establishing a mutually beneficial, proactive, cooperative environment within which to achieve contract objectives and resolve issues and implementing actions as required.

Patent: A statutory monopoly granted by the federal government for a limited time to an inventor to exclude others from making, using or selling the invention claimed in the patent.

Patent defect: Any defect, which exists at the time of acceptance and is not a latent defect.

Payment bond: A bond that assures payments as required by law to all persons supplying labor or material in the prosecution of the work provided for in the contract.

Peer review: The use of expert review panels or external advisory committees (in related disciplinary areas) to prioritize and evaluate research proposals.

Pension portability: The recognition and continuation in a successor service contract of the predecessor service contract employees' pension rights and benefits.

Performance-based contracting: Structuring all aspects of an acquisition around the purpose of the work to be performed as opposed to either the manner by which the work is to be performed or broad and imprecise statements of work.

Performance-based payments: A type of contract financing where payments are based on either specifically described events (e.g., milestones) or some measurable criterion of performance. It is the preferred financing method when the CO finds them practical and the contractor agrees to their use.

Performance bond: A bond that guarantees the contractor will fulfill the contract in accordance with its terms.

Personal services contract: A contract that, by its express terms or as administered, makes contractor personnel appear, in effect, Government employees; e.g., supervising the contractor's employees.

Phased acquisition: An incremental acquisition implementation comprised of several distinct phases where the realization of program/project objectives requires a planned, sequential acquisition of each phase.

Pre-award survey: An evaluation by a surveying activity of a prospective contractor's capability to perform a proposed contract.

Pre-contract costs: Costs incurred before the effective date of the contract directly pursuant to the negotiation and in anticipation of the contract award when such incurrence is necessary to comply with the proposed contract delivery schedule.

Price analysis: The process of examining and evaluating a proposed price without evaluating its separate cost elements and proposed profit.

Pricing: The process of establishing a reasonable amount or amounts to be paid for supplies or services.

Prime contract: A contract or purchase order entered directly between a contractor and the Government.

Privity of contract: The relationship of having a contract. A connection, mutuality of will, and interaction between the parties which they must occupy toward each other in order to form either an express or implied contract. For subcontractors, the Government has no legal basis except through the prime contractor.

PRLI: Purchase request line item, a subset of the total quantity broken out by quantities to be shipped to individual locations. Total quantity is the total of all PRLI quantities (applies to DLA contracts).

Procurement official: Any civilian or military official or employee of an agency who has participated personally and substantially in the conduct of the agency procurement concerned, including all officials and employees who are responsible for reviewing and approving the procurement.

Profit: The potential total remuneration that contractors may receive for contract performance over and above allowable costs.

Profit center: The smallest organizationally independent segment of a company charged by management with profit and loss responsibilities.

Progress payments: Payments to a contractor, under a fixed price contract for a specific percentage of his actual costs for work in process.

Progressive competition: A type of down-selection strategy for a phased acquisition.

Project Surveillance Plan (PSP): A plan developed by the Government, included in the contract, which describes how the contractor will assure quality performance.

Prompt Payment Act: A law enacted in order to ensure that companies transacting business with the Government are paid in a timely manner. For amounts not paid within the required period, the Government is obligated to pay interest at a rate established by the Secretary of the Treasury.

Proper invoice: An invoice that meets the minimum standards specified in the contract.

Proposal: Any offer or other submission used as a basis for pricing a contract, contract modification, or termination settlement or for securing payments thereunder.

Proposal modification: A change made to a proposal before the solicitation closing date and time, or made in response to an amendment, or made to correct a mistake at any time before award.

Proprietary data: That which provides information concerning the details of a contractor's proposal, wage rates, patent rights, trade secrets, or copyright laws, to the extent that such information is not disclosed by inspection or analysis of the product itself and to the extent that the contractor has protected such information from unrestricted use by others.

Protest: A written objection by an interested party to a solicitation by an agency for offers for a proposed contract for the acquisition of supplies or services or a written objection by an interested party to a proposed award or the award of such a contract.

Provision: A term or condition used only in solicitations and applying only before contract award.

Provisional rate: An alternate term for a billing rate.

Purchase order: An offer by the Government to buy supplies or services, including construction and research and development, upon specified terms and conditions, using simplified acquisition procedures.

Q

QBL: Qualified bidders list

QML: Qualified manufacturers list

QPL: Qualified products list

Qualification requirement: A government requirement for testing or other quality assurance demonstration that must be completed before award of a contract.

Qualified bidders list (QBL): A list of bidders who have had their products examined and tested and who have satisfied all applicable qualification requirements for that produce or have otherwise satisfied all applicable qualification requirements.

Qualified manufacturers list (QML): A list of manufacturers who have had their products examined and tested and who have satisfied all applicable qualification requirements for that product.

Qualified products list (QPL): A list of products that have been examined and tested and have satisfied all applicable qualification requirements.

Quality Assurance Provision (QAP): The QAP number identifies the requirements and standards for inspection of the material and rejection of parts that do not meet the requirements.

Quantity Variance: Based on each line item, the quantity variance allows a variation in shipment from the original line quantity. Maximum variation is +/- 5 percent. Variation is not issued as practice, but only where commercial package quantity varies from quantity specified, or manufacturing process requires variation. Variation is based on individual line item not total quantity.

Quick closeout: The settlement of indirect costs for a specific contract in advance of the determination of relevant final indirect cost rates. The use of quick closeout procedures generally is permitted only when the potential for audit differences between final and proposed indirect rates is low and/or the amounts of unsettled indirect costs are insignificant.

Quotation: The quoting of current prices for a requirement under the Simplified Acquisition Procedures. A quotation is not an offer; therefore, the government order placed in response to the quotation does not establish a contract. The action on the part of the offeror to perform shows intent and, therefore, establishes a contractual relationship.

R

Ratification: The act, by an official who has the authority to do so, of approving an unauthorized commitment.

R&D: Research and development

Reasonable cost: A cost is reasonable if, in its nature and amount, it does not exceed that which would be incurred by a prudent person in the conduct of competitive business.

Reconditioned: Restored to the original normal operating condition by readjustments and material replacement.

Recurring costs: Costs that vary only with the quantity being produced, such as labor and materials.

Reimbursable agreement: Agreements that provide for payment of allowable incurred costs to the extent prescribed in the contract. These contracts establish an estimated total cost and a ceiling that may not be exceeded, except at the performing party's own risk. To exceed the established ceiling and receive payment requires the approval of the other party.

Remanufactured: Factory rebuilt to original specifications.

Request for Information (RFI): A document used to obtain price, delivery, other market information, or capabilities for planning purposes when the government does not presently intend to issue a solicitation.

Request for Offer (RFO): The solicitation used to request offers for all authorized NASA *Mid-Range* procurements.

Request for Proposal (RFP): The government's invitation to prospective offerors to submit proposals based on the terms and conditions set forth in the RFP. Responses to RFPs are offers called "proposals."

Requirements contract: A contract that provides for filling all actual purchase requirements of designated activities, specific supplies, or services during a specified contract period, with deliveries to be scheduled by placing orders with the contractor.

Responsible: Term used to describe one of the principal criteria that a contractor must meet in order to be eligible for the award of a particular contract. A contractor generally is deemed to be responsible if it: has adequate financial resources to perform the contract; is capable of complying with the proposed performance of delivery schedule; has a satisfactory performance record; has a satisfactory record of integrity; has the necessary organization, experience, accounting, and operational controls and technical skills, or the ability to obtain them; has the necessary production, construction, and technical equipment and facilities, or the ability to obtain them; and is otherwise qualified and eligible to receive an award.

Responsive bidder: A bidder whose bid conforms to the terms and conditions of the IFB.

Retained earnings: The portion of after-tax net income of a corporation that is not paid out to shareholders in the form of dividends, but that instead is retained for use in the business.

RFI: Request for Information

RFO: Request for Offer

RFP: Request for Proposal

Risk: A measure of the inability to achieve program objectives within defined cost and schedule restraints. It has two considerations: the probability of failing to achieve a particular outcome, and the consequences of failing to achieve that outcome.

Risk management: The act or practice of controlling risk. The process for the identification, analysis, and treatment of loss exposure as well as the administration of techniques to accomplish the goals of a company in minimizing potential financial loss from such exposure.

Rule of ambiguity: If the wording in a contract is considered ambiguous, the ambiguity will be construed against the drafter of the language (usually the government).

S

SBA: Small Business Administration

SBA *PRO-Net*: An electronic database of procurement information for and about small businesses maintained by the Small Business Administration.

SBIR: Small Business Innovative Research

Scope of work (SOW): It is not always clear what precisely constitutes the "scope of work." Broadly, it defines the project and states the government's requirements.

SDB: Socially disadvantaged business

Service life: The period of usefulness of a tangible capital asset (or group of assets) to its current owner. The period may be expressed in units of time or output. The estimated service life of a tangible capital asset (or group of assets) is a current forecast of its service life and is the period over which depreciation cost is to be assigned.

SIC code: Standard Industrial Classification code

Simplified acquisition procedures: The methods prescribed in FAR Part 13 for making purchases of supplies or services.

Single process initiative (SPI): A DoD initiative, with NASA participation, that entails replacing government-unique specifications, standards, and processes with common commercial practices, whenever possible.

Size standards: Measures established by the SBA for the purpose of determining whether a business qualifies as a small business for purposes of implementing the socioeconomic programs enumerated in Part 19 of the Federal Acquisition Regulation. SBA size standards establish ceilings on either number of employees or the amount of annual revenue for each industry code contained in the SIC Manual published by the government.

Small business: A concern, including its affiliates, that is independently owned and operated, not dominant in the field of operation in which it is bidding on government contracts, and qualified as a small business under the criteria and size standards in 13 CFR Part 121.

Small Business Administration (SBA): The government agency that has primary responsibility for the advancement of small business. The SBA serves as a small business advocate through its many programs designed to assist small businesses in areas such as training, financing, and the identification of opportunities.

Small Business Innovative Research (SBIR) contract: A type of contract designed to foster technological innovation by small businesses. The SBIR contract program provides for a three-phased approach to research and development projects. The first phase is used to establish technological feasibility and ability of the contractor to fully develop the concept or idea; Phase II embodies the primary research effort; Phase III entails the effort to convert the technology to a commercial application.

Sole source acquisition: A contract for the purchase of supplies or services that is entered into or proposed to be entered into by an agency after soliciting and negotiating with only one source.

SOW: Statement of Work

Source Inspection/Acceptance: Where government inspection will take place, at the point of packaging and/or shipment.

Specification: A description of the technical requirements for items or materials that includes precise measurements, tolerances, materials, quality control requirements, and other requirements that control the processes of the contractor.

SPI: Single Process Initiative

Standard: A document that establishes engineering and technical limitations and applications of items, materials, processes, methods, designs, and engineering practices. It includes any related criteria deemed essential to achieve the highest practical degree of uniformity in materials or products or interchangeability of parts used in those products.

Standard cost: Any cost computed with the use of pre-established measures.

Standard Industrial Classification (SIC) code: A code representing a category within the Standard Industrial Classification System administered by the Statistical Policy Division of OMB. The system was established to classify all industries in the U.S. economy. A two-digit code designates each major industry group, which is coupled with a second two-digit code representing subcategories. Replaced by the North American Industrial Classification System (see NAICS).

Statement of Work (SOW): A document that defines service contract requirements in clear, concise language identifying specific work to be accomplished.

Subcontractor: Any supplier, distributor, vendor, or firm that furnished supplies or services to or for a prime contractor or another subcontractor. The government has no privity of contract with subcontractors.

Supplemental agreement: A contract modification that is accomplished by the mutual action of the parties.

Supplies: All property except land or interest in land.

Surety: An individual or corporation legally liable for the debt, default, or failure of a principal to satisfy a contractual obligation.

Suspension: An action taken by a suspending official under FAR 9.407 to disqualify a contractor temporarily from government contracting and government-approved subcontracting.

Synopsis: A notice of a proposed contract action furnished by an agency for publication at the Commerce Business Daily web site or the FedBizOpps web site.

T

Tangible capital asset: An asset that has physical substance, has more than minimal value, and is expected to be held by an enterprise for continued use or possession beyond the current accounting period for the service it yields.

Task order: An order for services placed against an established contract or with government sources.

Taxpayer Identification Number (TIN): The nine-digit number required by the IRS to be used by the offeror in reporting income tax and other returns. The TIN may be either a Social Security Number or an Employer Identification Number.

T4C: Termination for convenience

TCO: Termination contracting officer

T4D: Termination for default

Technical analysis: The examination and evaluation by personnel having specialized knowledge, skills, experience, or capability in engineering, science, or management of proposed quantities and kinds of materials, labor, processes, special tooling, facilities, and associated factors set forth in a proposal in order to determine and report on the need for and reasonableness of the proposed resources, assuming reasonable economy and efficiency.

Technical direction: A directive by a technical representative of the contracting officer (COTR) to the contractor that approves approaches, solutions, designs, or refinements; fills in details or otherwise completes the general description of work or documentation items; shifts emphasis among work areas or tasks; or furnishes similar instructions to the contractor.

Term form: A cost-plus-fixed-fee contract that describes the scope of work in general terms and obligates the contractor to devote a specified level of effort for a stated time period.

Termination Contracting Officer (TCO): A CO who specializes in the settlement of contracts terminated for the convenience of the government.

Termination costs: The incurrence of costs or the special treatment of costs that would not have arisen had the contract not been terminated.

Termination for convenience (T4C): The termination of a contract by the Government for reasons other than nonperformance or default when the government deems it to be in its interest to do so. A T4C is a unilateral contract action undertaken by the government under the provisions appearing at FAR 49 and the various T4C contract clauses. In a T4C action, the contractor generally is entitled to negotiate a settlement agreement for the purpose of providing an equitable recovery of costs reasonably incurred by the contractor in anticipation of fulfilling the contract and a reasonable profit thereon.

Termination for default (T4D): The termination of a contract by the Government for the failure of a contractor to perform the contract in accordance with its requirements. A T4D is a unilateral contract action undertaken by the government under the provisions appearing at FAR 49 (and especially FAR 49.4). In a T4D action, the contractor generally is not entitled to any payment for undelivered items and may be liable to the government for the repayment of progress payments or advances, liquidated or other damages, and the excess cost of acquiring the undelivered items from another source.

Time-and-materials (T&M) contract: A contract that provides for acquiring supplies or services on the basis of (1) direct labor hours at specified fixed hourly rates that include wages, overhead, general and administrative expenses, and profit, and (2) materials at cost, including, if appropriate, material handling costs as part of materials costs.

TIN: Taxpayer Identification Number

TINA: Truth in Negotiations Act

T&M: Time and materials

Truth in Negotiations Act (TINA): A public law enacted for the purpose of providing for full and fair disclosure by contractors in the conduct of negotiations with the government. The most significant provision included in TINA is the requirement that contractors submit certified cost and pricing data for negotiated procurements above a defined threshold.

Two-step sealed bidding: A combination of competitive procedures designed to obtain the benefits of sealed bidding when adequate specifications are not available.

U

UCA: Undefinitized contract action

Unallowable cost: Any cost that, under the provisions of any pertinent law, regulation, or contract, cannot be included in prices, cost reimbursements, or settlements under a government contract to which it is allocable.

Uncosted obligations: Obligations incurred for which costs have not been accrued. It represents materials or services ordered but not received or placed in use.

Undefinitized contract action (UCA): A new procurement action entered into by the government for which contractual terms, specifications, or final price or estimated cost and fee are not agreed to by the government and the contractor before performance is begun (letter contract or change order).

Unique and innovative concept: A product of original thinking that contains new, novel, or changed concepts, approaches, or methods.

Unliquidated obligations: Obligations incurred for which disbursements have not been made. The obligations may consist of an accounts payable (for goods or services received) or an obligation for goods and services ordered but not yet received.

Unsolicited proposal: A written proposal for a new or innovative idea that is submitted to an agency on the initiative of the offeror for the purpose of obtaining a contract with the government and that is not in response to a formal or informal request (other than an agency request constituting a publicized general statement of needs).

V

Value engineering (VE): The formal technique by which contractors may (1) voluntarily suggest methods for performing more economically and share in any resulting savings, or (2) be required to establish a program to identify and submit to the government methods for performing more economically.

Variable cost: A cost that varies in direct proportion to changes in volume, but which is uniform for each unit. In practice, some variable costs are difficult to distinguish from fixed costs. It has been said that all costs are fixed in the short run and variable in the long run.

Variance: The difference between a pre-established measure and an actual measure.

VE: Value engineering

Voluntary standard: A standard established by a private sector body and available for public use.

W

Walsh-Healy Act: A public law designed to prevent the practice of "bid brokering;" i.e., the practice of buying items and then reselling them to the government without the adding of any value to the item by the reseller. The Act provides that contracts subject to its provisions (generally contracts over $10,000) may be awarded only to "manufacturers" or "regular dealers," as defined.

Warranty: As used in FAR 46.701, a promise or affirmation given by a contractor to the government regarding the nature, usefulness, or condition of the supplies or performance of services furnished under the contract.

Weighted average cost: An inventory costing method under which an average unit cost is computed periodically by dividing the sum of the cost of beginning inventory plus the cost of acquisitions by the total number of units included in these two categories.

Weighted guidelines: A government technique for developing fee and profit negotiation objectives, within percentage ranges established by regulation.

Women-owned small business concern: A small business that is at least 51 percent owned by, and whose management and daily business operations are controlled by, one or more women.

Buying Offices

This Appendix identifies a number of government buying offices that should be contacted for opportunities. Many have their own web site, which include a lot of the information you will need. If you don't know their web address, we suggest that you start at the federal jumpstation maintained by NASA for the government. (http://prod.nais.nasa.gov/pub/fedproc/home.html.) The civilian agencies that are not specifically listed here may be contacted by calling your local PTAC office.

Organizational changes required by law, restructuring for efficiency or the impact of the E-Gov initiatives, have made us change the way in which we present this information. We have decided not to use as much in the way of specific offices and related information about what they buy, but rather list agency web sites that will give you access to the buying organization of those agencies. Many of these sites, especially for DoD, are gateways to the total organization. Some of the specialty-type buying offices we have retained the specific listings.

All the locations identified are the small business offices for that agency. Remember this small business specialist is your resource for that agency. They are employees of the agency and are a staff officer to the head of the agency. Use them to your advantage. Don't be afraid to ask reasonable questions.

SPECIAL DEPARTMENT OF DEFENSE BUYING OFFICES

The first listing is for the Department of Defense and some locations that specialize in items or services that are not normally bought by the commands and base, camps and stations.

There are three categories of goods and services that are purchased by special purchasing offices; the categories are merchandise for defense commissary stores, resale merchandise for the military exchange services, and motion pictures and videotape production.

The Defense Commissary Agency (DeCA)

DeCA is a chain of supermarkets (commissaries) providing quality goods at the lowest possible cost to authorized patrons. DeCA has three regional offices in the United States and one in Europe. For more information see web site http://www.commissaries.com/business/contracting.cfm

DeCA is not associated with any other military resale or retail activity. Other entities operate and manage these activities known as club systems, ship stores, or exchanges. DeCA is also not associated with dining facilities (mess halls, dining halls, galleys, etc.). The dining facilities are operated by the individual Armed Services to provide prepared meals for their members.

What DeCA Buys. DeCA has a preference for commercial-type products.

- Grocery Products—The resale products are those traditionally sold in commercial supermarkets. Commodities and products sold in the commissaries are restricted to those authorized by the U.S. Congress. (See the "Resale" section for more information.)

- Operational Support—Equipment, supplies and services required to support the operation of individual commissaries (stores).

- Administrative Support—Supplies and services to support the overall operation of the Agency.

Resale Focus. Resale includes both brand name and non-brand name products. Brand name products are those that have identifiable customer recognition, and are marketed, merchandised and commercially available and sold based on that brand. DeCA carries these products because the commissary patron prefers the brand name. Non-brand name products are products for which there is no customer preference and include meat, eggs, etc. and in-store resale operations (deli/bakery). They are procured competitively using commercial descriptions. (See the "Resale" section for more information.)

Other than Resale Focus. Other than resale means operational and administrative support items as defined above. (See the "Operational and Administrative Support Items" section for more information.) These acquisitions account for less than 5 percent of DeCA's total contractual awards.

Your Market Key for Brand Name Items. The first step in selling DeCA a brand name product is to make an item presentation to one of our buyers. The presentation is your opportunity to market your product and provide any unique information. Before selection, a brand name product must have a Universal Product Code (UPC) and be sold in commercial supermarkets. For more information regarding product UPC, you can contact Uniform Code Council Inc. at (937) 435-3870 or see web site http://www.uc-council.org. Details of your offer must be summarized on DeCA Form 40-33, Item Presentation Form, which may be obtained from a local commissary or from one of the points of contact under the "Getting Started" section.

For brand name resale items, your product's performance determines whether it remains in DeCA's stock assortment. DeCA continuously analyzes product sales information, and if sales trends indicate your product is moving, then replenishment quantities are ordered, if not, your product will be removed from the shelves. Specific time frames for measuring product performance will be explained during your presentation.

Products for national distribution are normally presented at the corporate headquarters at Fort Lee, VA. Products with regional or local distribution may be presented at one of the region offices or an individual commissary. DeCA small business specialists, category managers, or region buyers can help you decide which location is best for your presentation.

Defense Commissary Agency
Acquisition Management
1300 E Avenue, Building 11200
Fort Lee, Virginia 23801-1800
(804) 734-8740

Points of Contact/DeCA Headquarters/Ft Lee

Location	Topic	Name	Telephone
Business Diversity Office	Small Business (general and operational information)	SADBU	(804) 734-8740 Internet E-mail (smallbus@hqlee.deca.mil)
Information Technology (IT)	Electronic Data Interchange (EDI)	Derick Young, EDI Coordinator	(804) 734-8851 Internet E-mail (derrick.young@deca.mil)
Marketing Business Unit (MBU)	Resale Items	Chilled Foods Frozen Foods Edibles Non-Edibles Direct Store Delivery Produce	(804) 734-8232 (804) 734-8283 (804) 734-8221 (804) 734-8222 (804) 734-8381

		Operations	(804) 734-8387
		Meat Operations	(804) 734-8398
		Advertising	(804) 734-8410
		Promotions	(804) 734-8228
		Deli/Bakery	(804) 734-8382
		Seafood	(804) 734-8382

DeCA Region Locations and Points of Contact

REGION	LOCATION
DeCA Eastern Region	5151 Bonney Road, Suite 201 Virginia Beach, VA 23462-4314 (757) 462-3500 Small Business Specialist (757) 462-3112
DeCA Midwest Region	300 AFCOMS Way Kelly AFB, TX 78241-6132 (210) 925-6655 Small Business Specialist (210) 925-2475
DeCA Western/ Pacific Region	401 Beech Street McClellan AFB, CA 95652-1164 (916) 569-4697 Small Business Specialist (916) 569-4800
DeCA European Region	Gebaude 2780, Zimmer 109, Kapun AS, 67661 Vogelweh/Kaiserslautern GE 011-49-0631-3523-11

Military Exchange Services

The categories of merchandise and price limitations on goods sold by military exchange services in the continental United States are established by regulations approved by Congress. These limitations do not apply to overseas exchanges.

The buying offices and procedures for dealing with the exchanges are set forth below.

To sell to the Army and Air Force Exchange Service a firm must offer its product to the appropriate buyer at the Headquarters or the exchange region office. No merchandise is purchased by individual exchanges. The Headquarters buyers purchase all resale merchandise that is commonly stocked in post and base exchanges in the CONUS, and all resale merchandise of United States origin for overseas exchanges. Merchandise peculiar to a single exchange region is purchased by the regional offices.

The Army and Air Force Exchange Service (AAFES)
(http://www.aafes.com/pa/selling/index.html)

The Army and Air Force Exchange Service (AAFES) not only touches the lives of active-duty military, National Guard members, reservists, retirees and their families. It's a military organization with a two-fold mission:

- To provide quality merchandise and services to soldiers, airmen and their families wherever they're stationed around the world.

- To generate reasonable earnings to support Army and Air Force morale, welfare and recreation (MWR) programs.

This mission has remained essentially unchanged since a military exchange system was established in July 1895. The company buys goods and supplies from some 13,000 firms. Approximately 94 percent of these are small businesses.

AAFES policy is to cooperate to the fullest extent with all suppliers and manufacturers while maintaining the highest ethical business standards. AAFES is a staunch supporter of diverse suppliers. Determining factors for procuring merchandise from suppliers are quality products, competitive prices, on time delivery and customer demand.

Source list applications. Please use the new web-based system at http://partners.aafes.com/sourcelist/. For your convenience, the printable versions of the Source List Application are available.

- Source List Application/Retail Merchandise/General
  (http://www.aafes.com/pa/selling/srclist.htm)

- Source List Application/Concession & Vending
  (http://www.aafes.com/pa/selling/srclist_sdv.htm)

- Source List Application/Telecom
  (http://www.aafes.com/pa/selling/sourcelist_oct.pdf)

For information about Supplier Guidelines and Requirements, go to http://www.aafes.com/pa/selling/minority.html and pick "General Information" in the drop-down menu.

The Navy Exchange Service Command (http://www.navy-nex.com/command/contractor_vendor/cv-index.html)

The Navy Exchange Service Command (NEXCOM), headquartered in Hampton Roads, Virginia, operates the worldwide Navy Exchange System (NES). As the component of the Naval Supply Systems Command (NAVSUP) responsible for resale programs, NEXCOM's mission is to provide authorized customers, quality goods and services, at a savings, and to support quality of life programs.

The Navy Exchange System (NES) is a Navy retailing operation that provides quality products and a variety of services to the men and women of the Armed Forces, with special emphasis on Navy active-duty Sailors, retirees, reservists and their families. Navy Exchanges (NEXs) generally are located on or near Navy bases throughout the United States and around the world.

NEXCOM is self-supporting and uses almost no tax dollars for its operations. As a Non-Appropriated Fund Instrumentality (NAFI) of the U. S. Government, NEXCOM is subject to directives issued by the Departments of Defense and Navy, in addition to applicable Federal laws; however, procurement laws and regulations that apply to spending tax dollars, such as the Federal Acquisition Regulations (48 CFR 1, et seq.) do not generally apply to NES procurements.

Small and Disadvantaged Business Utilization (SADBU) Office. To assist prospective vendors in doing business with the NES, NEXCOM maintains a Small and Disadvantaged Business Utilization (SADBU) Office to provide guidance to small and disadvantaged businesses. The SADBU office provides information on how to do business with the NES. The NEXCOM SADBU specialist can be reached at:

> Navy Exchange Service Command
> Attn: Code K - SADBU Office
> 3280 Virginia Beach Blvd
> Virginia Beach, VA 23452-5724
> Phone: (757) 631-3696
> Fax: (757) 631-4508
> E-mail: small_business_office@nexnet.navy.mil

Authority to purchase items and services, both resale and to support NES operations, is limited to general and divisional merchandise managers, and buyers within the General Merchandising Group (Code M), contracting officers assigned to Corporate Contracts (Code K) and to overseas district offices located in Naples, Italy and Yokosuka, Japan, and to contracting officers that support the Ships Stores Afloat Program (Code A).

Four separate programs comprise the NES: Navy Exchanges, Navy Lodges, Ships Store Program and the Uniform Program Management Office.

Navy Exchanges. NEXs provide authorized customers with quality merchandise at affordable prices. Authorized customers who shop at a NEX save an average of 19 percent on items purchased—before sales tax. NEXs are considered a non-pay benefit for military personnel.

There are over 100 NEXs worldwide with sales volume ranging from $70,000 to over $150 million annually. NEX revenues worldwide are approximately $2 billion and contributions to Navy morale, welfare and recreation (MWR) have exceeded $2 billion since 1946.

Navy Exchanges are organized by region, into the following 12 districts:

District	*Location of Stores*
Northeast District	New England, New York, and New Jersey.
Tidewater District	Southeast Virginia and West Virginia.
Mid-Atlantic District	Pennsylvania, Maryland, and Washington DC area.
Great Lakes District	Illinois, Indiana, and Tennessee.
Southeast District	Eastern Florida, Georgia, South Carolina, Puerto Rico and Cuba.
Gulf Coast District	Western Florida, Mississippi, Louisiana, and Texas.
Northwest District	Washington State.
Central California District	Central California and Nevada.
Hawaii District; European District; Guam District; Japan District:	

See http://www.navy-nex.com/exchange/m-exchanges.html for additional information on individual Navy Exchanges.

NEXs consist of retail and service departments, and are operated in a similar manner to commercial retail enterprises, within limitations established by Congress and the Department of Defense. NEXs provide basic staple merchandise, including automotive supplies, candy and confections, food products, cameras and photo accessories, home furnishings, housewares, sporting goods, electrical appliances, consumer electronics, computers and software, luggage and leather goods, stationery, books and periodicals, greeting cards, hardware, garden supplies, pet supplies, cosmetics, toiletries and fragrances, uniforms and uniform accessories, clothing, domestics, family shoes, distilled spirits, wine, beer and soda and tobacco and smoking accessories.

Services available to authorized NEX customers include automotive service centers, fast food outlets, snack bars, food carts, mobile canteens, laundry and dry cleaning, vending machines, optical shops, photo finishing, specialty stores, barber and beauty salons, flower shops, video rental, car rental and other personalized services. Many of these services are provided through concession agreements established with local businesses. A summary of many of these services are provided below:

Direct Run Operations	*Contracted/License Agreements/Concessions*
Food services	National Brand Outlets
Haircare shops	Telecommunication services: AT&T, Sprint, PCS, Alltel, Cellular One, SunCom, Voice Stream
Auto service/gas dispensing	
Personalized services: Western Union, travelers checks, U-Haul, keys, stamps, etc.	Food services: McDonald's, Burger King, Wendy's, Subway, Blimpies, Bojangles, Pizza Hut, KFC, Taco Bell, Dunkin Donuts, Cinnabon, Seattle's Best, Applebees, Sbarros, Long John Silvers, etc.
Flower shops	
Video rental outlets	
Laundry/dry cleaning facilities & plants	
Optical shops	Vehicle Rental Enterprise, U-haul
Photo finishing & labs	Mail Boxes Etc (MBE)
NEXMARTs (combined Navy Exchange and DeCA Commissary)	Unbranded Outlets: Optometrists, Haircare shops, Video rental shops

Navy Lodges. Navy Lodges are motels operated by the Navy Lodge Program on or near Navy bases. With 41 locations worldwide, Navy Lodges provide temporary accommodations for authorized patrons who are in transit between duty stations, house hunting, on temporary assigned duty or on vacation. Go to http://www.navy-lodge.com/ for additional information on individual Navy Lodges.

Information regarding Navy Lodge operations, inquiries and correspondence should be directed to the Director, Navy Lodge Program, at:

Navy Lodge Program
1545 Crossways Boulevard, Suite 100
Chesapeake VA. 23320
Phone: (757) 424-8120
Fax: (757) 424-9350

Ships Store Program. Ships Stores Afloat and Military Sealift Command (MSC) exchanges are retail outlets on ships. However, because of space constraints aboard ships, merchandise is restricted to basic necessities and a limited selection of additional items.

Services include barber shops, laundry/dry cleaning, vending machines and video games. Contracts with local vendors are also available to supply merchandise and special orders to personnel aboard ships while those ships are in port.

Go to http://www.navy-nex.com/command/about_us/p-shipstores.html for additional information on Ships Store Afloat. Inquiries and correspondence should be directed to the Director, Ships Store Program, at:

Navy Exchange Service Command
Ships Store Program (Code A)
3280 Virginia Beach Boulevard
Virginia Beach VA 23452-5724
Phone: (757) 443-2085
Fax: (757) 443-2082

Military Sealift Command (MSC) Exchanges. In dealing with Military Sealift Command (MSC) exchanges, the same procedures are followed as that for NEX activities. Merchandise cannot be sold to individual MSC (USNS) ships directly. Such ships do not have contracting authority. Merchandise buying is accomplished by using bulletins/contracts prepared for NEXs and Ships Stores Afloat. Exchanges aboard MSC ships offer a moderate selection of basic necessities, snack items and general merchandise to meet crew and passenger requirements. Address mail to the MSC exchange division director at:

Commander, Military Sealift Command Pacific
Attn: MSC Exchange Sealift PM1 WL-3
9284 Balboa Avenue
San Diego, CA 92123-1591
Phone: (619) 553-2305

Uniform Program Management Office. As program manager for Navy uniforms, the Uniform Program Management Office (UPMO) is the only authorized source of certified Navy uniforms. The UPMO encompasses the management of government issue uniform items as well as commercially procured certified items for chiefs and officers.

Uniforms are sold to authorized patrons at over 100 uniform centers located around the world, the Uniform Support Center (USC) and through the command's website, www.navy-nex.com. The stock assortments at the uniform centers vary by location based on the mission of the base and the demographics of the area.

In addition to Navy uniform items, the UPMO also manages the U. S. Marine Corps mail order program and provides support for other services in quad services stores.

Go to http://www.navy-nex.com/command/about_us/p-uniformsupport.html for additional information on Uniform Program. Information regarding Navy uniform procurement procedures, inquiries and correspondence should be directed to the Director, Uniform Program Management Office, at:

Uniform Program Management Office
1545 Crossways Boulevard, Suite 100
Chesapeake, VA 23320
Phone: (757) 420-9116
Fax: (757) 420-4094

Buying Procedures—Resale Items for Navy Exchanges. The method of doing business with NEXs depends on the type of merchandise or service being offered for resale by the store. NEX buying is done by General Merchandise Group and by Corporate Contracts located at the NEXCOM Headquarters in Hampton Roads, Virginia. In addition, NEXs and districts receive merchandising guidance, policies and procedures from Headquarters.

In general, all buying for retail departments for all NEXs is done by NEXCOM. There is limited local buying in Japan, Europe and Pearl Harbor.

Categories of merchandise and price limitations on goods sold by NEXs in the continental United States are established by the Armed Services Exchange Regulations, issued by the Department of Defense. These limitations do not apply to overseas NEXs.

Go to http://www.navy-nex.com/command/contractor_vendor/merch/html/m-contacts.html for a directory of retail departments and buyer phone numbers. Inquiries and correspondence should be directed to a buyer or contracting officer as appropriate, at the address below.

Navy Exchange Service Command
3280 Virginia Beach Boulevard
Virginia Beach, VA 23452-5724

It is the policy of the NES to cooperate to the fullest extent possible with all suppliers and manufacturers, while maintaining the highest standards of business ethics in seeking to obtain suitable items for system operation and maintenance, or for resale to authorized customers. NEXCOM is as receptive to small business enterprises, including those that are minority or women-owned, as it is to large firms. Quality products, competitive prices and customer demand are the basic determining factors for the acquisition of merchandise and supplies.

NEXCOM, as a matter of policy, supports American businesses and the national workforce by seeking vendors and suppliers that are based in the United States and are consistent with its overall mission.

Appointments may be made by letter or telephone directly with the appropriate buyer, services or contract specialist. If there is a last minute emergency, and the buyer is not available, the divisional merchandise manager or the general merchandise manager will keep the appointment. If the services or contract specialist is not available, generally another specialist will keep the appointment or the appointment can be rescheduled.

Go to http://www.navy-nex.com/command/contractor_ vendor/merch/html/m-merchandising.html for additional information on doing business with the Merchandising Division.

Contract/Purchase Procedures—Services and Non-Resale Items. Contracting officers are primarily responsible for the procurement of all non-retail items and all services. This includes equipment, supplies and support services necessary for NES operations as well as revenue generating services. The latter includes concessions/license agreements, such as AT&T, McDonalds, Mail Boxes Etc. and car rental, as well as contracted services where NEX associates serve the customer, but a contractor provides services to the NEX such as U-Haul, Western Union, laundry/dry cleaning and photo finishing.

The role of a contracting officer is to evaluate requirements, determine most effective means of obtaining required equipment, supplies or services, solicit, evaluate, award and administer contracts as needed to fulfill each requirement. Larger procurements of items and services are solicited using a Request for Proposals (RFP), normally on a competitive basis, and subject to negotiation, in accordance with prescribed procedures. Awards are then issued to the successful offeror after supervisory approval, and as applicable, by the NEXCOM Contracts Review Board, consisting of senior members of the NEXCOM Corporate Contracts staff.

NEXCOM Corporate Contracts (Code K) presently consists of a main office located at the Headquarters in Hampton Roads, Virginia; and a satellite office is maintained in Pearl Harbor, Hawaii. There are also two overseas contracting offices in Naples, Italy and Yokosuka, Japan, assigned to District Europe and District Japan, respectively.

Go to http://www.navy-nex.com/command/contractor_vendor/cv-corp.html for additional information on participating in Corporate Contracts procurements.

The Marine Corps Exchange Program

U.S. Marine Corps Community Service (non-appropriated funds) buys products and services for the personal use of Marines. It is a diverse collection of activities, services, and programs which support the quality of life of the Marine Corps community, active duty, reserves and retired.

Marine Corps Market Points of Contact

Marine Corps Logistics Base
Barstow, CA
Barstow, CA 92331-5003
Phone: 760-256-8974
FAX: 800-256-7027

Marine Corps Exchange
Marine Corps Base
Camp Pendleton, CA 92055-5020
Phone: 760-725-6305
Phone: 760-385-0446

Marine Corps Exchange
MCAGCC
Twentynine Palms, CA 92278-8150
Phone: 760-830-6163
FAX: 760-830-7239

Marine Corps Exchange
MCRD/WRR
3800 Chosin Ave.
San Diego, CA 92140-5196
Phone: 619-297-2500
FAX: 619-543-9025

Marine Corps Exchange
MCAS Miramar
San Diego, CA 92145
Phone: 858-577-8651
FAX: 858-577-4122

Marine Corps Exchange
Marine Corps Air Station
Yuma, AZ 85369-9119
Phone: 520-341-2295
FAX: 520-344-1902

Marine Corps Exchange
HQBN Henderson Hall
P. O. Box 4009
Arlington, VA 22204-4009
Phone: 703-979-8420
FAX: 703-979-0972

Marine Corps Exchange
Marine Corps Air Station
Beaufort, SC 29904-5003
Phone: 843-522-7888
FAX: 843-522-7077

Marine Corps Exchange
MCB Quantico
P.O. Box 229
Quantico, VA 22134-5003
Phone: 703-640-8800
Phone: 703-640-6708

Marine Corps Exchange
Marine Corps Recruit Depot/ERR
Parris Island, SC 29905-3301
Phone: 843-525-3301
FAX: 843-525-2872

Marine Corps Exchange
Norfolk, VA 23551-5003
Phone: 757-423-1187

Marine Corps Exchange
Marine Corps Logistics Base
814 Radford Blvd., Bldg. 7500
Albany, GA 31704-1128
Phone: 229-888-6801
Phone: 229-439-0324

Marine Corps Exchange
Marine Corps Air Station
Cherry Point, NC 28533-5003
Phone: 252-447-7041
FAX: 252-447-2922

Marine Corps Exchange
Marine Corps Base Hawaii
Kaneohe Bay, HI 96863-5018
Phone: 808-254-7515
FAX: 808-254-7504

Marine Corps Exchange
Marine Corps Base
Camp Lejeune, NC 28547-2539
Phone: 910-451-2434
Phone: 910-451-3355

Marine Corps Exchange
MCAS Iwakuni Japan
FPR AP 96310-1866
Phone: 011-81-6117-53-5641
Fax: 011-81-827-21-7363

COMPUTER SYSTEMS

Activities Involved in Procurement of ADPE, Software, Maintenance and Services for the military

Department of the Army

CECOM Acquisition Center
Navy Information System and
Acquisition Agency
Washington Operation Office
2461 Eisenhower Ave.
Alexandria, VA 22331-0700
Tel: (703) 325-5793

**Defense Supply Service-
Washington**
5200 Army Pentagon
Washington, DC 20310-5210
Tel: (703) 697-6024

Department of the Navy

Management Center
Code OOX1, Bldg. 176-4
Washington Navy Yard
Washington, DC 20374-5070
Tel: (202) 433-4337

**Naval Fleet and Industrial
Supply Center**
Long Beach Detachment
Code, PA, Bldg. 53, 2nd Floor
Long Beach, CA 90822-5074
Tel: (310) 901-3794

CECOM - Acquisition Center
ATTN: AMSEL-IE-SB
Fort Huachuca, AZ 85613-5000
Tel: (520) 538-7870

Naval Fleet and Industrial Supply Center
Washington Navy Yard,
Building 200
901 M Street S. E., Code OOA
Washington, DC 20374-2000
Tel: (202) 433-2957

Department of Air Force Electronic System Division
275 Randolph Road
Hanscom AFB, MA 01731-5000
Tel: (617) 377-4973

Naval Fleet and Industrial Supply Center
Code 09B
Philadelphia Detachment
Philadelphia, PA 19112-5083
Tel: (215) 697-9555

SSC/PK
375 Libby Street
Maxwell AFB
Gunter Annex, AL 36114-3207
Tel: (334) 416-5614

Defense Information System Agency
701 South Courthouse Road
Arlington, VA 22204-2199
Tel: (703) 607-6920

Defense Logistics Agency
Administrative Support Center
Office of Contracting
ATTN: Deputy for Small Business
8725 John J. Kingman Road
Suite 0119, Room 1134
Fort Belvoir, VA 22206-6220
Tel: (703) 767-1161

Motion Picture And Videotape Productions

Motion picture and videotape productions are purchased only from qualified producers. To obtain an application form for acceptance on the qualified Film Producers List or the Qualified Videotape Producers List, contact the Joint Visual Information Activity Office,

601 North Fairfax Street,
Room 334, Alexandria,
Virginia 22314-2007,
telephone (703) 428-0636

They serve as an executive agent for all Federal agencies, including the Department of Defense. To become qualified, producers submit sample films or videotapes to a review board. Ultimately, contracts are placed by authorized procurement offices of the Army, Navy and Air Force. In order for a producer to receive a contract from an authorized procurement office, the producer must first be approved for the appropriate qualified list.

Note: audiovisual services such as processing or graphics, and audiovisual equipment are purchased by the requiring post, camp, station, or installation.

Authorized Military Service procurement offices are:

Army

Joint Visual Information Activity Washington - Contracting 601 N. Fairfax Street, Room 334 Alexandria, VA 22314-2007 703-428-1122

Joint Visual Information Activity - Production 601 N. Fairfax Street, Room 334 Alexandria, VA 22314-2007 703-248-1118

Navy and Marine Corps

Navy Imaging Command
Anacostia Naval Station
Production Contracting Department
Building 168
Washington, DC 20374-1681
(202) 433-5775

U.S. Army Installation Management Agency
(http://www.ima.army.mil/demo/sites/local/)

The agency will oversee all Army-wide installation management, including environmental programs, construction, morale and welfare, family care, force protection landscaping, logistics, public works, etc., and the planning, programming and budgeting that resource these functions. The IMA structure enables the Army to establish standards, resource to standard, and deliver equitable services from installation to installation.

The IMA is headquartered in the National Capital Region, with seven regional offices located at Fort Monroe, Va.; Fort McPherson, Ga.; Rock Island Arsenal, Ill.; Fort Sam Houston, Texas; Heidelberg, Germany; Fort Shafter, Hawaii; and Seoul, Korea.

As a field operating agency under the Army's Assistant Chief of Staff for Installation Management, IMA is at the center of the Army's initiative to mold installation support functions into a corporate structure, enabling equitable, efficient and effective management of Army installations worldwide. The IMA will support readiness, promote well-being of soldiers, civilians and family members, and preserve infrastructure and environment.

DEPARTMENT OF VETERANS AFFAIRS

The buying offices of the Department of Veterans Affairs are divided into dozens of regions serving hundreds of facilities. Each facility has a point of contact person assigned the task of working with small business contractors.

To get the latest facility and contact information, log onto http://www.va.gov/osdbu/contacts/conactspec.htm.

GOVERNMENT R&D BUYING OFFICES

The government encourages participation by small concerns, including those owned by women and by disadvantaged persons, in its R&D programs. The government seeks the most advanced scientific knowledge attainable and the best possible equipment and systems that can be devised and produced. It is the government's policy (FAR 35.008), in awarding an R&D contract, to select the organization "...that proposes the best ideas or concepts and has the highest competence in the specific field of science or technology involved." You should evaluate your firm critically before seeking a government R&D contract. Be sure that your firm is as well qualified as others who may want the same award.

The web sites on this list point to small business specialists at the research organizations for the Small Business Innovation Research (SBIR) and the Small business Technical Transfer (STTR) programs.

- US Army Research Office:
  http://www.aro.army.mil/arowash/rt/sbir/sbir.htm

- US Navy: http://www.navysbir.com/

- US Air Force: http://www.afrl.af.mil/sbir/index.htm

- DARPA: http://www.darpa.mil/sbir/

- Defense Threat Reduction Agency:
  http://www.dtra.mil/dtralink_12Oct04/business_opp/procurement/acq_sbir.cfm

- Missile Defense Agency: http://www.winbmdo.com/

- Special Operations Command:
  http://soal.socom.mil/index.cfm?page=sadbu&sb=sbir

- National Geospatial Intelligence Agency:
  http://www.nga.mil/

- Chemical and Biological Defense:
  http://www.aro.army.mil/arowash/rt/cbdsbir/index.htm

Other Federal Agencies SBIR/STTR web sites

- Department of Health and Human Services:
  http://grants.nih.gov/grants/funding/sbir.htm

- NASA: http://sbir.hq.nasa.gov/

- Department of Energy: http://sbir.er.doe.gov/sbir/

- National Science Foundation: http://www.eng.nsf.gov/sbir/

- Department of Agriculture:
  http://www.csrees.usda.gov/funding/sbir/sbir.html

- Department of Education:
  http://www.ed.gov/offices/IES/SBIR/

- Environmental Protection Agency:
  http://es.epa.gov/ncerqa/sbir/

- Department of Transportation:
  http://www.volpe.dot.gov/sbir/index.html

- Department of Homeland Security:
  http://www.hsarpasbir.com/

- US SBA: http://www.sbaonline.sba.gov/SBIR/

GUIDE FOR PREPARING UNSOLICITED PROPOSALS

An unsolicited proposal is a written proposal independently originated and developed by the offeror and submitted to federal agency for the purpose of obtaining a contract. To be considered for acceptance, an unsolicited proposal must be innovative and unique and in sufficient detail to allow a determination that the agency support would benefit the agency's mission responsibilities. An unsolicited proposal is not a response to an agency request or an advance proposal for an agency requirement that could be met by competitive methods.

There is no particular format to be followed in preparation of unsolicited proposals. Elaborate proposals are discouraged. The proposal should contain the following information to permit consideration in an objective and timely manner:

Basic Information

Offeror's name, address, and type of organization; e.g., profit, nonprofit, educational, small business, minority business, women-owned business.

Names and telephone numbers of technical and business personnel to be contacted for evaluation or negotiation purposes.

Names of other federal, state, and local agencies, or other parties, if any, receiving the proposal or funding the proposed effort.

Date of submission and signature of a person authorized to represent and contractually obligate the offeror.

Technical Information

A concise, descriptive title and an abstract (200-300 words) stating the basic purpose, summary of work, and expected end result of the proposed effort.

A reasonably complete narrative in which the relevance of the proposed work to the agency mission is discussed. State the problems to be addressed; the specific objectives of the research, and the expected consequences of successful completion of the research, including potential economic and other benefits.

Provide a full and complete description of the work to be performed, the method of approach, and the extent of effort to be employed. Indicate an estimated period of time in which to accomplish the objectives, and criteria by which success of the project can be evaluated.

Names and biographical information on the key personnel who would be involved in the project.

Any support needed from the agency; e.g., facilities, equipment, material.

Supporting Information

A breakdown of the proposed cost or price in sufficient detail for meaningful evaluation. Show the estimated cost of materials and how you established it. Show the estimated costs of labor by category (engineering, manufacturing, test, etc.) and show the salary rates for each category. Show the indirect expense rates (manufacturing and engineering overheads, general and administrative expenses) to be applied. Explain the basis for the labor and indirect expense rates included in your cost breakdown (e.g., current experienced rates, projected from current experience, budgetary, etc.). Identify and explain the basis for any other cost elements included in your proposal.

A statement as to the proposed duration of the effort, the type of contract preferred, and the length of time for which the proposal is valid (a 6-month minimum is suggested).

A brief description of any previous or ongoing R&D work performed in the field or in related fields. Describe briefly the facilities and any special equipment available to perform the proposed effort.

Unsolicited proposals may include proprietary data which the offeror does not want disclosed to the public or used by the government for any purpose other than proposal evaluation. The government cannot assume responsibility for use of such data unless it is specifically and clearly marked with the following legend on the title page:

Use and Disclosure of Data

The data in this proposal shall not be disclosed outside the government and shall not be duplicated, used, or disclosed in whole or in part for any purpose other than to evaluate the proposal; provided that if a contract is awarded to the offeror as a result of or in connection with the submission of these data, the Government shall have the right to duplicate, use, or disclose the data to the extent provided in the contract. This restriction does not limit the Government's right to use information contained in the ata if it is obtainable from another source without restriction. The data subject to this restriction are contained in Sheets _____. Each restricted sheet should be marked with the following legend: "Use or disclosure of proposal data is subject to the restriction on the title page of this proposal."

MILITARY BUYING OFFICES BY DoD COMPONENT

The offices are identified by their DoD component. The web sites are gateways to the agency locations. Most web addresses are for the small business office, which is a valuable resource to utilize.

Office of the Under Secretary of Defense AT&L
Office of Small and Disadvantaged Business Utilization
Address:1777 North Kent St.
Rosslyn Plaza North Suite 9100
Arlington, VA 22209-2100
Phone: 703-588-8631
Fax: 703-588-7561
Web: www.acq.osd.mil/sadbu

Office of the Secretary of the Army
Office of Small and Disadvantaged Business Utilization
Address: 106 Army Pentagon

Washington, DC 20310-0106

Phone: 703-697-2868

Fax: 703-693-3898

Web: www.sellingtoarmy.info, then open the "Locations" tab to find Army Activities

Office of the Secretary of the Navy
Office of Small and Disadvantaged Business Utilization

Address: 720 Kennon Street SE
Washington Navy Yard
Bldg. 36, Room 207
Washington, DC 20374-5015

Phone: 202-685-6485

Fax: 202-685-6865

Web: www.hq.navy.mil/sadbu, then open "Navy Contracting Activities"

Office of the Secretary of the Air Force
Office of Small and Disadvantaged Business Utilization

Address: 1060 Air Force Pentagon
Washington, DC 20330-1060

Phone: 703-696-1103

Fax: 703-696-1170

Web: www.selltoairforce.org, open the "Locator" tab and then select either the Small Business Specialist or Major Command link

Defense Information Systems Agency
Office of Small and Disadvantaged Business Utilization

Address: 701 S. Courthouse Rd.
D04 Room 1108B
Arlington VA 22204-2199

Phone: 703-607-6436

Fax   703-607-4173

Web: www.disa.mil/main/sadbu.html

Defense Logistics Agency
Office of Small and Disadvantaged Business Utilization

Address: 8725 John J. Kingman Blvd, Suite 2533
                Fort Belvoir, VA 22060-6221
Phone: 703-767-1662
Fax: 703-767-9446
Web: www.dla.mil/db

Missile Defense Agency
Office of Small and Disadvantaged Business Utilization
Address: 7100 Defense Pentagon
                Washington, DC 20301-7100
Phone: 703-697-8017
Fax: 703-767-9446
Web: www.acq.osd.mil/mda/mdalink/html/mdalink.html,
                then click on "Doing Business" tab

Defense Intelligence Agency
Office of Small and Disadvantaged Business Utilization
Address: McDill Blvd., Bldg. 6000
                Bolling AFB
                Washington, DC 20340-0002
Phone: 202-231-2822
Fax: 202-231-2831
Web: www.dia.mil/Business/disadvantage.html

National Geospatial-Intelligence Agency
Office of Small and Disadvantaged Business Utilization
Address: 4600 Sangamore Rd.
                Bethesda, MD, 20816-5003
Phone: 301-227-7855
Web: http://www.nga.mil/portal/site/nga01, then click
on "Business Opportunity" tab

United States Special Operations Command
Office of Small and Disadvantaged Business Utilization
Address: 2418 Florida Keys Ave.
                MacDill Air Force Base
                Tampa, FL 33621-5323
Phone: 813-828-7338

Web: soal.socom.mil/index.cfm?page=sadbu

Defense Threat Reduction Agency
Office of Small and Disadvantaged Business Utilization
Address: 8725 John J. Kingman Rd., MS 6201
                Ft. Belvoir, VA 22060-6201
Phone: 703-767-5870
Web: www.dtra.mil/business_opp/small/index.cfm

Defense Advanced Research Projects Agency
Office of Small and Disadvantaged Business Utilization
Address: 3701 N. Fairfax Dr.
                Arlington, VA 22203-1714
Phone: 703-526-4170
Fax: 703-696-2208
Web: http://www.darpa.mil/sbirl

GSA FSS ACQUISITION CENTERS

GSA Federal Supply Service (FSS) provides federal customers with the products, services and programs to meet their supply, service, procurement, vehicle purchasing and leasing, travel and transportation, and personal property management requirements.

The Office of Commercial Acquisition provides a variety of product and service opportunities for companies interested in doing business with the government. Check out the web site at http://www.gsa.gov/Portal/gsa/ep/contentView.do?contentType=GSA_OVERVIEW&contentID=11479&noc=T. Work with your local PTAC to make sure you have explored every opportunity.

The mission of the Office of Commercial Acquisition is to provide commercial solutions to customers worldwide and reduce costs of government. It works with more than 14,000 commercial firms to produce more than 7.5 million products and services, covering a variety of items, from hardware to scientific and information technology.

The office is composed of the following centers:

- Information Technology Center

- Services Acquisition Center

- National Furniture Center

- Office Supplies and Administrative Services

- Center for Facilities Maintenance and Hardware

- General Products

- Management Services Center

- Enterprise GWAC Center

- IT GWAC Center

- Small Business GWAC Center

Appendix **3**

Web Sites

Following is a consolidated listing of the web sites that have merit from our perspective, but is not intended to be a comprehensive list. Remember that the Internet is a dynamic environment and changing constantly. We have made every effort to assure that these sites are "live," but also know that they change quite frequently.

To help you understand the variety of locations using the Internet, the following information is provided for the last part of the URL address:

.biz = a business	.info = information provider
.com = commercial entity	.mil = military entity
.edu = educational entity	.net = network entity
.gov = government entity	.org = an organization

If you get to a site that does not respond, try backing up the address by eliminating the part of the address after the last "/". Keep doing this until you get a hit. Then look around that location for a way back to the area in which you are interested.

These first URLs we mention are those that we feel are important sites to be aware of for federal acquisition purposes. We have included some comments in regards to the sites to help you their purpose.

PRODUCT/SERVICE CODING

FSC: http://fpdcapp.gsa.gov/pls/fpdsweb/PscWiz

The Federal Supply Code (FSC) is the first four digits of the National Stock Number (NSN) that is used to identify categories of supplies and equipment. Important for inventorying items in federal supply system.

NAICS: http://www.census.gov/epcd/www/naics.html

The SBA used the NAICS code to classify a business as a small business. When included in a company profile, it helps the government determine whether there are a sufficient number of small businesses available to set the requirement aside for small business bidding only.

VENDOR CODING

CAGE Code: http://www.dlis.dla.mil/cageserv.asp

The government automatically assigns the CAGE Code when a company registers in CCR. The CAGE Code is a five-position code that identifies contractors doing business with the federal government, NATO member nations, and other foreign governments. The CAGE Code is used to support a variety of mechanized systems throughout the government and provides for a standardized method of identifying a given facility at a specific location. The code may be used for a variety of purposes: facility clearance, a pre-award survey, automated bidders lists, identification of debarred bidders, fast pay processes, etc.

The Defense Logistics Information Service (DLIS) has sole responsibility for assigning and maintaining the CAGE Code Master File.

DUNS Number:
https://eupdate.dnb.com/requestoptions/government/ccrreg/

The Digital Uniform Numbering System (DUNS) Number is a distinctive nine-digit identification sequence, that links you to a wealth of quality information products and services originating exclusively from Dun & Bradstreet. The D-U-N-S Number, free for the asking, is an internationally recognized common company identifier in EDI and global electronic commerce transactions.

DATABASES LISTING OPPORTUNITIES

DoD database of award information:
http://web1.whs.osd.mil/peidhome/peidhome.htm

Links to DoD activities: http://www.defenselink.mil/

FedBizOpps: http://www.eps.gov/

This is the official federal site to post business opportunities $25,000 or more.

CREDIT CARD INFORMATION

List of credit card holders for the Army:
http://purchasecard.saalt.army.mil/news.htm

IMPORTANT VENDOR DATABASES

Dynamic small business search: http://www.ccr.gov

This site is a search-only site used by the government buyers and prime contractors to identify small businesses for contracting opportunities. It is a great passive marketing tool for a small business. All registration for federal contract work is through CCR.

CCR: http://www.ccr.com/

This is the major registration site for the federal government. Truly a one-stop registration point, registering here will ensure that federal contract documents will have proper vendor information.

ORCA: http://orca.bpn.gov/

ORCA (Online Representations and Certifications Application) is an e-Government initiative designed by the Integrated Acquisition Environment (IAE) to replace the paper-based Representations and Certifications (Reps and Certs) process. This will allow a firm to provide this information on an annual basis instead of for each offer submitted.

ELECTRONIC COMMERCE HELP

Electronic Commerce: http://www.acq.osd.mil/ec/

THE BEST HELP

PTAC: http://www.dla.mil/db

This is the resource everyone should check out.

Small Business Specialists:
http://www.acq.osd.mil/sadbu/publications/sbs/sbs.html

A great resource. This is your "inside" person.

SBA Resources

SBA: http://www.sba.gov/

SBDC: http://www.sba.gov/sbdc/

SCORE: http://www.score.org/

Regional SBA: http://www.sba.gov/regions/states.html

SBA's Women Business Offices:
http://www.sba.gov/womeninbusiness

SBA's Online Women's Business Center:
http://www.onlinewbc.org/

Subcontracting Opportunities

Subcontracting Opportunities: http://web.sba.gov/subnet

DoD Primes:
http://www.acq.osd.mil/sadbu/publications/subdir/index.html

This directory lists over 3,700 large businesses with DoD contracts. It includes contact information.

GSA Stuff

GSA: http://www.gsa.gov/

GSA FSS: http://www.fss.gsa.gov/

Special Small Business Programs

SBIR (DoD):
http://www.acq.osd.mil/sadbu/sbir/homepg.htm#sbirsttr

If you do research, this is the site for you.

SBIR (Fed'l): http://www.sba.gov/expanding/sbir.html

Ditto for this site as well.

Mentor-Protégé (DoD):
http://www.acq.osd.mil/sadbu/mentor_protege/

Would you like to work with a large prime contractor and enhance your business capabilities? Here is a site to start the process.

Mentor-Protégé (Fed'l):
http://www.sba.gov/8abd/indexmentorprogram.html

Would you like to work with a large prime contractor and enhance your business capabilities? Well here is a site to start the process.

REGULATIONS

FAR: http://www.safaq.hq.af.mil/contracting/toolkit/
You have to know the rules, and here is the place to do that.

DFARS: http://farsite.hill.af.mil/Vfdfar.htm
Friendly sites to look up the regulations.

MORE SITES TO KNOW ABOUT

NAICS Code revisions for 2002: http://www.bls.gov/bls/naics.htm

Great search capability for government web sites:
http://www.firstgov.gov

Good links to related sites: http://www.wingovcon.com

GENERAL LIST OF SITES

The following list of sites provides a broad spectrum of resources that may help you in doing government contracting. We have attempted to break them out into a number of categories to help in your search. Remember that sites change, and if you find that a URL is no longer valid, use the backing up methods discussed at the beginning of this appendix.

Web Site	URL
Commercial and Other Non-Government Sites	
American Bar Association.	http://www.abanet.org
Business Owner's Toolkit	http://www.toolkit.cch.com/
The Federal Marketplace	http://www.fedmarket.com
Govcon	http://www.govcon.com
ISBC	http://www.isbc.com
NCMA	http://www.ncmahq.org
APTAC	http://aptac-us.org
SBIR-National Conference Center	http://www.zyn.com/sbir/
Wingovcon	http://www.wingovcon.com
Government Sites	
abm online	http://www.abm.rda.hq.navy.mil
ARNet	http://www.arnet.gov

Defense Finance and Accounting Service   http://www.dfas.mil
Department of the Treasury--Electronic Funds Transfer Notice of Proposed
Rulemaking   http://www.fms.treas.gov/eft/
Department of the Treasury Financial Management Service
                                   http://www.fms.treas.gov
DITCO headquarters   http://www.ditco.disa.mil
DOD's Small and Disadvantaged Business Utilization Office
                                   http://www.acq.osd.mil/sadbu
Electronic Commerce Office   http://www.acq.osd.mil/ec
FAA Acquisition Toolset   http://fast.faa.gov
Federal Procurement Data System   http://www.fpdc.gov
GPO   http://www.access.gpo.gov
SBA Gopher
                    http://www.sbaonline.sba.gov/gopher/Ecedi/Facts
SSA's Office of Acquisition and Grants' Acquisition Information Page
                                   http://www.ssa.gov/oag/
UNICOR Catalog   http://www.unicor.gov
White House home page   http://www.whitehouse.gov

NASA Procurement Addresses
NAIS   http://procurement.nasa.gov
NASA   http://www.nasa.gov
NASA Electronic Handbooks   http://lincoln.gsfc.nasa.gov/ehbs.html
Ames Research Center
                    http://server-mpo.arc.nasa.gov/Services/Proc/home.html
Dryden Flight Research Center   http://www.dfrc.nasa.gov/Procure
Goddard Space Flight Center   http://genesis.gsfc.nasa.gov/procure.htm
Kennedy Space Center   http://www.ksc.nasa.gov/procurement/
Lewis Research Center
                    http://www.lerc.nasa.gov/Other_Groups/Procure/home.htm
NASA Commercial Technology Network http://nctn.hq.nasa.gov/
NASA Headquarters   http://www.hq.nasa.gov/

Contract Activities
Acquisition Reform--Air Force   http://www.safaq.hq.af.mil/acq_ref/
Acquisition Reform Net of NPR   http://www.arnet.gov/
Acquisition Systems Management   http://www.acq.osd.mil/
Air Force Acquisition Home Page   http://www.safaq.hq.af.mil/
                                   http://www.safaq.hq.af.mil/contracting/
Army, AMC, TACOM-ARDEC Acquisition Ctr.   http://procnet.pica.army.mil/
Bureau of Engraving & Printing Office of Procurement
                                   http://www.ustreas.gov/
Bureau of Land Management   http://www.blm.gov/nhp/info/index.htm
U.S. Department of Transportation http://www.dot.gov/
Defense Advanced Research Projects http://www.arpa.mil/cmo/
Defense Logistics Agency   http://www.dla.mil/
Defense Procurement Homepage   http://www.acq.osd.mil/dpap/
Defense Supply Center Columbus   http://www.dscc.dla.mil/
Defense Supply Center Richmond   http://www.dscr.dla.mil/
Defense Supply Center Philadelphia http://www.dscp.dla.mil/

Department of Agriculture
Rural Bus.-Coop. Service   http://www.rurdev.usda.gov/
Procurement   http://www.usda.gov/procurement
Farm Service Agency   http://www.fsa.usda.gov/amb/
Department of Energy   http://www.doe.gov/engine/content.do

Department of Health & Human Serv.-Grants
http://www.os.dhhs.gov
Department of Housing and Urban Development
http://www.hud.gov/offices/cpo/index.cfm
Department of Interior   http://www.doi.gov
Department of Justice   http://www.usdoj.gov/07business/index.html
Department of Treasury   http://www.ustreas.gov/
Department of Veterans Affairs   http://www.va.gov/OSDBU/
Dept. of Defense Acquisition Reform   http://www.acq.osd.mil/ar/
Dept. of Defense Acquisition Web (AC QWEB)   http://www.acq.osd.mil
Dept. of Defense Ballistic Missile Defense Organization Acquisition
http://www.acq.osd.mil/mda/mdalink/html/mdalink.html
Federal Prison Industry--Unicor   http://www.unicor.gov/
Government Printing Office
http://www.access.gpo.gov/#business
Government Printing Office-Procurement Information on the Internet
http://www.access.gpo.gov/procurement/info-net.html
Information on the Internet
http://www.access.gpo.gov/procurement/info-net.html
Illinois Department of Commerce and Community Affairs
http://www.commerce.state.il.us/
Interior Department Electronic Acquisition Sys.
http://www.nbc.gov/g2b.html
NASA Acquisition Internet Service   http://procurement.nasa.gov
National Coordination Office for High Performance Computing and Communications
http://www.hpcc.gov/
National Imagery and Mapping Agency   http://164.214.2.59/
National Institute of Standards and Technology
http://www.nist.gov/admin/od/contract/contract.htm
National Oceanic and Atmospheric Admin.--Western Administrative Support Center
http://www.wasc.noaa.gov/wasc/proc.htm
National Science Foundation   http://www.nsf.gov/about/contracting/
Navy Acquisition & Business Management   http://www.abm.rda.hq.navy.mil/
Navy Acquisition Reform Office
http://www.abm.rda.hq.navy.mil/navyaos/content/view/full/131
Office of Federal Procurement Policy   http://www.arnet.gov/
Office of the Under Secretary of Defense for Acquisition and Technology
http://www.acq.osd.mil/
Securities and Exchange Commission   http://www.sec.gov/
Small Business Administration   http://www.sbaonline.sba.gov
Social Security Administration   http://www.ssa.gov/oag/
State of California Contracts Register   http://www.dgs.ca.gov
State, Provincial & Pacific Rim Purchasing/Contracting Offices
http://www.primaryaccess.com/
Tri-Service Contract Solicitation Network   http://tsn.wes.army.mil/
Govt. Printing Office Procurement Services
http://www.access.gpo.gov/procurement/index.html
Patent and Trademark Office Acquisitions
http://www.uspto.gov/web/offices/ac/comp/proc/acquisitions/
U.S. Postal Service   http://www.usps.gov/business/
United States Geological Survey   http://www.usgs.gov/contracts/index.html

Business and Economic Development Programs
Bureau of Land Mgt.   http://www.blm.gov
California Trade and Commerce Agency
http://commerce.ca.gov/state/ttca/ttca_homepage.jsp

Center for Innovation   http://www.und.nodak.edu/dept/purchase/index.html
Defense Technical Information Center-Small Business Program
                              http://www.dtic.mil/dtic/sbir/
Dept. of Energy-Small Business Information
                              http://www.pr.doe.gov/small.html
EntreWorld-Entrepreneurial Leadership http://www.entreworld.org/
Mentor-Protege Program-NASA   http://www.hq.nasa.gov/
Minority Business Development Agency http://www.doc.gov/
Office of Small and Disadvantaged Business Utilization:
         -Air Force   http://www.sellingtoairforce.org
         -Bureau of Land Management http://www.doi.gov/diversity/
         -Department of Agriculture   http://www.usda.gov/
         -Department of Commerce   http://www.osec.doc.gov/osdbu/
         -Department of Justice   http://www.usdoj.gov/jmd/osdbu
         -DOD   http://www.acq.osd.mil/sadbu
         -Government Printing Office http://www.access.gpo.gov/
         -Housing and Urban Development   http://www.hud.gov/
         -NASA   http://www.hq.nasa.gov/office/codek
         -with their 'Women-Owned Business Representatives (WOBREP)
                              http://www.osec.doc.gov/
Procurement Points of Contact GPO
               http://www.access.gpo.gov/procurement/pp002.html
Securities and Exchange Commission: Small Business Information
                              http://www.sec.gov/
Small Business Advancement National Center
                              http://www.sbaer.uca.edu/
Small Business Development Centers   http://www.sbaonline.sba.gov/SBDC/
Small Business Innovative Research:
         -Defense Technical Information Center
                              http://www.dtic.mil/dtic/sbir/
         - NASA   http://nctn.oact.hq.nasa.gov/
Small Business Office Directors- U. S. Govt.
                          http://www.usda.gov/da/smallbus/sbdirect.htm
Small Business Personnel:
         -Dept. of Agriculture http://www.usda.gov/da/smallbus/sbcoord.htm
         -DOD   http://www.acq.osd.mil/
         -HUD   http://www.hud.gov/
         -NASA   http://www.hq.nasa.gov/office/codek/
         -National Institute of Standards and Technology
                              http://www.nist.gov/
Small Business Regulatory Compliance Assistance
                              http://www.dol.gov/

Women-Owned Business Resources
Am. Society of Women Entrepreneurs (ASWE)
                              http://www.membership.com/
BizWomen   http://www.bizwomen.com/
Business Owner's Toolkit   http://www.toolkit.cch.com/
Entrepreneurs and Small Business Information   http://www.lowe.org/
EntreWorld-Entrepreneurial Leadership http://www.entreworld.org/
Guide for Minority, Women Owned, and Small Businesses—HUD
                              http://www.hud.gov/
Home Office Association of America (HOAA)   http://www.hoaa.com/
Inc Online   http://www.inc.com/
Minority Business Entrepreneur (MBE) Magazine http://www.mbemag.com/
National Association for Female Executives   http://www.nafe.com/

National Foundation for Women Business Owners http://www.nfwbo.org/
SCORE-Free Business Counseling   http://www.scn.org/
Women In Technology International   http://www.witi.com/
Women Organization Directory   http://www.feminist.org
Women's Business Exclusive (MrgE)   http://www.mbemag.com

How to Do Business Resources

Contracting Opportunities with GSA   http://www.gsa.gov/Portal/home.jsp
Bureau of Land Mgt.   http://www.blm.gov/natacq/BUDS/proc6.html
Dept. of Energy   http://www.pr.doe.gov/
Dept. of Justice   http://www.usdoj.gov/jmd/pss/doin_bus.htm
Dept. of Veterans Affairs   http://www.va.gov/oa&mm/busopp/dbwva1.htm
Environ. Protection Agency   http://www.epa.gov/oam/
Federal Government   http://www.business.gov/busadv/maincat.cfm?catid=24
Navy   http://www.abm.rda.hq.navy.mil/doing.html
Small Business Admin.   http://www.sba.gov/SBDC/13cfr130.html
Govt. Printing Office http://www.access.gpo.gov/procurement/pub1050.pdf
U. S. Postal Service   http://www.usps.gov/business/ldb.htm
Dept. of Interior   http://www.doi.gov/osdbu/

Acquisition Forecast for Business Opportunities

Navy   http://www.ntsc.navy.mil
Social Security Admin.   http://www.ssa.gov/
Government Printing Office
    http://www.access.gpo.gov/procurement/nb001.html
Air Force   http://www.safaq.hq.af.mil/
Defense Advanced Research Projects Agency
    http://www.arpa.mil/baa/
Dept. of Agriculture   http://www.usda.gov/wps/portal/usdahome
Farm Service Agency   http://www.fsa.usda.gov/amb/solic.htm
Dept. of Justice   http://www.usdoj.gov/07business/07_5.html
Dept. of Veterans Affairs   http://www.va.gov/oa&mm/busopp/index.htm
EPA   http://www.epa.gov/oam/
Federal Communications Commission   http://www.fcc.gov/ocbo/
General Services Admin.   http://www.gsa.gov/
Govt. Printing Office
    http://www.access.gop.gov/bidopps/central/index.shtml
HUD   http://www.hud.gov/cts/
National Institute of Standards and Technology
    http://www.nist.gov/admin/od/contract/business.htm
Navy Solicitations   http://www.abm.rda.hq.navy.mil/
U. S. Postal Service   http://www.usps.gov/business/
Subcontracting Opportunities with DOD
    http://www.acq.osd.mil/sadbu/publications/

Financial/Venture Capital Resources

America's Business Funding Directory   http://www.businessfinance.com/
Ben Franklin Technology Center   http://www.benfranklin.org/
Business Owner's Toolkit   http://www.toolkit.cch.com/
Center for Innovation
    http://www.und.nodak.edu/dept/cibd/default.htm
Creative Investment Research   http://www2.ari.net/cirm/
Defense Loan and Technical Assistance Program
    http://www.sbaonline.sba.gov/business_finances/delta/
Kansas Technology Enterprise Corporation (KTEC)
    http://www.ktec.com/

MoneyHunter   http://www.moneyhunter.com/
SBA Financing Your Business   http://www.sba.gov/financing/
SBA's Export Working Capital Program Loans
            http://www.sbaonline.sba.gov/business_finances/export/
SBA's International Loan Program
            http://www.sbaonline.sba.gov/business_finances/inter/
SBA's Minority and Women's Prequalification Pilot Loan Program
            http://www.sbaonline.sba.gov/business_finances/prequal/
SBA's Qualified Employee Trusts Loans
            http://www.sbaonline.sba.gov/business_finances/qet/
SBA's Surety Bond Program   http://www.sba.gov/financing/
SBA's Veterans Loan Program
            http://www.sbaonline.sba.gov/business_finances/vets/
SBA's 7(a) Loan Guaranty Program — Certified and Preferred
            http://www.sba.gov/financing/sbaloan/snapshot.html
SBA's Certified Development Company (504 Loan) Program
            http://www.sba.gov/financing/indexloans.html
SBA's Secondary Market Program
            http://www.sba.gov/financing/indexloans.html
Shareware Programs for Financing a Business
            http://www.sbaonline.sba.gov/shareware/finfile.html
Small Business Investment Companies
            http://www.sbaonline.sba.gov/INV/

General Contracting Resources
Bid Protest--GAG Decisions
            http://www.gao.gov/decisions/bidpro/bidpro.htm
Bureau of Economic Analysis   http://www.bea.doc.gov/
Bureau of Export Administration   http://www.bxa.doc.gov/
Commercial Advocates Forum   http://www.acq.osd.mil/dpap
Comptroller General Decisions   http://www.gao.gov/decisions/decision.htm
Congressional Legislation/Bills   http://thomas.loc.gov/
Congressional Record   http://thomas.loc.gov/
Davis-Bacon Wage Determination Database   http://davisbacon.ntis.gov
Debarred List of Parties Excluded from Federal Procurement and
Nonprocurement Programs   http://www.arnet.gov/epls/
Defense Acquisition University   http://www.acq.osd.mil/dau/
Defense Technical Information Center   http://www.dtic.mil/dtic/
Dept. of Defense Electronic Commerce Office   http://www.acq.osd.mil/ec/
Dept. of Treasury E-mail Notification   http://www.fms.treas.gov/
Economic Development Administration   http://www.doc.gov/eda/
Federal Community   http://www.firstgov.gov
Federal Depository Libraries by State/Area Code
            http://www.gpoaccess.gov/libraries.html
Federal Depository Library Gateway
            http://www.access.gpo.gov/su_docs/aces/aaces004.html
Federal Discount Lodging Directory   http://www.usgov.digital.com/
Federal Information Center   http://fic.info.gov/
Federal Procurement Data System (FPDS) Contract Data Information
            http://www.fpdc.gov
Federal Supply Schedule
      http://www.gsa.gov/Portal/content/orgs_content.jsp?contentOID=
                              22892&contentType=1005
FedWorld Information Network (NTIS) http://www.fedworld.gov
General Accounting Office Decisions   http://www.gao.gov/
            http://www.access.gpo.gov/su_docs/multidb.html

General Accounting Office Decisions (Searchable)
          http://www.access.gpo.gov/su_docs/aces/aces170.shtml
Government Information Xchange   http://www.info.gov/
Government Printing Office (GPO) Access   http://www.access.gpo.gov/
Government Printing Office Access
          http://www.access.gpo.gov/su_docs/multidb.html
Legislative Information on the Internet   http://thomas.loc.gov
National Technology Transfer Center (NTTC)   http://www.nttc.edu/
NAICS   http://www.census.gov/epcd/naics02/
NASA Procurement Synopsis Search   http://procurement.nasa.gov/
NASA Technology Transfer Center   http://www.nttc.edu/
Standard Industrial Class. Codes Construction   http://www.opsafesite.com/
Standard Industrial Classifications Codes
          http://www.sba.gov/regulations/siccodes
Standard Industrial Classifications Codes Search
          http://www.osha.gov/oshstats/sicser.html
U. S. Govt. Information Sources (Virtual Library)
          http://www.nttc.edu/resources/government/govresources.asp
U. S. Business Advisor Home Page   http://www.business.gov
U. S. Federal Court Opinions/Decisions
          http://www.ll.georgetown.edu/Fed-Ct/index.bk
U. S. Patent and Trademark Office   http://www.uspto.gov/
U. S. Statistics Database   http://www.stat-usa.gov/
U. S. Trade Representative   http://www.ustr.gov/index.html

Laws, Regulations, and Other Related Procurement Documents
Air Force FAR Supplement   http://www.hq.af.mil/
Bid Protest: GAO Administrative Practice & Procedure, Regulations, and Govt. Contracts
          http://www.gao.gov/decisions/bidpro/new.reg/regulation.htm
Code of Federal Regulations   http://www.gpoaccess.gov/cfr/index.html
          http://www.gpoaccess.gov/multidb.html
          http://www.law.cornell.edu/regs.html
Congressional Legislation/Bills   http://thomas.loc.gov/
Defense Acquisition Circulars   http://www.acq.osd.mil/dp/dacs/
Defense FAR Supplement   http://www.acq.osd.mil/dp/dars/dfars.html
Dept. of Ag. Procure. Regulations & Notices
          http://www.usda.gov/procurement
Dept. of Ag. Procurement Regulatory Info.
          http://www.usda.gov/da/procure/procreg.htmment
Dept. of Defense Contracting Regulations
          http://www.acq.ods.mil/dp/dars
Dept. of Energy Acquisition Regulations   http://www.doe.gov
Dept. of Energy Procurement and Property Regs.
          http://www.energy.gov
DOD and Navy Instructions, Manuals, Standards, Flowcharts and Guidebooks
          http://www.spawar.navy.mil/
DOD Contracting Regulations   http://www.acq.osd.mil.dp/dars
DOD Directives and Instructions   http://www.dtic.mil/whs/directives
DOD FAR Supplement   http://www.dtic.mil/dfars/
DOD Single Stock Point for Specs. & Standards   http://www.dodssp.daps.mil/
          http://forms.deps.dla.mil
          http://neds.deds.dla.mil
Federal Acquisition Regulations   http://www.arnet.gov/far/
Federal Acquisition Regulations and NASA FAR Supplement (Searchable)
          http://procurement.nasa.gov/FAR/

Fed'l Information Resources Management Reg.
              http://www.itpolicy.gsa.gov/firmr/firmrtoc.htm
FedWorld Information Network (NTIS) http://www.fedworld.gov
Freedom of Information Act (FOIA): A Citizen's Guide on Using the FOIA and the Privacy Act of 1974 to Request Government Records
              http://foia.larc.nasa.gov/
FOIA: NASA Information
              http://www.hq.nasa.gov/office/pao/FOIA/general.html
GSA Procurement Regulations   http://www.gsa.gov
Information Technology Issues   http://www.itpolicy.gsa.gov/
Labor Laws and Executive Orders
              http://www.dol.gov/cgi-bin/consolid.pl?regs+statutes
Legislative Information on the Internet http://thomas.loc.gov/
NASA Center's Unique Clauses
              http://www.ksc.nasa.gov/procurement/uniq_cls.htm
National Industrial Security Program Operating Manual (NISPOM)
              http://www.tscm.com/Nispom.html
National Institute of Standards and Technology   http://www.nist.gov/
OMB Circulars (Searchable)   http://www.ucop.edu/cgi-bin/cgcircular.pl
Uniform Commercial Code   http://www.law.cornell.edu/
United States Code   http://www.law.cornell.edu/
US Postal Service Procurement Manual http://www.usps.gov/
World Wide Web Home Page Guidelines and Best Practices
              http://www.dtic.mil/staff/cthomps/guidelines/
Zip Codes   http://www.usps.gov/ncsc/lookups/lookup_zip+4.html

Employment and Labor Resources
Dept. of Labor--Employment & Training Admin. http://www.doleta.gov/
Dept. of Labor--Women Bureau   http://www.dol.gov/
Dept. of Labor Posters   http://www.dol.gov/
Labor Laws and Executive Orders
              http://www.dol.gov/cgi-bin/consolid.pl?regs+statutes
Labor Laws and Regulations [DOL]   http://www.doleta.gov/
Occupational Safety and Health Admin. (OSHA)
              http://www.osha.gov/index.html
Office of Federal Contract Compliance Programs
              http://www.dol.gov/
Office of Labor-Management Standards (OLMS)   http://www.dol.gov/
Small Business Regulatory Compliance Assistance
              http://www.dol.gov/
U. S. Census Bureau   http://www.census.gov/
U. S. Census Bureau Business Statistics http://www.census.gov/econ/www/
U. S. Department of Labor   http://www.dol.gov/
U. S. Dept. of Interior Vacancy Announcements   http://www.usgs.gov/
U. S. Office of Compliance   http://www.compliance.gov/index.html
U. S. Office of Government Ethics   http://www.access.gpo.gov/
U. S. Office of Special Counsel for Prohibited Personnel Practices
              http://www.osc.gov/osc/index.html
U.S. Equal Employment Opportunity Commission http://www.eeoc.gov/
U.S. Merit Systems Protection Board   http://www.access.gpo.gov/
Wage and Hour Division   http://www.dol.gov/

Professional Organizations and Publications
American Arbitration Association   http://www.adr.org/
Association of Proposal Mgt. Professionals   http://www.apmp.org/
Entrepreneurs and Small Business Information   http://www.lowe.org/

EntreWorld-Entrepreneurial Leadership   http://www.entreworld.org/
Front-Line Procurement Professional's Forum   http://www.arnet.gov/
Home Office Association of America (HOAA)   http://www.hoaa.com/
Inc Online   http://www.inc.com/
Job Web--Nat. Assoc. of Colleges & Employers   http://www.jobweb.org//
Minority Business Entrepreneur (MBE) Magazine   http://www.mbemag.com/
National Association for Female Executives   http://www.nafe.com/
National Association of Development Org.   http://www.nado.org/
National Association of Management and Technical Assistance Centers
    http://www.namtac.com/
National Association of Purchasing Management   http://www.napm.org
Project Management Institute   http://www.pmi.org/
National Contract Management Association (NCMA)
    http://www.ncmahq.org
National Council for Urban Economic Developmt.   http://iedconline.org/
National Foundation for Women Business Owners   http://www.nfwbo.org/
National Institute of Governmental Purchasing   http://www.nigp.org/
Northeast-Midwest Institute   http://www.nemw.org/
Society of Cost Estimating and Analysis   http://www.sceaonline.net/
Women In Technology International   http://www.witi.com/
Women's Business Exclusive (WBE)
    http://www.mbemag.com/html/WBEwelcome.html

Federal Acquisition Regulation Outline

The following is the Table of Contents of the FAR, the "Bible" for federal procurement. By reviewing it, you can see that the regulations contained in the FAR are organized and presented in a way that will help you quickly locate the specific section you need to get the answer to your question.

Federal Acquisition Regulation
Table of Contents

Part 10 — Market Research

Part 11 — Describing Agency Needs

Part 12 — Acquisition of Commercial Items

FAR   Parts 13 - 18   Contracting Methods, Contract Types

Subchapter C   Contracting Methods and Contract Types

Part 13 — Simplified Acquisition Procedures

Part 14 — Sealed Bidding

Part 15 — Contracting by Negotiation

Part 16 — Types of Contracts

Part 17 — Special Contracting Methods

Part 18 — (Reserved)

FAR   Parts 19 - 26   Socioeconomic Programs

Subchapter D   Socioeconomic Programs

Part 19 — Small Business Programs

Part 20 — (Reserved)

Part 21 — (Reserved)

Part 22 — Application of Labor Laws to Government Acquisitions

Part 23 — Environment, Conservation, Occupational Safety, and Drug-Free Workplace

Part 24 — Protection of Privacy and Freedom of Information

Part 25 — Foreign Acquisition

Part 26 — Other Socioeconomic Programs

FAR   Parts 27 - 41   General Requirements, Special Categories

Subchapter E   General Contracting Requirements

Part 27 — Patents, Data, and Copyrights

Part 28 — Bonds and Insurance

Part 29 — Taxes

Part 30 — Cost Accounting Standards

Part 31 — Contract Price Principles and Procedures

Part 32 — Contract Financing

Part 33 — Protests, Disputes, and Appeals

Subchapter F   Special Categories Of Contracting

Part 34 — Major System Acquisition

Part 35 — Research and Development Contracting

Part 36 — Construction and Architect-Engineering Contracts

Part 37 — Service Contracting

Part 38 — Federal Supply Schedule Contracting

Part 39 — Acquisition of Information Resources

Part 40 — (Reserved)

Part 41 — Acquisition of Utility Services

FAR   Parts 42 - 51   Contract Management

Subchapter G   Contract Management

Part 42 — Contract Administration

Part 43 — Contract Modifications

Part 44 — Subcontracting Policies and Procedures

Part 45 — Government Property

Part 46 — Quality Assurance

Part 47 — Transportation

Part 48 — Value Engineering

Part 49 — Termination of Contracts

Part 50 — Extraordinary Contractual Actions

Part 51 — Use of Government Sources by Contractors

Appendices

Common Contracting Forms

Following are the forms most commonly used in the federal procurement process.

Standard Form 18

REQUEST FOR QUOTATION *(THIS IS NOT AN ORDER)*		THIS RFQ ☐ IS ☐ IS NOT A SMALL BUSINESS SET-ASIDE			PAGE OF PAGES
1. REQUEST NO.	2. DATE ISSUED	3. REQUISITION/PURCHASE REQUEST NO.	4. CERT. FOR NAT. DEF. UNDER BDSA REG. 2 AND/OR DMS REG. 1	RATING	

5a. ISSUED BY

6. DELIVER BY *(Date)*

5b. FOR INFORMATION CALL *(NO COLLECT CALLS)*

7. DELIVERY

NAME

TELEPHONE NUMBER

☐ FOB DESTINATION ☐ OTHER *(See Schedule)*

AREA CODE | NUMBER

9. DESTINATION

a. NAME OF CONSIGNEE

8. TO:

a. NAME	b. COMPANY	b. STREET ADDRESS
c. STREET ADDRESS		c. CITY
d. CITY	e. STATE	f. ZIP CODE	d. STATE	e. ZIP CODE

10. PLEASE FURNISH QUOTATIONS TO THE ISSUING OFICE IN BLOCK 5a ON OR BEFORE CLOSE OF BUSINESS *(Date)*

IMPORTANT: This is a request for information, and quotations furnished are not officers. If you are unable to quote, please so indicate on this form and return it to the address in Block 5a. This request does not commit the Government to pay any costs incurred in the preparation of the submission of this quotation or to contract for supplies or service. Supplies are of domestic origin unless otherwise indicated by quoter. Any representations and/or certifications attached to this Request for Quotation must be completed by the quoter.

11. SCHEDULE *(Include applicable Federal, State and local taxes)*

ITEM NO. (a)	SUPPLIES/ SERVICES (b)	QUANTITY (c)	UNIT (d)	UNIT PRICE (e)	AMOUNT (f)

12. DISCOUNT FOR PROMPT PAYMENT	a. 10 CALENDAR DAYS (%)	b. 20 CALENDAR DAYS (%)	c. 30 CALENDAR DAYS (%)	d. CALENDAR DAYS NUMBER	PERCENTAGE

NOTE: Additional provisions and representations ☐ are ☐ are not attached.

13. NAME AND ADDRESS OF QUOTER	14. SIGNATURE OF PERSON AUTHORIZED TO SIGN QUOTATION	15. DATE OF QUOTATION
a. NAME OF QUOTER		
b. STREET ADDRESS	16. SIGNER	
	a. NAME *(Type or print)*	b. TELEPHONE AREA CODE
c. COUNTY		
d. CITY	e. STATE	f. ZIP CODE	c. TITLE *(Type or print)*	NUMBER

AUTHORIZED FOR LOCAL REPRODUCTION
Previous edition not usable

FormFlow/Delrina Inc.

STANDARD FORM 18 (REV. 6-95)
Prescribed by GSA-FAR (48 CFR) 53.215-1(a)

Standard Form 26

AWARD/CONTRACT	1. THIS CONTRACT IS A RATED ORDER UNDER DPAS (15 CFR 350)	RATING	PAGE	OF	PAGES

2. CONTRACT *(Proc. Inst. Ident.)* NO.	3. EFFECTIVE DATE	4. REQUISITION/PURCHASE REQUEST/PROJECT NO.

5. ISSUED BY	CODE		6. ADMINISTERED BY *(If other than Item 5)*	CODE	

7. NAME AND ADDRESS OF CONTRACTOR *(No., street, county, State and ZIP Code)*

8. DELIVERY

☐ FOB ORIGIN   ☐ OTHER *(See below)*

9. DISCOUNT FOR PROMPT PAYMENT

10. SUBMIT INVOICES   ITEM
*(4 copies unless other-
wise specified)* TO THE
ADDRESS SHOWN IN

CODE   FACILITY CODE

11. SHIP TO/MARK FOR	CODE		12. PAYMENT WILL BE MADE BY	CODE	

13. AUTHORITY FOR USING OTHER THAN FULL AND OPEN COMPETITION:

☐ 10 U.S.C. 2304(c) (   )   ☐ 41 U.S.C. 253(c) (   )

14. ACCOUNTING AND APPROPRIATION DATA

15A. ITEM NO.	15B. SUPPLIES/SERVICES	15C. QUANTITY	15D. UNIT	15E. UNIT PRICE	15F. AMOUNT

15G. TOTAL AMOUNT OF CONTRACT ► $

16. TABLE OF CONTENTS

(X)	SEC.	DESCRIPTION	PAGE(S)	(X)	SEC.	DESCRIPTION	PAGE(S)
		PART I - THE SCHEDULE				PART II - CONTRACT CLAUSES	
	A	SOLICITATION/CONTRACT FORM			I	CONTRACT CLAUSES	
	B	SUPPLIES OR SERVICES AND PRICES/COSTS				PART III - LIST OF DOCUMENTS, EXHIBITS AND OTHER ATTACH.	
	C	DESCRIPTION/SPECS./WORK STATEMENT			J	LIST OF ATTACHMENTS	
	D	PACKAGING AND MARKING				PART IV - REPRESENTATIONS AND INSTRUCTIONS	
	E	INSPECTION AND ACCEPTANCE			K	REPRESENTATIONS, CERTIFICATIONS AND OTHER STATEMENTS OF OFFERORS	
	F	DELIVERIES OR PERFORMANCE					
	G	CONTRACT ADMINISTRATION DATA			L	INSTRS., CONDS., AND NOTICES TO OFFERORS	
	H	SPECIAL CONTRACT REQUIREMENTS			M	EVALUATION FACTORS FOR AWARD	

CONTRACTING OFFICER WILL COMPLETE ITEM 17 OR 18 AS APPLICABLE

17. ☐ CONTRACTOR'S NEGOTIATED AGREEMENT *(Contractor is required to sign this document and return _____ copies to issuing office.)* Contractor agrees to furnish and deliver all items or perform all the services set forth or otherwise identified above and on any continuation sheets for the consideration stated herein. The rights and obligations of the parties to this contract shall be subject to and governed by the following documents: (a) this award/contract, (b) the solicitation, if any, and (c) such provisions, representations, certifications, and specifications, as are attached or incorporated by reference herein. *(Attachments are listedc herein.)*

18. ☐ AWARD *(Contractor is not required to sign this document.)* Your offer on Solicitation Number _____, including the additions or changes made by you which additions or changes are set forth in full above, is hereby accepted as to the items listed above and on any continuation sheets. this award consummates the contract which consists of the following documents: (a) the Government's solicitation and your offer, and (b) this award/contract. No further contractual document is necessary.

19A. NAME AND TITLE OF SIGNER *(Type or print)*		20A. NAME OF CONTRACTING OFFICER	
19B. NAME OF CONTRACTOR	19C. DATE SIGNED	20B. UNITED STATES OF AMERICA	20C. DATE SIGNED
BY _____ *(Signature of person authorized to sign)*		BY _____ *(Signature of Contracting Officer)*	

NSN 7540-01-152-8069
Previous edition is unusable

STANDARD FORM 26 (REV. 4-85)
Prescribed by GSA - FAR (48 CFR) 53.214(a)

Standard Form 30 (front)

AMENDMENT OF SOLICITATION/MODIFICATION OF CONTRACT			1. CONTRACT ID CODE	PAGE	OF	PAGES
2. AMENDMENT/MODIFICAITON NO.		3. EFFECTIVE DATE	4. REQUISITION/PURCHASE REQ. NO.	5. PROJECT NO. (If applicble)		
6. ISSUED BY	CODE		7. ADMINISTERED BY (If other than Item 6)	CODE		

8. NAME AND ADDRESS OF CONTRACTOR (No., street, county, State and ZIP Code)	(X)	9A. AMENDMENT OF SOLICITATION NO.
		9B. DATED (SEE ITEM 11)
		10A. MODIFICATION OF CONTRACT/ORDER NO.
		10B. DATED (SEE ITEM 11)
CODE	FACILITY CODE	

11. THIS ITEM ONLY APPLIES TO AMENDMENTS OF SOLICITATIONS

☐ The above numbered solicitation is amended as set forth in Item 14. The hour and date specified for receipt of Offers ☐ is extended, ☐ is not extended.

Offers must acknowledge receipt of this amendment prior to the hour and date specified in the solicitation or as amended, by one of the following methods:

(a)By completing items 8 and 15, and returning _____ copies of the amendment; (b) By acknowledging receipt of this amendment on each copy of the offer submitted; or (c) By separate letter or telegram which includes a reference to the solicitation and amendment numbers. FAILURE OF YOUR ACKNOWLEDGMENT TO BE RECEIVED AT THE PLACE DESIGNATED FOR THE RECEIPT OF OFFERS PRIOR TO THE HOUR AND DATE SPECIFIED MAY RESULT IN REJECTION OF YOUR OFFER. If by virtue of this amendment your desire to change an offer already submitted, such change may be made by telegram or letter, provided each telegram or letter makes reference to the solicitation and this amendment, and is received prior to the opening hour and date specified.

12. ACCOUNTING AND APPROPIRATION DATA (If required)

13. THIS ITEM ONLY APPLIES TO MODIFICATION OF CONTRACTS/ORDERS.
IT MODIFIES THE CONTRACT/ORDER NO. AS DESCRIBED IN ITEM 14.

CHECK ONE	A. THIS CHANGE ORDER IS ISSUED PURSUANT TO: (Specify authority) THE CHANGES SET FORTH IN ITEM 14 ARE MADE IN THE CONTRACT ORDER NO. IN ITEM 10A.
	B. THE ABOVE NUMBERED CONTRACT/ORDER IS MODIFIED TO REFLECT THE ADMINISTRATIVE CHANGES (such as changes in paying office, appropriation date, etc.) SET FORTH IN ITEM 14, PURSUANT TO THE AUTHORITY OF FAR 43.103(b).
	C. THIS SUPPLEMENTAL AGREEMENT IS ENTERED INTO PURSUANT TO AUTHORITY OF:
	D. OTHER (Specify type of modification and authority)

E. IMPORTANT: Contractor ☐ is not, ☐ is required to sign this document and return _____ copies to the issuing office.

14. DESCRIPTION OF AMENDMENT/MODIFICATION (Organized by UCF section headings, including solicitation/contract subject matter where feasible.)

Except as provided herein, all terms and conditions of the document referenced in Item 9A or 10A, as heretofore changed, remains unchanged and in full force and effect.

15A. NAME AND TITLE OF SIGNER (Type or print)		16A. NAME AND TITLE OF CONTRACTING OFFICER (Type or print)	
15B. CONTRACTOR/OFFEROR	15C. DATE SIGNED	16B. UNITED STATES OF AMERICA	16C. DATE SIGNED
(Signature of person authorized to sign)		(Signature of Contracting Officer)	

NSN 7540-01-152-8070
Previous edition unusable

STANDARD FORM 30 (REV. 10-83)
Prescribed by GSA FAR (48 CFR) 53.243

Standard Form 30 (back)

INSTRUCTIONS

Instructions for items other than those that are self-explanatory, are as follows:

(a) <u>Item 1 (Contract ID Code)</u>. Insert the contract type identification code that appears in the title block of the contract being modified.

(b) <u>Item 3 (Effective date)</u>.

    (1) For a solicitation amendment, change order, or administrative change, the effective date shall be the issue date of the amendment, change order, or administrative change.

    (2) For a supplemental agreement, the effective date shall be the date agreed to by the contracting parties.

    (3) For a modification issued as an initial or confirming notice of termination for the convenience of the Government, the effective date and the modification number of the confirming notice shall be the same as the effective date and modification number of the initial notice.

    (4) For a modification converting a termination for default to a termination for the convenience of the Government, the effective date shall be the same as the effective date of the termination for default.

    (5) For a modification confirming the contacting officer's determination of the amount due in settlement of a contract termination, the effective date shall be the same as the effective date of the initial decision.

(c) <u>Item 6 (Issued By)</u>. Insert the name and address of the issuing office. If applicable, insert the appropriate issuing office code in the code block.

(d) <u>Item 8 (Name and Address of Contractor)</u>. For modifications to a contract or order, enter the contractor's name, address, and code as shown in the original contract or order, unless changed by this or a previous modification.

(e) <u>Item 9, (Amendment of Solicitation No. - Dated), and 10, (Modification of Contract/Order No. - Dated)</u>. Check the appropriate box and in the corresponding blanks insert the number and date of the original solicitation, contract, or order.

(f) <u>Item 12 (Accounting and Appropriation Data)</u>. When appropriate, indicate the impact of the modification on each affected accounting classification by inserting one of the following entries.

    (1) Accounting classification
        Net increase $ _____

    (2) Accounting classification
        Net decrease $ _____

NOTE: If there are changes to multiple accounting classifications that cannot be placed in block 12, insert an asterisk and the words "See continuation sheet".

(g) <u>Item 13</u>. Check the appropriate box to indicate the type of modification. Insert in the corresponding blank the authority under which the modification is issued. Check whether or not contractor must sign this document. (See FAR 43.103.)

(h) <u>Item 14 (Description of Amendment/Modification)</u> .

    (1) Organize amendments or modifications under the appropriate Uniform Contract Format (UCF) section headings from the applicable solicitation or contract. The UCF table of contents, however, shall not be set forth in this document

    (2) Indicate the impact of the modification on the overall total contract price by inserting one of the following entries:

        (i) Total contract price increased by $ _____

        (ii) Total contract price decreased by $ _____

        (iii) Total contract price unchanged.

    (3) State reason for modification.

    (4) When removing, reinstating, or adding funds, identify the contract items and accounting classifications.

    (5) When the SF 30 is used to reflect a determination by the contracting officer of the amount due in settlement of a contract terminated for the convenience of the Government, the entry in Item 14 of the modification may be limited to --

        (i) A reference to the letter determination; and

        (ii) A statement of the net amount determined to be due in settlement of the contract.

    (6) Include subject matter or short title of solicitation/contract where feasible.

(i) <u>Item 16B</u>. The contracting officer's signature is not required on solicitation amendments. The contracting offier's signature is normally affixed last on supplemental agreements.

STANDARD FORM 30 (REV. 10-83) BACK

Standard Form 33

SOLICITATION, OFFER AND AWARD	1. THIS CONTRACT IS A RATED ORDER UNDER DPAS (15 CFR 700)	RATING	PAGE	OF	PAGES

2. CONTRACT NUMBER	3. SOLICITATION NUMBER	4. TYPE OF SOLICITATION	5. DATE ISSUED	6. REQUISITION/PURCHASE NUMBER
		☐ SEALED BID (IFB) ☐ NEGOTIATED (RFP)		

7. ISSUED BY	CODE	8. ADDRESS OFFER TO (If other than Item 7)

NOTE: In sealed bid solicitations "offer" and "offeror" mean "bid" and "bidder".

SOLICITATION

9. Sealed offers in original and _____ copies for furnishing the supplies or services in the Schedule will be received at the place specified in Item 8, or if handcarried, in the depository located in _____ until _____ local time _____

(Hour) (Date)

CAUTION - LATE Submissions, Modifications, and Withdrawals: See Section L, Provision No. 52.214-7 or 52.215-1. All offers are subject to all terms and conditions contained in this solicitation.

10. FOR INFORMATION CALL:	A. NAME	B. TELEPHONE (NO COLLECT CALLS)			C. E-MAIL ADDRESS
		AREA CODE	NUMBER	EXT.	

11. TABLE OF CONTENTS

(X)	SEC.	DESCRIPTION	PAGE(S)	(X)	SEC.	DESCRIPTION	PAGE(S)
		PART I - THE SCHEDULE				PART II - CONTRACT CLAUSES	
	A	SOLICITATION/CONTRACT FORM			I	CONTRACT CLAUSES	
	B	SUPPLIES OR SERVICES AND PRICES/COSTS				PART III - LIST OF DOCUMENTS, EXHIBITS AND OTHER ATTACH.	
	C	DESCRIPTION/SPECS./WORK STATEMENT			J	LIST OF ATTACHMENTS	
	D	PACKAGING AND MARKING				PART IV - REPRESENTATIONS AND INSTRUCTIONS	
	E	INSPECTION AND ACCEPTANCE			K	REPRESENTATIONS AND CERTIFICATIONS AND OTHER STATEMENTS OF OFFERORS	
	F	DELIVERIES OR PERFORMANCE					
	G	CONTRACT ADMINISTRATION DATA			L	INSTRS., CONDS., AND NOTICES TO OFFERORS	
	H	SPECIAL CONTRACT REQUIREMENTS			M	EVALUATION FACTORS FOR AWARD	

OFFER (Must be fully completed by offeror)

NOTE: Item 12 does not apply if the solicitation includes the provisions at 52.214-16, Minimum Bid Acceptance Period.

12. In compliance with the above, the undersigned agrees, if this offer is accepted within _____ calendar days (60 calendar days unless a different period is inserted by the offeror) from the date for receipt of offers specified above, to furnish any or all items upon which prices are offered at the price set opposite each item, delivered at the designated point(s), within the time specified in the schedule.

13. DISCOUNT FOR PROMPT PAYMENT (See Section I, Clause No. 52.232-8)	10 CALENDAR DAYS (%)	20 CALENDAR DAYS (%)	30 CALENDAR DAYS (%)	CALENDAR DAYS (%)

14. ACKNOWLEDGMENT OF AMEND-MENTS (The offeror acknowledges receipt of amendments to the SOLICITATION for offerors and related documents numbered and dated):	AMENDMENT NO.	DATE	AMENDMENT NO.	DATE

15A. NAME AND ADDRESS OF OFFER-OR	CODE	FACILITY	16. NAME AND TITLE OF PERSON AUTHORIZED TO SIGN OFFER (Type or print)

15B. TELEPHONE NUMBER			15C. CHECK IF REMITTANCE ADDRESS IS DIFFERENT FROM ABOVE - ENTER SUCH ADDRESS IN SCHEDULE.	17. SIGNATURE	18. OFFER DATE
AREA CODE	NUMBER	EXT.	☐		

AWARD (To be completed by Government)

19. ACCEPTED AS TO ITEMS NUMBERED	20. AMOUNT	21. ACCOUNTING AND APPROPRIATION

22. AUTHORITY FOR USING OTHER THAN FULL AND OPEN COMPETITION: ☐ 10 U.S.C. 2304(c) ( ) ☐ 41 U.S.C. 253(c) ( )	23. SUBMIT INVOICES TO ADDRESS SHOWN IN (4 copies unless otherwise specified)	ITEM

24. ADMINISTERED BY (If other than Item 7)	CODE	25. PAYMENT WILL BE MADE BY	CODE

26. NAME OF CONTRACTING OFFICER (Type or print)	27. UNITED STATES OF AMERICA (Signature of Contracting Officer)	28. AWARD DATE

IMPORTANT - Award will be made on this Form, or on Standard Form 26, or by other authorized official written notice.

AUTHORIZED FOR LOCAL REPRODUCTION
Previous edition is unusable

STANDARD FORM 33 (REV. 9-97)
Prescribed by GSA - FAR (48 CFR) 53.214(c)

Standard Form 129 (front)

SOLICITATION MAILING LIST APPLICATION

1. TYPE OF APPLICATION	2. DATE	OMB No.: 9000-0002
☐ INITIAL ☐ REVISION		Expires: 10/31/97

NOTE: Please complete all items on this form. Insert N/A in items not applicable. See reverse for instruction.

Public reporting burden for this collection of information is estimated to average .58 hours per response, including the time for reviewing instructions, searching existing data sources, gathering and maintaining the data needed, and completing and reviewing the collection of information. Send comments regarding this burden estimate or any other aspect of this collection of information, including suggestions for reducing this burden, to the FAR Secretariat (MVR), Federal Acquisition Policy Division, GSA, Washington, DC 20405.

3. SUBMIT TO

a. FEDERAL AGENCY'S NAME

b. STREET ADDRESS

c. CITY	d. STATE	e. ZIP CODE

4. APPLICANT

a. NAME

b. STREET ADDRESS	c. COUNTY

d. CITY	e. STATE	e. ZIP CODE

5. TYPE OF ORGANIZATION (Check one)

☐ INDIVIDUAL ☐ NON-PROFIT ORGANIZATION

☐ PARTNERSHIP ☐ CORPORATION, INCORPORATED UNDER THE LAWS OF THE STATE OF:

6. ADDRESS TO WHICH SOLICITATIONS ARE TO BE MAILED (If different than Item 4)

a. STREET ADDRESS	b. COUNTY

c. CITY	d. STATE	e. ZIP CODE

7. NAMES OF OFFICERS, OWNERS, OR PARTNERS

a. PRESIDENT	b. VICE PRESIDENT	c. SECRETARY

d. TREASURER	e. OWNERS OR PARTNERS

8. AFFILIATES OF APPLICANT

NAME	LOCATION	NATURE OF AFFILIATION

9. PERSONS AUTHORIZED TO SIGN OFFERS AND CONTRACTS IN YOUR NAME (Indicate if agent)

NAME	OFFICIAL CAPACITY	TELEPHONE NUMBER AREA CODE	NUMBER

10. IDENTIFY EQUIPMENT, SUPPLIES, AND/OR SERVICES ON WHICH YOU DESIRE TO MAKE AN OFFER (See attached Federal Agency's supplemental listing and instruction, if any)

11a. SIZE OF BUSINESS (See definitions on reverse)	11b. AVERAGE NUMBER OF EMPLOYEES (including affiliates) FOR FOUR PRECEDING CALENDAR QUARTERS	11c. AVERAGE ANNUAL SALES OR RECEIPTS FOR PRECEDING THREE FISCAL YEARS
☐ SMALL BUSINESS (If checked, complete Items 11B and 11Ci) ☐ OTHER THAN SMALL BUSINESS		$

12. TYPE OF OWNERSHIP (See definitions on reverse) (Not applicable for other than small businesses)	13. TYPE OF BUSINESS (See definitions on reverse)	
☐ DISADVANTAGED BUSINESS ☐ WOMAN-OWNED BUSINESS	☐ MANUFACTURER OR PRODUCER ☐ SERVICE ESTABLISHMENT	☐ CONSTRUCTION CONCERN ☐ RESEARCH AND DEVELOPMENT ☐ SURPLUS DEALER

14. DUNS NO. (If available)	15. HOW LONG IN PRESENT BUSINESS?

16. FLOOR SPACE (Square Feet/M²)

a. MANUFACTURING	b. WAREHOUSE

17. NET WORTH

a. DATE	b. AMOUNT $

18. SECURITY CLEARANCE (If applicable, check highest clearance authorized)

FOR	TOP SECRET	SECRET	CONFIDENTIAL	c. NAMES OF AGENCIES GRANTING SECURITY CLEARANCES	d. DATES GRANTED
a. KEY PERSONNEL					
b. PLANT ONLY					

The information supplied herein (including all pages attached) is correct and neither the applicant nor any person (or concern) in any connection with the applicant as a principal or officer, so far as is known, is now debarred or otherwise declared ineligible by any agency of the Federal Government from making offers for furnishing materials, supplies, or services to the Government or any agency thereof.

19a. NAME OF PERSON AUTHORIZED TO SIGN (Type or print)	20. SIGNATURE	21. DATE SIGNED
19b. TITLE OF PERSON AUTHORIZED TO SIGN (Type or print)		

AUTHORIZED FOR LOCAL REPRODUCTION
Previous edition not usable

STANDARD FORM 129 (REV. 12-96)
Prescribed by GSA - FAR (48 CFR) 53.214(e)

Standard Form 129 (back)

INSTRUCTIONS

Persons or concerns wishing to be added to a particular agency's bidder's mailing list for supplies or services shall file this properly completed Solicitation Mailing List Application, together with such other lists as may be attached to this application form, with each procurement office of the Federal agency with which they desire to do business. If a Federal agency has attached a Supplemental Commodity list with instructions, complete the application as instructed. Otherwise, identify in Item 10 the equipment, supplies, and/or services on which you desire to bid. (Provide Federal Supply Class or Standard Industrial Classification codes, if available.) The application shall be submitted and signed by the principal as distinguished from an agent, however constituted.

After placement on the bidder's mailing list of an agency, your failure to respond (submission of bid, or notice in writing, that you are unable to bid on that particular transaction but wish to remain on the active bidder's mailing list for that particular item) to solicitations will be understood by the agency to indicate lack of interest and concurrence in the removal of your name from the purchasing activity's solicitation mailing for items concerned.

SIZE OF BUSINESS DEFINITIONS
(See Item 11A.)

a. Small business concern - A small business concern for the purpose of Government procurement is a concern, including its affiliates, which is independently owned and operated, is not dominant in the field of operation in which it is competing for Government contracts, and can further qualify under the criteria concerning number of employees, average annual receipts, or the other criteria, as prescribed by the Small Business Administration. (See Code of Federal Regulations, Title 13, Part 121, as amended, which contains detailed industry definitions and related procedures.)

b. Affiliates - Business concerns are affiliates of each other when either directly or indirectly (i) one concern controls or has the power to control the other, or (ii) a third party controls or has the power to control both. In determining whether concerns are independently owned and operated and whether or not affiliation exists, consideration is given to all appropriate factors including common ownership, common management, and contractual relationship. (See Items 8 and 11A.)

c. Number of employees - (Item 11B) In connection with the determination of small business status, "number of employees" means the average employment of any concern, including the employees of its domestic and foreign affiliates, based on the number of persons employed on a full-time, part-time, temporary or other basis during each of the pay periods of the preceding 12 months. If a concern has not been in existence for 12 months, "number of employees" means the average employment of such concern and its affiliates during the period that such concern has been in existence based on the number of persons employed during each of the pay periods of the period that such concern has been in business.

TYPE OF OWNERSHIP DEFINITIONS
(See Item 12.)

a. "Disadvantaged business concern" - means any business concern (1) which is at least 51 percent owned by one or more socially and economically disadvantaged individuals; or, in the case of any publicly owned business, at least 51 percent of the stock of which is owned by one or more socially and economically disadvantaged individuals; and (2) whose management and daily business operations are controlled by one or more of such individuals.

b. "Women-owned business" - means a business that is at least 51 percent owned by a woman or women who are U.S. citizens and who also control and operate the business.

TYPE OF BUSINESS DEFINITIONS
(See Item 13.)

a. "Manufacturer or producer" - means a person (or concern) owning, operating, or maintaining a store, warehouse, or other establishment that produces, on the premises, the materials, supplies, articles or equipment of the general character of those listed in Item 10, or in the Federal Agency's Supplemental Commodity List, if attached.

b. "Service establishment" - means a concern (or person) which owns, operates, or maintains any type of business which is principally engaged in the furnishing of nonpersonal services, such as (but not limited to) repairing, cleaning, redecorating, or rental of personal property, including the furnishing of necessary repair parts or other supplies as a part of the services performed.

• COMMERCE BUSINESS DAILY - The Commerce Business Daily, published by the Department of Commerce, contains information concerning proposed procurements, sales, and contract awards, For further information concerning this publication, contact your local Commerce Field Office.

STANDARD FORM 129 (REV. 12-96) **BACK**

Standard Form 254 (page 1)

STANDARD FORM (SF)

254

Architect-Engineer and Related Services Questionnaire

Form Approved
OMB No. 9000-0004

Public reporting burden for this collection of information is estimated to average 1 hour per response, including the time for reviewing instructions, searching existing data sources, gathering and maintaining the data needed, and completing and reviewing the collection of information. Send comments regarding this burden estimate or any other aspect of this collection of information, including suggestions for reducing this burden, to the FAR Secretariat (VRS), Office of Federal Acquisition and Regulatory Policy, GSA, Washington, D.C. 20406; and to the Office of Management and Budget, Paperwork Reduction Project (9000-0004), Washington, D.C. 20503.

Purpose:
The policy of the Federal Government in acquiring architectural, engineering, and related professional services is to encourage firms lawfully engaged in the practice of those professions to submit annually a statement of qualifications and performance data. Standard Form 254, "Architect-Engineer and Related Services Questionnaire," is provided for that purpose. Interested A-E firms (including new, small, and/or minority firms) should complete and file SF 254's with each Federal agency and with appropriate regional or district offices for which the A-E is qualified to perform services. The agency head for each proposed project shall evaluate these qualification resumes, together with any other performance data on file or requested by the agency, in relation to the proposed project. The SF 254 may be used as a basis for selecting firms for discussions, or for screening firms preliminary to inviting submission of additional information.

Definitions:
"Architect-Engineer Services" are defined in Part 36 of the Federal Acquisition Regulation.
"Parent Company" is that firm, company, corporation, association or conglomerate which is the major stockholder or highest tier owner of the firm completing this questionnaire, i.e., Firm A is owned by Firm B which is, in turn, a subsidiary of Corporation C. The "parent company" of Firm A is Corporation C.
"Principals" are those individuals in a firm who possess legal responsibility for its management. They may be owners, partners, corporate offices, associates, administrators, etc.
"Discipline" as used in this questionnaire, refers to the primary technological capability of individuals in the responding firm. Possession of an academic degree, professional registration, certification, or extensive experience in a particular field of practice normally reflects an individual's primary technical discipline.
"Joint Venture" is a collaborative undertaking by two or more firms or individuals for which the participants are both jointly and individually responsible.
"Consultant," as used in this questionnaire, is a highly specialized individual or firm having significant input and responsibility for certain aspects of a project and possessing unusual or unique capabilities for assuring success of the finished work.
"Prime" refers to that firm which may be coordinating the concerted and complementary inputs of several firms, individuals or related services to produce a completed study or facility. The "prime" would normally be regarded as having full responsibility and liability for quality of performance by itself as well as by subcontractor professionals under its jurisdiction.

"Branch Office" is a satellite, or subsidiary extension, of a headquarters office of a company, regardless of any differences in name or legal structure of such a branch due to local or state laws. "Branch offices" are normally subject to the management decisions, bookkeeping, and policies of the main office.

Instructions of Filing (Numbers below correspond to numbers contained in form):

1. Type accurate and complete name of submitting firm, its address, and zip code.
   1a. Indicate whether form is being submitted in behalf of a parent firm or a branch office. (Branch office submissions should list only personnel in, and experience of, that office.)
2. Provide date the firm was established under the name shown in question 1.
3. Show date on which form is prepared. All information submitted shall be current and accurate as of this date.
4. Enter type of ownership, or legal structure, of firm (sole proprietor, partnership, corporation, joint venture, etc.).
   Check appropriate boxes indicating if firm is (a) a small business concern; (b) a small business concern owned and operated by socially and economically disadvantaged individuals; and (c) Woman-owned (See 48 CFR 19.101 and 52.219-9).
5. Branches of subsidiaries of large or parent companies, or conglomerates, should insert name and address of highest-tier owner.
   5a. If present firm is the successor to, or outgrowth of, one or more predecessor firms, show name(s) of former entity(ies) and the year(s) of their original establishment.
6. List not more than two principals from submitting firm who may be contacted by the agency receiving this form. (Different principals may be listed on forms going to another agency.) Listed principals must be empowered to speak for the firm on policy and contractual matters.
7. Beginning with the submitting office, list name, location, total number of personnel, and telephone numbers for all associated or branch offices. (including any headquarters or foreign offices) which provide A-E and related services.
   7a. Show total personnel in all offices. (Should be sum of all personnel, all branches.)
8. Show total number of employees, by discipline, in submitting office. (*If form is being submitted by main or headquarters office, form should list total employees, by discipline, in all offices.) While some personnel may be qualified in several disciplines, each person should be counted only once in accord with his or her primary function. Include clerical personnel as "administrative." Write in any additional disciplines -- sociologists, biologists, etc. -- and number of people in each, in blank spaces.

NSN 7540-01-152-8073

254-104

STANDARD FORM 254 (REV. 11-92)

Standard Form 254 (page 2)

STANDARD
FORM (SF)
254

Architect-Engineer
and Related Services
Questionnaire

9. Using chart (below) insert appropriate index number to indicate range of professional services fees received by submitting firm each calendar year for last five years, most recent year first. Fee summaries should be broken down to reflect the fees received each year for (a) work performed directly for the Federal Government (not including grant and loan projects) or as a sub to other professionals performing work directly for the Federal Government; (b) all other domestic work, U.S. and possessions, including Federally-assisted projects; and (c) all other foreign work.

Ranges of Professional Services Fees

INDEX		INDEX	
1.	Less than $100,000	5.	$1 million to $2 million
2.	$100,000 to $250,000	6.	$2 million to $5 million
3.	$250,000 to $500,000	7.	$5 million to $10 million
4.	$500,000 to $1 million	8.	$10 million or greater

10. Select and enter, in numerical sequence, **not more than thirty** (30) "Experience Profile Code" numbers from the listing (next page) which most accurately reflect submitting firm's demonstrated technical capabilities and project experience. **Carefully review list.** (It is recognized some profile codes may be part of other services or projects contained on list; firms are encouraged to select profile codes which best indicate type and scope of services provided on past projects.) For each code number, show total number of projects and gross fees (in thousands) received for profile projects performed by firm during past few years. If firm has on or more capabilities not included on list, insert same in blank spaces at end of list and show numbers in question 10 on the form. In such cases, the filled-in listing **must** accompany the complete SF 254 when submitted to the Federal agencies.

11. Using the "Experience Profile Code" numbers in the same sequence as entered in item 10, give details of at least one recent (within last five years) representative project for each code number, up to a **maximum** of thirty (30) separate projects, or portions of projects, for which firm was responsible. (Project examples may be used more than once to illustrate different services rendered on the same job. Example: a dining hall may be part of an auditorium or educational facility.) Firms which select less than thirty "profile codes" may list two or more project examples (to illustrate specialization) for each code number so long as total of all project examples does not exceed thirty (30). After each code number in question 11, show: (a) whether firm was "P," the prime professional, or "C," a consultant, or "JV," part of a joint venture on that particular project (new firms, in existence less than five (5) years may use the symbol "IE" to indicate "Individual Experience" as opposed to firm experience); (b) provide name and location of the specific project which typifies firm's (or individual's) performance under that code category; (c) give name and address of the owner

of that project (if government agency indicate responsible office); (d) show the estimated construction cost (or other applicable cost) for that portion of the project for which the firm was primarily responsible. (Where no construction was involved, show approximate cost of firm's work); and (e) state year when work on that particular project was, or will be, completed.

12. The completed SF 254 should be signed by a principal of the firm, preferably the chief executive officer.

13. Additional data, brochures, photos, etc. should not accompany this form unless specifically requested.

NEW FIRMS (not reorganized or recently-amalgamated firms) are eligible and encouraged to seek work from the Federal Government in connection with performance of projects for which they are qualified. Such firms are encouraged to complete and submit Standard Form 254 to appropriate agencies. Questions on the form dealing with personnel or experience may be answered by citing experience and capabilities of individuals in the firm, based on performance and responsibility while in the employee of others. In so doing, notation of this fact should be made on the form. In question 9, write in "N/A" to indicate "not applicable" for those years prior to firm's organization.

STANDARD FORM 254 PAGE 2 (REV. 11-92)

Standard Form 254 (page 3)

Experience Profile Code Numbers for use with questions 10 and 11

001 Acoustics, Noise Abatement
002 Aerial photogrammetry
003 Agricultural Development; Grain Storage; Farm Mechanization
004 Air Pollution Control
005 Airports; Navaids; Airport Lighting;
006 Airports; Terminals & Hangars; Freight Handling
007 Arctic Facilities
008 Auditoriums & Theatres
009 Automation; Controls; Instrumentation
010 Barracks; Dormitories
011 Bridges
012 Cemeteries (Planning & Relocation)
013 Chemical Processing & Storage
014 Churches; Chapels
015 Codes; Standards; Ordinances
016 Cold Storage; Refrigeration; Fast Freeze
017 Commercial Building (low rise); Shopping Centers
018 Communication Systems; TV; Microwave
019 Computer Facilities; Computer Service
020 Conservation and Resource Management
021 Construction Management
022 Corrosion Control; Cathodic Protection; Electrolysis
023 Cost Estimating
024 Dams (Concrete,Arch)
025 Dams (Earth; Rock); Dikes; Levees
026 Desalination (Process & Facilities)
027 Dining Halls; Clubs; Restaurants
028 Ecological & Archeological Investigations
029 Educational Facilities; Classrooms
030 Electronics
031 Elevators; Escalators; People-Movers
032 Energy Conservation; New Energy Sources
033 Environmental Impact Studies, Assessments or Statements
034 Fallout Shelters; Blast-Resistant Design
035 Field Houses; Gyms; Stadiums
036 Fire Protection
037 Fisheries; Fish Ladders
038 Forestry & Forest Products
039 Garages; Vehicle Maintenance Facilities; Parking Decks
040 Gas Systems (Propane; Natural; Etc.)

041 Graphic Design
042 Harbors; Jetties; Piers, Ship Terminal Facilities
043 Heating; Ventilating; Air Conditioning
044 Health Systems Planning
045 Highrise; Air-Rights-Type Buildings
046 Highways; Streets; Airfield Paving; Parking Lots
047 Historical Preservation
048 Hospital & Medical Facilities
049 Hotels; Models
050 Housing (Residential, Multi-Family; Apartments; Condominiums)
051 Hydraulics & Pneumatics
052 Industrial Buildings; Manufacturing Plants
053 Industrial Processes; Quality Control
054 Industrial Waste Treatment
055 Interior Design; Space Planning
056 Irrigation; Drainage
057 Judicial and Courtroom facilities
058 Laboratories; Medical Research Facilities
059 Landscape Architecture
060 Libraries; Museums; Galleries
061 Lighting (Interiors; Display; Theatre, Etc.)
062 Lighting (Exteriors; Streets; Memorials; Athletic Fields, Etc.)
063 Materials handling Systems; Conveyors; Sorters
064 Metallurgy
065 Microclimatology; Tropical Engineering
066 Military Design Standards
067 Mining & Mineralogy
068 Missile Facilities (Silos; Fuels; Transport)
069 Modular Systems Design; Pre-Fabricated Structures or Components
070 Naval Architecture; Off-Shore Platforms
071 Nuclear Facilities; Nuclear Shielding
072 Office Building; Industrial Parks
073 Oceanographic Engineering
074 Ordnance; Munitions; Special Weapons
075 Petroleum Exploration; Refining
076 Petroleum and Fuel (Storage and Distribution)
077 Pipelines (Cross-Country - Liquid & Gas)
078 Planning (Community, Regional Areawide and State)
079 Planning (Site, Installation, and Project)
080 Plumbing & Piping Design
081 Pneumatic Structures; Air-Support Buildings
082 Postal Facilities
083 Power Generation, Transmission. Distribution
084 Prisons & Correctional Facilities

085 Product, Machine & Equipment Design
086 Radar; Sonar; Radio & Radar Telescopes
087 Railroad; Rapid Transit
088 Recreation Facilities (Parks, Marinas, Etc.)
089 Rehabilitation (Buildings; Structures; Facilities)
090 Resource Recover; Recycling
091 Radio Frequency Systems &Shieldings
092 Rivers; Canals; Waterways; Flood Control
093 Safety Engineering; Accident Studies; OSHA Studies
094 Security Systems; Intruder & Smoke Detection
095 Seismic Designs & Studies
096 Sewage Collection, Treatment and Disposal
097 Soils & Geologic Studies; Foundations
098 Solar Energy Utilization
099 Solid Wastes; Incineration; Land Fill
100 Special Environments; Clean Rooms, Etc.
101 Structural Design; Special Structures
102 Surveying; Platting; Mapping; Flood Plain Studies
103 Swimming Pools
104 Storm Water Handling & Facilities
105 Telephone Systems (Rural; Mobile; Intercom, Etc.)
106 Testing Inspection Services
107 Traffic & Transportation Engineering
108 Towers (Self-Supporting & Guyed Systems)
109 Tunnels & Subways
110 Urban Renewals; Community Development
111 Utilities (Gas & Steam)
112 Value Analysis; Life-Cycle Costing
113 Warehouses & Depots
114 Water Resources; Hydrology; Ground Water
115 Water Supply; Treatment and Distribution
116 Wind Tunnels; Research/Testing Facilities
117 Zoning; Land Use Studies
201 _____
202 _____
203 _____
204 _____
205 _____

STANDARD FORM 254 PAGE 3 (REV. 11-92)

Standard Form 254 (page 4)

STANDARD FORM (SF) **254**

Architect-Engineer and Related Services Questionnaire

1. Firm Name/Business Address:

1a. Submittal is for ☐ Parent Company ☐ Branch or Subsidiary Office

2. Year Present Firm Established

3. Date Prepared:

4. Specify type of ownership and check below, if applicable.

A. Small Business
B. Small Disadvantaged Business
C. Woman-owned Business

5. Name of Parent Company, if any:

5a. Former Parent Company Name(s), if any, and Year(s) Established:

6. Names of not more than Two Principals to Contact: Title/Telephone

1)
2)

7. Present Offices: City / State / Telephone / No. Personnel Each Office

7a. Total Personnel

8. Personnel by Discipline: (List each person only once, by primary function.)

Administrative	Electrical Engineers	Oceanographers	
Architects	Estimators	Planners: Urban/Regional	
Chemical Engineers	Geologist	Sanitary Engineers	
Civil Engineers	Hydrologists	Soils Engineers	
Construction Inspectors	Interior Designers	Specification Writers	
Draftsmen	Landscape Architects	Structural Engineers	
Ecologists	Mechanical Engineers	Surveyors	
Economists	Mining Engineers	Transportation Engineers	

9. Summary of Professional Services Fees Received: (Insert index number)

Last 5 Years (most recent year first)

	19	19	19	19	19
Direct Federal contract work, including overseas					
All other domestic work					
All other foreign work*					

*Firms interested in foreign work, but without such experience, check here: ☐

Ranges of Professional Services Fees
INDEX
1. Less than $100,000
2. $100,000 to $250,000
3. $250,000 to $500,000
4. $500,000 to $1 million
5. $1 million to $2 million
6. $2 million to $5 million
7. $5 million to $10 million
8. $10 million or greater

STANDARD FORM 254 PAGE 4 (REV. 11-92)

Standard Form 254 (page 5)

Profile of Firm's Project Experience, Last 5 Years

Profile	Number of	Total Gross Fees (in thousands)	Profile Code		Number of Projects	Total Gross Fees (in thousands)	Profile Code		Number of Projects	Total Gross Fees (in thousands)
1)			11)				21)			
2)			12)				22)			
3)			13)				23)			
4)			14)				24)			
5)			15)				25)			
6)			16)				26)			
7)			17)				27)			
8)			18)				28)			
9)			19)				29)			
10)			20)				30)			

11. Project examples, Last 5 Years

Profile Code	"P," "C," "JV," or "IE"	Project Name and Location	Owner Name and Address	Cost of Work (in thousands)	Completion Date (Actual
		1.			
		2			
		3			
		4			
		5			
		6			
		7			

STANDARD FORM 254 PAGE 5 (REV. 11-92)

Standard Form 254 (page 6)

STANDARD FORM 254 PAGE 6 (REV. 11-92)

8	9	10	11	12	13	14	15	16	17	18	19

Standard Form 254 (page 7)

20													
21													
22													
23													
24													
25													
26													
27													
28													
29													
30													

12. The foregoing is a statement of facts

Typed Name and Title: _____

Date:

STANDARD FORM 254 PAGE 7 (REV. 11-92)

Standard Form 255 (page 1)

STANDARD FORM (SF) **255**	**Architect-Engineer and Related Services Questionnaire for Specific Project**	Form Approved OMB No. 9000-0005

Public reporting burden for this collection of information is estimated to average 1.2 hours per response, including the time for reviewing instructions, searching existing data sources, gathering and maintaining the data needed, and completing and reviewing the collection of information. Send comments regarding this burden estimate or any other aspect of this collection of information, including suggestions for reducing this burden, to the FAR Secretariat (VRS), Office of Federal Acquisition and Regulatory Policy, GSA, Washington, D.C. 20405; and to the Office of Management and Budget, Paperwork Reduction Project (9000-0005), Washington, D.C. 20503.

Purpose:

This form is a supplement to the "Architect-Engineer and Related Services Questionnaire" (SF 254). Its purpose is to provide additional information regarding the qualifications of interested firms to undertake a specific Federal A-E project. Firms, or branch offices of firms, submitting this form should enclose (or already have on file with the appropriate office of the agency) a current (within the past year) and accurate copy of the SF 254 for that office.

The procurement official responsible for each proposed project may request submission of the SF 255 "Architect-Engineer and Related Services Questionnaire for Specific Project" in accord with applicable civilian and military procurement regulations and shall evaluate such submissions as well as related information contained on the Standard Form 254, and any other performance data on file with the agency, and shall select firms for subsequent discussions leading to contract award in conformance with Public Law 92-582. This form should only be filed by an architect-engineer or related services firm when requested to do so by the agency or by a public announcements. Responses should be as complete and accurate as possible, contain data relative to the specific project for which you wish to be considered, and should be provided, by the required due date, to the office specified in the request or public announcement.

This form will be used only for the specified project. Do not refer to this submittal in response to other requests or public announcements.

Definitions:

"**Architect-Engineer Services**" are defined in Part 36 of the Federal Acquisition Regulation.
"**Principals**" are those individuals in a firm who possess legal responsibility for its management. They may be owners, partners, corporate officers, associates, administrators, etc.
"**Discipline**," as used in this questionnaire, refers to the primary technological capability of individuals in the responding firm. Possession of an academic degree, professional registration, certification, or extensive experience in a particular field of practice normally reflects an individual's primary technical discipline.
"**Joint Venture**" is a collaborative undertaking by two or more firms or individuals for which the participants are both jointly and individually responsible.
"**Key Persons, Specialists, and Individual Consultants,**" as used in this questionnaire, refer to individuals who will have major project responsibility or will provide unusual or unique capabilities for the project under consideration.

Instructions for Filing (Numbers below correspond to numbers contained in form):

1. Give name and location of the project for which this form is being submitted.
2. Provide appropriated data from the Commerce Business Daily (CBD) identifying the particular project for which this form is being filed.
   2a. Give the date of the Commerce Business Daily in which the project announcement appeared, or indicate "not applicable" (N/A) if the source of the announcement is other than the CBD.
   2b. Indicate Agency identification or contract number as provided in the CBD announcement.
3. Show name and address of the individual or firm (or joint venture) which is submitting this form for the project.
   3a. List the name, title, and telephone number of that principal who will serve as the point of contact. Such an individual must be empowered to speak for the firm on policy and contractual matters and should be familiar with the programs and procedures of the agency to which this form is directed.
   3b. Give the address of the specific office which will have responsibility for performing the announced work.
4. Insert the number of consultant personnel by discipline proposed for subject project on line (A). Insert the number of in-house personnel by discipline proposed for subject project on line (B). While some personnel may be qualified in several disciplines, each person should be counted only once in accord with his or her primary function. Include clerical personnel as "administrative." Write in any additional disciplines -- sociologists, biologists, etc. -- and number of people in each, in blank spaces.
5. Answer only if this form is being submitted by a joint venture of two or more collaborating firms. Show the names and addresses of all individuals or organizations excepted to be included as part of the joint venture and describe their particular areas of anticipated responsibility (ie., technical disciplines, administration, financial, sociological, environment, etc.).
   5a. Indicate, by checking the appropriate box, whether this particular joint venture has worked together on other projects.
Each firm participating in the joint venture should have a Standard Form 254 on file with the contracting office receiving this form. Firms which do not have such forms on file should provide same immediately along with a notation at the top of page 1 of the form regarding their association with this joint venture submittal.

NSN 7540-01-152-8074
Previous edition not usable.

STANDARD FORM 255 (REV. 11-92)
Prescribed by GSA - FAR (48 CFR) 53. 236-2(2)

Standard Form 255 (page 2)

STANDARD FORM (SF) **255**

Architect-Engineer and Related Services Questionnaire for Specific Project

Standard Form 255
General Services Administration
Washington, D.C. 20405

6. If respondent is not a joint venture, but intends to use outside (as opposed to in-house or permanently and formally affiliated) consultants or associates, he should provide names and addresses of all such individuals or firms, as well as their particular areas of technical/professional expertise, as it relates to this project. Existence of previous working relationships should be noted. If more than eight but less than consultants or associates are anticipated, attach an additional sheet containing requested information.

7. Regardless of whether respondent is a joint venture or an independent firm, provide brief resumes of key personnel expected to participate on this project. Care should be taken to limit resumes to only those personnel and specialists who will have major project responsibilities. Each resume must include: (a) name of each key person and specialist and his or her title, (b) the project assignment or role which that person will be expected to fulfill in connection with this project, (c) the name of the firm or organization, if any, with whom that individual is presently associated, (d) years of relevant experience with present firm and other firms, (e) the highest academic degree achieved and the discipline covered (if more than one highest degree, such as two Ph.D.'s, list both), the year received and the particular technical/professional discipline which that individual will bring to the project, (f) if registered as an architect, engineer, surveyor, etc., show only the field of registration and the year that such registration was first acquired. If registered in several states, do not list states, and (g) a synopsis of experience, training, or other qualities which reflect individual's potential contribution to this project. Include such data as: familiarity with Government or agency procedures, similar type of work performed in the past, management abilities, familiarity with the geographic area, relevant foreign language capabilities, etc. Please limit synopsis of experience to directly relevant information.

8. List up to ten projects which demonstrate the firm's or joint venture's competence to perform work similar to that likely to be required on this project. The more recent such projects, the better. Prime consideration will be given to projects which illustrate respondent's capability for performing work similar to that being sought. Required information must include: (a) name and location of project, (b) brief description of type and extent of services provided for each project (submissions by joint ventures should indicate which member of the joint venture was the prime on that particular project and what role it played), (c) name and address of the owner of that project (if Government agency, indicate responsible office), and name and phoone number of individual to contact for reference (preferably the project manager), (d) completion date (actual when available, otherwise estimated), (e) total construction cost of completed project (or where no construction was involved, the approximate cost of your work) and that portion of the cost of the project for which the named firm was/is responsible.

9. List only those projects which the A-E firm or joint venture, or members of the joint venture, are currently performing under direct contract with an agency or department of the Federal Government. Exclude any grant or loan projects being financed by the Federal Government but being performed under contract to other non-Federal Government entities. Information provided under each heading is similar to that requested in the preceding Item 8, except for (d) "Percent Complete." Indicate in this item the percentage of A-E work completed upon filing this form.

10. Through narrative discussion, show reason why the firm or joint venture submitting this questionnaire believes it is especially qualified to undertake the project. Information provided should include, but not be limited to, such data as: specialized equipment available for this work, any awards or recognition received by a firm or individuals for similar work, required security clearances, special approaches or concepts developed by the firm relevant to this project, etc. Respondents may say anything they wish in support of their qualifications. When appropriate, respondents may supplement this proposal with graphic material and photographs which best demonstrate design capabilities of the team proposed for this project.

11. Completed forms should be signed by the chief executive officer of the joint venture (thereby attesting to the concurrence and commitment of all members of the joint venture), or by the architect-engineer principal responsible for the conduct of the work in the event it is awarded to the organization submitting this form. Joint ventures selected for subsequent discussions regarding this project must make available a statement of participation signed by a principal of each member of the joint venture. ALL INFORMATION CONTAINED IN THE FORM SHOULD BE CURRENT AND FACTUAL.

STANDARD FORM 255 PAGE 2 (REV.11-92)

Standard Form 255 (page 3)

STANDARD FORM (SF) **255** Architect-Engineer and Related Services Questionnaire for Specific Project	1. Project Name/Location for which Firm is Filing:	2a. Commerce Business Daily Announcement Date, if any:	2b. Agency Identification Number, if any:

3. Firm (or Joint-Venture) Name & Address

3a. Name, Title & Telephone Number of Principal to Contact

3b. Address of office to perform work, if different from Item 3

4. Personnel by Discipline: (List each person only once, by primary function.) Enter proposed consultant personnel to be utilized on this project on line (A) and in-house personnel on line (B).

(A)___ (B)___	Administrative	(A)___ (B)___	Electrical Engineers	(A)___ (B)___	Oceanographers
(A)___ (B)___	Architects	(A)___ (B)___	Estimators	(A)___ (B)___	Planners: Urban/Regional
(A)___ (B)___	Chemical Engineers	(A)___ (B)___	Geologists	(A)___ (B)___	Sanitary Engineers
(A)___ (B)___	Civil Engineers	(A)___ (B)___	Hydrologists	(A)___ (B)___	Soils Engineers
(A)___ (B)___	Construction Inspectors	(A)___ (B)___	Interior Designers	(A)___ (B)___	Specification Writers
(A)___ (B)___	Draftsmen	(A)___ (B)___	Landscape Architects	(A)___ (B)___	Structural Engineers
(A)___ (B)___	Ecologists	(A)___ (B)___	Mechanical Engineers	(A)___ (B)___	Surveyors
(A)___ (B)___	Economists	(A)___ (B)___	Mining Engineers	(A)___ (B)___	Transportation Engineers
				___	Total Personnel

5. If submittal is by JOINT-VENTURE list participating firms and outline specific areas of responsibility (including administrative, technical and financial) for each firm: (Attach SF 254 for each if not on file with Procuring Office.)

5a. Has this Joint-Venture previously worked together? ☐ Yes ☐ No

STANDARD FORM 255 PAGE 3 (REV 11/92)

Standard Form 255 (page 4)

6. If respondent is not a joint-venture, list outside key Consultants/Associates anticipated for this project (Attach SF 254 for Consultants/Associates listed, if not already on file with the Contracting Office).		
Name & Address	Specialty	Worked with Prime before (Yes or No)
1)		
2)		
3)		
4)		
5)		
6)		
7)		
8)		

STANDARD FORM 255 PAGE 4 (REV. 11-92)

Standard Form 255 (page 5)

7. Brief resume of key persons, specialists, and individual consultants anticipated for this project.

a. Name & Title:

b. Project Assignment:

c. Name of Firm with which associated:

d. Years experience: With this Firm _____   With Other Firms _____

e. Education: Degree(s)/Year/Specialization

f. Active Registration: Year First Registered/Discipline

g. Other Experience and Qualifications relevant to the proposed project:

a. Name & Title:

b. Project Assignment:

c. Name of Firm with which associated:

d. Years experience: With this Firm _____   With Other Firms _____

e. Education: Degree(s)/Year/Specialization

f. Active Registration: Year First Registered/Discipline

g. Other Experience and Qualifications relevant to the proposed project:

STANDARD FORM 255 PAGE 5 (REV.11-92)

Standard Form 255 (page 6)

7. Brief resume of key persons, specialists, and individual consultants anticipated for this project.

a. Name & Title:

b. Project Assignment:

c. Name of Firm with which associated:

d. Years experience: With this Firm _____ With Other Firms _____

e. Education: Degree(s)/Year/Specialization

f. Active Registration: Year First Registered/Discipline

g. Other Experience and Qualifications relevant to the proposed project:

a. Name & Title:

b. Project Assignment:

c. Name of Firm with which associated:

d. Years experience: With this Firm _____ With Other Firms _____

e. Education: Degree(s)/Year/Specialization

f. Active Registration: Year First Registered/Discipline

g. Other Experience and Qualifications relevant to the proposed project:

STANDARD FORM 255 PAGE 6 (REV 11-92)

Standard Form 255 (page 7)

7. Brief resume of key persons, specialists, and individual consultants anticipated for this project.

a. Name & Title:

b. Project Assignment:

c. Name of Firm with which associated:

d. Years experience: With this Firm _____ With Other Firms _____

e. Education: Degree(s)/Year/Specialization

f. Active Registration: Year First Registered/Discipline

g. Other Experience and Qualifications relevant to the proposed project:

a. Name & Title:

b. Project Assignment:

c. Name of Firm with which associated:

d. Years experience: With this Firm _____ With Other Firms _____

e. Education: Degree(s)/Year/Specialization

f. Active Registration: Year First Registered/Discipline

g. Other Experience and Qualifications relevant to the proposed project:

STANDARD FORM 255 PAGE 7 (REV 11-92)

Standard Form 255 (page 8)

7. Brief resume of key persons, specialists, and individual consultants anticipated for this project.

a. Name & Title:

b. Project Assignment:

c. Name of Firm with which associated:

d. Years experience: With this Firm _____ With Other Firms _____

e. Education: Degree(s)/Year/Specialization

f. Active Registration: Year First Registered/Discipline

g. Other Experience and Qualifications relevant to the proposed project:

a. Name & Title:

b. Project Assignment:

c. Name of Firm with which associated:

d. Years experience: With this Firm _____ With Other Firms _____

e. Education: Degree(s)/Year/Specialization

f. Active Registration: Year First Registered/Discipline

g. Other Experience and Qualifications relevant to the proposed project:

STANDARD FORM 255 PAGE 8 (REV.11-92)

Standard Form 255 (page 9)

8. Work by firms or joint-venture members which best illustrates current qualifications relevant to this project (list not more than 10 projects).

a. Project Name & Location	b. Nature of Firm's Responsibility	c. Project Owner's Name& Address and Project Manager's Name & Phone Number	d. Completion Date (actual or estimated)	e. Estimated Cost (in Thousands) Entire Project	Work for Which Firm Was/Is Responsible
(1)					
(2)					
(3)					
(4)					
(5)					
(6)					
(7)					
(8)					
(9)					
(10)					

STANDARD FORM 255 PAGE 9 (REV. 11-92)

Standard Form 255 (page 10)

9. All work by firms or joint-venture members currently being performed directly for Federal agencies.

a. Project Name & Location (Cols. NOT divided like item 8)	b. Nature of Firm's Responsibility	c. Agency (Responsible Office) Name and Address and Project Manager's Name & Phone Number	d. Percent Complete	e. Estimated Cost (in Thousands) Entire Project	e. Estimated Cost (in Thousands) Work for Which Firm Is Responsible

STANDARD FORM 255 PAGE 10 (REV 1-92)

Standard Form 255 (page 11)

10. Use this space to provide any additional information or description of resources (including any computer design capabilities) supporting your firm's qualifications for the proposed project

11. The foregoing is a statement of facts.

Signature: _____

Typed Name and Title: _____

Date: _____

STANDARD FORM 255 PAGE 11 (REV 11-92)

Standard Form 1403 (page 1)

PREAWARD SURVEY OF PROSPECTIVE CONTRACTOR
(GENERAL)

| 1. SERIAL NO. *(For surveying activity use)* | OMB NO.:9000-0011 Expires: 10/31/97 |

Public reporting burden for this collection of information is estimated to average 24 hours per response, including the time for reviewing instructions, searching existing datasources, gathering and maintaining the data needed, and completing and reviewing the collection of information. Send comments regarding this burden estimate or any other aspect of this collection of information, including suggestions for reducing this burden, to the FAR Secretariat (VRS), Office of Federal Acquisition and Regulatory Policy, GSA, Washington, DC 20405; and to the Office of Management and Budget, Paperwork Reduction Project (9000-0011), Washington, DC 20503.

SECTION I - REQUEST *(For Completion by Contracting Office)*

| 2. NAME AND ADDRESS OF SURVEYING ACTIVITY | 3. SOLICITATION NO. | 4. TOTAL OFFERED PRICE $ |
| | 5. TYPE OF CONTRACT | |

6A. NAME AND ADDRESS OF SECONDARY SURVEY ACTIVITY
(For surveying activity use)

7A. NAME AND ADDRESS OF PROSPECTIVE CONTRACTOR

6B. TELEPHONE NO. *(Include AUTOVON, WATS, or FTS, if available)*

7B. FIRM'S CONTACT

7C. TELEPHONE NO. *(with area code)*

8. WILL CONTRACTING OFFICE PARTICIPATE IN SURVEY?
☐ YES ☐ NO

13. NAME AND ADDRESS OF PARENT COMPANY *(If applicable)*

9. DATE OF REQUEST

10. DATE REPORT REQUIRED

11. PROSPECTIVE CONTRACTOR REPRESENT THAT IT ☐ IS, ☐ IS NOT A SMALL BUSINESS CONCERN.

12. WALSH-HEALY CON ACT *(Check applicable box(es))*

A. IS NOT APPLICABLE

B. IS APPLICABLE AND PROSPECTIVE CONTRACTOR REPRESENTS HIS CLASSIFICATION AS:
☐ MANUFACTURER ☐ REGULAR DEALER
☐ OTHER *(Specify)*

14A. PLANT AND LOCATION *(If different from Item 7, above)*

15A. NAME OF REQUESTING ACTIVITY CONTRACTING OFFICER

14B. POINT OF CONTACT

14C. TELEPHONE NO. *(with area code)*

15B. SIGNATURE

16A. NAME OF CONTACT POINT AT REQUESTING ACTIVITY *(If different from Item 15A)*

15C. TELEPHONE NO. *(Include AUTOVAN, WATS or FTS, if available)*

17. RETURN PREAWARD SURVEY TO THIS ADDRESS:

16B. TELEPHONE NO. *(Include AUTOVON, WATS, or FTS, if available)*

ATTN:

SECTION II - DATA *(For Completion by Conracting Office)*

18A. ITEM NO.	18B. NATIONAL STOCK NUMBER (NEW) AND NOMENCLATURE		18C. TOTAL QUANTITY	18D. UNIT PRICE	18E. DELIVERY SCHEDULE				
					(a)	(b)	(c)	(d)	(e)
		SOLICITED							
		OFFERED		$					
		SOLICITED							
		OFFERED		$					
		SOLICITED							
		OFFERED		$					
		SOLICITED							
		OFFERED		$					
		SOLICITED							
		OFFERED		$					
		SOLICITED							
		OFFERED		$					
		SOLICITED							
		OFFERED		$					
		SOLICITED							
		OFFERED		$					

AUTHORIZATION FOR LOCAL REPRODUCTION
Previous edition is usable.

STANDARD FORM 1403 (REV. 9-88)
Prescribed by GSA FAR (48 CFR) 53.209-1(a)

Standard Form 1403 (page 2)

SECTION III - FACTORS TO BE INVESTIGATED

19. MAJOR FACTORS	CHK. (a)	SAT. (b)	UN-SAT. (c)	20. OTHER FACTORS (Provide specific requirements in Remarks)	CHK. (a)	SAT. (b)	UN-SAT. (c)
A. TECHNICAL CAPABILITY				A. GOVERNMENT PROPERTY CONTROL			
B. PRODUCTION CAPABILITY				B. TRANSPORTATION			
C. QUALITY ASSURANCE CAPABILITY				C. PACKAGING			
D. FINANCIAL CAPABILITY				D. SECURITY			
E. ACCOUNTING SYSTEM				E. SAFETY			
21. IS THIS A SHORT FORM PREAWARD REPORT? (For completion by surveying activity)				F. ENVIRONMENTAL/ENERGY CONSIDERATION			
				G. FLIGHT OPERATIONS/FLIGHT SAFETY			
☐ YES ☐ NO				H. OTHER (Specify)			
22. IS A FINANCIAL ASSISTANCE PAYMENT PROVISION IN THE SOLICITATION? (For completion by contracting activity)							
☐ YES ☐ NO							

23. REMARKS (For Contracting Activity Use)

SECTION IV - SURVEYING ACTIVITY RECOMMENDATIONS

24. RECOMMEND	25A. NAME AND TITLE OF SURVEY APPROVING OFFICIAL	25B. TELEPHONE NO.
☐ A. COMPLETE AWARD ☐ B. PARTIAL AWARD (Quantity _____) ☐ C. NO AWARD	25C. SIGNATURE	25D. DATE

STANDARD FORM 1403 (REV. 9-88) **BACK**

Standard Form 1404

PREAWARD SURVEY OF PROSPECTIVE CONTRACTOR TECHNICAL	SERIAL NO. *(For surveying activity use)*	OMB NO.:**9000-0011** Expires: 10/31/97
	PROSPECTIVE CONTRACTOR	

Public reporting burden for this collection of information is estimated to average 24 hours per response, including the time for reviewing instructions, searching existing data sources, gathering and maintaining the data needed, and completing and reviewing the collection of information. Send comments regarding this burden estimate or any other aspect of this collection of information, including suggestions for reducing this burden, to the FAR Secretariat (VRS), Office of Federal Acquisition and Regulatory Policy, GSA, Washington, DC 20405; and to the Office of Management and Budget, Paperwork Reduction Project (9000-0011), Washington, DC 20503.

1. RECOMMENDED

☐ a. COMPLETE AWARD   ☐ b. PARTIAL AWARD *(Quantity: _____)*   ☐ c. NO AWARD

2. NARRATIVE *(Include the following information concerning key personnel who will be involved with the prospective contract: (1) Names, qualifications/experience and length of affiliation with prospective contractor; (2) Evaluate technical capabilities with respect to the requirements of the proposed contract or item classifications); (3) Description of any technical capabilities which the prospective contractor lacks. Comment on the prospective contractor's efforts to obtain the needed technical capabilities.)*

IF CONTINUATION SHEETS ATTACHED - MARK HERE ☐

3. FIRM HAS AND/OR UNDERSTANDS *(Give explanation for any items marked "NO" in 2. Narrative)*

a. SPECIFICATIONS	☐ YES ☐ NO	b. EXHIBITS	☐ YES ☐ NO
c. DRAWINGS	☐ YES ☐ NO	d. TECHNICAL DATA REQUIREMENTS	☐ YES ☐ NO

4. SURVEY MADE BY	a. SIGNATURE AND OFFICE *(Include typed or printed name)*	b. TELEPHONE NO. *(include area code)*	c. DATE SIGNED
5. SURVEY REVIEWING OFFICIAL	a. SIGNATURE AND OFFICE *(Include typed or printed name)*	b. TELEPHONE NO. *(include area code)*	c. DATE REVIEWED

AUTHORIZED FOR LOCAL REPRODUCTION
Previous edition is usable.

STANDARD FORM 1404 (REV. 9-88)
Prescribed by GSA - FAR (48 CFR) 53.209-1(b)

Standard Form 1405 (page 1)

PREAWARD SURVEY OF PROSPECTIVE CONTRACTOR PRODUCTION	SERIAL NO. *(For surveying activity use)*	OMB No.: **9000-0011** Expires: 09/30/91
	PROSPECTIVE CONTRACTOR	

Public reporting burden for this collection of information is estimated to average 24 hours per response, including the time for reviewing instructions, searching existing data sources, gathering and maintaining the data needed, and completing and reviewing the collection of information. Send comments regarding this burden estimate or any other aspect of this collection of information, including suggestions for reducing this burden, to the FAR Secretariat (VRS), Office of Federal Acquisition and Regulatory Policy, GSA, Washington, DC 20405; and to the Office of Management and Budget, Paperwork Reduction Project (9000-0011), Washington, DC 20503.

SECTION I - RECOMMENDATION

1. RECOMMENDED

☐ COMPLETE AWARD   ☐ b. PARTIAL AWARD *(Quantity: —————)*   ☐ c. NO AWARD

2. NARRATIVE *(Cite those sections of this report which substantiate the recommendations. List any other backup information in this space or on attached sheet if necessary. Identify any formal systems reviews and state results.)*

IF CONTINUATION SHEETS ATTACHED - MARK HERE ☐

	a. SIGNATURE AND OFFICE *(Include typed or printed name)*	b. TELEPHONE NUMBER *(Include are code)*	c. DATE SIGNED
3. SURVEY MADE BY			
4. SURVEY REVIEWING OFFICIAL	a. SIGNATURE AND OFFICE *(Include typed or printed name)*	b. TELEPHONE NUMBER *(Include are code)*	c. DATE REVIEWED

AUTHORIZED FOR LOCAL REPRODUCTION
Previous edition not usable

STANDARD FORM 1405 (REV. 9-88)
Prescribed by GSA-FAR (48 CFR) 53.209-1(c)

Standard Form 1405 (page 2)

SECTION II - PLANT FACILITIES

1. SIZE OF TRACT		4. DESCRIPTION AND TYPE OF BUILDING(S)
		☐ OWNED
2. SQUARE FEET UNDER ROOF	3. NO. OF BUILDINGS	☐ LEASED *(Give expiration date)*

5. SPACE					6. MISCELLANEOUS PLANT OBSERVATIONS		
	TYPE	SQUARE FEET	ADE-QUATE	INADE-QUATE	*(Explain any items marked "NO" on an attached sheet.)*	YES	NO
MANUFACTURING	a. TOTAL MANUFACTURING SPACE				a. GOOD HOUSEKEEPING MAINTAINED		
	b. SPACE AVAILABLE FOR OFFERED ITEM				b. POWER AND FUEL SUPPLY ADEQUATE TO MEET PRODUCTION		
	c. TOTAL STORAGE SPACE				c. ALTERNATE POWER AND FUEL SOURCE AVAILABLE		
STORAGE	d. FOR INSPECTION LOTS				d. ADEQUATE MATERIAL HANDLING EQUIPMENT AVAILABLE		
	e. FOR SHIPPING QUANTITIES				e. TRANSPORTATION FACILITIES AVAILABLE FOR SHIPPING PRODUCT		
	f. SPACE AVAILABLE FOR OFFERED ITEM				**OTHER** *(Specify)* f.		
					g.		
	g. AMOUNT OF STORAGE THAT CAN BE CONVERTED FOR MANUFAC-TURING, IF REQUIRED				h.		

SECTION III - PRODUCTION EQUIPMENT

	LIST MAJOR EQUIPMENT REQUIRED *(Include GFP and annotate it as such)* (a)	QUANTITY REQUIRED FOR PROPOSED CONTRACT (b)	TOTAL QTY. REQD. DUR-ING LIFE OF PROPOSED CONTRACT (c)	QUANTITY ON HAND (d)	CONDI-TION (e) G F P	QUANTITY SHORT* *(Col. (c) minus (d))* (f)	SOURCE, IF NOT ON HAND (g)	VERIFIED DELIVERY DATE (h)
MANUFACTURING	1.							
SPECIAL TOOLING	2.							
SPECIAL TEST	3.							

* Coordinate shortage information for financial implications.

STANDARD FORM 1405 (REV. 9-88) PAGE 2

Standard Form 1405 (page 3)

SECTION IV - MATERIALS, PURCHASED PARTS AND SUBCONTRACTS
1. PARTS/MATERIALS/SUBCONTRACTS WITH LONGEST LEAD TIME OR CRUCIAL ITEMS

DESCRIPTION (a)	SOURCE (b)	VERIFIED DELIVERY DATE TO MEET PROD. (c)

2. DESCRIBE THE MATERIAL CONTROL SYSTEM, INDICATING WHETHER IT IS CURRENTLY OPERATIONAL, AND EVALUATE ITS ABILITY TO MEET THE NEEDS OF THE PROPOSED ACQUISITION.

SECTION V - PERSONNEL

1. NUMBER AND SOURCE OF EMPLOYEES

TYPE OF EMPLOYEES	NO. ON BOARD	ADD. NO. REQUIRED	AVAIL. YES	AVAIL. NO	SOURCE
a. SKILLED PRODUCTION					
b. UNSKILLED PRODUCTION					
c. ENGINEERING					
d. ADMINISTRATIVE					
e. TOT. (Lines A thru D)					

2. SHIFTS ON WHICH WORK IS TO BE PERFORMED
☐ FIRST ☐ SECOND ☐ THIRD

3. UNION AFFILIATION

AGREEMENT EXPIRATION DATE ▶

4. RELATIONSHIP WITH LABOR INDICATES PROBLEMS AFFECTING TIMELY PERFORMANCE OF PROPOSED CONTRACT (If "Yes," explain on attached sheet)
☐ YES ☐ NO

SECTION VI - DELIVERY PERFORMANCE RECORD

STANDARD FORM 1405 (REV. 9-88) PAGE 3

Standard Form 1405 (page 4)

SECTION VII - RELATED PREVIOUS PRODUCTION (*Government*)

| PAST YEAR PRODUCTION | | GOVERNMENT CONTRACT NUMBER* | PERFORMANCE | | QUANTITY | DOLLAR VALUE ($000) |
ITEM NOMENCLATURE (a)	NATIONAL STOCK NO. (NSN) (b)	(c)	ON SCHED. (d)	DELIN-QUENT (e)	(f)	(g)

* Identify identical items by an asterisk(*) after the Government contract number.

SECTION VIII - CURRENT PRODUCTION
(Government and civilian concurrent production schedule using same equipment and/or personnel as offered item)

ITEM(S) (Include Government Contract No., if applicable. Identify unsatisfactory performance with asterisk(*).)	MONTHLY SCHEDULE OF CONCURRENT DELIVERIES (*Quantity*)										
	1st	2nd	3rd	4th	5th	6th	7th	8th	9th	10th	BAL.
1. BEING PRODUCED											
2. PENDING AWARD											

SECTION IX - ORGANIZATION AND MANAGEMENT DATA

Provide the following information in SECTION I NARRATIVE:

1. Describe the relationship between management production, and inspection. Attach an organization chart, if available.

2. Describe the prospective contractor's production control system. State whether or not it is operational.

3. Evaluate the prospective contractor's production control system in terms of (a) historical effectiveness, (b) the proposed contract, and (c) total production during performance of the proposed contract.

4. Comment on or evaluate other areas unique to this survey (include all special requests by the contracting office and any other information pertinent to the proposed contractor item classification).

STANDARD FORM 1405 (REV. 9-88) PAGE 4

Standard Form 1406 (page 1)

PREAWARD SURVEY OF PROSPECTIVE CONTRACTOR QUALITY ASSURANCE	SERIAL NO. *(For surveying activity use)*	OMB No.:**9000-0011** Expires: 10/31/2000
	PROSPECTIVE CONTRACTOR	

Public reporting burden for this collection of information is estimated to average 24 hours per response, including the time for reviewing instructions, searching existing data sources, gathering and maintaining the data needed, and completing and reviewing the collection of information. Send comments regarding this burden estimate or any other aspect of this collection of information, including suggestions for reducing this burden, to the FAR Secretariat (MVR), Federal Acquisition Policy Division, GSA, Washington, DC 20405.

SECTION I - RECOMMENDATION

1. RECOMMEND: ☐ AWARD ☐ NO AWARD *(Provide full substantiation for recommendation in 4. NARRATIVE)*

2. IF PROSPECTIVE CONTRACTOR RECEIVES AWARD, A POST AWARD CONFERENCE IS RECOMMENDED. ☐ YES ☐ NO

3. AN ON-SITE SURVEY WAS PERFORMED. ☐ YES ☐ NO

4. NARRATIVE

IF CONTINUATION SHEETS ATTACHED - MARK HERE ☐

5. SURVEY MADE BY		6. SURVEY REVIEWING OFFICIAL	
A. SIGNATURE	B. DATE SIGNED	A. SIGNATURE	B. DATE REVIEWED
C. NAME		C. NAME	
D. OFFICE		D. OFFICE	
E. AREA CODE / F. TELEPHONE NUMBER / G. EXT.		E. AREA CODE / F. TELEPHONE NUMBER / G. EXT.	

AUTHORIZED FOR LOCAL REPRODUCTION
Previous edition is not usable.

STANDARD FORM 1406 (REV. 11-97)
Prescribed by GSA FAR (48 CFR) 53.209-1(d)

Standard Form 1406 (page 2)

SECTION II - COMPANY AND SOLICITATION DATA

1. BRIEFLY DESCRIBE HOW QUALITY ASSURANCE RESPONSIBILITIES ARE ACCOMPLISHED.

2. QUALITY ASSURANCE OFFICIALS CONTACTED

A. NAME	B. TITLE	C. YEARS OF QUALITY ASSURANCE EXPERIENCE

3. APPLICABLE CONTRACT QUALITY REQUIREMENTS

A. NUMBER	B. TITLE	C. TAILORING *(If any)*

4. ☐ IDENTICAL OR ☐ SIMILAR ITEMS HAVE BEEN ☐ PRODUCED, ☐ SUPPLIED, OR ☐ SERVICED BY PROSPECTIVE CONTRACTOR

   (If similar items, identify:)

SECTION III - EVALUATION CHECKLIST

STATEMENTS		YES	NO
1. These items (where applicable to the contract) are understood by the prospective contractor.	A. Exhibits, technical data, drawings, specifications, and approval requirements.		
	B. Preservation, packaging, packing, and marking requirements.		
	C. Other *(Specify)*		
2. Records available indicate that the prospective contractor has a satisfactory quality performance record during the past twelve (12) months for similar items.			
3. Used, reconditioned, or remanufactured material and former Government surplus material will be furnished by the prospective contractor. *(If Yes, explain in Section I NARRATIVE)*			
4. Prospective contractor will require unusual assistance from the Government. *(If Yes, explain in Section I NARRATIVE)*			
5. Did prospective contractor fulfill commitments to correct deficiencies, as proposed on previous surveys, when awarded that contract? *(If No, explain in Section I NARRATIVE)*			
6. Quality verification personnel	NUMBER SKILLED _____ NUMBER SEMI-SKILLED _____		
7. Quality verification to production personnel ratio.	RATIO _____ : _____		
THE FOLLOWING ARE AVAILABLE AND ADEQUATE. *(If not applicable, show "N/A" in "Yes" column.)*			
8. Inspection and test equipment, gauges, and instruments for first article and production *(including solicitation specified equipment)*.			
9. Calibration/metrology program.			
10. Quality system procedures and controls.			
11. Control of specifications, drawings, changes and modifications, work/process instructions.			
12. System for determining inspection, test, and measurement requirements.			
13. Purchasing: Processes for selecting qualified suppliers and assuring the quality of purchased materials.			
14. Product identification, segregation, traceability, and maintenance.			
15. Government furnished property controls.			
16. Process controls.			
17. Nonconforming product: System for timely identification, disposition, correction of deficiencies, and corrective and preventative action.			
18. Preservation, storage, packaging, packing, marking, and delivery controls.			
19. Records *(such as: inspection, test, status, corrective actions, calibration, etc.)*			
20. Controls for investigation of customer complaints and correction of deficiencies.			
21. Design controls system.			
22. Computer software *(deliverable and/or non-deliverable)* quality assurance program.			
23. Management review and internal quality audits.			
24. Quality assurance training program.			
25. Installation and servicing quality assurance program.			
26. Statistical techniques.			

STANDARD FORM 1406 (REV. 11-97) **BACK**

Standard Form 1407 (page 1)

PREAWARD SURVEY OF PROSPECTIVE CONTRACTOR FINANCIAL CAPABILITY	SERIAL NO. *(For surveying activity use)*	OMB No.:9000-0011 Expires: 09/30/91
	PROSPECTIVE CONTRACTOR	

Public reporting burden for this collection of information is estimated to average 24 hours per response, including the time for reviewing instructions, searching existing data sources, gathering and maintaining the data needed, and completing and reviewing the collection of information. Send comments regarding this burden estimate or any other aspect of this collection of information, including suggestions for reducing this burden, to the FAR Secretariat (VRS), Office Federal Acquisition and Regulatory Policy, GSA, Washington, DC 20405; and to the Office of Management and Budget, Paperwork Reduction Project (9000-0011), Washington, DC 20503.

SECTION I - RECOMMENDATION

1. RECOMMENDED

☐ a. COMPLETE AWARD   ☐ b. PARTIAL AWARD (Quantity: _____)   ☐ c. NO AWARD

2. TOTAL OFFERED PRICE

3. NARRATIVE *(Cite those sections of the report which substantiate the recommendation. Give any other backup information in this space or on an additional sheet, if necessary.)*

IF CONTINUATION SHEETS ATTACHED - MARK HERE ☐

4. SURVEY MADE BY	a. SIGNATURE	b. TELEPHONE NUMBER *(Include area code)*	c. DATE SIGNED
5. SURVEY REVIEWING OFFICIAL	a. SIGNATURE	b. TELEPHONE NUMBER *(Include area code)*	c. DATE REVIEWED

AUTHORIZED FOR LOCAL REPRODUCTION
Previous edition is usable.

STANDARD FORM 1407 (REV. 9-88)
Prescribed by GSA - FAR (48 CFR) 53.209-1(e)

Standard Form 1407 (page 2)

SECTION II - GENERAL

1. TYPE OF COMPANY

☐ CORPORATION   ☐ PARTNERSHIP

☐ SUBSIDIARY   ☐ DIVISION

☐ PROPRIETORSHIP   ☐ OTHER *(Specify)*

2. YEAR ESTABLISHED:

3. NAME AND ADDRESS OF:

a. PARENT CO.

b. SUBSIDIARIES

SECTION III - BALANCE SHEET/PROFIT AND LOSS STATEMENT

PART A - LATEST BALANCE SHEET

1. DATE	2. FILED WITH

3. FINANCIAL POSITION

a. Cash	$
b. Accounts Receivable	
c. Inventory	
d. Other Current Assets	
e. Total Current Assets	
f. Fixed Assets	
g. Current Liabilities	
h. Long Term Liabilities	
i. Total Liabilities	
j. Net Worth	
4. WORKING CAPITAL *(Current Assets less Current Liabilities)*	

5. RATIOS

a. CURRENT ASSETS TO CURRENT LIABILITIES	b. ACID TEST *(Cash, temporary investments held in lieu of cash and current receivables to current liabilities)*	c. TOTAL LIABILITIES TO NET WORTH

PART B - LATEST PROFIT AND LOSS STATEMENT

1. CURRENT PERIOD		2. FILED WITH
a. FROM	b. TO	

3. NET SALES	a. CURRENT PERIOD	$
	b. First prior fiscal year	
	c. Second prior fiscal year	

4. NET PROFITS BEFORE TAXES	a. CURRENT PERIOD	$
	b. First prior fiscal year	
	c. Second prior fiscal year	

PART C - OTHER

1. FISCAL YEAR ENDS *(Date):*

2. BALANCE SHEETS AND PROFIT AND LOSS STATEMENTS HAVE BEEN CERTIFIED	a. THROUGH *(Date)*	b. BY *(Signature)*

3. OTHER PERTINENT DATA

SECTION IV - PROSPECTIVE CONTRACTOR'S FINANCIAL ARRANGEMENTS

Mark "X" in appropriate column.	YES	NO
1. USE OF OWN RESOURCES		
2. USE OF BANK CREDITS		
3. OTHER *(Specify)*		

4. INDEPENDENT ANALYSIS OF FINANCIAL POSITION SUPPORTS THE STATEMENTS SHOWN IN ITEMS 1, 2, AND 3   ☐ YES   ☐ NO *(If "NO", explain)*

SECTION V - GOVERNMENT FINANCIAL AID

1. TO BE REQUESTED IN CONNECTION WITH PERFORMANCE OF PROPOSED CONTRACT

Mark "X" in appropriate column.	YES	NO
a. PROGRESS PAYMENT(S)		
b. GUARANTEED LOAN		
c. ADVANCE PAYMENTS		

2. EXPLAIN ANY "YES" ANSWERS TO ITEMS 1a, b, AND c.

3. FINANCIAL AID CURRENTLY OBTAINED FROM THE GOVERNMENT

Complete items below only if Item a., is marked "YES."

a. PROSPECTIVE CONTRACTOR RECEIVES GOVERNMENT FINANCING AT PRESENT	b. IS LIQUIDATION CURRENT?	c. AMOUNT OF UNLIQUIDATED PROGRESS PAYMENTS OUTSTANDING	DOLLAR AMOUNTS	(a) AUTHORIZED	(b) IN USE
☐ YES ☐ NO	☐ YES ☐ NO $		a. Guaranteed loans	$	$
			b. Advance payments	$	$

4. LIST THE GOVERNMENT AGENCIES INVOLVED	5. SHOW THE APPLICABLE CONTRACT NOS.

STANDARD FORM 1407 *(REV. 9-88)* **PAGE 2**

Standard Form 1407 (page 3)

SECTION VI - BUSINESS AND FINANCIAL REPUTATION

1. COMMENTS OF PROSPECTIVE CONTRACTOR'S BANK

2. COMMENTS OF TRADE CREDITORS

3. COMMENTS AND REPORTS OF COMMERCIAL FINANCIAL SERVICES AND CREDIT ORGANIZATIONS *(Such as, Dun & Bradstreet, Standard and Poor, etc.)*

4. MOST RECENT CREDIT RATING ▶	a. DATE	b. BY

5. DOES PRICE APPEAR UNREALISTICALLY LOW? ☐ YES ☐ NO *(If Yes, explain in Section I NARRATIVE)*

6. DESCRIBE ANY OUTSTANDING LIENS OR JUDGMENTS

SECTION VII - SALES (000'S) FOR NEXT SIX QUARTERS

CATEGORY	1	2	3	4	5	6	TOTAL
1. CURRENT CONTRACT SALES (Backlog)	$	$	$	$	$	$	$
A. GOVERNMENT (Prime & Subcontractor)							
B. COMMERCIAL							
2. ANTICIPATED ADDITIONAL SALES							
A. GOVERNMENT (Prime & Subcontractor)							
B. COMMERCIAL							
3. TOTALS							

STANDARD FORM 1407 (REV. 9-88) **PAGE 3**

Standard Form 1408 (page 1)

	SERIAL NO. *(For surveying activity use)*	OMB No.:9000-0011 Expires: 10/31/97
PREAWARD SURVEY OF PROSPECTIVE CONTRACTOR ACCOUNTING SYSTEM	PROSPECTIVE CONTRACTOR	

Public reporting burden for this collection of information is estimated to average 24 hours per response, including the time for reviewing instructions, searching existing data sources, gathering and maintaining the data needed, and completing and reviewing the collection of information. Send comments regarding this burden estimate or any other aspect of this collection of information, including suggestions for reducing this burden, to FAR Secretariat (VRS), Office of Federal Acquisition and Regulatory Policy, GSA, Washington, DC 20405; and to the Office of Management and Budget, Paperwork Reduction Project (9000-0011), Washington, DC 20503.

SECTION I - RECOMMENDATION

1. PROSPECTIVE CONTRACTOR'S ACCOUNTING SYSTEM IS ACCEPTABLE FOR AWARD OF PROSPCTIVE CONTRACT

☐ YES ☐ NO *(Explain in 2. NARRATIVE)*

☐ YES, WITH A RECOMMENDATION THAT A FOLLOW ON ACCOUNTING SYSTEM REVIEW BE PERFORMED AFTER CONTRACT AWARD
(Explain in 2. NARRATIVE)

2. NARRATIVE *(Clarification of deficiencies, and other pertinent comments,. If additional space is required, continue on plain sheets of paper.)*

IF CONTINUATION SHEETS ATTACHED - MARK HERE ☐

	a. SIGNATURE AND OFFICE *(Include typed or printed name)*	b. TELEPHONE NO. *(include area code)*	c. DATE SIGNED
3. SURVEY MADE BY			
4. SURVEY REVIEWING OFFICIAL	a. SIGNATURE AND OFFICE *(Include typed or printed name)*	b. TELEPHONE NO. *(include area code)*	c. DATE REVIEWED

AUTHORIZED FOR LOCAL REPRODUCTION
Previous edition usable

STANDARD FORM 1408 (REV. 9-88)
Prescribed by GSA
FAR (48 CFR) 53.209-1(f)

Standard Form 1408 (page 2)

SECTION II - EVALUATION CHECKLIST			
MARK"X" IN THE APPROPRIATE COLUMN *(Explain any deficiencies in SECTION I NARRATIVE)*	YES	NO	NOT APPLIC-CABLE
1. EXCEPT AS STATED IN SECTION I NARRATIVE, IS THE ACCOUNTING SYSTEM IN ACCORD WITH GENERALLY ACCEPTED ACCOUNTING PRINCIPLES APPLICABLE IN THE CIRCUMSTANCES?			
2. ACCOUNTING SYSTEM PROVIDES FOR:			
a. Proper segregation of direct costs from indirect costs.			
b. Identification and accumulation of direct costs by contract.			
c. A logical and consistent method for the allocation of indirect costs to intermediate and final cost objectives. (A contract is a final cost objective.)			
d. Accumlation of costs under general ledger control.			
e. A timekeeping system that identifies employees' labor by intermediate or final cost objectives.			
f. A labor distribution system that charges direct and indirect labor to the appropriate cost objectives.			
g. Interim (at least monthly) determination of costs charged to a contract through routine posting of books of account.			
h. Exclusion from costs charged to government contracts of amounts which are not allowable in terms of FAR31, Contract Cost Principles and Procedures, or other contract provisions.			
i. Identification of costs by contract line item and by units (as if each unit or line item were a separate contract) if required by the proposed contract.			
j. Segregation of preproduction costs from production costs.			
3. ACCOUNTING SYSTEM PROVIDES FINANCIAL INFORMATION:			
a. Required by contract clauses concerning limitation of cost (FAR52.232-20 and 21) or limitation on payments (FAR52.216-16).			
b. Required to support requests for progress payments.			
4. IS THE ACCOUNTING SYSTEM DESIGNED, AND ARE THE RECORDS MAINTAINED IN SUCH A MANNER THAT ADEQUATE, RELIABLE DATA ARE DEVELOPED FOR USE IN PRICING FOLLOW-ON ACQUISITONS?			
5. IS THE ACCOUNTING SYSTEM CURRENTLY IN FULL OPERATION? (If not, describe in Section I Narrative which portions are (1) in operation, (2) set up, but not yet in operation, (3) anticipated, or (4) nonexistent.)			

GSA FORM 1408 (REV. 9-88) **BACK**

Standard Form 1447 (page 1)

SOLICITATION/CONTRACT BIDDER/OFFEROR TO COMPLETE BLOCKS 11, 13, 15, 21, 22, & 27	1. THIS CONTRACT IS A RATED ORDER UNDER DPAS (15 CFR 350)	RATING	PAGE OF OF

2. CONTRACT NO.	3. AWARD/EFFECTIVE DATE	4. SOLICITATION NUMBER	5. SOLICITATION TYPE	6. SOLICITATION ISSUE DATE
			☐ SEALED BIDS (IFB) ☐ NEGOTIATED (RFP)	

7. ISSUED BY CODE

8. THIS ACQUISITION IS

☐ UNRESTRICTED

☐ SET ASIDE: ____ % FOR

☐ SMALL BUSINESS

SIC: ____ SIZE STANDARD: ____

☐ LABOR SURPLUS AREA CONCERNS

☐ COMBINED SMALL BUSINESS & LABOR SURPLUS AREA CONCERNS

☐ OTHER

NO COLLECT CALLS

9. (AGENCY USE)

10. ITEMS TO BE PURCHASED *(BRIEF DESCRIPTION)*

☐ SUPPLIES   ☐ SERVICES

11. IF OFFER IS ACCEPTED BY THE GOVERNMENT WITHIN ____ CALENDAR DAYS (60 CALENDAR DAYS UNLESS OFFEROR INSERTS A DIFFERENT PERIOD) FROM THE DATE SET FORTH IN BLK 9 ABOVE, THE CONTRACTOR AGREES TO HOLD ITS OFFERED PRICES FIRM FOR THE ITEMS SOLICITED HEREIN AND TO ACCEPT ANY RESULTING CONTRACT SUBJECT TO THE TERMS AND CONDITIONS STATED HEREIN.

12. ADMINISTERED BY CODE

13. CONTRACTOR OFFEROR CODE ____ FACILITY CODE ____

14. PAYMENT WILL BE MADE BY CODE

TELEPHONE NO. ____ DUNS NO. ____

☐ CHECK IF REMITTANCE IS DIFFERENT AND PUT SUCH ADDRESS IN OFFER

SUBMIT INVOICES TO ADDRESS SHOWN IN BLOCK:

15. PROMPT PAYMENT DISCOUNT

16. AUTHORITY FOR USING OTHER THAN FULL AND OPEN COMPETITION ☐ 10 U.S.C. 2304 ( ) ☐ 41 U.S.C. 253 ( )

17. ITEM NO.	18. SCHEDULE OF SUPPLIES/SERVICES	19. QUANTITY	20. UNIT	21. UNIT PRICE	22. AMOUNT

23. ACCOUNTING AND APPROPRIATION DATA

24. TOTAL AWARD AMOUNT (FOR GOVT. USE ONLY)

☐ **25. CONTRACTOR IS REQUIRED TO SIGN THIS DOCUMENT AND RETURN ____ COPIES TO ISSUING OFFICE. CONTRACTOR AGREES TO FURNISH AND DELIVER ALL ITEMS SET FORTH OR OTHERWISE IDENTIFIED ABOVE AND ON ANY CONTINUATION SHEETS SUBJECT TO THE TERMS AND CONDITIONS SPECIFIED HEREIN.**

☐ **26. AWARD OF CONTRACT: YOUR OFFER ON SOLICITATION NUMBER SHOWN IN BLOCK 4 INCLUDING ANY ADDITIONS OR CHANGES WHICH ARE SET FORTH HEREIN, IS ACCEPTED AS TO ITEMS:**

27. SIGNATURE OF OFFEROR/CONTRACTOR	28. UNITED STATES OF AMERICA *(SIGNATURE OF CONTRACTING OFFICER)*
NAME AND TITLE OF SIGNER *(TYPE OR PRINT)*	DATE SIGNED	NAME OF CONTRACTING OFFICER	DATE SIGNED

NSN 7540-01-218-4386

STANDARD FORM 1447 (5-88)
Prescribed by GSA - FAR (48 CFR) 53.215-1(g)

Standard Form 1447 (page 2)

NO RESPONSE FOR REASONS CHECKED	
CANNOT COMPLY WITH SPECIFICATIONS	CANNOT MEET DELIVERY REQUIREMENT
UNABLE TO IDENTIFY THE ITEM(S)	DO NOT REGULARLY MANFACTURE OR SELL THE TYPE OF ITEMS INVOLVED
OTHER (Specify)	

WE DO | WE DO NOT, DESIRE TO BE RETAINED ON THE MAILING LIST FOR FUTURE PROCUREMENT OF THE TYPE OF ITEM(S) INVOLVED

NAME AND ADDRESS OF FIRM (Include ZIP Code)

SIGNATURE

TYPE OR PRINT NAME AND TITLE OF SIGNER

FROM:

AFIX
STAMP
HERE

TO:

SOLICITATION NO. _____

DATE AND LOCAL TIME _____

STANDARD FORM 1447 (5-88) BACK

Standard Form 1449 (page 1)

SOLICITATION/CONTRACT/ORDER FOR COMMERCIAL ITEMS *OFFEROR TO COMPLETE BLOCKS 12, 17, 23, 24, & 30*	1. REQUISITION NUMBER	PAGE 1 OF

2. CONTRACT NO.	3. AWARD/EFFECTIVE DATE	4. ORDER NUMBER	5. SOLICITATION NUMBER	6. SOLICITATION ISSUE DATE

7. FOR SOLICITATION INFORMATION CALL: ▶	a. NAME	b. TELEPHONE NUMBER *(No collect calls)*	8. OFFER DUE DATE/ LOCAL TIME

9. ISSUED BY CODE	10. THIS ACQUISITON IS	11. DELIVERY FOR FOB DESTINATION UNLESS BLOCK IS MARKED	12. DISCOUNT TERMS

10. THIS ACQUISITON IS
☐ UNRESTRICTED
☐ SET ASIDE: % FOR
☐ SMALL BUSINESS
☐ HUBZONE SMALL BUSINESS
☐ 8(A)
NAICS:
SIZE STANDARD:

11. DELIVERY FOR FOB DESTINATION UNLESS BLOCK IS MARKED
☐ SEE SCHEDULE

☐ 13a. THIS CONTRACT IS A RATED ORDER UNDER DPAS (15 CFR 700)
13b. RATING

14. METHOD OF SOLICITATION
☐ RFQ   ☐ IFB   ☐ RFP

15. DELIVER TO CODE	16. ADMINISTERED BY CODE

17a. CONTRACTOR/ OFFEROR CODE FACILITY CODE	18a. PAYMENT WILL BE MADE BY CODE

TELEPHONE NO.

☐ 17b. CHECK IF REMITTANCE IS DIFFERENT AND PUT SUCH ADDRESS IN OFFER

18b. SUBMIT INVOICES TO ADDRESS SHOWN IN BLOCK 18a UNLESS BLOCK BELOW IS CHECKED ☐ SEE ADDENDUM

19. ITEM NO.	20. SCHEDULE OF SUPPLIES/SERVICES	21. QUANTITY	22. UNIT	23. UNIT PRICE	24. AMOUNT

(Use Reverse and/or Attach Additional Sheets as Necessary)

25. ACCOUNTING AND APPROPRIATION DATA	26. TOTAL AWARD AMOUNT *(For Govt. Use Only)*

☐ 27a. SOLICITATION INCORPORATES BY REFERENCE FAR 52.212-1, 52.212-4. FAR 52.212-3 AND 52.212-5 ARE ATTACHED. ADDENDA ☐ ARE ☐ ARE NOT ATTACHED

☐ 27b. CONTRACT/PURCHASE ORDER INCORPORATES BY REFERENCE FAR 52.212-4. FAR 52.212-5 IS ATTACHED. ADDENDA ☐ ARE ☐ ARE NOT ATTACHED

28. CONTRACTOR IS REQUIRED TO SIGN THIS DOCUMENT AND RETURN _____ COPIES TO ISSUING OFFICE. CONTRACTOR AGREES TO FURNISH AND DELIVER ALL ITEMS SET FORTH OR OTHERWISE IDENTIFIED ABOVE AND ON ANY ADDITIONAL SHEETS SUBJECT TO THE TERMS AND CONDITIONS SPECIFIED HEREIN.

29. AWARD OF CONTRACT: REF. _____ OFFER DATED _____ . YOUR OFFER ON SOLICITATION (BLOCK 5), INCLUDING ANY ADDITIONS OR CHANGES WHICH ARE SET FORTH HEREIN, IS ACCEPTED AS TO ITEMS:

30a. SIGNATURE OF OFFEROR/CONTRACTOR	31a. UNITED STATES OF AMERICA *(SIGNATURE OF CONTRACTING OFFICER)*

30b. NAME AND TITLE OF SIGNER *(Type or print)*	30c. DATE SIGNED	31b. NAME OF CONTRACTING OFFICER *(Type or print)*	31c. DATE SIGNED

AUTHORIZED FOR LOCAL REPRODUCTION
PREVIOUS EDITION IS NOT USABLE

STANDARD FORM 1449 (REV. 4/2002)
Prescribed by GSA - FAR (48 CFR) 53.212

Standard Form 1449 (page 2)

19. ITEM NO.	20. SCHEDULE OF SUPPLIES/SERVICES	21. QUANTITY	22. UNIT	23. UNIT PRICE	24. AMOUNT

32a. QUANTITY IN COLUMN 21 HAS BEEN

☐ RECEIVED ☐ INSPECTED ☐ ACCEPTED, AND CONFORMS TO THE CONTRACT, EXCEPT AS NOTED: _____

32b. SIGNATURE OF AUTHORIZED GOVERNMENT REPRESENTATIVE	32c. DATE	32d. PRINTED NAME AND TITLE OF AUTHORIZED GOVERNMENT REPRESENTATIVE

32e. MAILING ADDRESS OF AUTHORIZED GOVERNMENT REPRESENTATIVE	32f. TELPHONE NUMBER OF AUTHORZED GOVERNMENT REPRESENTATIVE
	32g. E-MAIL OF AUTHORIZED GOVERNMENT REPRESENTATIVE

33. SHIP NUMBER	34. VOUCHER NUMBER	35. AMOUNT VERIFIED CORRECT FOR	36. PAYMENT	37. CHECK NUMBER
☐ PARTIAL ☐ FINAL			☐ COMPLETE ☐ PARTIAL ☐ FINAL	
38. S/R ACCOUNT NUMBER	39. S/R VOUCHER NUMBER	40. PAID BY		

41a. I CERTIFY THIS ACCOUNT IS CORRECT AND PROPER FOR PAYMENT		42a. RECEIVED BY *(Print)*
41b. SIGNATURE AND TITLE OF CERTIFYING OFFICER	41c. DATE	
		42b. RECEIVED AT *(Location)*
		42c. DATE REC'D *(YY/MM/DD)* 42d. TOTAL CONTAINERS

STANDARD FORM 1449 (REV. 4/2002) BACK

DD Form 250

MATERIAL INSPECTION AND RECEIVING REPORT	Form Approved OMB No. 0704-0248

The public reporting burden for this collection of information is estimated to average 30 minutes per response, including the time for reviewing instructions, searching existing data sources, gathering and maintaining the data needed, and completing and reviewing the collection of information. Send comments regarding this burden estimate or any other aspect of the collection of information, including suggestions for reducing the burden, to Department of Defense, Washington Headquarters Services, Directorate for Information Operations and Reports (0704-0248), 1215 Jefferson Davis Highway, Suite 1204, Arlington, VA 22202-4302. Respondents should be aware that notwithstanding any other provision of law, no person shall be subject to any penalty for failing to comply with a collection of information if it does not display a currently valid OMB control number.

PLEASE DO NOT RETURN YOUR COMPLETED FORM TO THE ABOVE ADDRESS.
SEND THIS FORM IN ACCORDANCE WITH THE INSTRUCTIONS CONTAINED IN THE DFARS, APPENDIX F-401.

1. PROCUREMENT INSTRUMENT IDENTIFICATION (CONTRACT) NO.	ORDER NO.	6. INVOICE NO./DATE	7. PAGE	OF	8. ACCEPTANCE POINT

2. SHIPMENT NO.	3. DATE SHIPPED	4. B/L TCN		5. DISCOUNT TERMS

9. PRIME CONTRACTOR CODE	10. ADMINISTERED BY CODE

11. SHIPPED FROM (If other than 9) CODE	FOB:	12. PAYMENT WILL BE MADE BY CODE

13. SHIPPED TO CODE	14. MARKED FOR CODE

15. ITEM NO.	16. STOCK/PART NO. DESCRIPTION (Indicate number of shipping containers - type of container - container number.)	17. QUANTITY SHIP/REC'D*	18. UNIT	19. UNIT PRICE	20. AMOUNT

21. CONTRACT QUALITY ASSURANCE

a. ORIGIN

☐ CQA ☐ ACCEPTANCE of listed items has been made by me or under my supervision and they conform to contract, except as noted herein or on supporting documents.

DATE	SIGNATURE OF AUTHORIZED GOVERNMENT REPRESENTATIVE

TYPED NAME:

TITLE:

MAILING ADDRESS:

COMMERCIAL TELEPHONE NUMBER:

b. DESTINATION

☐ CQA ☐ ACCEPTANCE of listed items has been made by me or under my supervision and they conform to contract, except as noted herein or on supporting documents.

DATE	SIGNATURE OF AUTHORIZED GOVERNMENT REPRESENTATIVE

TYPED NAME:

TITLE:

MAILING ADDRESS:

COMMERCIAL TELEPHONE NUMBER:

22. RECEIVER'S USE

Quantities shown in column 17 were received in apparent good condition except as noted.

DATE RECEIVED	SIGNATURE OF AUTHORIZED GOVERNMENT REPRESENTATIVE

TYPED NAME:

TITLE:

MAILING ADDRESS:

COMMERCIAL TELEPHONE NUMBER:

* If quantity received by the Government is the same as quantity shipped, indicate by (X) mark; if different, enter actual quantity received below quantity shipped and encircle.

23. CONTRACTOR USE ONLY

DD FORM 250, AUG 2000   PREVIOUS EDITION IS OBSOLETE. | Reset |

DD Form 1707 (page 1)

INFORMATION TO OFFERORS OR QUOTERS SECTION A – COVER SHEET		Form Approved OMB No. 9000-0002 Expires Oct 31, 2004

The public reporting burden for this collection of information is estimated to average 30 minutes per response, including the time for reviewing instructions, searching existing data sources, gathering and maintaining the data needed, and completing and reviewing the collection of information. Send comments regarding this burden estimate or any other aspect of this collection of information, including suggestions for reducing the burden, to Department of Defense, Washington Headquarters Services, Directorate for Information Operations and Reports (9000-0002), 1215 Jefferson Davis Highway, Suite 1204, Arlington, VA 22202-4302. Respondents should be aware that notwithstanding any other provision of law, no person will be subject to any penalty for failing to comply with a collection of information if it does not display a currently valid OMB control number.
PLEASE DO NOT RETURN YOUR FORM TO THE ABOVE ADDRESS. RETURN COMPLETED FORM TO THE ADDRESS IN BLOCK 4 BELOW.

1. SOLICITATION NUMBER SP0600-03-R-0114	2. *(X one)* ☐ a. INVITATION FOR BID (IFB) ☒ b. REQUEST FOR PROPOSAL (RFP) ☐ c. REQUEST FOR QUOTATION (RFQ)	3. DATE/TIME RESPONSE DUE 25 November 2002/3:00 PM Eastern Standard Time

INSTRUCTIONS

NOTE: The provision entitled "Required Central Contractor Registration" applies to most solicitations.
1. If you are not submitting a response, complete the information in Blocks 9 through 11 and return to the issuing office in Block 4 unless a different return address is indicated in Block 7.
2. Offerors or quoters must include full, accurate, and complete information in their responses as required by this solicitation (including attachments). "Fill-ins" are provided on Standard Form 18, Standard Form 33, and other solicitation documents. Examine the entire solicitation carefully. The penalty for making false statements is prescribed in 18 U.S.C. 1001.
3. Offerors or quoters must plainly mark their responses with the Solicitation Number and the date and local time for bid opening or receipt of proposals that is in the solicitation document.
4. Information regarding the timeliness of response is addressed in the provision of this solicitation entitled either "Late Submissions, Modifications, and Withdrawals of Bids," or "Instructions to Offerors – Competitive Acquisition."

4. ISSUING OFFICE *(Complete mailing address, including ZIP Code)* SEE BLOCK 8B	5. ITEMS TO BE PURCHASED *(Brief description)*		
	Marine Gas Oil	NSN: 9140-01-313-7776	31,668,300 GL
	Fuel Oil, Intermediate 180	NSN: 9140-01-271-5280	1,043,000 GL
	Fuel Oil, Intermediate 380	NSN: 9140-01-235-2832	2,482,000 GL
	DIESEL FUEL, GRADE #2	NSN: 9140-01-456-9443	1,410,000 GL

6. PROCUREMENT INFORMATION *(X and complete as applicable.)*

☒	a. THIS PROCUREMENT IS UNRESTRICTED.
☐	b. THIS PROCUREMENT IS _____ % SET-ASIDE FOR SMALL BUSINESS. THE APPLICABLE NAICS CODE IS:
☐	c. THIS PROCUREMENT IS _____ % SET-ASIDE FOR HUB ZONE CONCERNS. THE APPLICABLE NAICS CODE IS:
☐	d. THIS PROCUREMENT IS RESTRICTED TO FIRMS ELIGIBLE UNDER SECTION 8(a) OF THE SMALL BUSINESS ACT.

7. ADDITIONAL INFORMATION:
THE NOTES ON THIS DD FORM 1707 PROVIDE INFORMATION THAT WARRANT YOUR SPECIAL ATTENTION PRIOR TO PREPARATION OF YOUR PROPOSAL. ADDRESS YOUR PROPOSAL TO:

ATTN: BID CUSTODIAN
DESC-CPC ROOM 3815
8725 JOHN J. KINGMAN RD. SUITE 4950
FORT BELVOIR, VA 22060-6222

8. POINT OF CONTACT FOR INFORMATION

a. NAME *(Last, First, Middle Initial)* ARMSTRONG, GARRELL L.	b. ADDRESS *(Include ZIP Code)* DESC-PHB ROOM 3815 8725 JOHN J. KINGMAN RD. SUITE 4950 FORT BELVOIR, VA 22060-6222
c. TELEPHONE NUMBER *(Include Area Code and Extension)* -703-767-8457	d. E-MAIL ADDRESS garmstrong@desc.dla.mil

9. REASONS FOR NO RESPONSE *(X all that apply)*

☐ a. CANNOT COMPLY WITH SPECIFICATIONS ☐ b. UNABLE TO IDENTIFY THE ITEMS(S) ☐ c. CANNOT MEET DELIVERY REQUIREMENT	☐ d. DO NOT REGULARLY MANUFACTURE OR SELL THE TYPE OF ITEMS INVOLVED ☐ e. OTHER

10. MAILING LIST INFORMATION *(X one)*
WE ☐ DO ☐ DO NOT DESIRE TO BE RETAINED ON THE MAILING LIST FOR FUTURE PROCUREMENT OF THE TYPE INVOLVED.

11a. COMPANY NAME	b. ADDRESS
c. ACTION OFFICER	
(1) TYPED OR PRINTED NAME *(Last, First, Middle Initial)*	(2) TITLE
(3) SIGNATURE	(4) DATE SIGNED *(YYYYMMDD)*

DD FORM 1707, FEB 2002   PREVIOUS EDITION IS OBSOLETE.

CCR Worksheet (page 1)

Central Contractor Registration Worksheet

You may use this CCR Worksheet to collect the information required to register in CCR, then go to www.ccr.gov to register.

(M) = Mandatory field. Data must be entered for registration to be complete.

General Information

DUNS Number[1] **(M)**:_____CAGE Code[2] **(M)** if foreign:_____

Legal Business Name **(M)**:_____

Doing Business As:_____

Tax ID[3] **(M)**:_____ **OR** Social Security Number:_____

Division Name:_____ Division Number:_____

Corporate Web Page URL (Company website address): _____

Physical Address **(M)**:_____

City **(M)**:_____State **(M)**:_____Zip/Postal Code **(M)**:_____

Country **(M)**:_____

Mailing Address **(M)**:☐ Check if same as physical address

Business Name:_____

Mailing Address (PO Box is acceptable):_____

City:_____State:_____Zip/Postal Code:_____

Country:_____

Business Start Date **(M)**(mm/dd/yyyy):_____Number of Employees **(M)**:_____

Fiscal Year Close Date **(M)** (mm/dd):_____   Annual Revenue **(M)**:_____

Type of Organization (M):
☐ Corporate Entity (Not Tax Exempt)   ☐ Corporate Entity (Tax Exempt)

State of Incorporation:_____ or Country (if other than US):_____

☐ Sole Proprietorship   ☐ Partnership   ☐ U.S. Government Entity
                                                     ☐ Federal ☐ State ☐ Local

☐ Foreign Government   ☐ International Organization   ☐ Other

---

1   Data Universal Numbering System (DUNS)– Call Dun & Bradstreet at 1-800-333-0505 or 1-610-882-7000 if unsure.
2   Commercial and Government Entity (CAGE) Code – If you do not have a CAGE Code, one will be assigned to you, call DLIS – Defense Logistics Information Services at 1-888-352-9333 Option 3 if unsure, or check CAGE search web http://www.dlis.dla.mil/cage_welcome.asp
3   Taxpayer Identification Number (TIN) – Call the IRS at 1-800-829-1040 if unsure. The TIN may be used by the Government to collect and report on any delinquent amounts arising out of the offeror's relationship with the Government (31 U.S.C. 7701 (c) (3)).

Page 1 of 5
07/22/2002   CCR Registration Worksheet

CCR Worksheet (page 2)

Owner Information (M) if Sole Proprietorship:

Name:_____

U.S. Phone:_____ Ext.:_____

Non U.S. Phone:_____ Ext.:_____

Fax (U.S. Only):_____

Email:_____

Business Type(s) (M) Check all that apply:

- ☐ 8(a) Program Participant
- ☐ American Indian Owned
- ☐ Hub Zone Business
- ☐ Minority Owned Business (Must choose one below):
  - ☐ Subcontinent Asian (Asian-Indian) American
  - ☐ Asian-Pacific American
  - ☐ Black American
  - ☐ Hispanic American
  - ☐ Native American
  - ☐ No Representation/None of the above
- ☐ Large Business
- ☐ Small Business
- ☐ Small Disadvantaged Business
- ☐ Woman Owned Business
- ☐ Veteran Owned Business
- ☐ Service Disabled Veteran Owned

- ☐ Construction Firm
- ☐ Educational Institution
- ☐ Emerging Small Business
- ☐ Foreign Supplier
- ☐ Historically Black College/Univ.
- ☐ Labor Surplus Area Firm
- ☐ Limited Liability Company
- ☐ Manufacturer of Goods
- ☐ Minority Institution
- ☐ Municipality
- ☐ Nonprofit Institution
- ☐ Research Institute
- ☐ S Corporation
- ☐ Service Location
- ☐ Sheltered Workshop (JWOD)
- ☐ Tribal Government

Party Performing Certification (M) if approved for 8a certification through the Small Business Administration (SBA)

Certifier's Name: _____

Address: _____

City: _____ State: _____ Zip/Postal Code: _____

Country: _____

Goods and Services:

NAICS Codes (M) North American Industrial Classification Code to identify what product or service your business provides (6 digit numeric). Search on
http://www.census.gov/epcd/www/naicstab.htm

NAICS Code:_____ NAICS Code:_____ NAICS Code: _____

NAICS Code:_____ NAICS Code:_____ NAICS Code:_____

07/22/2002

CCR Worksheet (page 3)

SIC Codes (M) Standard Industrial Classification Codes identify what type of activity your business performs (4 or 8 digit numeric). Search on http://www.osha.gov/oshstats/sicser.html

SIC Code:_____ SIC Code:_____ SIC Code: _____

SIC Code:_____ SIC Code:_____ SIC Code:_____

Financial Information:
EFT –Electronic Funds Transfer Information
Financial Institution Name: _____
(Bank name for Electronic Funds Transfer)   (If Non-US business, EFT is optional)

ABA Routing Number **(M)** (9digits):_____

Must indicate type of account **(M)**

Account Number **(M)**:_____ ☐ Checking OR ☐ Savings

Lockbox Number:_____

Automated Clearing House (ACH=Bank) **(M)** at least one method of contact must be entered

ACH U.S. Phone Number:_____

ACH Fax (U.S. Only):_____

ACH Non-U.S. Phone:_____

ACH Email:_____

Remittance Address (M): (what is the "Remit to" name and address on your invoice/bill?)

Business Name **(M)**:_____

Address **(M)**:_____ _____

City **(M)**:_____ State **(M)**: _____ Zip/Postal Code **(M)**: _____

Country **(M)**:_____

Accounts Receivable Contact (M):

Name **(M)**:_____

Email **(M)**:_____

U.S. Phone **(M)**:_____ Ext.:_____

Non U.S. Phone:_____ Ext.:_____

Fax (U.S. Only):_____
Do you (the Registrant) use or accept Credit Cards   ☐ Yes   ☐ No
as a method of Purchase or Payment? **(M)**.

CCR Worksheet (page 4)

Registration Acknowledgement and Point of Contact Information:

Note: The Registrant acknowledges that the information provided is current, accurate, and complete.

CCR Point of Contact (M)

Name:_____

Email:_____

U.S. Phone:_____Ext.:_____

Non U.S. Phone:_____Ext.:_____

Fax (U.S. Only):_____

CCR Alternate Point of Contact (M)

Name:_____

Email :_____

U.S. Phone:_____Ext.:_____

Non U.S. Phone:_____ Ext.:_____

Fax (U.S. Only):_____

For the following POCs, may identify two persons for each category

Government Business Point of Contact (If name is entered, all fields are mandatory

Name:_____

Email:_____

Address:_____

City:_____ State:_____ Zip Code:_____

U.S. Phone:_____Ext.:_____

Non U.S. Phone:_____Ext.:_____

Fax (U.S. Only):_____

E-Business Point of Contact (If name is entered, all fields are mandatory)

Name:_____

Email:_____

Address:_____

07/22/2002

Page 4 of 5
CCR Registration Worksheet

CCR Worksheet (page 5)

City: _____ State: _____ Zip Code: _____

U.S. Phone: _____ Ext.: _____

Non U.S. Phone: _____ Ext.: _____

Fax (U.S. Only): _____

Past Performance Point of Contact (If name is entered, all fields are mandatory)(PPAIS)

Name: _____

Email: _____

Address: _____

City: _____ State: _____ Zip Code: _____

U.S. Phone: _____ Ext.: _____

Non U.S. Phone: _____ Ext.: _____

Fax (U.S. Only): _____

Marketing Partner ID (MPIN) _____
(Used in PPAIS and TEDS systems) (Must be 9 alphanumeric, no spaces, no symbols.)
MPIN is Mandatory if entering Past Performance POC.

You may enter your registration directly on the web at **www.ccr.gov**

Read the CCR Handbook **http://www.ccr.gov/handbook.cfm** for further information.

E-mail address CCR@dlis.dla.mil

For registration assistance call 1-888-227-2423 or 1-616-961-4725

07/22/2002

Page 5 of 5
CCR Registration Worksheet

Numbered Notes Used on FedBizOpps

One of the main ways that you can find out about contracting opportunities is to religiously review the FedBizOpps web site (http://www.fedbizopps.gov). FedBizOpps lists notices of proposed government procurement actions, contract awards, and other procurement information.

When you read a notice in FedBizOpps, you will often see reference to numbered notes within the text. (For example, you may see such phrases as "Notes 12 and 26 apply" or "See Note(s) 22 and 23.") The purpose of these numbered notes, which are similar to footnotes, is to avoid the unnecessary repetition of information that appears in various announcements. Whenever a numbered note is included in a notice, the note referred to must be read as part of the item or section in which it appears.

Following is a list of numbered notes and their meaning.

Numbered Notes

1. The proposed contract is 100 percent set aside for small business concerns.

2. A portion of the acquisition is set aside for small business concerns.

3. The proposed contract is a labor surplus area set-aside. (This note is deleted as of 7/21/99.)

4. The proposed contract is 100 percent set aside for small disadvantaged business concerns (SDB). Offers from concerns other than SDBs will not be considered. (This note is deleted as of 11/24/99.)

5. The proposed contract is 100 percent set aside for Historically Black Colleges and Universities (HBCUs) and Minority Institutions (MIs). Offers from other than HBCUs and MIs will not be considered.

6. The proposed contract is a total small disadvantaged business set aside or is being considered as a total small disadvantaged business set aside. (This note is deleted as of 11/24/99.)

7. The proposed contract is 100 percent set aside for Historically Black Colleges, Universities and Minority Institutions or is partially set aside for Historically Black Colleges, Universities and Minority Institutions.

8. The solicitation document contains information that has been designated as "Militarily Critical Technical Data." Only businesses that have been certified by the Department of Defense, United States/Canada Joint Certification Office, and have a valid requirement may have a copy of the solicitation document. All requests for copies of the solicitation document must include a certified copy of DD Form 2345, Militarily Critical Technical Data Agreement. To obtain certification, contact: Commander, Defense Logistics Information Service (DLIS), ATTN: U.S./Canada Joint Certification Office, 74 Washington Avenue North, Battle Creek, MI 49017-3084 or call the DLIS at (800)-352-3572. The DLIS Unites States/Canada Joint Certification Lookup service is available via the Internet at: http://www.dlis.dla.mil/ccal/.

9. Interested parties may obtain copies of Military and Federal Specifications and Standards, Qualified Product Lists, Military Handbooks, and other standardization documents from the DoD Single Stock Point (DODSSP), in Philadelphia, PA. Most documents are available in Adobe PDF format from the ASSIST database via the Internet at http://assist.daps.mil.

Users may search for documents using the ASSIST-Quick Search and, in most cases, download the documents directly via the Internet using standard browser software.

Documents not available for downloading from ASSIST can be ordered from the DODSSP using the ASSIST Shopping Wizard, after establishing a DODSSP Customer Account by following the registration procedures or by phoning the DoDSSP Special Assistance Desk at (215) 697-2179 (DSN: 442-2179).

Users not having access to the Internet may contact the DODSSP Special Assistance Desk at (215) 697-2179 (DSN:

442-2179) or mail requests to the DODSSP, Bldg. 4/D, 700 Robbins Avenue, Philadelphia, PA 19111-5094. Patterns, Drawings, Deviations Lists, Purchase Descriptions, etc., are not stocked at the DODSSP.

10. Reserved.

11. Reserved

12. One or more of the items under this acquisition may be subject to an Agreement on Government Procurement approved and implemented in the United States by the Trade Agreements Act of 1979. All offers shall be in the English language and in U.S. dollars. All interested suppliers may submit an offer.

13. The proposed contract is restricted to domestic sources under the authority of FAR 6.302-3. Accordingly, foreign sources, except Canadian sources, are not eligible for award.

14. Reserved

15. Reserved

16. Reserved

17. Reserved

18. Reserved

19. Reserved

20. Reserved

21. Reserved

22. The proposed contract action is for supplies or services for which the Government intends to solicit and negotiate with only one source under the authority of FAR 6.302. Interested persons may identify their interest and capability to respond to the requirement or submit proposals. This notice of intent is not a request for competitive proposals. However, all proposals received within forty-five days (thirty days if award is issued under an existing basic ordering agreement) after date of publication of this synopsis will be considered by the Government. A determination by the Government not to compete with this proposed contract based upon responses to this notice is solely within the discretion of the Government. Information received will normally be considered solely for the purpose of determining whether to conduct a competitive procurement.

23. Award will be made only if the offeror, the product/service or the manufacturer meets qualification requirement at time

of award, in accordance with FAR clause 52.209-1 or 52.209-2. The solicitation identifies the office where additional information can be obtained concerning qualification requirements and is cited in each individual solicitation.

24. Architect-Engineer firms which meet the requirements described in this announcement are invited to submit: (1) a Standard Form 254, Architect-Engineer and Related Services Questionnaire, (2) a Standard Form 255, Architect-Engineer and Related Services Questionnaire for Specific Project, when requested, and (3) any requested supplemental data to the procurement office shown. Firms having a current Standard Form 254 on file with the procurement office shown are not required to register this form. Firms desiring to register for consideration for future projects administered by the procurement office (subject to specific requirements for individual projects) are encouraged to submit annually, a statement of qualifications and performance data, utilizing Standard Form 254, Architect-Engineer and Related Services Questionnaire. Firms responding to this announcement before the closing date will be considered for selection, subject to any limitations indicated with respect to size and geographic location of firm, specialized technical expertise or other requirements listed. Following an initial evaluation of the qualification and performance data submitted, three or more firms that are considered to be the most highly qualified to provide the type of services required, will be chosen for negotiation. Selection of firms for negotiation shall be made through an order of preference based on demonstrated competence and qualifications necessary for the satisfactory performance of the type of professional services required, that include: (1) professional capabilities; (2) specialized experience and technical competence, as required; (3) capacity to accomplish the work in the required time; (4) past performance on contracts with respect to cost control, quality of work, and compliance with performance schedules; (5) geographical location and knowledge of the locality of the project, provided that application of the criterion leaves an appropriate number of qualified firms, given the nature and size of the project; (6) any other special qualification required under this announcement by the contracting activity. In addition to the above qualifications, special qualifications in the Department of Defense include the volume of work previously awarded to the firm by the Department of Defense, with the object of effecting an equitable distribution of Department of Defense architect engineer contracts among qualified architect-engineer firms including small and small disadvantaged business firms, and firms that have not had prior Department of Defense contracts.

25. Information submitted should be pertinent and specific in the technical area under consideration, on each of the following qualifications: (1) Experience: An outline of previous projects, specific work previously performed or being performed and any in-house research and development effort; (2) Personnel: Name, professional qualifications and specific experience of scientist, engineers and technical personnel who may be assigned as a principal investigator and/or project officer; (3) Facilities: Availability and description of special facilities required to perform in the technical areas under consideration. A statement regarding industry security clearance. Any other specific and pertinent information as pertains to this particular area of procurement that would enhance our consideration and evaluation of the information submitted.

26. Based upon market research, the Government is not using the policies contained in Part 12, Acquisition of Commercial Items, in its solicitation for the described supplies or services. However, interested persons may identify to the contracting officer their interest and capability to satisfy the Government's requirement with a commercial item within 15 days of this notice.

27. The proposed contract is set aside for HUBZone small business concerns. Offers from other than HUBZone small business concerns will not be considered.

28. The proposed contract is set-aside for Very Small Business Concerns (VSB). A VSB is a small business concern whose headquarters is located within the geographic area served by a district designated by SBA; and which, together with its affiliates, has no more than 15 employees and has average annual receipts that do not exceed $1 million. Offers from other than very small business concerns will not be considered.

Sample Documents

Following is a collection of sample documents you can use to help draft similar, more personalized versions for your business when participating in the federal procurement process.

Sample Non-Disclosure Agreement

SAMPLE NON-DISCLOSURE AGREEMENT

_____, ("COMPANY") and

_____, ("RECIPIENT") agree:

_____ and its designees may from time to time disclose to RECIPIENT certain confidential information or trade secrets generally regarding:

_____

_____

RECIPIENT agrees that RECIPIENT shall not disclose the information so conveyed, unless in conformity with this agreement, and shall protect the same from disclosure with reasonable diligence.

As to all information which COMPANY claims is confidential, RECIPIENT shall reduce the same to writing prior to disclosure and shall conspicuously mark the same as "confidential," "not to be disclosed" or with other clear indication of its status. If the information which COMPANY is disclosing is not in written form, for example, a machine or device, shall be required prior to or at the same time that the disclosure is made to provide written notice of the secrecy claimed by . agrees upon reasonable notice to return the confidential tangible material provided by it by upon reasonable request.

The obligation of non-disclosure shall terminate when if any of the following occurs:

(a) The confidential information becomes known to the public without the fault of RECIPIENT , or;

(b) The information is disclosed publicly by COMPANY , or ;

(c) a period of 60 months passes from the disclosure, or;

(d) the information loses its status as confidential through no fault of RECIPIENT.

In any event, the obligation of non-disclosure shall not apply to information which was known to prior to the execution of this agreement.

Dated: _____   Dated: _____

_____   _____

_____   _____
Printed Name   Printed Name

Sample Request for Quotation

REQUEST FOR QUOTATION (THIS IS NOT AN ORDER)				
DLA, DEFENSE SUPPLY CENTER COLUMBUS 3990 EAST BROAD STREET P.O. BOX 16704 COLUMBUS, OH 43216-5010				
REQUEST NO.	**DATE ISSUED**	**RETURN BY**	**DELIVER BY:**	**PURCHASE REQUEST NUMBER**
SP075000QA331	03/07/00	03/21/00	AWD DT + 90	YPC99347001065
BUYER CODE	**BUYER NAME**		**BUYER PHONE**	**BUYER FAX**
LDAC3	Julie Brill		(614) 692-1278	(614) 693-1574
NSN or Part Number			**Unit of Issue**	**Quantity**
2910-01-263-3224			EA	65
Rating	**FOB**		**Standard Industrial Classification Code**	**Small Business Size Standard**
DOA4	DESTINATION		3714	0

```
SEE CONTINUATION SHEETS TO COMPLETE QUOTE INFORMATION.
Quoters may respond:  (1) electronically via the DSCC Internet
Bid Board System (DIBBS) at http://dibbs.dsccols.com;  by
facsimile to the buyer's fax number, or (2) by hard copy via
mail or other physical delivery to the address listed above.
Quoter must also complete the following:

a.  Quotation is valid for 90 days from return quote date unless otherwise
    indicated:_____ .

b.  FOB Point _____  Destination
                _____  Origin        Shipping Point (City,State)_____

c.  If delivery period shown above is unacceptable, provide
    best possible delivery:  _____

d.  Quoter's CAGE Code:  _____
    Quoter's Address (Name, Street, City, State, ZIP):

        _____
        _____
        _____
        _____

e.  Remittance Address (Name, Street, City, State, ZIP):  applicable
    only if EFT does not apply.

        _____
        _____
        _____
        _____

f.  Vendor FAX Number:
    Vendor Telephone Number:
    Vendor E-Mail Number:
```

Sample Request for Quotation (page 2)

ITEM DESCRIPTION

```
NSN or Part Number: 2910-01-263-3224

TANK, FUEL, ENGINE
"CLASS I OZONE DEPLETING CHEMICALS ARE NOT TO BE
USED NOR INCORPORATED IN ANY ITEMS TO BE
DELIVERED UNDER THIS CONTRACT.  THIS PROHIBITION
SUPERSEDES ALL SPECIFICATION REQUIREMENTS BUT
DOES NOT ALLEVIATE ANY PRODUCT REQUIREMENTS.
SUBSTITUTE CHEMICALS MUST BE SUBMITTED FOR
APPROVAL UNLESS THEY ARE AUTHORIZED BY THE
SPECIFICATION REQUIREMENTS."
IF AQLS ARE LISTED IN THE SPECIFICATION(S)
OR DRAWING(S) THEY MAY BE USED TO ESTABLISH THE
AUTHORIZED SAMPLE SIZE, HOWEVER, THE ACCEPTANCE
NUMBER FOR THIS CONTRACT IS ZERO; I.E., THIS
CONTRACT REQUIRES A SAMPLING PLAN THAT ACCEPTS
ON ZERO DEFECTS AND REJECTS ON ONE OR MORE
DEFECT(S).
DLAD 52.246-9004, PRODUCT VERIFICATION TESTING,
APPLIES.  THIS CLAUSE IS A GOVERNMENT OPTION
THAT CAN ONLY BE INVOKED UPON THE COGNIZANT
CONTRACT ADMINISTRATION OFFICE NOTIFYING THE
CONTRACTOR THAT PVT SAMPLES ARE TO BE SELECTED.
I/A/W DWG NR 19207 12338583
REFNO DTD 01/22/86
AMEND NR  C DTD 10/16/90
"DETAILED DRAWING (ONE ITEM)"
I/A/W DWG NR 19207 12338588
BASIC DTD 07/29/86
AMEND NR  E DTD 10/07/92
"DETAILED DRAWING (ONE ITEM)"
I/A/W DWG NR 19207 12338588
REFNO DTD 08/18/87
AMEND NR  A DTD 09/26/90
SUPPLEMENTAL QUALITY ASSURANCE PROVISIONS
(SQAP) ALL TYPES.
I/A/W DWG NR 19207 12339975
REFNO DTD 07/23/86
"DETAILED DRAWING (ONE ITEM)"
```

LINE ITEM 0001

PURCHASE REQUEST	QUANTITY	UNIT OF ISSUE	UNIT PRICE
YPC99347001065	50	EA	

PACKAGING DATA

```
PREP FOR DELIVERY

    PKGING DATA - MIL-STD-2073-1C, 01 OCT 1996
    QUP = 001: PRES MTHD = AE: CLNG/DRY = 1: PRESV MAT = 00:
    WRAP MAT = XX: CUSH/DUNN MAT = XX: CUSH/DUNN THKNESS = X:
    UNIT CONT = D3: OPI = O:
    INTRMDTE CONT = YY: INTRMDTE CONT QTY = AAA:
    PACK CODE = U:
```

Sample Request for Quotation (page 3)

```
      MARKING SHALL BE IN ACCORDANCE WITH MIL-STD-129.
      SPECIAL MARKING CODE: 00 - NO SPECIAL MARKING.
      PALLETIZATION SHALL BE IN ACCORDANCE WITH DC1636P001 REV B
      DATED 99238
      SUPPLEMENTAL INSTRUCTIONS


      DOD BAR CODE MARKING REQUIRED IN ACCORDANCE WITH
      MIL-STD-129 (LATEST REVISION) MARKING AND BAR
      CODING IN ACCORDANCE WITH AIM BC1.
```

SHIPPING DATA

```
FREIGHT SHIPPING ADDRESS

SW3108
TRANSPORTATION OFFICER
DDSP - NEW CUMBERLAND FACILITY
BUILDING MISSION   DOOR 113-134
NEW CUMBERLAND PA     17070-5002

NON-MILSTRIP
RDD: 04/04/00
```

LINE ITEM 0002

PURCHASE REQUEST	QUANTITY	UNIT OF ISSUE	UNIT PRICE
YPC99347001065	15	EA	

PACKAGING DATA

```
PREP FOR DELIVERY

    PKGING DATA - MIL-STD-2073-1C, 01 OCT 1996
    MIL-STD-2073 PACKAGING DATA SAME AS PRIOR LINE
```

SHIPPING DATA

```
PARCEL POST ADDRESS

SW3200
DEF DIST DEPOT SAN JOAQUIN
SAN JOAQUIN   TRACY
PO BOX   96001
STOCKTON CA     95296-0130


FREIGHT SHIPPING ADDRESS

SW3200
DEF DIST DEPOT SAN JOAQUIN
SAN JOAQUIN   TRACY
25600 S CHRISMAN ROAD RECV WHS 10
TRACY CA     95376-5000

NON-MILSTRIP
```

Sample Request for Quotation (page 4)

```
RDD: 04/04/00
```

PROCUREMENT HISTORY FOR NSN: 2910012633224

TYPE	CAGE	CONTRACT NUMBER	QUANTITY	UNIT COST	AWD DATE
STK	32783	SP075000V0436	000040	360.00000	10/19/99
STK	9R012	SP075099M2671	000030	369.28000	09/07/99
STK	32783	SP075099M2486	000024	392.10000	04/30/99

APPLICABLE CLAUSES

All clauses and provisions listed within this individual
solicitation are contained in the DSCC Master Solicitation
(S9C/S9E) dated JUNE 1999. This document can be found at (
www.dscccols.com). Current changes to the aforementioned
Master Solicitation are contained within this solicitation and
will supersede any outdated information contained in the Master
Solicitation. The clauses/provisions incorporated by reference
have the same force and effect as if they were in full text;
however, those having no bearing on the instant acquisition
become self-deleting. In the event of an inconsistency between
the Master Solicitation and the individual solicitation, the
provision of the individual solicitation shall govern.
For Simplified Acquisitions (under $100,000) quoters may respond
electronically via the DSCC Internet Bid Board System (DIBBS) at
http://dibbs.dscccols.com or by facsimilie to the buyer's fax
number.

SECTION B

B02 -
QUANTITY BREAK (DLAD 52.213-9000) (MAR 1988)

B03 - DSCC WEB SITE
     The DSCC Master Solicitation is available on the Internet
via the DSCC Web Site at
http://dibbs.dscccols.com/Refs/ProvClauses/.
Also, the full text of FAR/DFARS/DLAD clauses incorporated by
reference may be accessed electronically at
http://www.procregs.hq.dla.mil/icps.htm .

B04 - ALTERNATE DISPUTE RESOLUTION (ADR)

B15 - ADVANCE NOTICE OF DELIVERY TO CONSIGNEES (OTHER THAN AIR
OR WATER TERMINALS (AUG 1985)

B30 - MANUFACTURER'S PART NUMBER
Prior to or at the time the offer is submitted, the contractor
shall inform the buyer if any discrepancy exists between the
physical/functional description and the specifications/drawings.
ALL OFFERS MUST PROVIDE THE FOLLOWING INFORMATION:
Offer based on:

Sample Request for Quotation (page 5)

```
Manufacturer's Name:

Manufacturer's P/N:

Actual Bare Item Part Number Marking:



SECTION C

C - Y2K
COMPLIANT NOTICE


SECTION D

D02a -
PACKAGING AND MARKING REQUIREMENTS (DSCC 52.246-9C41)
(AUG 1999)


D03 - PACKING LIST/INVOICE/SHIPPING DOCUMENTS (AUG 1999) (DSCC
52.211-9C17)


D07 - LABELS (AUG 1999) (DSCC 52.211-9C18)


D08 - SPECIAL HANDLING DATA/ACKNOWLEDGEMENT (AUG 1999)
(DSCC 52.211-9C20)


SECTION E

E01 -
CLAUSES INCORPORATED BY REFERENCE (FAR 52.252-2) (FEB
1998)


E02 - INSPECTION OF SUPPLIES-FIXED PRICE (FAR 52.246-2)
(AUG 1996)


E03 - INSPECTION AT ORIGIN (DSCC 52.246-9C01) (FEB 1993)
     (c)  Inspection Points:
            SUPPLIES
CLIN(s)
          ( )  Same as Offeror
          ( )  Other (CAGE, Name, Street Address, City,
            State and Zip Code)
          ( )


          ( )


            PACKAGING
CLIN(s)
          ( )  Same as Offeror
          ( )  Same as above
          ( )  Other (CAGE, Name, Street Address, City,
            State and Zip Code)
          ( )
```

Sample Request for Quotation (page 6)

```
           (  )



E04 - ACCEPTANCE AT ORIGIN (DSCC 52.246-9C02) (NOV 1995)


E06 - MATERIAL INSPECTION AND RECEIVING REPORT
(DFARS 252.246-7000) (DEC 1991)


E15 - CERTIFICATE OF CONFORMANCE (FAR 52.246-15)(APR 1984)


E18 - PRODUCT VERIFICATION TESTING (DLAD 52.246-9004) (AUG
1997)


E21 - WARRANTY - ACCEPTANCE OF SUPPLIES (DSCC 52.246-9C10)
(JUN 1989)


E23 - SUBSTITUTION OF ITEM AFTER AWARD (DSCC 52.246-9C13)
(JAN 1999)


E28 - DOCUMENTATION OF PART NUMBER CHANGE (DSCC 52.246-9C30)
(JUN 1997)
The offer certifies that the part number (P/N) requested in the
Request for Quotation (RFQ) has been changed from CAGE -
P/N                    to P/N                    and that this is
a part number change
only.
Reason for change is



E32 - RECORDS RETENTION REQUIREMENTS (DSCC 52.204-9C01)
(JUN 1980)


SECTION F

F01 -
SOLICITATION CLAUSES INCORPORATED BY REFERENCE
(FAR 52.252-2) (FEB 1998)


F05 - SHIPPING INSTRUCTIONS (DOMESTIC) (DSCC 52.247-9C02)
(JUN 1999)


F20 - REQUIRED DELIVERY WITH DELIVERY EVALUATION FACTOR
(DSCC 52.211-9C09)(OCT 1999)
     (a)  This clause applies to CLIN(s) ALL          .
The Government's intent is to meet the Required Delivery Schedule
at the best possible price.  Offers will be evaluated in
accordance with Provision M26, Delivery Evaluation Factor (DEF).
The Government requires delivery to be made according to the
following schedule:
          REQUIRED DELIVERY SCHEDULE
```

Sample Request for Quotation (page 7)

```
        (Contracting Officer to insert specific details)
ITEM NO.    QUANTITY    WITHIN DAYS AFTER DATE OF CONTRACT
ALL         65          90
```

It is intended to award without discussions regarding delivery; therefore, it is in the offeror's best interest to provide the best delivery. If the offeror proposes no other delivery schedule below, the Required Delivery Schedule will apply.

           OFFEROR'S PROPOSED DELIVERY SCHEDULE

```
ITEM NO.    QUANTITY    WITHIN DAYS AFTER DATE OF CONTRACT
```

(b) Application of the Delivery Evaluation Factor set forth below in (c) may result in award to other than the lowest priced acceptable offeror. (e.g., award to an offeror with a higher offered price and a better/shorter delivery schedule). The formula reflected below is used in DEF calculations and is for evaluation purposes only. This calculation is applied to each line (CLIN and subCLIN) for which an offer has been made. The total amount for each line (CLIN and subCLIN) is added together for each offer received.

[Total Offered Price per line x Evaluation Factor] x [Offered Delivery per line - Govt's Required Delivery] + Price Adjustment per line = Evaluated Offer per Line

(c) If a DEF award is made based on paying a DEF price differential and the delivery/ship date is made after the contract due date (CDD) because of a contractor-caused delay, the award price may be automatically reduced for late delivery using the Award Reduction Formula reflected below. In this circumstance, recoupment/consideration may also be required. When calculating the recoupment/consideration amount, the applicable DEF factor reflected in the solicitation will be used.

Unit Price x Evaluation Factor (See Clause F20a) x Delinquent Quantity x Number of Days Delinquent + Administrative Costs (when applicable)

Reductions may be up to, but not exceeding 25% of the total contract price or 150% of the price differential, whichever is greater, plus the administrative cost(s) of modifying the contract to provide for a revised delivery schedule.

(d) This clause does not affect or limit the Government's right under the Default Clause of this contract.

(e) Attention is directed to the contract award provision of the solicitation which provides that a written award or acceptance of an offer mailed or otherwise furnished to the successful offeror results in a binding contract. The Government will mail or otherwise furnish to the offeror an award or notice of award not later than the day the award is dated. Therefore, the offeror shall compute the time available for performance beginning with the award date on the contract, in lieu of the date the written notice of award is received from the Contracting Officer through the ordinary mails. The Government will evaluate an offer that proposes delivery based on the Contractor's date of receipt of the contract or notice of award by adding five days for delivery of the award through the ordinary mails.

Sample Request for Quotation (page 8)

NOTE: Unless otherwise specified in the individual solicitation or contract, ACCELERATED DELIVERY is acceptable and desired at no additional cost to the Government.

SECTION I

I01 -
CLAUSES INCORPORATED BY REFERENCE (FAR 52.252-2)
(FEB 1998)
The following changes have been made to the Master Solicitation:
FAR 52.223-2 Clean Air and Water (Deleted)
FAR 52.225-8 Duty-Free Entry (FEB 2000)
FAR 52.225-13 Restriction on Certain Foreign Purchases (FEB 2000)
FAR 52.225-14 Inconsistency between English and Translation
              of Contract (FEB 2000)
FAR 52.225-15 Sanctioned European Union Country End
              Products (FEB 2000)
FAR 52.226-1 Utilization of Indian Organizations and
              Indian-Owned Economic Enterprises (FEB 2000)
FAR 52.248-1 Value Engineering (FEB 2000)

I17 - The following must be completed for offers/quotations
based on supplying surplus materials:
        GOVERNMENT SURPLUS MATERIAL (MAY 1999) - DLAD 52.211-9000
(a) With respect to the surplus supplies being offered, the
Offeror represents that:
        (1) The supplies are unused and in good condition.
        (2) The supplies were purchased by the Offeror from the
Government selling agency or other source contract date, and the
contract number. If the supplies were purchased from the
Government by a source other than the Offeror, also identify that
source and its address. If complete information is not
available, attach an explanation as to when, where, and how the
property was acquired.)
Government Selling Agency or Other Source:

Contract Date (Month, Year):
Contract Number:
        (3) The supplies ( ) have ( ) have not been
altered, modified, or refurbished, and (ii) ( ) do ( )
do not contain cure dated components. (If the supplies are to be
reconiditioned or altered, attach a complete description of the
work to be done.
        (4) The Offeror ( ) has ( ) does not have the
supplies. (If the Offeror does not have the supplies, attach an
explanation as to how the offered quantities will be secured.)
        (5) If items have data plates attached, the Offeror has
furnished a copy of information contained thereon, which is
stated below:

        (6) The offered item(s) ( ) are ( ) are not in
their original package. (If the original package is being used,
state here all markings and data including contract number, cited
on the package, and provide a copy or facsimile of package
markings.)
Contract Number:
NSN:
Cage Code:
Part Number:
Other Markings/Data:
(b) The Offeror agrees that in the event of award and

Sample Request for Quotation (page 9)

notwithstanding the provisions of this solicitation, inspection
and acceptance of the surplus supplies will be performed at
origin or destination subject to all applicable provisions for
origin or destination inspection.
(c) Failure to provide the information requested by this
clause may result in rejection of the offer for failure to meet
the requirements of the solicitation.

I58 - HAZARDOUS MATERIAL IDENTIFICATION AND MATERIAL SAFETY
DATA (FAR 52.223-3) (JAN 1997)
     MATERIAL IDENTIFICATION NO. (If none, insert "None")

I63 - HAZARD WARNING LABELS (DFARS 252.223-7001) (DEC 19961)
     MATERIAL (If none, insert "None") ACT

I64 - MATERIAL SAFETY DATA SHEETS AND HAZARD WARING LABELS
(DLAD 52.223-9000) (MAR 1992)
          (2) Check here ( ) if an MSDS accompanies your
offer. Where this is the case, the MSDS must be identified to
the offer, and must cite the solicitation number and the
applicable CAGE code of the manufacturer, the part number, and,
where so identified, the National Stock Number (NSN).

I74 - SUBCONTRACTS FOR COMMERCIAL ITEMS AND COMMERCIAL
COMPONENTS (far 52.244-6) (APR 1998)

I78 - CONFIGURATION CONTROL - ENGINEERING CHANGES, DEVIATIONS
AND WAIVERS (DSCC 52.248-9C01)(APR 1996)

I89 - NOTICE OF TOTAL SMALL BUSINESS SET-ASIDE (FAR 52.219-6)
(JUL 1996)
( ) Alternate I (OCT 1995)

SECTION K

K01
- SOLICITATIONS PROVISIONS INCORPORATED BY REFERNCE
(FAR 52.252-1) (FEB 1998)

K06 - TAXPAYER IDENTIFICATION (FAR 52.204-3) (OCT 1998)
     (d) Taxpayer Identification Number (TIN).
          ( ) TIN: .
          ( ) TIN has been applied for.
          ( ) TIN is not required because:
               ( ) Offeror is a nonresident alien, foreign
corporation, or foreign partnership that does not have income
effectively connected with the conduct of a trade or business in
the U.S. and does not have an office or place of business or a

Sample Request for Quotation (page 10)

```
fiscal paying agent in the U.S.;
              ( )  Offeror is an agency or instrumentality
of a foreign government;
              ( )  Offeror is an agency or instrumentality
of a Federal, state, or local government;
              ( )   Other.  State basis.

     (e)  Type of Organization.
          ( )  Sole proprietorship;
          ( )  Partnership;
          ( )  Corporate entity (not tax-exempt);
          ( )  Corporate entity (tax-exempt);
          ( )  Foreign government;
          ( )  International organization per 26 CFR
1.6049-4;
          ( )  Other
     (f)  Common Parent.
          ( )  Offeror is not owned or controlled by a
common parent as defined in paragraph (a) of this provision.
          ( )  Name and TIN of common parent:
Name:
TIN:


K08 - DATA UNIVERSAL NUMBERING SYSTEM (DUNS) NUMBER
(FAR 52.204-6) (JUN 1999)


K27 - SMALL BUSINESS PROGRAM REPRESENTATION (FAR 52.219-1)
(MAY 1999)
     (a)(1) The standard industrial classification (SIC) code for
this acquisition is 3714   (insert SIC code).
          (2) The small business size standard is 500       (insert
size standard).
          (3) The small business size standard for a concern which
submits an offer in its own name, other than on a construction or
service contract, but which proposes to furnish a product which
it did not itself manufacture, is 500 employees.
     (b) Representations. (1) The offeror represents as part of
its offer that it ( ) is, ( ) is not a small business
concern.
          (2) (Complete only if offeror represented itself as a
small business concern in paragraph (b)(1) of this provision.)
The offeror represents, for general statistical purposes, that it
( ) is, ( ) is not a small disadvantaged business
concern as defined in 13 CFR 124.1002.
          (3) (Complete only if offeror represented itself as a
small business concern in paragraph (b)(1) of this provision.)
The offeror represents as part of its offer that it ( ) is,
( ) is not a women-owned small business concern.
(X) ALTERNATE I (NOV 1999)
The
offeror represents
(i)  It ( ) is, ( ) is not a HUBZone small
business concern
(ii)  It ( ) is, ( ) is not a joint venture
that complies with the requirements of 13 CFR part 126,
The offeror shal enter
the name or names of the HUBZone small business concern or
concerns that are participating in the joint venture:

ALTERNATE II (NOV 1999)
          (5)  (Complete if offeror represented itself as
disadvantaged in paragraph (b)(2) of this provision).  (The
```

Sample Request for Quotation (page 11)

offeror shall check the category in which its ownership falls):
( )   Black American.
( )   Hispanic American.
( )   Native American (American Indians, Eskimos,
Aleuts, or Native Hawaiians).
( )   Asian-Pacific American (persons with origins from
Burma, Thailand, Malaysia, Indonesia, Signapore, (Kampuchea),
Vietnam, Korea, The Philippines, U.S. Trust Territory of the
Pacific Islands (Republic of Palau), Republic of the Marshall
Islands, Federated States of Micronesia, the Commonwealth of the
Northern Marianna Islands, Guam, Samoa, Macao, Hong Kong, Fiji,
Tonga, Kiribati, Tuvalu, or Nauru).
( )   Subcontinent Asian (Asian-Indian) American
(persons with origins from India, Pakistan, Bangladesh, Sri
Lanka, Bhutan, the Maldives Islands, or Nepel).
( )   Individual/concern, other than one of the
preceding.

K33 - PREVIOUS CONTRACTS AND COMPLIANCE REPORTS (FAR 52.222-22)
(FEB 1999)
The offeror represents that --
(a)   It ( ) has, ( ) has not participated in a
previous contract or subcontract subject to the Equal Opportunity
clause of this solicitation;
(b)   It ( ) has, ( ) has not filed all required
compliance reports

K34 - AFFIRMATIVE ACTION COMPLIANCE (FAR 52.222-25)
(APR 1984)
The offeror represents that
(a)   it ( ) has developed and has on file, ( ) has
not developed and does not have on file, at each establishment,
affirmative action programs required by the rules and regulations
of the Secretary of Labor (41 CFR 60-1 and 60-2), or
(b)   it ( ) has not previously had contracts subject to
the written affirmative action programs requirement of the rules
and regulations of the Secretary of Labor.

K39 - INFORMATION FOR DUTY-FREE ENTRY EVALUATION
(DFARS 252.225-7003) (MAR 1998)
(a)   Is the offer based on furnishing any supplies (i.e.,
end items, components, or material) of foreign origin other than
those for which duty-free entry is to be accorded pursuant to the
Duty-Free Entry -- Qualifying Country End Products and Supplies
clause of this solicitation?
( )   Yes   ( )   No
(b)   If the answer in paragraph (a) is yes, answer the
following questions:
(1)   Are such foreign supplies now in the United
States?   ( )   Yes   ( )   No
(2)   Has the duty on such foreign supplies been paid?
( )   Yes   ( )   No
(3)   If the answer to paragraph (b)(2) is no, what
amount is included in the offer to cover such duty?
$

SECTION L

L01
- SOLICITATION PROVISIONS INCORPORATED BY REFERENCE

Sample Request for Quotation (page 12)

```
(FAR 52.252-1) (FEB 1998)
The following changes have been made to the Master Solicitation:
FAR 52.225-10   Notice of Buy American Act/Balance of Payments
                Program Requirement Construction
                Materials (FEB 2000)
FAR 52.225-12   Notice of Buy American Act/Balance of Payments
                Program Requirement-Construction Materials under
                Trade Agreements (FEB 2000)


L03 - AVAILABILITY OF SPECIFICATIONS LISTED IN THE DOD INDEX OF
SPECIFICATIONS AND STANDARDS (DODISS) AND DESCRIPTIONS LISTED IN
THE ACQUISITION MANAGEMENT SYSTEMS AND DATA REQUIREMENTS CONTROL
LIST, DoD 5010.12-L. (FAR 52.211-2) (DEC 1999)


L07 - AVAILABILITY OF DRAWINGS, PURCHASE DESCRIPTIONS OR
DEVIATIONS LISTS (DSCC 52.211-9C13) (OCT 1996)


L09 - CONDITIONS FOR EVALUATION OF OFFERS OF SURPLUS MATERIAL
(DLAD 52.211-9003) (JUN 1999)
The Agency will evaluate offers of surplus material when
the contracting officer determines the offeror is
otherwise in line for award, after adding the cost of evaluation
($200 for internal evaluation and, if applicable, an additional
$500 for Engineering Support Activity (ESA) evaluation plus any
additional fees required for special testing and/or
inspection).


L25 - AGENCY PROTESTS (DLAD 52.233-9000) (SEP 1999)


SECTION M


M01 - SOLICITATION PROVISIONS INCORPORATED BY REFERENCE
(FAR 52.252-1) (FEB 1998)


M07 - AUTOMATED BEST VALUE SYSTEM (ABVS) (DSCC 52.215-9C10)
(FEB 2000)
(a)  Award against this solicitation shall be made based on a
comparative assessment of offerors' prices, quoted deliveries,
and past performance.  Award may be made to other than the
low-priced, technically acceptable, responsible offeror.  The
Government retains the right to award to the offeror with the
lowest quoted or lowest evaluated price.  Price, quoted delivery,
and past performance will be evaluated equally when making a
comparative analysis of offers.  The past performance factor
considers quality performance and delivery performance to be of
equal value.
(b) Past Performance:
     (1)  Past performance information is maintained for
performance under all procurements with the Defense Logistics
Agency (DLA).  Overall performance is evaluated as is performance
in each Federal Supply Class (FSC).  This information is used to
generate ABVS ratings which are based on the following
indicators:
Delivery Delinquencies
- Number
- Severity
- Contractor caused Terminations, Cancellations, and Withdrawals
```

Sample Request for Quotation (page 13)

For administrative purposes, the delivery rating period excludes the most recent 60 days. For ABVS purposes, delinquent lines represent shipments not shipped and/or received in their entirety by the Contract Delivery Date (CDD).
Quality Complaints
- Product Nonconformances/Laboratory Test Failures
- Packaging Nonconformances
For administrative purposes, the quality rating period excludes the most recent 30 days.
NOTE: The above 60 and 30 day offset periods are NOT grace periods.

(2) An offeror's past performance is an indicator of performance risk and will be evaluated first on the basis of past performance in the same Federal Supply Class (FSC) as the supplies being solicited. The Contracting Officer may consider the volume of business on which the performance score is based as a measure of confidence in the FSC score. A vendor's overall score may be evaluated when a satisfactory measure of confidence cannot be obtained from the FSC score or if a vendor has no FSC score. The Contracting Officer may also take into consideration any other available and relevant past performance data.

(3) An offeror with no performance history in any FSC procured
by DLA will be identified as a new offeror and will not be scored by ABVS on performance. However, any other available and relevant past performance data may be considered in rendering an award decision. Regardless, the status of being a new offeror will not be grounds for disqualification for an award. New offerors may be considered more favorably than scored offerors with a poor performance record. Also, the desirability of expanding the supplier base and possible competition enhancement in future procurements will be considered in the source selection decision when new offerors are present.

(4) ABVS ratings do not determine an offeror's award eligibility, or technical acceptability, nor does it constitute a responsibility or non-responsibility determination.

(5) By accessing the DSCC Internet Bid Board System (DIBBS), (http://dibbs.dscccols.com/), each offeror will be provided the opportunity to review their ABVS scores and negative historical performance data. For any questions or challenges to negative performance data, please forward requests/challenges to an ABVS Administrator at the below cited address, or telephone/fax an Administrator at one of the provided numbers:
Mail requests to: Defense Supply Center, Columbus
                      ATTN: DSCC-PAMB
                      P. O. Box 3990
                      Columbus OH   43216-5010
Telephone Numbers: (614) 692-1381
                    (614) 692-3383
Facsimile (FAX) Number: (614) 692-4170

(6) When a discrepancy between contractor data and Government data occurs, the Government will make every effort to resolve the discrepancy expeditiously. However, the Government may make an award decision despite the existence of an unresolved challenge. The Government is the final authority for resolution of disputed data and its use in the source selection process.
(c) Price. In making an award decision, the Government may consider price as follows:

(1) Offered Price - The Government will evaluate the reasonableness of the offered price after a price analysis of offers is performed.

(2) Evaluated Price - If required, the evaluation process may include the Factor (DEF), the Small Disadvantaged Business Concerns (SDBC) preference, and/or any other applicable price

Sample Request for Quotation (page 14)

evaluation factor(s).
(d) Delivery. The quoted delivery will be evaluated in comparison with the delivery required on the solicitation.
(e) General Basis for Award. Award will be made to the offeror whose proposal conforms to the terms and conditions of the solicitation and which represents the best value to the Government. In making the best value determination, the Government will make a comparative assessment of the proposals with regard to price, delivery, and past performance. The following considerations may affect the trade-off determination:
- Whether or not an item is used in a weapons system or is a personnel support item
- Item delivery and quality history
- Inventory status
- Delivery schedule/urgency of the item
- Limited number of supply sources
- Benefits from obtaining new sources
- Difference in price

M26 - DELIVERY EVALUATION FACTOR (DEF) (DSCC 52.211-9C12) (OCT 1999)

(a) Offers will be evaluated based upon the delivery offered in DSCC Clause F20, Required Delivery with Delivery Evaluation Factor, and the formula set forth below in paragraph (c) of this provision. The Evaluated Price may include additive CLIN(s) and/or the value of any option CLIN(s). Calculations of the Evaluated Price are made on a line-by-line (CLIN-by-CLIN, subCLIN-by-subCLIN) basis for which an offer has been received. However, offers could be awarded on a total price basis only or by a CLIN/line basis.
For evaluation purposes only:
7 Offers with a Proposed Delivery Schedule which meets/is the same as the Required Delivery Schedule will be evaluated without an adjustment to their offered price.
7 Offers with a Proposed Delivery Schedule shorter/earlier than the Required Delivery Schedule will also be evaluated without an adjustment to their offered price.
7 Offers with a Proposed Delivery Schedule longer/later than the Required Delivery Schedule will have the evaluation factor adjustment added to their offered price.

(b) The DEF is based upon separate Center factors for Construction (S9C) FSCs/items and Electronic (S9E) FSCs/items. Currently, the factor for S9C FSCs/items is .00118; while for S9E FSCs/items, it is .00256. The factor represents the day/cost ratio (the cost per day due to late delivery) and is expressed as a portion of the overall contract cost.
(c) For DEF evaluation purposes only, the formula reflected below is used for this acquisition to calculate the DEF Price Adjustment and the Evaluated Price per line/CLIN.
[Total Offered Price per line x Evaluation Factor]   x [Offered Delivery per line - Govt's Required Delivery] + Price Adjustment per line = Evaluated Price per line

Example:
DEF Factor: .00256 per day
Total Quantity: 30 ea   CLIN 0001 - 20 ea;   CLIN 0002 - 10 ea
Option Quantity: 30 ea
Govt's Required Delvy: CLIN 0001 - 90 days; CLIN 0002 - 60 days
FAT Delivery and Approval Time: 180 days

	(a)	(b)	(c)	(d)	(e)
				Govt's	Total

Sample Request for Quotation (page 15)

CLIN	Quantity	Offered Unit Price	Offered Delivery	Required Delivery	Evaluation Factor
0001	20	$1,375.00	60	90	$27,500.00
0002	10	$1,500.00	60	60	$15,000.00
5001AA	20	$1,375.00	60	90	$27,500.00
5001AB	10	$1,500.00	60	60	$15,000.00
9907	1	$1,000.00	180	180	---
(f)		(g)		(h)	(i)

Evaluation Factor	Difference in Offered and Govt's Required Delivery (d-c)	Price Adjustment (exfxg)	Evaluated Price (Per Line) (e+h)
.00256	-30	0	$27,500.00
.00256	0	0	$15,000.00
.00256	-30	0	$27,500.00
.00256	0	0	$ 1,000.00
	Total Evaluated Price		$86,000.00

PART VII MASTER SOLICITATION - PALLETIZATION NO. DC1636P001 - 96150 - APPLIES

Sample Quality Assurance Manual (page 1)

(Company Name, Address and Telephone Number--Can be Letterhead)

Sample Quality Assurance Manual

Copy Number: _____

Issue Date: _____

Approved By:

_____   _____

Name: Name:

Title: (Quality Head)   Title (Company Head)

Sample Quality Assurance Manual (page 2)

Quality Assurance Manual

Section: Revision
Revision: _____
Approved: _____
Date: _____
Page: of____

Quality Manual Revision Status

Rev Description of Change	Date	Approved by
A. Clarification of Responsibilities	06/06/99	John Supplier

Sample Quality Assurance Manual (page 3)

Quality Assurance Manual

Section: Revision
Revision: _____
Approved: _____
Date: _____
Page: of____

Table of Contents

Section   Element

1.0   Scope and Policy
2.0   Amendments and Revisions to the Quality Manual
3.0   Organization
4.0   Quality Program
5.0   Procurement Document Control
6.0   Instructions, Procedures and Drawings
7.0   Document Control
8.0   Control of Purchased Items
9.0   Identification and Control of Items
10.0 Inspection
11.0 Control of Measuring and Test Equipment
12.0 Control of Nonconforming Articles
13.0 Corrective Action
14.0 Quality Records

Appendix

A.   Receiving Report
B.   Calibration Intervals
C.   Shipping Document

Sample Quality Assurance Manual (page 4)

Quality Assurance Manual	Section:	Revision
	Revision:	_____
	Approved:	_____
	Date:	_____
	Page:	of____

1.0   Scope

This manual describes (Insert Company's Name) Quality System Policies and Procedures. These policies and procedures control all activities from Supplier procurement to customer shipment of articles.

1.1   Policy

The quality program is developed to assure customer satisfaction by providing quality products. We will perform all activities in a manner, which meets or exceeds the expectations of our customers.

1.2   Application

The quality System described herein is mandatory for all activities performed at (Location or Company's Name) to assure product conformance to the applicable drawing, catalog item specification and/or contract requirement.

Sample Quality Assurance Manual (page 5)

Quality Assurance Manual

Section:	Revision
Revision:	_____
Approved:	_____
Date:	_____
Page:	of____

2.0   Amendments and Revisions to the Quality Manual

2.1 Revision Control

This manual will be revised by Quality Assurance as required. Whenever revisions occur, all holders of controlled copies will be distributed copies of the application revised pages, including a new revision page describing the changes.

2.2 Reviews

Management reviews of operations are continuous and any problems indicated with the Quality Program or its implementation will be addressed and corrected as directed by Management.

Sample Quality Assurance Manual (page 6)

Quality Assurance Manual	Section: _Revision_ Revision: _____ Approved: _____ Date: _____ Page: of____

3.0   Organization

    3.1   Quality Manager

The Quality Manager reports directly to (Title of Person) and is delegated authority and organizational freedom to identify and evaluate quality problems and to initiate, recommend or provide solutions.

    3.2   Responsibilities

The Quality Manager is responsible for:

        a. Update and distribution control of the Quality Manual as required.

        b. Planning to meet customer's quality requirements.

        c. Determining inspection points within the system.

        d. Approval of quality work instructions.

        e. Directing inspection activities.

        f. Surveillance of procurement documents.

        g. Approval of Suppliers.

        h. Maintaining a listing of approved suppliers.

        i. Monitoring procedures to assure compliance

        j. Reviewing and maintaining Quality Records.

        k. Calibration of Measuring and Test Equipment.

        1. Approval of disposition of Nonconforming Articles

        m. Corrective action coordination

Sample Quality Assurance Manual (page 7)

Quality Assurance Manual	Section:	Revision
	Revision:	_____
	Approved:	_____
	Date:	_____
	Page:	of____

4.0   Quality Program

    4.1   Documentation

The Quality Program is documented within this manual and may be supported at any point by desk or work instructions that may be selected to increase control of a quality function. Desk or work instructions affecting Quality shall be approved by the Quality Manager.

    4.2   Planning

The Quality Program is planned to control products from the requirements of a customer order to include procurement practices, receipt of material, receipt inspection of supplier material, handling and storage to the eventual shipment of an article to our customer.

    4.3   Indoctrination and Training

Employees are indoctrinated and trained, as necessary, to assure that suitable proficiency is achieved and maintained throughout our operation systems. Training is performed as "On the Job Training" under the direct supervision of management. Procedural changes are implemented by training of any individual(s) affected by the change.

Sample Quality Assurance Manual (page 8)

Quality Assurance Manual	Section:	Revision
	Revision:	_____
	Approved:	_____
	Date:	_____
	Page:	of____

5.0   Procurement Document Control

    5.1   System of Procurement

Procurement documents are (computer) (manually) generated and include appropriate technical and quality requirements. When a customer has special requirements, such as a Certified Material Test Report (CMTR), our program is designed to include the requirement into our procurement documents.

    5.2   Review and Approval

Procurement documents are reviewed and approved by the Purchasing Manager. The Quality Manager performs random surveillance of procurement documents semi-annually and documents the results.

    5.3   Changes to Documents

Changes to procurement documents are subject to the same level of control as in preparation of the original document.

Quality Assurance Manual	Section:	Revision
	Revision:	
	Approved:	
	Date:	
	Page:	of___

6.0   Instructions and Drawings

6.1   Work Instructions

Work or desk instruction are utilized in support of this Quality Manual to improve the control of a specific operation or evaluation, but in no circumstances shall these documents supersede or change the requirements of this manual.

6.2   Drawings

Drawings, specifications and/or catalog criteria shall be used to control the technical requirements of products offered to our customers.

Sample Quality Assurance Manual (page 10)

Quality Assurance Manual	Section: _____ Revision
	Revision: _____
	Approved: _____
	Date: _____
	Page: ____ of ____

7.0   Document Control

     7.1   Current Issues

The latest issue of drawings, specifications, catalogs, work instructions and Customer orders will be utilized to control articles throughout the operations system.

     7.2   Modification or Design Changes

Obsolete documents caused by modification or design change will be identified as such and removed from use.

Sample Quality Assurance Manual (page 11)

Quality Assurance Manual	Section:	Revision
	Revision:	_____
	Approved:	_____
	Date:	_____
	Page:	of____

8.0   Control of Purchased Items

    8.1   Incoming Articles

Receipt of purchased articles is documented on a Receiving Report (Appendix A). The requirements of the Purchase Order are (included in) (attached to) the Receiving Report to provide the inspection function with complete criteria for evaluation of the receipt.

    8.2   Inspection

Articles are inspected in accordance with the requirements of the receiving documents. As a minimum, all articles are inspected for count, identification and damage.

    8.3   Certifications

Certifications and Certified Material Test Reports (CMTRs) are reviewed for compliance and accuracy of contents as required by procurement documents. Certified reports or other proof of Quality used as a basis for acceptance shall be (validated by independent testing on an annual basis) (validated by audit of the supplier on a triennial basis).

    8.4   Rejected Articles

Rejected articles will be documented as nonconforming on the Receiving Report to prevent inadvertent use or further processing. The Quality Manager will approve final disposition.

    8.5   Acceptance

Acceptance of the receipt will be documented on the Receiving Report as accepted and the identity of the inspector will be included by initialing the document.

Sample Quality Assurance Manual (page 12)

Quality Assurance Manual	Section:	Revision
	Revision:	_____
	Approved:	_____
	Date:	_____
	Page:	of____

9.0   Identification and control of Items

The Original Equipment Manufacturer (OEM) articles will retain their identity through our receipt, stocking and delivery function traceable to the procurement and receipt documents containing acceptance status.

Sample Quality Assurance Manual (page 13)

Quality Assurance Manual		Section:	Revision
		Revision:	_____
		Approved:	_____
		Date:	_____
		Page:	of____

10.0 Inspection

10.1 Stock

Stock reinspection will be implemented on specific articles in storage as a result of a customer complaint or any suspected Quality problem concerning an article. Rejected articles will be identified or segregated and disposition in accordance with control of nonconforming material. Accepted articles will be returned to the stock location.

10.2 Final Inspection

Inspection of articles to be delivered to a customer will be accomplished prior to packaging for identification, damage and in accordance with the shipping document. The customer ordered requirements are included (with) (in) the shipping document. Rejected articles will be identified or segregated and disposition in accordance with control of nonconforming material. Accepted articles will be identified on the shipping document as accepted by (signature) (stamp impression) (initials)

10.3 Shipping Inspection

Inspection of the packaging will include evaluation to determine adequacy to preclude damage during delivery and any special requirements directed by the customer order. Customer requirements for Certifications and/or Certified Material Test Reports will be included with the articles.

Sample Quality Assurance Manual (page 14)

Quality Assurance Manual	Section:	Revision
	Revision:	_____
	Approved:	_____
	Date:	_____
	Page:	of ____

11.0   Control Of Measuring and Test Equipment

    11.1   Commercial Equipment

Calibration of normal commercial equipment (i.e., rulers, tape, measures, levels, and other similar devices) is not required. It is the responsibility of the user to report worn or damaged equipment to management to prevent inadvertent use.

    11.2   Special Devices

Calibration will be performed and maintained at prescribed intervals in accordance with Appendix B. An Outside Calibration Laboratory is contracted to supply this service. The supplier is certified and performs calibrations traceable to recognized national Standards.

    11.3   Identification of Equipment

Each item is identified with current status of calibration and the user is responsible to verify an item is serviceable. Items too small to be identified are serialized, and calibration status is maintained by a traceable record supporting a calibration recall system.

Sample Quality Assurance Manual (page 15)

Quality Assurance Manual		Section:	Revision
		Revision:	_____
		Approved:	_____
		Date:	_____
		Page:	of ____

12.0   Control of Nonconforming Articles

    12.1   Disposition

All nonconforming articles are reviewed to determine disposition; the disposition is documented on the accompanying paperwork.

    12.2   Approval of Dispositions

        A. The quality Manager approves all dispositions of nonconforming articles as follows:

            1. Return to Supplier
            2. Rework to Specification
            3. Scrap

        B. Customer approval of the following dispositions shall be requested and required prior to delivery of articles:

            1. Use as Is (waiver)
            2. Repair to a Useable Condition

12.3.1.1.1   Reworked and repaired items are reinspected and/or tested in accordance with disposition instructions.

Sample Quality Assurance Manual (page 16)

Quality Assurance Manual

Section:	Revision
Revision:	_____
Approved:	_____
Date:	_____
Page:	of____

13.0   Corrective Action

Conditions adverse to quality shall be promptly identified and corrected. In the case of significant conditions adverse to Quality, the cause of the condition shall be determined and action planned to correct and preclude repetition.

13.1 Customer Complaints

Responses to Customer complaints will be documented by letter or on forms required by the customer. Responses will include cause of the condition, actions taken to prevent a future occurrence and effective date.

Sample Quality Assurance Manual (page 17)

Quality Assurance Manual

Section: Revision
Revision: _____
Approved: _____
Date: _____
Page: of____

14.0   Quality Records

    14.1   Retention

Quality records traceable to an article or lot of articles will be stored by the identifying part number. Quality records traceable to a Customer will be stored by the Customer's Order Number. The retention of Quality records is a minimum of three years or as otherwise directed by a Customer Order Requirement.

Sample Quality Assurance Manual (page 18)

Quality Assurance Manual

Appendix A

Page

Receiving Report

> INCLUDE A COPY OF YOUR COMPANY'S EFFORT OR WHATEVER IS USED
> TO INDICATE RECEIVED ARTICLES.

Form should include identity of Supplier, item, quantity received, any special requirements, and space
for indicating evidence of inspection, status of acceptance, disposition and identity of inspector.

Sample Quality Assurance Manual (page 19)

Quality Assurance Manual

Appendix B

Page

CALIBRATION INTERVALS:

Equipment	Interval
Master Gage Block Set	Two Years
Thread plug and ring gages	Six Months
Micrometer	One Week
Caliper	One Year
Surface Plate	Three Years
Volt/Ohm Meter	One Year
Hole Plug Gage	After Each Use

NOTE: Items and Intervals are for example only and do not accurately describe tools your company may use or property interval which must be determined by use potential wear and calibration history of each item

Sample Quality Assurance Manual (page 20)

Quality Assurance Manual

Appendix C

Page

Shipping Document

INCLUDE A COPY OF YOUR COMPANY'S REPORT OR WHATEVER IS USED TO SHIP PRODUCTS TO CUSTOMERS.

The form should contain any special conditions included in the customer's order such as, Requirements for data, test reports, certifications, marking or packaging. The form should also include some space to indicate evidence of acceptance by inspection was performed.

Sample Mentor-Protégé Program Agreement Template (page 1)

Department of Defense
Office of Small and Disadvantaged Business Utilization

Mentor-Protégé Program

Agreement Template

Companies that have been approved as mentors in the DoD Mentor-Protégé Program and have identified a protégé firm must submit a signed mentor-protégé agreement for each mentor-protégé relationship to the Director, Small and Disadvantaged Business Utilization (SADBU), Office of the Under Secretary of Defense (Acquisition, Technology and Logistics [OUSD (AT&L)]) for approval. For companies seeking direct reimbursement of developmental assistance costs, your submission should be made through the cognizant Military Department/Defense Agency SADBU Office. For companies seeking credit of developmental assistance costs, your submission should be made through the Defense Contract Management Agency (DCMA). Regardless of the agreement type, an information copy must be submitted to the OUSD SADBU.

Please Note:

    Credit Only Agreements: *Developmental assistance costs may only be incurred after receipt of an approval letter from DCMA. Note: Official start date is the date of OUSD (AT&L) approval letter.*

    Direct Reimbursed Agreements: *Developmental assistance costs may only be incurred upon the award of a contract modification that incorporates a separate line item for the mentor-protégé agreement. Note: Official start date is the date of the contract modification.*

The following template is provided as a guide to assist in the preparation of the mentor-protégé agreement, however at a minimum all elements below must be addressed. Attachments/addendums are welcome.

Sample Mentor-Protégé Program Agreement Template (page 2)

1. **Agreement Information:** *Check the agreement type that applies and provide the following.*

   Credit _____   OR   Direct Reimbursement _____

   Period of Performance: *State the period of time (in months) over which the developmental assistance will be performed - not to exceed three years.*

Number of Months:	
Anticipated Start Date:	
Anticipated Completion Date	

   For Direct Reimbursable: *Please provide the following.*

Military Department or Defense Agency:	
Contract Number (*if known*):	

   Estimated Cost of Agreement: *Provide an estimate of the total cost of the developmental assistance provided by the mentor. Include a cost breakdown of each year of effort - to be fully funded - by element of costs (i.e., employee labor, HBCUs/MIs/PTACs/SDBDCs, and incidental costs.)*

	(*Expressed in whole dollar amounts*)		
	Year 1	**Year 2**	**Year 3**
Employee Labor:	$	$	$
HBCU/MI/PTAC/SBDC:	$	$	$
Other Direct Costs:	$	$	$
Subtotal:	$	$	$
Total Estimated Cost: (*all budgeted years*)			$

   For Direct Reimbursement agreements please contact the Military Department/Defense Agency for additional guidance on the format and level of detail of your estimated cost submission. Be prepared to furnish a more detailed cost breakdown of the labor categories.

2. **Mentor Eligibility.** *Provide a statement (be sure to include the date of approval) that the Mentor has been previously approved under the DoD Mentor-Protégé Program and is still eligible to participate as a mentor, (provide a copy of approval letter, if available) or attach the Mentor Application.*

3. **Mentor Firm Information.** *Provide the following.*

Name of Firm:	
Address:	
Telephone/ext.:	
Fax:	
Homepage:	
Industry:	
Cage Code:	

Sample Mentor-Protégé Program Agreement Template (page 3)

4. **Mentor Historical Background.** *Provide a __brief__ summary about the company, including the company profile, and historical and recent activities and accomplishments under their Small Disadvantaged Business and Mentor-Protégé Programs. Indicate whether your company has been a small disadvantaged business (SDB), woman-owned small business, or 8(a). If a graduated 8(a), please include graduation date.*

5. **DoD Subcontract Awards to Protégé.** *The number and total dollar amount of DoD subcontract awards made to the identified protégé firm by the mentor firm during the two preceding fiscal years (if any). Please note fiscal year here represent the government's fiscal year which runs October 1 through September 30.*

Total DoD Subcontract Awards to this Protégé		
Fiscal Year	Number	Dollar Amount
FY-____		$
FY-____		$

6. **Federal Agency Subcontract Awards to Protégé.** *The number and total dollar amount of Federal Agency subcontract awards made to the identified protégé firm by the mentor firm during the two preceding fiscal years (if any). Please note fiscal year here represent the government's fiscal year which runs October 1 through September 30.*

Total Federal Agency Subcontract Awards to this Protégé		
Fiscal Year	Number	Dollar Amount
FY-____		$
FY-____		$

7. **Potential Subcontracts.** *The anticipated number, dollar value, and type of subcontracts to be awarded the protégé firm consistent with the extent and nature of mentor firm's business, and the period of time over which they will be awarded. Please note fiscal year here represent the government's fiscal year which runs October 1 through September 30.*

Estimated Potential Subcontract Awards to this Protégé			
Fiscal Year	Number	Dollar Amount	Type
FY-____		$	
FY-____		$	
FY-____		$	

Sample Mentor-Protégé Program Agreement Template (page 4)

8. **Protégé Eligibility.** *Provide a statement that the protégé firm is currently eligible pursuant to one of the following criteria below:*

An entity may qualify as a protégé firm if it is —

(1.) *A Small Disadvantaged Business (SDB) concern as defined by section 8(d)(3)(C) of the Small Business Act (15 U.S.C. 637(D)(3)(C)) which is —*
  (i) *Eligible for the award of Federal contracts; and*
  (ii) *A small business according to the SBA size standard for the North American Industry Classification System (NAICS) code which represents the contemplated supplies or services to be provided by the protégé firm to the mentor firm; and*
  (iii) *Certified by the Small Business Administration as an SDB.*

(2.) *A business entity that meets the criteria in above and is owned and controlled by either an Indian tribe as defined by section 8(a)(13) of the Small Business Act (15 U.S.C. 637(a)(13)) or a Native Hawaiian Organization as defined by section 8(a)(15) of the Small Business Act (15 U.S.C. 637(a)(15)); and is certified by the Small Business Administration as an SDB.*

(3.) *A qualified organization employing the severely disabled which self certifies that it meets the criteria for such entities defined in Pub. L. 102-172, section 8064A.*

(4.) *A woman-owned small business which self certifies that it meets the criteria for such entities in accordance with the DFARS and by the Small Business Act (15 U.S.C. 637(d)(3)(D).*

9. **Protégé Firm Information.** *Provide the following.*

Name of Firm:			
Address:			
Telephone/ext.:			
Fax:			
Homepage:			
Industry/Bus. Type: *(e.g. Svc – 80% Mfg – 20%)*	Construction:		
	Manufacturing:		
	R&D:		
	Service:		
Year Established:			
Number of Employees:			
Annual Gross Revenue: *(for previous Corporate fiscal year)*			
SDB Dates:	Entrance Date:	Expiration Date:	
8(a) Dates:	Entrance Date:	Expiration Date:	

Sample Mentor-Protégé Program Agreement Template (page 5)

North American Industrial Classification System Codes (NAICS). *The NAICS code which represents the contemplated supplies or services to be provided by the protégé firm to the mentor firm and a statement that at the time the agreement is submitted for approval, the protégé firm, if an SDB or a woman-owned small business concern, does not exceed the size standard for the appropriate NAICS code.*

	Code	Title
Primary NAICS		
Additional NAICS		

Percent (%) Owned. *Provide percent of the Protégé Firm currently owned by the Mentor Firm.*

% Mentor Owned:	

Protégé-Obtained DoD Subcontract Awards. *The number and total dollar amount of DoD subcontract awards obtained by the protégé firm during the two preceding fiscal years (if any). Please note fiscal year here represent the government's fiscal year which runs October 1 through September 30.*

Total DoD Subcontract Awards			
Fiscal Year	**Number**	**Funded Contract Value**	**Dollar Amount Received**
FY-		$	$
FY-		$	$
FY-		$	$

Protégé-Obtained DoD Prime contract Awards. *The number and total dollar amount of DoD Prime contract awards obtained by the protégé firm during the two preceding fiscal years (if any). Please note fiscal year here represent the government's fiscal year which runs October 1 through September 30.*

Total DoD Prime Contract Awards			
Fiscal Year	**Number**	**Funded Contract Value**	**Dollar Amount Received**
FY-		$	$
FY-		$	$
FY-		$	$

10. **Protégé Firm Historical Background.** *Provide a <u>brief</u> summary about the company, including the company profile, and historical and recent activities and accomplishments. Indicate whether your company is a small disadvantaged business (SDB), woman-owned small business, or an organization that employs the severely disabled person. Include a description of the company's ability to participate in the DoD Mentor-Protégé Program without impairing the company's day-to-day operations (i.e., business management, revenue stream).*

Sample Mentor-Protégé Program Agreement Template (page 6)

11. **Protégé Firm's Previous Program Participation.** *Provide the following information if the protégé firm has previously participated in the DoD Mentor-Protégé Program. Provide a statement (separate enclosure to this agreement) that there will be no duplication of effort (i.e., developmental assistance provided by the mentor firm) previously provided to the protégé firm under prior agreements. This must be agreed upon and presented on letterhead from both the mentor and protégé firms.*

Previous Mentor Firm Name:	
Sponsoring Military Dept./Agency: *(e.g., Army, Navy, Air Force, DISA, DIA, DLA, NGA)*	
Type: *(credit or direct reimbursed)*	
Period of performance of previous agreement: *(in months)*	
Termination Date: *(if applicable)*	
Termination Reason: *(if applicable)*	

12. **Developmental Assistance Program.** *Describe the developmental program for the protégé firm specifying the type of assistance planned. Provide how this plan will address the protégé's identified needs to enhance their ability to perform successfully under contracts or subcontracts within DoD and other federal agencies. Your developmental assistance program is not expected to conform to only the examples listed below, nor is your developmental assistance program expected to provide assistance in all of the examples cited. Please also note that some examples cited under (a)(i) and (a)(ii) may be interchangeable within the two categories. Types of developmental assistance allowable under the program are:*

(a) Assistance by mentor firm personnel in —
  (i) General Business Management/Corporate Infrastructure: (See example list below)

> *Example List*
> - *Organizational Planning Management*
>   - *Strategic planning, business planning, legal/risk management, proposal development*
> - *Business Development/Marketing/Sales*
>   - *Market research, product forecasting, web-based marketing, e-commerce*
> - *Human Resource Management*
> - *Financial Management*
> - *Contract Management*
> - *Facilities and Plant Management – security, heath & safety, OSHA standards*

  (ii) Engineering and technical: (See example list below)

> *Example List*
> - *Quality Management Programs*
>   - *ISO 9000 certification, SEI/CMM certification*
> - *Logistic Systems*
>   - *Supply chain management, transportation management*
> - *Sensing & Imagery*
> - *Environmental Remedial System Design*
> - *Hazardous Material Control*
> - *Metal Machining*
> - *Fiber Optics System Design*
> - *Network Systems*

Sample Mentor-Protégé Program Agreement Template (page 7)

> o *Design and engineering, implementation*
> - *Information System Design*
> - *Tooling Design & Fabrication*
> - *Product Assembly Technique*
> - *Supply Chain Management*

(iii) Any other assistance designed to develop the capabilities of the protégé firm under the developmental program.

(b) Award of subcontracts under DoD contracts or other contracts on a non-competitive basis.

(c) Payment of progress payments for the performance of subcontracts by a protégé firm in amounts as provided for in the subcontract; but in no event may any such progress payment exceed 100 percent of the costs incurred by the protégé firm for the performance of the subcontract. Provision of progress payments by a mentor firm to a protégé firm at a rate other than the customary rate for small disadvantaged businesses shall be implemented in accordance with FAR 32.504(c).

(d) Advance payments under such subcontracts. Mentor firms must administer advance payments in accordance with FAR Subpart 32.4.

(e) Loans.

(f) Investment(s) in the protégé firm in exchange for an ownership interest in the protégé firm, not to exceed 10 percent of the total ownership interest. Investments may include but not be limited to cash, stock, contributions in kind, etc.

(g) Assistance obtained by the mentor firm for the protégé firm from one or more of the following:
> *(i) Small Business Development Centers (SBDC) established pursuant to section 21 of the Small Business Act (15 U.S.C. 648).*
> *(ii) Entities providing procurement technical assistance pursuant to chapter 142 of Title 10 U.S.C. (Procurement Technical Assistance Centers.)*
> *(iii) Historically Black Colleges and Universities.*
> *(iv) Minority Institutions of higher education.*

13. **Value to the Department of Defense.** Provide a summary of the value(s) this agreement will bring in support of the DoD's, Military Departments'/Other Defense Agencies', and the Warfighters' mission(s).

Sample Mentor-Protégé Program Agreement Template (page 8)

14. Milestones. *Define milestones for providing the identified developmental assistance. (Gantt chart) The charts will be submitted with the agreement execution and updated charts will be submitted to program managers every calendar quarter. (See example below)*

Example Gantt Chart

15. Metrics. *The success of the Mentor-Protégé program will be measured quarterly by a system of metrics designed to ensure adherence to the milestones outlined in the program plan, achieve complete technology transfers in the business and achievement of revenue and contracting awards. The Mentor, following review by the Protégé will submit the quarterly status to the Military Department/Defense Agency, Program Manager. An information copy will also be sent to the OUSD (AT&L) SADBU Mentor-Protégé Program Manager. Program progress will be measured quarterly and in the semi annual reports. In addition to the developmental assistance plan, provide factors to assess the protégé firm's developmental progress under the Program. Mandatory metrics will include but are not limited to the following:*

> *The quantitative measures for the success of this program will include:*
> - *Planned tasks started on time: planned tasks behind schedule*
> - *Planned tasks completed on time; planned completions behind schedule*
> - *Development program on/off schedule*
> - *The number of certifications completed and in progress*
> - *Agreement budget variance report by task area/developmental assistance categories (see section 12(a) of this template for assistance category)*
> - *The number of DoD prime/sub contracts, Federal subcontracts, other contracts awarded to Protégé*
> - *Annual revenue of Protégé*
> - *Status of Semi-Annual report submission.*

Sample Mentor-Protégé Program Agreement Template (page 9)

16. **Termination Procedures (Mentor).**

Voluntary: *Provide the procedures for the mentor firm to notify the protégé firm in writing at least 30 days in advance of the mentor firm's intent to voluntarily withdraw its participation in the Program. Mentor firms may only voluntarily terminate the mentor-protégé agreement if they no longer want to be a participant in the Program as a mentor firm.*

For Cause: *Provide procedures for the mentor firm to terminate the mentor-protégé agreement for cause which provide —*

- *The protégé firm shall be furnished a written notice by the Mentor firm of the proposed termination, stating the specific reasons for such action, at least 30 days in advance of the effective date of such proposed termination.*

- *The protégé firm shall have 30 days to respond to such notice of proposed termination, and may rebut any findings believed to be erroneous and offer a remedial program.*

- *Upon prompt consideration of the protégé firm's response, the mentor firm shall either withdraw the notice of proposed termination and continue the protégé firm's participation, or issue the notice of termination.*

The decision of the mentor firm regarding termination for cause, conforming with the requirements of this section, shall be final and is not reviewable by the DoD.

17. **Voluntary Termination Procedures (Protégé).** *Provide procedures for a protégé firm to notify the mentor firm in writing at least 30 days in advance of the protégé firm's intent to voluntarily terminate the mentor-protégé agreement.*

18. **Additional Terms and Conditions.** *Describe any other additional terms and conditions as may be agreed upon by both parties.*

All correspondence and inquiries by OUSD (AT&L), Military Departments, and Defense Agencies will be addressed to the Points of Contact that you provide below.

19. **Mentor Firm Point of Contact (POC).**

Name:	
Title:	
Address:	
Telephone/ext.:	
Fax:	
E-mail:	

Sample Mentor-Protégé Program Agreement Template (page 10)

20. Protégé Firm Point of Contact (POC).

Name:	
Title:	
Address:	
Telephone/ext.:	
Fax:	
E-mail:	

21. Procuring Contracting Officer (PCO). *(Direct reimbursable agreements only)*

Name:	
Title:	
Address:	
Telephone/ext.:	
Fax:	
E-mail:	

22. Mentor Firm's Cognizant Administrative Contracting Officer (ACO).

Name:	
Title:	
Address:	
Telephone/ext.:	
Fax:	
E-mail:	

23. Mentor Firm's Cognizant Defense Contract Management Agency (DCMA) Contract Administration Office (CAO).

Name:	
Title:	
Address:	
Telephone/ext.:	
Fax:	
E-mail:	

Sample Mentor-Protégé Program Agreement Template (page 11)

24. Protégé Firm's Cognizant Defense Contract Management Agency (DCMA) Contract Administration Office (CAO)

Name:	
Title:	
Address:	
Telephone/ext.:	
Fax:	
E-mail:	

25. Report & Review Requirement. *Attach a statement from each firm indicating their willingness to comply with the Program's reporting and review requirements (i.e., the semi-annual reports, the annual performance reviews that will be conducted by the Defense Contract Management Agency (DCMA). The protégé must also include in their statement they will provide data on employment and revenues for two years after the conclusion of the agreement.*

26. Signature of Each Party. *The Mentor and Protégé are required to sign and date this agreement.* **Titles of the individuals must also be included.** *Please note: a mentor firm may not require an SDB concern to enter into a mentor-protégé agreement as a condition for being awarded a contract by the mentor firm including a subcontract under a DoD contract awarded to the mentor firm.*

<u>Mentor</u>   <u>Protégé</u>

_____   _____
Printed Name   Printed Name

_____   _____
Signature   Signature

_____   _____
Title   Title

_____   _____
Date   Date

Index

... *Formulating and Writing an Effective Business Plan?*

Business Plans That Work for Your Small Business now in its second edition-clearly translates complicated marketing and financial concepts into down-to-earth practical advice, explains all the essential elements and formulas, and offers concrete examples throughout. Five newly developed sample plans from real small businesses provide readers with the blueprints for their own plans, as well as a wealth of detailed information about how a successful small business should operate.

This book will appeal not only to budding entrepreneurs who are planning a new venture on paper to see whether it will fly, but also to new or existing business owners who need a business plan document as part of a business loan application, and to established owners who want to create a plan for internal use.

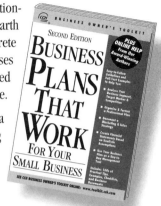

304 pages / Book No. 0-5246-200 **$19.95***

... *Protecting Your Assets and Limiting Your Liability?*

Safe Harbors: An Asset Protection Guide for Small Business Owners is a one-of-a-kind book offering the latest techniques for preserving family wealth and legally avoiding personal liability when structuring, funding and operating a small business. Unfortunately, many small business owners retain a lawyer only after a financial crisis strikes, and usually by then it's too late, often resulting in the loss of the business and possibly a home, investments, savings, and other assets, and maybe those of your spouse as well. Almost all of these problems are preventable with solid advance planning.

Taken together, all of the strategies in this guide form a multi-layered approach to asset protection, often presenting an insurmountable barrier to personal or business creditors, even in the worst of financial circumstances. The emphasis is on easy-to-understand techniques that business owners can undertake on their own, with little or no legal assistance. Sample forms with instructions make it easy to carry out the author's advice, and extensive appendices provide detailed information on state and federal laws.

$19.95* *500 pages / Book No. 0-5436-200*

... *Securing the Necessary Financing for Your Business?*

Small Business Financing: How and Where To Get It, now in its newly revised second edition, thoroughly but simply discusses each source of debt and equity capital, whether public or private—from bookstrapping and IPOs to commercial loans and SBA-guaranteed programs, and everything in between. This book covers methods for determining the amount of capital needed, choosing an appropriate source and type of financing, selecting a business form, and planning successful applications or presentations.

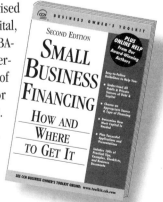

Sample forms are integrated into the text to facilitate learning the details and the data-gathering skills needed for the financing process. A handy glossary is included to take the mystery out of dealing with bankers and other financial professionals.

224 pages / Book No. 0-5142-200 **$17.95***

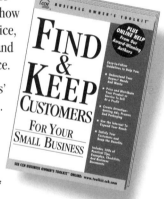